Charles I and the Aristocracy, 1625–1642

This is a major new study of Charles I's relationship with the English aristocracy. Rejecting the traditional emphasis on the 'The Crisis of the Aristocracy', Professor Richard Cust highlights instead the effectiveness of the king and the Earl of Arundel's policies to promote and strengthen the nobility. He reveals how the peers reasserted themselves as the natural leaders of the political nation during the Great Council of Peers in 1640 and the Long Parliament. He also demonstrates how Charles deliberately set out to cultivate his aristocracy as the main bulwark of royal authority, enabling him to go to war against the Scots in 1639 and then build the royalist party that provided the means to fight parliament in 1642. The analysis is framed throughout within a broader study of aristocratic honour and the efforts of the heralds to stabilise the social order.

RICHARD CUST is Professor of Early Modern History at the University of Birmingham. His most recent book is *Charles I. A Political Life* (2005), and he is a Fellow of the Royal Historical Society.

Charles I and the Aristocracy, 1625–1642

Richard Cust

CAMBRIDGE
UNIVERSITY PRESS

CAMBRIDGE UNIVERSITY PRESS
Cambridge, New York, Melbourne, Madrid, Cape Town,
Singapore, São Paulo, Delhi, Mexico City

Cambridge University Press
The Edinburgh Building, Cambridge CB2 8RU, UK

Published in the United States of America by Cambridge University Press, New York

www.cambridge.org
Information on this title: www.cambridge.org/9781107009905

First published 2013

Printed and bound in the United Kingdom by the MPG Books Group

A catalogue record for this publication is available from the British Library

Library of Congress Cataloguing in Publication data
Cust, Richard.
Charles I and the aristocracy, 1625–1642 / Richard Cust.
pages cm
Includes bibliographical references and index.
ISBN 978-1-107-00990-5 (hardback : alk. paper)
1. Charles I, King of England, 1600–1649 – Relations with nobility.
2. Great Britain – Politics and government – 1625–1649. 3. Great Britain. Parliament – History – 17th century. 4. Nobility – Great Britain – History – 17th century. 5. Great Britain – History – Charles I, 1625–1649. I. Title.
DA397.C87–2013
941.06′2 – dc23 2013013110

ISBN 978-1-107-00990-5 Hardback

For Ann

Contents

Illustrations

Abbreviations

AC	Arundel Castle Archives
APC	*Acts of the Privy Council*
BL	British Library
BRO	Bedfordshire Record Office
Bodl.L.	Bodleian Library, Oxford
CA	College of Arms
Cases in the Court of Chivalry	*Cases in the High Court of Chivalry 1634–1640*, ed. R.P. Cust and A.J. Hopper (Harleian Society, new ser., 18, 2006)
Ceremonies of Charles I	*Ceremonies of Charles I*, ed. A.J. Loomie (Bronx, NY: Fordham University Press, 1987)
CJ	*Journals of the House of Commons*
Chamberlain	John Chamberlain, *The Letters of John Chamberlain*, ed. N.E. McLure, 2 vols. (American Philosophical Society, 12, 1939)
Clarendon, *History*	Edward, Earl of Clarendon, *The History of the Rebellion*, ed. W.D. MacRay, 6 vols. (Oxford: Clarendon Press, 1888)
Clarendon, *Life*	Edward, Earl of Clarendon, *The Life of Edward, Earl of Clarendon*, 3 vols. (Oxford, 1828)
Clarendon SP	*State Papers Collected by Edward Earl of Clarendon*, 2 vols. (Oxford, 1767)
Collins Letters	*Letters and Memorials of State*, ed. A. Collins, 2 vols. (London, 1746)
Commons Debates 1621	*Commons Debates in 1621*, ed. W. Notestein, F.H. Relf & H. Simpson, 7 vols. (New Haven, CT: Yale University Press, 1635)
Constitutional Documents	*Constitutional Documents of the Puritan Revolution 1625–1660*, ed. S.R. Gardiner (Oxford: Clarendon Press, 3rd edn., 1906)
Court and Times	*Court and Times of Charles I*, ed. T. Birch, 2 vols. (London, 1848)

CSP Dom.	*Calendar of State Papers Domestic*
CSP Ven.	*Calendar of State Papers and Manuscripts Relating to English Affairs . . . in Venice*, vols.19–24, 1625–42 (London: HMSO, 1912–24)
D'Ewes Journal	*The Journal of Sir Simonds D'Ewes from the Beginning of the Long Parliament to the Opening of the Trial of Strafford*, ed. W. Notestein (New Haven, CT: Yale University Press, 1923)
DRO	Devon Record Office
EHR	*English Historical Review*
Evelyn	*The Diary and Correspondence of John Evelyn*, ed W. Bray (London: Routledge and Sons, 1890)
FSL	Folger Shakespeare Library, Washington DC
Gardiner, *History*	S.R. Gardiner, *The History of England 1603–1642*, 10 vols. (London: Longman, Green & Co, 1883–4)
GEC	*The Complete Peerage of England, Ireland and Scotland*, by G.E. Cokayne, 13 vols. (London: St Catherine Press, 1910–1959)
Hardwicke SP	*Hardwicke State Papers*, 2 vols. (London, 1778)
Hist.	*History*
HJ	*Historical Journal*
HoP	History of Parliament
Holles Letters	*The Letters of John Holles*, ed. P.R. Seddon, 3 vols. (Transactions of the Thoroton Soc. XXXI, XXXV, XXXVI, 1975–86)
HMC	Historical Manuscripts Commission
HR	*Historical Research*
Hunt.L.	Huntington Library, California
JBS	*Journal of British Studies*
JMH	*Journal of Modern History*
Lismore Papers	*Lismore Papers*, ed. A.B. Grosart, 10 vols. (London, 1886–8)
Letters of Henrietta Maria	*Letters of Queen Henrietta Maria*, ed. M.A.E. Green (London, 1857)
LJ	*Journals of the House of Lords*
LRO	Leicestershire Record Office
NLW	National Library of Wales
NRO	Northamptonshire Record Office
NUL	Nottingham University Library

Oxf.DNB	*Oxford Dictionary of National Biography; from the earliest times to the year 2000*, ed. H.C.G. Mathew, 61 vols. (Oxford: Oxford University Press, 2004)
PA	Parliamentary Archives
P & P	*Past & Present*
Private Journals	*The Private Journals of the Long Parliament 3 January to 5 March 1642*, ed. W.H. Coates, A.S. Young and V.F. Snow (New Haven, CT: Yale University Press, 1982)
Proceedings in Parliament 1614	*Proceedings in Parliament 1614*, ed. M. Jansson (Philadelphia, PA: Temple University Press, 1985)
Proceedings in Parliament 1625	*Proceedings in Parliament 1625*, ed. M. Jansson & W.B. Bidwell (New Haven, CT: Yale University Press, 1987)
Proceedings in Parliament 1626	*Proceedings in Parliament 1626*, ed. W.B. Bidwell & M. Jansson, 4 vols. (New Haven, CT: Yale University Press, 1991–6)
Proceedings in Parliament 1628	*Proceedings in Parliament 1628*, ed. R.C. Johnson, M.F. Keeler, M.J. Cole & W.B. Bidwell, 6 vols. (New Haven, CT: Yale University Press, 1977–83)
Proceedings of the Short Parliament	*Proceedings of the Short Parliament of 1640*, ed. E.S. Cope and W.H. Coates (Camden Society, 4th ser., 19, 1977)
Proceedings in the Long Parliament	*Proceedings in the Opening Session of the Long Parliament*, ed. M. Jansson, 7 vols. (New York: University of Rochester Press, 2000–2007)
Proclamations	*Stuart Royal Proclamations*, ed. J.F. Larkin and P.L. Hughes, 2 vols. (Oxford: Oxford University Press, 1973–83)
Rushworth	J. Rushworth, *Historical Collections*, 7 vols. (London, 1659–1701)
SHC	Surrey History Centre
Somers Tracts	*A Collection of Rare and Valuable Tracts of the Most Interesting Subjects; but chiefly such as relate to the History and Constitution of these Kingdoms. . .*, 13 vols (London, 1809–15)
SRO	Staffordshire Record Office
Strafforde Letters	*The Earl of Strafforde's Letters and Dispatches*, 2 vols., ed W. Knowler (London, 1729)

TRHS	*Transactions of the Royal Historical Society*
Walker, *Discourses*	Sir Edward Walker, *Historical Discourses on Several Occasions* (London, 1705)
Warwick Memoirs	Sir Philip Warwick, *Memoirs of the Reign of Charles I* (Edinburgh, 1813)
WCLA	Windsor Castle, St George's Chapel, Library and Archive

The original spelling of manuscripts has been retained, but punctuation has been modernised to aid the sense.

Preface

This book began life as a research project on the Court of Chivalry. I wish to thank the Arts and Humanities Research Council for funding the project and granting me a research fellowship. I am also indebted to the Huntington Library in California for awarding me a Mayers Fellowship and Birmingham University for allowing me study leave to complete the research and writing up. I am very grateful to all those who helped with the project. Andrew Hopper acted as research assistant and collaborator throughout, and its successful completion owed an enormous amount to his initiative and enthusiasm. Robert Yorke, archivist at the College of Arms, supported the project from the outset, and his knowledge and hospitality made research at the college a great pleasure. I have also been able to draw on the expertise of Adrian Ailes, Clive Cheeseman, Timothy Duke, David Gelber and Nigel Ramsay for which I am very grateful.

In writing the book I have relied heavily on the work of others and benefited enormously from their insights. I am particularly indebted to John Adamson, Ronald Asch, Jan Broadway, Alexandra Gajda, Paul Hammer, Cynthia Herrup, Clive Holmes, Brendan Kane, Noah Millstone, Kevin Sharpe, Malcolm Smuts, Christopher Thompson, Nicholas Tyacke and John Walter. In the latter stages I have been able to draw on the expertise of those who work on the Stuart history sections at the History of Parliament, among whom Stephen Roberts and Andrew Thrush have been especially helpful. Tom Cogswell, Ann Hughes and Peter Lake have, as always, been particularly generous in commenting on my work and sharing their understanding and ideas. I owe an enormous amount to their insights and encouragement. Finally, I want to record my continuing debt to Conrad Russell, who supervised my early research and whose ideas and approaches have done much to shape this book.

On a personal level, I could not have completed the book without the support and encouragement of my friends. I am particularly grateful to John Bourne, Jacqueline Eales, Anthony Fletcher, Elaine Fulton, Jeff Goodman, Tara Hamling, Eric Ives, George Lukowski, Graeme Murdock, William Purkis, Robert Swanson, Angela Trikic, Nigel and Diana

Wood, and my friends at Lichfield Cricket Club and in the history department at Birmingham University. I also wish to thank Elizabeth Friend-Smith at Cambridge University Press for her patience and encouragement. Above all, I am more grateful than I can easily express to Ann, Alice and David, for their support, encouragement and so much else besides. They make it all worthwhile.

Richard Cust
Lichfield

Introduction

At the first Privy Council meeting of Charles I's reign, early in April 1625, the Earl Marshal, Thomas Howard, Earl of Arundel and Surrey, set out a bold agenda for the reform of the honours system and the resurrection of the aristocracy. As discussion turned to the reforms to be implemented at the start of the new reign, he proposed that it was both 'honourable and necessary to limit honours; that titles should not be distributed broadcast as in the past, but only to persons of quality and of noble birth'. He then elaborated on this under three headings: first, the need 'to maintain the ancient nobility'; second, the damage done by sale of office and title; and third the importance of the king letting 'his council share in the things he wishes to announce [and] publishing them as having been discussed with the councillors'.[1]

This was a bold and risky move because it would inevitably be seen as an attack on the royal favourite, the Duke of Buckingham, who was largely responsible for the continuing traffic in titles. Sure enough, Buckingham immediately spoke against it, arguing that the earl was casting aspersions on the memory of the late king and seeking to restrict the present king's capacity to reward merit. Arundel found himself isolated in the face of the favourite's disapproval. However, he had calculated that Charles would be sympathetic to this idea of a return to the traditional status quo and, in this, he was proved correct. A few days later the king came down to the council in person and issued an instruction that 'henceforth no honors shall pass either in England or Ireland until the Erle Marshall be first acquainted therewith.'[2] But getting Charles to agree in principle was often much easier than getting him to commit himself in practice, and when push came to shove he sided with Buckingham. During 1626 he allowed the favourite to persuade him that the needs of the war against France and Spain justified a new round of selling honours and creating titles. The abuses that Arundel complained of continued apace and he

[1] *CSP Ven 1625–1626*, pp. 12, 21. [2] *APC 1625–1626*, p. 24.

found himself a marked man, first of all barred from the royal court and then stripped of the authority of his office of Earl Marshal.[3]

In April 1625 the reforms proposed by Arundel had become particularly pressing because the English aristocracy appeared to be facing the threat of terminal decline. Social commentators lined up to pronounce on the diminishing respect for the noble order and the waning of their power and authority. The newsletter writer, Joseph Mede, picked up on calls for a 'resumption of honours . . . the number of our nobility being grown too great for . . . the ancient and due esteem of that order'; the Venetian ambassador echoed a general complaint that 'the number' of 'titled persons' had been 'so constantly multiplied that they are no longer distinguishable from common people'; and the poet, Michael Drayton, lamented that now the worthless 'Drone . . . dares grow/To any title Empire can bestow'.[4] Perhaps, the most evocative analysis was offered by Sir Henry Spelman who, in his *History of Sacrilege*, completed in the early 1630s, looked back on what he saw as 50 years of noble decline. He recalled that as a young man, he had witnessed 'with what great respect, observance and distance principal men of countries applied themselves to some of the meanest barons'. But now, as a consequence of the 'ancient honour of nobility' being granted 'to the meanest of people . . . the whole body of the baronage is . . . fallen so much from their ancient lustre, magnitude and estimation' that even 'inferior gentlemen' would 'accost' them with a 'familiarity' that made him wonder at 'the declination of the one or the arrogance of the other'.[5] This was a trend that most contemporaries believed had been exacerbated by the ascendancy of Buckingham. Not only was the continuing sale of honours draining away the honour and prestige of the order, but his determination to dominate royal counsels had led to a sidelining of the 'ancient nobility' and their displacement from their traditional role as *consiliarii nati*, a king's 'natural counsellors'. Arundel saw it as his main purpose in politics to reverse this trend and restore the English aristocracy to their 'ancient lustre' and 'magnitude'. This was the agenda he set out in 1625 and following Buckingham's assassination in August 1628 he was able to claw his way back into royal favour and embark on the programme that he had outlined in 1625, this time with the wholehearted support of the king.

[3] K. Sharpe, 'The Earl of Arundel, his circle and the opposition to the duke of Buckingham, 1618–1628', in *Faction and Parliament*, ed. K. Sharpe (Oxford: Oxford University Press, 1978), pp. 219–34.

[4] *Court and Times*, i.335; *CSP Ven. 1626–1628*, p. 607; R. McCoy, 'Old English honour in an evil time: Aristocratic principle in the 1620s', in *The Stuart Court and Europe*, ed. R.M. Smuts (Cambridge: Cambridge University Press, 1996), p. 149.

[5] H. Spelman, *The History and Fate of Sacrilege* (London, 1698), p. 224; L. Stone, *The Crisis of the Aristocracy 1558–1641* (Oxford: Oxford University Press, 1965), pp. 747–8.

This book is a study of the policies implemented by Charles and Arundel in pursuit of this programme. It focuses on two closely related themes: first, the royal project to revive and reinforce the status of the aristocracy, and at the same time fashion them into a loyal, court-based, 'royalist party' capable of upholding the monarchy; and second the efforts made by the king and his Earl Marshal to reform the honours system. In this context 'the aristocracy' will be understood as synonymous with the English 'nobility', or more precisely the parliamentary peerage. During the seventeenth century 'aristocracy' was generally used in its original, Aristotelian, sense to refer to a system of government in which the 'best men', equipped with the virtue and capacity to rule in the interests of the state and its citizens, wielded power. This was what Arundel had in mind when he insisted on the need for the 'ancient nobility' to resume their traditional role in counselling the king. But 'aristocracy' and 'aristocrat' have also long been understood by political and social commentators (particularly since the era of the French Revolution) to refer to the elite groupings at the top of various societies. In this sense the term has generally been used interchangeably with 'nobility' or 'noblemen' (derived from the Roman *nobiles* or 'known') to describe those whose birth, wealth and status set them apart as a social elite. This has also been qualified in the English context where a distinction has generally been drawn between *nobilitas maior* and *nobilitas minor*, the former consisting of those peers who were summoned to sit in parliament and who enjoyed a limited range of privileges, such as freedom from arrest and outlawry, and the latter the gentry classes, comprising knights, esquires and gentlemen.[6] It is with the former group that we will be mainly concerned in this study: the 120 or so English peers who sat in the House of Lords.[7]

The aim will be to trace the fortunes of the English aristocracy through the various schemes and policies promoted by the king and his Earl Marshal to restore their 'ancient lustre' and recruit them as the main source of political support for the crown. The lack of a sustained investigation of this topic is one of the more surprising gaps in the recent historiography of early Stuart England. It has long been a staple theme of continental studies of state building and the rise of absolutism, with often exhaustive analyses of monarchs' policies in dealing with their noble elites. Yet the last detailed exploration of the topic for early Stuart England was 45 years ago in Lawrence Stone's *magnum opus* on *The Crisis of the Aristocracy*; and there Stone's main preoccupation was with the inflation of honours rather

6 W. Doyle, *Aristocracy; A Very Short Introduction* (Oxford: Oxford University Press, 2010), pp. 1–7; Stone, *Crisis of the Aristocracy*, pp. 53–5.

7 The number of peers in the House of Lords stood at 99 in June 1625, 126 in 1628, 112 in April 1640 and 123 in March 1642: *Proceedings in Parliament 1625*, pp. 583–90; *Proceedings in Parliament 1628*, v.15–24; *LJ*, iv.45; PA, HL/PO/JO/5/1/8.

than crown policy towards the nobility more generally.[8] This omission is the more remarkable because it was an area of government that Charles, himself, took very seriously indeed. In contemporary parlance, he was the 'fount of honour', which meant that he was responsible for distributing titles and regulating honours in such a way that virtuous service of crown and commonwealth was seen to be rewarded, and the existing social hierarchy was maintained. He shared the view of his father that the exercise of this particular prerogative was the sphere in which monarchs 'doe most expresse the image of that imortall God which hath placed them on their thrones. [It was] their chiefest calling and worthiest of their care'. He also recognised that it was crucial to the maintenance of royal authority. He described his nobles as those 'persons in rank and degree nearest to the royal throne', who, 'having received honour from himself and his royal progenitors, he doubted not would . . . be moved in honour and dutiful affection'. He regarded them as his natural partners in government, standing alongside the bishops as one of the twin pillars on which rested the effective management of the state.[9] If his monarchy was to prosper and flourish it was as important to him to promote the welfare of his nobles and respect for the honours system as it was to promote Laudian reform in the church. Yet, whereas the campaign for the latter has been analysed exhaustively, the former has received only cursory treatment. Caroline Hibbard has shown that Charles took a close and persistent interest in the welfare of aristocrats, going out of his way to arbitrate their quarrels, arrange dynastic marriages and satisfy their legitimate ambitions for honour; while Kevin Sharpe in *The Personal Rule of Charles I*, sees the king as embarking on a self-conscious policy to enhance the prestige and 'ancient lustre' of the nobility.[10] Beyond this, however, there has been little attempt to explore the directions in which the king's concerns might have taken him.

This study will seek to fill the gap and then move on to analysing the political responses of the aristocracy in the crucial period from the First Bishops War in 1639 to the outbreak of the English Civil War in 1642. The emphasis will be on exploring how far the aristocracy were willing to perform the role that Charles had assigned to them, and the degree to which his efforts to fashion them into a 'royalist party' were successful. Much of the recent work in this area has highlighted the extent of aristocratic dissidence, most notably John Adamson's powerful

8 Stone, *Crisis of the Aristocracy*, ch. III and pp. 750–2.

9 BL, Lansdowne MS 152, fo. 38; Rushworth, ii.1163.

10 C. Hibbard, 'The Theatre of Dynasty', in *The Stuart Court and Europe*, ed. R.M. Smuts (Cambridge: Cambridge University Press, 1996), pp. 156–76; K. Sharpe, *The Personal Rule of Charles I* (New Haven, CT: Yale University Press), pp. 417–22.

and ground-breaking study *The Noble Revolt* that analyses the role of a group of noble rebels in precipitating the civil war.[11] Here, however, the main focus will be on the other side of the aristocratic equation. I will concentrate on the 60 per cent of the politically active nobility who eventually sided with the king in the summer of 1642 and provided him with the support needed to take on his enemies and actually fight a civil war.

The second theme of the book picks up on the other main aspect of Arundel's 1625 agenda: the more general need to reform the system for granting and affirming honours and titles. There was a long history behind Arundel's proposals at the April council meeting. They were the latest version of a succession of initiatives promoted since the mid sixteenth century by Earl Marshals and the heraldic establishment to get to grips with the problem of how to restore the integrity of what can broadly be described as 'the honours system'. 'Honour' in early modern England is generally best understood as the qualities, sets of values and standards of behaviour that entitled an individual to status and esteem. In this sense, as contemporaries readily acknowledged, it was inseparable from 'aristocracy'. 'Aristocrats' and 'nobles' were those who possessed and displayed 'honourable' attributes such as virtue, courage and antiquity of lineage, which qualified them for elevated social rank.[12] However, the term 'honour' or 'honours' could also be used to describe the formal titles and marks of distinction conferred on those regarded as 'noble'. From the mid sixteenth century the processes for granting and affirming these were becoming increasingly institutionalised in response to growing anxieties over the maintenance of order and hierarchy. The Earl Marshal and the heralds, who were officially responsible for regulating 'honours', established an increasingly formalised system for controlling claims to titles, the right to display arms and precedence within the noble order. Such concerns continued to command attention in Charles's reign, the more so because of the sale of titles and apparent downgrading of 'quality and noble birth' that Arundel alluded to. These topics have often been seen by early modern historians as of interest only to antiquarians and specialists in heraldry. But medieval historians, such as Maurice Keen and Peter Coss, have demonstrated that they are central to understanding the self-image and conduct of the ruling elite, and they are therefore of immediate relevance to any analysis of Charles's relationship with his

[11] J. Adamson, *The Noble Revolt. The Overthrow of Charles I* (London: Weidenfeld & Nicolson, 2007); M.E. James, *English Politics and the Concept of Honour 1485–1642* (Past & Present Supplement 3, 1978), pp. 84–8; McCoy, 'Old English Honour', pp. 133–55.

[12] Doyle, *Aristocracy*, pp. 32–5; J. Powis, *Aristocracy* (Oxford: Blackwell, 1984), pp. 8–14.

aristocracy.[13] Alongside an analysis of specific policies directed towards the peerage this book will explore the Crown's efforts to promote and defend honour more broadly by investigating the effectiveness of reforms instituted by Charles and Arundel in the Court of Chivalry and Office of Arms. To begin with, however, it is important to analyse the context for all this, by examining the pressures and challenges faced by the aristocracy and the honours system prior to Charles's reign.

[13] M. Keen, *Chivalry* (New Haven, CT: Yale University Press, 1984), chs. 7–9; M. Keen, *The Origins of the English Gentleman* (Stroud: Tempus, 2002); P.R. Coss, *The Knight in Medieval England 1000–1400* (Stroud: Alan Sutton Publishing, 1993); P.R. Coss and M. Keen (eds.), *Heraldry, Pageantry and Social Display in Medieval England* (Woodbridge: The Boydell Press, 2002).

1 The honours system in late Tudor and early Stuart England

Heralds and Earl Marshals in late Tudor England

All over Europe in the late sixteenth and early seventeenth century there was a tightening up of definitions of nobility. Everywhere there was concern to limit the rise of social upstarts, prevent those who did not have secure titles from claiming noble privileges, such as tax exemption, and fix in place existing hierarchies in the face of unprecedented social mobility. A status that much of the time depended on collective social judgment and relatively relaxed assumptions about wealth and status became a matter of providing legal proofs of noble descent or the right to bear arms.[1] England has often been seen as a special case in matters relating to nobility because its gentry and aristocracy did not enjoy the extensive privileges of their European counterparts. Nonetheless during the late Tudor period there was a similar concerted effort to tighten up the regulation of status. Once again, the main reason was anxiety over the problems of maintaining order and degree, prompted, in particular, by the concern that the aristocracy and gentry were being deprived of the means to carry out their traditional roles of governing and defending their country. There was general agreement that something must be done to stabilise the social order and ensure that the different ranks within it discharged their customary duties. What this should be, however, was subject to a wide variety of proposals. Humanists urged fundamental changes in education, Protestant reformers advocated a moral and spiritual crusade and the 'commonwealthmen' promoted inquests into evils such as enclosure, backed by judicial and executive action.[2] One concrete

[1] R.G. Asch, *Nobilities in Transition 1550–1700* (London: Arnold, 2003), ch. 1; J. Dewald, *The European Nobility 1400–1800* (Cambridge: Cambridge University Press, 1996), pp. 19–32; I.A.A. Thompson, '*Hidalgo* and *pechero*: the language of "estates" and "castes" in early-modern Castile', in *Language, History and Class*, ed. P. Corfield (Oxford: Blackwell, 1991), pp. 53–78. I am grateful to Ronald Asch for advice on this issue.

[2] Stone, *Crisis of the Aristocracy*, pp. 22–36; J.P. Cooper, 'Ideas of gentility', in J.P. Cooper, *Land, Men and Beliefs in Early Modern History* (London: The Hambledon Press, 1983), pp. 51–4; Q. Skinner, *The Foundations of Modern Political Thought*, 2 vols. (Cambridge:

outcome of all this energy and industry was a great raft of regulatory bills and statutes, covering everything from poor relief and vagrancy to the regulation of dress and manners, culminating in the Statute of Artificers of 1563 that, by codifying all the existing rules relating to wage assessments and apprenticeship, sought to provide a template for the lives of the non-noble classes.[3] Another was to give much greater powers to those whose professional responsibility it was to supervise matters relating to noble status: the heralds.

The heralds had become established in England in the fourteenth and fifteenth centuries, with the power to grant and regulate coats of arms, direct heraldic funerals and conduct visitations of the local gentry.[4] These powers were considerably extended in the mid Tudor period when the crown entrusted the heralds with a primary role in policing the honours system and acting as the arbiters of order and degree. The first royal visitation commission, granted to Thomas Benolt, Clarenceux King of Arms, in 1530 was expanded in 1552 to give them specific responsibility for ensuring that there was 'discent, order and due reformacon' in the display of coats of arms and other 'tokens of nobilitie and honour', and that none 'beare and use the same', 'except they be lineally descended of blode and name' from ancestors approved 'by the the lawe of armes'. For the first time the crown also spelled out sanctions, stipulating that any abuses were to be reported to the Privy Council and the Earl Marshal.[5] Then in July 1555 the heralds were granted a new charter that established the three kings of arms, six heralds and three pursuivants as the Office of Arms, 'a corporation with perpetual succession'. They were endowed with estates and a settled base at Derby House where they were able to set up a library to keep their 'records, rolls and pedigrees', thus providing an unprecedented genealogical and armorial resource.[6] However, the biggest step forward took place in the 1560s, with a series of reforms

Cambridge University Press, 1978), i.224–8, 240; A. Fletcher and D. MacCulloch, *Tudor Rebellions* (Harlow: Longman, 5th edn, 2004), pp. 6, 10–11.

3 G.R. Elton, *The Parliament of England 1559–1581* (Cambridge: Cambridge University Press, 1981), pp. 262–75; S.T. Bindoff, 'The Statute of Artificers', in *Elizabethan Government and Society*, ed. C.H. Williams (London: Athlone Press, 1961), pp. 56–94; G.R. Elton, *The Tudor Constitution* (Cambridge: Cambridge University Press, 1960), pp. 466–70.

4 A. Ailes, 'The development of the heralds' visitations in England and Wales', *The Coat of Arms*, 3rd ser., 5 (2009), 7–23. I am grateful to Adrian Ailes for valuable advice on this topic. See also A. Ailes, 'Elias Ashmole's "Heraldical Visitacion" of Berkshire 1665–6' (Oxford University DPhil thesis, 2008); A.R. Wagner, *Heralds of England* (London: HMSO, 1967).

5 *Munimenta Heraldica*, ed. G.D. Squibb (Harleian Soc., new ser., 4, 1985), pp. 131–2; *Visitations of the North*, pt. 1 (Surtees Soc., 122, 1912), p. 199.

6 *Munimenta Heraldica*, pp. 20–7; Wagner, *Heralds of England*, pp. 182–3.

managed by the young Earl Marshal, Thomas Howard, 4th Duke of Norfolk, and his mentor, Lord Burghley.[7]

The Earl Marshal had emerged as the crown minister responsible for overseeing the honours system since the lapse of the office of Lord High Constable in 1521, following the treason and execution of the Duke of Buckingham. However, Norfolk was the first to develop this role to the full and by the end of the 1560s he had transformed the scope and range of the heralds' activities. There were initial indications of this in a new visitation commission issued to Norroy in June 1561. Picking up on the language of social reform, its declared aim was to ensure that 'every person and persons, bodys politique, corporate and others, may be the better knowen in his or their estate, degree and misteries, without confusion or disorder', and, in particular, that 'the nobilitye' be 'preserved in every degree as apperteyneth as well in honor and in worship'.[8] To this end the heralds were equipped with new powers. Their primary task remained to investigate coats of arms and pedigrees, and record these in their register. But they were now given authority 'to reprove, comptroll and make infamous' by public proclamation and humiliation any who 'shall usurpe or take upon him or them any name or title of honour or dignitie, as esquire, gentleman, or other'. In other words, they were now being made responsible for monitoring the critical divide between gentleman and commoner. Armed with these powers, from July 1561 onwards, the provincial kings began an extensive round of visitations which, by the mid 1570s, had covered virtually every county in England. In earlier visitations the main emphasis had been on authorising coats of arms but in this round descents and marriages became the primary focus of attention, with the recording of sometimes lengthy pedigrees in the visitation office books and the first appearance of the rectilinear format of the modern family tree in place of the earlier narrative descents. This led to a much fuller and more comprehensive visitation process, with a substantial rise in the number of gentry families being included and far more detailed information on descents, often accompanied by 'proofs' in the form of charters, indentures, seals and 'church notes'.[9]

7 Cecil was a professed admirer of the duke as an exemplar to the nobility, writing of him in October 1565 when several of the reforms relating to the heralds were being put in place, 'I think England hath not had in this age a nobleman more likely to prove a father and stay to his country': C. Read, *Mr Secretary Cecil and Queen Elizabeth* (London: Jonathan Cape, 1955), p. 332.

8 *Visitations of the North*, pp. 204–6; *Calendar of the Patent Rolls 1560–3*, p. 92.

9 Ailes, 'Development of heralds' visitations', 15–21; Wagner, *Heralds of England*, pp. 185–6, 206; A.R. Wagner, *The Records and Collections of the College of Arms* (London: Burkes Peerage, 1952), pp. 69–70, 78–81.

However, the extension and reform of the visitation process was only part of Norfolk and Burghley's campaign. On 5 December 1566 a bill for 'Confirming the Letters Patents and Corporation of the kings [and] Heralds of Arms' was given a first reading in the House of Commons.[10] As well as enshrining the charter of 1555, it proposed that the ancient Earl Marshal's court, the High Court of Chivalry, should be re-established as the 'Court of the Company of the kings and Herraulds of the Office of Arms'. It was to continue to have oversight of all matters relating to 'heraldrie . . . and the ancient law of arms'; but its remit was to be extended to a general oversight of the honours system. It would now have the power to resolve disputes about descents or pedigrees, enforce the registration of funeral certificates for noblemen and gentlemen, curb the activities of illegal arms painters and prevent the defacing of monuments. Furthermore, as back up to the new authority given to the heralds, it would determine any questions that related to the 'using or usurping of any title, name or addicon of esquire or gentleman'. Finally, it was to become a court of record, meeting twice yearly at set times under the supervision of the Earl Marshal and heralds, which meant that its proceedings were to be officially recorded and became valid as fact in legal proceedings. Had this bill become law it would have equipped the Elizabethan regime with a powerful mechanism for regulating the upper classes. However, for reasons that are unclear, it never progressed beyond its first reading.

Nonetheless Norfolk was able to further extend his own and the heralds' powers in a series of regulations issued from 1561 onwards and codified in the 'Earl Marshal's Orders' of 18 July 1568. These stipulated first of all that grants made by the kings of arms were to be authorised by the Earl Marshal or one of his deputies (Burghley or Leicester) and then recorded in a register that was to be presented to the Earl Marshal once a year for inspection; then, second that the executors of deceased nobles and gentleman be required to provide a funeral certificate giving their date of death, place of burial and habitation and family details, even where there had been no herald in attendance. All this documentation would be kept alongside the visitation books to provide a comprehensive record of the descents, marriages, residences and coats of arms of the landed elite.[11]

Taken together these reforms would have established the Earl Marshal as the principal arbiter of honour and degree, equipped to address many of the concerns raised by commentators and moralists, and offer the

10 *CJ*, i.79; the full text is in CA, Heralds, vol. II, fos. 743–52.

11 *Munimenta Heraldica*, pp. 97–105; Wagner, *Heralds of England*, pp. 110, 187, 197; Ailes, 'Development of heralds' visitations', 16–17.

prospect of fixity and stability that contemporaries craved. However, much of the impetus behind these schemes drained away when Norfolk was imprisoned in the Tower in 1569 and subsequently executed for treason. It was not until the 1630s, when Charles and Arundel embarked on their concerted campaign to resurrect the status of the peerage and reform the honours system, that such a comprehensive programme was revived.

Under Norfolk's successor, the Earl of Shrewsbury, the regulation of grants of arms and claims to gentility was much more lax. The earl was in the north for much of the 1570s and 1580s, acting as jailer to Mary Queen of Scots, and in his absence the heralds operated largely unsupervised. Norfolk's order for a register of new grants of arms was ignored and the kings of arms were able to make grants simply on their own authority. It was during this period that the heralds acquired their reputation for venality. Sir Thomas Smith's famous description in the *De Republica Anglorum* (1583) – of how 'a king of heraulds shal also give [a gentleman] for money armes newly made and invented which the title shall beare that the said herauld hath perused and seen olde registers where his auncestors in times past had borne the same'[12] – helped to establish an image which stuck. Even Robert Cooke, Clarenceux King of Arms, writing in 1587, had to admit that 'no one thing doth so mightily empaire their credit and estimacon in this age as doethe the badd opinion conceived of them for granting of armes unto new gentlemen.'[13] With controls relaxed, the numbers of grants reached record levels. It has been calculated that there were at least 740 during the 1570s and 700 during the 1580s, compared with more typical totals of 300–400 per decade.[14] This profligacy, however, was not simply a function of the acquisitiveness of the heralds. It was also a reflection of the flexibility and inclusiveness of contemporary understandings of who was entitled to call himself a gentleman.

The early Tudors developed a relatively open-ended approach that allowed for wealth, reputation and service as appropriate qualifications.[15]

12 Sir Thomas Smith, *De Republica Anglorum*, ed. M. Dewar (Cambridge: Cambridge University Press, 1982), p. 72.

13 'The givinge of armes no wayes hurtfull to the commonwealthe written by Clarenceux Cooke 1587': BL, Lansdowne MS 255, fos. 190–3. There are further copies of this at BL, Cotton MS Faustina E.1, fos. 161–3, 164–5 where it is attributed to Robert Glover. However, as Cooper has pointed out ('Ideas of gentility', p. 67n), Cooke is the more likely author as it fits with his need to defend the practice at this time.

14 The decadal totals are calculated in E. Elmhirst, 'The Fashion for Heraldry', *Coat of Arms*, iv (1956), 47–50, based on the evidence of docket books, drafts and copies: 1550–9 (300), 1560–9 (580), 1570–9 (740), 1580–9 (700), 1590–9 (300), 1600–9 (440), 1610–9 (440), 1620–9 (340), 1630–9 (240), 1640–9 (120).

15 M. Keen, *Origins of the English Gentleman* (Stroud: Tempus, 2002), ch. 7.

The 1530 visitation commission included a clause stating that grants of arms could be made to 'any person or persons' who had earned them by the 'service doon to us or to other, that be encreased or augmented to possessions and riches hable to maynteyn the same. So that they be . . . men of good honest reputacyon'; and garter king of arms defined 'possessions and riches hable to maynteyne the same' as either a landed income of £10 p.a., or movable goods amounting to £300.[16] This was an acknowledgement of the situation that prevailed in the late medieval period when an income of £10 p.a. had generally been recognised as a threshold for acceptance as a gentleman.[17] But it was not seen as helpful by those commentators and legislators who sought to control social mobility. References to wealth and reputation appeared to open the way for 'upstartes' and 'new men'. Later commissions, therefore, stipulated much tighter requirements based on 'blood and name' and the 'lawe of armes'. Nonetheless, the fact that the Henrician commission had sanctioned a relatively permissive entitlement provided a precedent that was picked up by later commentators and regularly cited in grants of arms.[18]

This approach was bolstered by the widespread currency given to Sir Thomas Smith's famous description of a gentleman in the *De Republica Anglorum*. Smith was careful to stress the qualities of virtue, and 'race and blood', which went towards making a gentlemen, but then went on to describe what he saw as the contemporary reality: that wealth and reputation were often the key determinants. In Smith's version, 'whosoever studieth the lawes of the relme, who studieth in the universities, who professeth liberall sciences, and to be shorte, who can live idly and without manuall labour, and will beare the port, charge and countenance of a gentleman, he shall be called master . . . and shall be taken for a gentleman'.[19] Smith's description came to be widely used as an authoritative statement of who qualified for gentility. Cooke quoted large chunks of it verbatim in his 1587 treatise 'The givinge of armes no wayes hurtfull to the commonwealthe' that justified the grants of arms he had been making to 'new gentlemen' and lawyers, and other heralds, cited Smythe

16 Ailes, 'Ashmole's "Heraldicall Visitacion"', p. 43.

17 Keen, *Origins of the Gentleman*, pp. 109–10.

18 For heralds' justifying the rise of '*novi homines*', see Ailes, 'Ashmole's "Heraldicall Visitacion"', pp. 50–1; BL, Cotton Faustina E.1, fo. 163. For examples of grants of arms that cite 'reputation' and 'good deserts', see *A Collection of Miscellaneous Grants of Arms Part 1*, ed. W.A. Littledale (Harleian Soc, 76, 1925), pp. 15, 25, 37, 41–2, 51.

19 Smith, *De Republica Anglorum*, p. 72; W. Harrison, *Harrison's Description of England*, ed. F.J. Furnivall (London: New Shakespeare Soc., 1877), pt. i, 128–9. Smith probably borrowed the wording from Harrison's *Description* which he read in draft during the 1570s; but it was his description that made its mark on the contemporary consciousness: D.M. Palliser, *The Age of Elizabeth* (Harlow: Longman, 2nd edn, 1992), pp. 459–60.

as an apparently unimpeachable source.[20] The generally permissive approach that prevailed in the mid Elizabethan period was reinforced by the relaxed priorities of the common law, which generally allowed 'vulgar reputation' as sufficient grounds for claiming the title of a gentleman in legal proceedings.[21] However, such views did not go unchallenged and over the same period there was a reaction against them that brought about a considerable tightening of definitions by the end of the century.

Leading the way were two highly influential works on heraldry: Gerard Legh's *The Accedence of Armorie* (1562) and John Ferne's *The Blazon of Gentrie* (1586). These were the most widely read examples of an increasingly fashionable literary genre that did much to establish 'blood and arms' as the 'gold standard' for assessing gentility.[22] Legh and Ferne looked back to medieval traditions set out in *The Boke of St Albans* and Nicholas Upton's *De Studio Militaris* and traced the origins of gentility back to biblical times, first of all to the division between the descendants of Noah and then to Christ himself, 'a gentleman of blood' according to Ferne.[23] These authors also picked up on the notion that 'true noble stock' came to exist only after several generations within the same family had lived as gentlemen. For Ferne (like Upton and *The Boke*) it required five generations following the first grant of arms to purge ignoble origins and create a gentleman of 'blood and coat armour perfect'. For Legh, Robert Glover, William Segar and most other heraldic writers three generally sufficed, and this became the customary benchmark for the heralds. The stress on biblical origins and longevity of descent

20 BL, Lansdowne MS 255, fos. 190–3. John Doddridge, barrister and member of the Elizabethan Society of Antiquaries, cited it in the Abergavenny peerage case in 1588: G.D. Squibb, *The High Court of Chivalry* (Oxford: Oxford University Press, 1959), p. 172.

21 Keen, *Origins of the Gentleman*, pp. 101–2; Cooper, 'Ideas of Gentlity', p. 62. As the Jacobean Norroy, Sir Richard St George, pointed out, 'additions of titles given very base & unworthye men, or assumed by themselves without just and lawfull authoritye . . . at assises, sessions, publique meetings [and] in private instruments between partie and partie', continually undermined the heralds' efforts to tighten controls: CA, Phillipps MS 13084, vol. 8, fos. 338–9.

22 J.F.R. Day, 'Primers of Honor: heraldry, heraldry books and English renaissance literature', *Sixteenth Century Journal*, xxi (1990), pp. 93–103; Gerard Legh, *The Accedence of Armorie* (London, 1562) was reprinted in 1568, 1576, 1591, 1597 and 1612 (my references are to the 1612 edition); Sir John Ferne, *The Blazon of Gentrie* (London, 1586). Other influential works by heraldic authors that sought to tighten up and restrict definitions of gentility (Cooper, 'Ideas of gentility', p. 58) included Robert Glover's 'Nobility, Politicke and Civill', which did not appear in print until 1610 when it was published as part of Thomas Milles' *The Catalogue of Honour* (London, 1610) and William Segar's *Honor, Military and Civill* (London, 1602), which was a synthesis of earlier work.

23 In fact Ferne and Legh were drawing on only part of this tradition which, as Cooper and Keen have pointed out, was in itself open ended and ambiguous: Cooper, 'Ideas of gentility', pp. 46–8; Keen, *Origins of the Gentleman*, pp. 76, 104, 106, 110, 124.

enabled these authors to argue that nobles and gentry were a race apart, united by a purity of blood that carried within it special qualities distinguishing them from plebeians and commoners. They did not attempt to challenge the conventional view that gentility was based on virtue, and that it represented an acknowledgement of an individual's virtuous achievements.[24] But they insisted that those descended of gentle stock were more likely to display virtuous qualities, partly due to the environment in which they were raised and partly to a natural propensity to emulate their forbears.[25] 'Gentleness' was most visible, according to Legh, in those families where 'children who beeing brought up in vertue, and perceiving the advauncement of their progenitors, endeavoured themselves to walke in their parents' steppes'.[26] This enabled heraldic writers to get around the argument – often advanced by humanists and derived from Cicero – that this meant that 'new men', risen into the ranks of the gentry by their own achievements, were as worthy, if not worthier, than established families. For these authors, the highest form of gentility was 'perfect' or 'mixed noblenes', where virtue and gentle blood were combined.

The emphasis on lineage and blood was elaborated in their discussions of pedigree and coat armour. Recording and validating these two aspects of gentility had, of course, long been one of the primary professional functions of the heralds. But in the hands of these authors it was elevated into something much more significant: the basis for a new branch of knowledge that provided the key to understanding matters of honour and status. Legh praised it as the science of sciences, which 'made the distinction between the gentle and the ungentle in whom there is much difference as between virtue and vice'.[27] The heralds themselves were seen as being transformed from what Ferne described as amateurish retired knights to highly skilled professionals, equipped to advise and adjudicate on all matters relating to honour and coat armour.[28] The pursuit of this branch of knowledge was often endowed with semi-mystical overtones that enhanced its authority. Ferne referred to the 'secret emblemes or sacred sculptures of the coat armour' in which were 'figured out' a whole history of a family's virtuous achievements, as well as its relationships and

[24] Ferne, *Glorie*, pp. 14, 26–7; Legh, *Accedence of Armorie*, p. 17; Milles, *Catalogue*, pp. 17–21; Segar, *Honor, Military and Civill*, pp. 203, 209, 228

[25] Ferne, *Blazon of the Gentrie*, pp. 2–3, 14, 26–7, 87, 162; Legh, *Accedence of Armorie*, pp. 16, 17, 19, 209–10; Milles, *Catalogue of Honour*, pp. 10, 11–12, 17–21; Segar, *Honor, Military and Civill*, pp. 114, 121, 203, 209, 228; see also, R.P. Cust, 'Catholicism, antiquarianism and gentry honour: the writings of Sir Thomas Shirley', *Midland History*, 23 (1998), 48–51.

[26] Legh, *Accedence of Armorie*, p. 16.

[27] Cooper, 'Ideas of Gentility', p. 58.

[28] Ferne, *Blazon of Gentrie*, pp. 74, 91, 152.

descents.[29] Legh described a visit to the library of an imaginary 'Heraught Marshall' – surely intended to evoke the library at Derby House – in which were preserved all the records of 'true nobility', set out in a series of huge ledgers, recording descents, pedigrees and coat armour.[30]

The elevation of this branch of knowledge was assisted by significant advances in the techniques for studying genealogy and heraldry. From the 1560s onwards, the heralds began to research these matters with far greater professionalism. On visitations they began examining charters, indentures and seals provided by the gentry, sometimes copying them out as proof of a descent or coats of arms. They also started to record the displays of heraldry found in church windows or on monuments, and deposited the resulting 'church notes' at Derby House to provide a further archive of armorial 'evidences'. Robert Glover, Somerset herald, took these processes a stage further. In the 1570s and 1580s he formalised the use of rectilinear pedigrees and began systematically transcribing the records he had seen, not only as proof of descent, but also for their more general interest as historical sources.[31] By the 1590s 'genealogical science' was providing the tools and inspiration for the burgeoning study of family and local history, and the new fashion for creating elaborate (often bogus) pedigrees. Generations of peers and gentlemen became enthusiastic students of their ancestral heritage, poring over muniments to establish the distinguished achievements of their forbears and, if possible, trace their line back to the Norman Conquest.[32]

The effect of all this was to reinforce and popularise the basic message of the heraldic writers: that gentility was a status that implied a whole series of complex relationships and obligations. To accord it to an individual simply because of wealth or reputation was to pander to the ignorance of the 'vulgar multitude' and ignore the importance of nobler associations with honour, lineage and virtue. Ferne was particularly exercised by the problem of 'so many craftsmen, so many mercers & shopkeepers, retaylors, cooks, victaylours, and taverne-holders, millioners and such lyke' who had been 'suffered to clothe themselves with the coates of gentlemen'. To remedy this he urged his contemporaries to adopt the principle that 'the name of gentleman can not by common right apperteine to any except to those of coat armors', and that the heralds make it their prime function 'to denounce all such' who tried to claim the title without this qualification. He then went on to outline a scale

29 *Ibid.*, p. 26. 30 Legh, *Accedence of Armorie*, pp. 217–18.

31 Ailes, 'Development of heralds' visitations', 16–21; Wagner, *Heralds of England*, pp. 206–7; 'Robert Glover (1543/4–1588)', *Oxf.DNB*.

32 J. Broadway, 'No Historie So Meete' (Manchester: Manchester University Press, 2006), pp. 62–3, 152–60; Cust, 'Catholicism, antiquarianism and family honour', 40–70.

of degrees of gentility that combined this principle with his insistence that only the gentleman of five descents was 'perfect'. At the top of his hierarchy was 'the gentleman of auncestry with blood and coat armour perfect'; then 'of blood and coate armour perfect, but not of auncestrie'; next 'of blood perfect and coat armour unperfect', then 'of coate armour unperfect' and finally the group that he sought to have excluded, those who were 'neither of bloud nor coat armour'.[33] This proved too elaborate and limiting to be incorporated into general usage. However, it was picked up and reiterated by later generations of heralds;[34] and, by the 1590s, Ferne's general message, that only those in possession of coats of arms and a respectable lineage were fully entitled to be called gentleman, was beginning to resonate widely.

Concern to restore order and degree began to appear more urgent because of the widespread experience of social dislocation during the final decade of the sixteenth century; and this was compounded by a heightened sensitivity to the dangers of 'popularity' and social 'levelling'. Puritan challenges to the established church hierarchy, evidence of 'democracy' leading to disorder in town government and the political turmoil caused by the Earl of Essex at court, were all interpreted as indications that the 'inferior multitude' was being stirred up to threaten hierarchy and degree.[35] Such concerns leaked into anxiety about the preservation of the honours system. William Segar, appointed Norroy in 1597 and Garter in 1604, denounced 'Peevish precisenese which loves no heraldry' and that derided 'Degrees in bloode [as] the steps of pride and scorne'.[36] And John Raven, Rouge Dragon pursuivant during the 1590s, spelt out the danger presented by 'these paritistes [who] would have one condicon & qualitye in all creatures'. Drawing extensively on Ferne's *Blazon of Gentrie*, he explained that this was an affront to the

[33] Ferne, *Blazon of Gentrie*, pp. 68, 89–91.

[34] For example Sir Richard St George, Norroy, revived Ferne's categories and approach in an important Jacobean attempt to grapple with the whole problem of defining gentility: CA, Phillipps MS 13084, vol. 5, fos. 301–2, 'A note of Sir Richard St George about precedency', *c.* 1615.

[35] J.A. Sharpe, 'Social strain and social dislocation, 1585–1603', in *The Reign of Elizabeth I. Court and Culture in the Last Decade*, ed. J.A. Guy (Cambridge: Cambridge University Press, 1995), pp. 192–211; Stone, *Crisis of the Aristocracy*, pp. 30–1; D.M. Hirst, *The Representative of the People* (Cambridge: Cambridge University Press, 1975), pp. 47–8; R.P. Cust, 'Patriots and popular spirits: narratives of conflict in early Stuart politics', in *The English Revolution c. 1590–1720*, ed. N.R.N. Tyacke (Manchester: Manchester University Press, 2007), pp. 54–7.

[36] Guillim, *Display of Heraldrie*, prefatory verses by Segar. In similar vein William Wyrley and Sampson Erdeswicke, and also John Ferne, condemned those 'that be so precise' that they disallowed the setting up of funeral monuments to the gentry: W. Wyrley, *The True Use of Armories* (London, 1592), pp. 21, 25; Ferne, *Blazon of Gentrie*, p. 83.

natural order created by God, the biblical distinctions between noble and ignoble, and 'the pollicye of all countries and commonwealths', by which those 'of the best families, whoe excel in virtue and valor . . . deservedly obteyn the right of nobility, with most honourable ensigns to them and their posterity'. Without the maintenance of such honourable distinctions, 'all thinges goe to havocke and confusion . . . every one taketh his owne way, there aryseth all horror and disorder'.[37]

These anxieties gave greater urgency to the reforming efforts of the decade. In January 1592, following the Earl of Shrewsbury's death, the office of Earl Marshal was entrusted to a commission headed by Burghley who had always taken a keen interest in matters relating to descent and antiquities.[38] Burghley recognised that the honours system was in urgent need of reform and highlighted the problem in the queen's patent to the lords commissioners, which he probably drafted. In what was to become a consistent refrain of the complaint literature of the decade, this emphasised the dangers in the casual proliferation of grants of arms, made 'to persons of base birth, or of mean vocation & quality of living'. Not only did this endanger the established hierarchy, it had also brought about 'the dishonour of our nobility and chivalry, and . . . the disgrace of sundry families of ancient blood'.[39] As in the mid Tudor period, the status of the aristocracy, and its capacity to govern and defend the country, appeared to be under threat.

The lords commissioners did their best to address the problem by reissuing Norfolk's 'Orders' of 1568 and revising the standard order of precedence among peers at public ceremonies, which had become a cause of contention.[40] They also conducted a lengthy inquest that exposed George Rotherham's attempt to claim the barony of Grey of Ruthen, on the basis of a pedigree that had been forged by William Dethick garter king of Arms. This became something of a *cause célèbre*, exposing the danger to title and property right posed by false or inaccurate pedigrees.[41] However, diligent as Burghley was, he had limited time and energy to devote to reforming the heralds and his instinct was to fall back on repeating the formulae of the 1560s. It was only when a new

37 BL, Harleian MS 1154, fos. 65v–63v (reverse pagination). Raven set out these concerns in an address to the Norfolk gentry at the start of a county visitation in 1613. I am indebted to Adrian Ailes for this reference.

38 Wagner, *Heralds of England*, pp. 203, 209, 215, 221.

39 BL, Additional MS 6297, fo. 3. For examples of the complaint literature, see Wyrley, *True Use of Armories*, pp. 2, 7, 19–20; Wagner, *Heralds of England*, pp. 203–4.

40 Joseph Edmondson, *A Complete Body of Heraldry*, vol. 1 (London, 1780), pp. 151–3; G.D. Squibb, *Precedence in England and Wales* (Oxford: Oxford University Press, 1981), pp. 98–100.

41 Squibb, *High Court of Chivalry*, pp. 36–7; Wagner, *Heralds of England*, p. 215.

Earl Marshal was appointed in December 1597 that the cause of reform gained major impetus.

The queen's nominee was Robert Devereux, 2nd Earl of Essex, who had a point to prove. The Earl Marshalship was his first major civil office and, therefore, an important test of his ability to make the all-important transition from military commander to civilian councillor. It also conferred on him the status of senior member of the aristocracy, with all the responsibilities that this entailed for overseeing the honour system and protecting the interests of his fellow peers.[42] Essex threw himself into the role with considerable energy. One of his first moves was to encourage his trusted adviser, Lord Henry Howard, younger brother of the 4th Duke of Norfolk and himself a longstanding student of matters relating to honour and nobility, to draw up guidance on what he should do as Earl Marshal.[43] Howard wrote 'A briefe discourse of the right use of giving armes with the late abuses about that matter, and the best meanes by which they may be reformed orderly', which ran to over 50 folios. This was far more wide ranging than anything put forward by Burghley. It included the radical proposal that all grants of arms made since his brother's order for a register in 1568 should be called in, investigated, and, if found wanting, invalidated. 'By this means', Howard insisted, 'yow shall take awaye the leaven that infects the lumpe of dowe, make upp the breache that lett in the popular invasion and once againe give honour unto armes.' The treatise was presented to Essex just as he was about to depart for Ireland in early 1599, and he had no opportunity to implement it.[44] But, during 1598, he did pursue two, very significant, initiatives, probably with Howard's advice.

One of these was to begin in earnest to confront the problem of duelling. This was an issue that was beginning to cause concern in the late 1590s after a series of high profile combats appeared to challenge order and royal authority. The practice of the 'duel of honour' or 'private combat' developed in England in the late sixteenth century. Prior to the

42 A.M. Gajda, *The Earl of Essex and Late Elizabethan Political Culture* (Oxford: Oxford University Press, 2012), pp. 175–8; P.J. Hammer, 'How to become an Elizabethan Statesman: Lord Henry Howard, the Earl of Essex and the politics of friendship', *English Manuscript Studies, 1100–1700*, 13(2007), 20–1. I am grateful to Alex Gajda for valuable discussions of Essex's Earl Marshalship.

43 Hammer, 'How to become an Elizabethan statesmen', 1–25; 'Henry Howard, Earl of Northampton (1540–1614)', *Oxf.DNB*.

44 FSL, MS V. b. 7, pp. 97–8. I am grateful to Paul Hammer for advice on this manuscript. See also, Hammer, 'How to become an Elizabethan statesman', 9; L.L. Peck, *Northampton. Patronage and Politics at the Court of James I* (London: George Allen & Unwin, 1982), pp. 156–60.

1580s most of these combats were chaotic and relatively harmless affairs, being fought with the heavy broadsword with a single cutting edge, and the buckler or shield. As Lawrence Stone observed, these weapons often 'allowed the maximum muscular effort and the most spectacular show of violence with the minimum threat to life and limb'. By the 1580s, however, the broadsword was giving way to the much more dangerous rapier, with a needle sharp point with which it was all too easy to kill a man by running him through the vital organs. It was recognised that if its use was allowed to continue unregulated large numbers of young nobles and gentlemen would kill each other. So there was a concerted effort at educating the gentry in the proper use of the rapier, and moves to control and restrict the practice. The first fencing school opened at Blackfriars in London in 1576 and by the turn of the century fencing was firmly established as one of the skills required of a young aristocrat. At the same time, among lawyers, social commentators and defenders of the traditional English martial arts there was the beginnings of reaction against this dangerous and new fangled Italianate practice.[45]

Responsibility for regulating duels fell within the remit of the Earl Marshal who traditionally had oversight of all forms of judicial combat; but it was also a particularly significant issue for Essex who himself had a reputation as a duellist and was patron to Vincente Saviolo, the most famous fencing master in London.[46] If he was to demonstrate his credentials as a responsible, civilian minister, it was important that he show his resolve in dealing with such matters. The individuals Essex chose to make an example of were two middling gentry from Suffolk: Anthony Felton, a justice of the peace, and Edmund Withipool, a militia captain. This enabled him to sidestep the thorny issues that would have arisen had he picked on members of the peerage. In April–May 1598 the two men were summoned before a high-powered tribunal and imprisoned, with Withipool, the main perpetrator, being forced to apologise publicly to Felton and promise to defend his honour 'against any that would by his former unadvised act seeke to impaire it'.[47] The case was widely publicised, with a copy of the judges' verdict circulating separately. Essex also consulted the heralds over how to deal with such matters in the future and William Segar, newly appointed Norroy, responded by

45 Stone, *Crisis of the Aristocracy*, pp. 242–50; M. Peltonen, *The Duel in Early Modern England* (Cambridge: Cambridge University Press, 2003), pp. 44–79, 94–7.

46 Gajda, *Earl of Essex*, p. 177; 'Vincente Saviolo (d.1595)', *Oxf.DNB*.

47 Bodl.L., Ashmole MS 856, pp. 105–6; Squibb, *High Court of Chivalry*, pp. 39–40. The case was still being referred to as an important precedent in the 1621 Parliament: *Commons Debates 1621*, iii.218, v.159.

drawing up 'A briefe discourse touching injuries', the first anti-duelling treatise to emerge from official circles in England. This rehearsed what, over the following decades, was to become the most familiar argument against duelling: that 'whosoever taketh revenge by himself to be done goeth about to take God's office out of his hand and power from the magistrate.'[48] The aim of Essex's policy on duelling was to bear down on some of the unacceptable aspects of aristocratic honour culture in the interests of promoting royal authority and good government. This approach was to be picked up again under James and Charles. However, the main priority of his Earl Marshalship was not to diminish the aristocratic order, but to reinforce and strengthen it.

This priority became apparent in his second major initiative, which was to reconstitute the Court of Chivalry to hear a dispute over rival claims to the Abergavenny peerage. Full-dress sittings of the court resumed, probably for the first time since the 1560s. The survival of a seating plan for the session held at Essex House on 25 November 1598 makes clear the dignity and significance of the occasion. The Earl Marshal sat at the centre of a raised stage, flanked by senior peers, who included Lord Buckhurst and the Earls of Sussex, Rutland and Cumberland, and the Lord Chief Justices. Around a table at the foot of the stage sat Garter, Clarenceux, the officials of the court and Lord Henry Howard, who probably had a hand in supervising the arrangements. Then at a further table behind them sat the parties to the case, Edward Neville and Lady Fane, together with their counsel who included Francis Bacon.[49] There were several hearings, but no clear conclusion was reached. Lady Fane's claim, as the heir general, was stronger at law; but, as Essex himself pointed out, she was 'incapable' of exercising the dignity herself 'in respect of her sexe' and he was concerned that in such a case in the future 'if an heire female noblye descended should mache herself with him who is scant a gentleman' this would 'disparage' the title. The Earl Marshal therefore recommended that the matter be referred back to the queen for

48 CA, Heralds, vol. III, fo. 1210. Segar established himself as an authority in such matters, in 1602 dealing with the judicial combats in his much better known *Honour Military and Civill*. His tract predated the consultations undertaken at Northampton's behest with members of the Society of Antiquaries in 1602 that Peltonen (*The Duel*, pp. 99–104) identifies as the earliest such debate in quasi-official circles.

49 CA, R.19, fo. 180v; Squibb, *High Court of Chivalry*, pp. 157–8. G.D. Squibb the historian of the court's jurisdiction points out that evidence about sittings of the court in the Elizabethan period is far from clear, although it was unlikely that anything of the scale and formality of Essex's proceedings had been witnessed since Norfolk's Earl Marshalship: *High Court of Chivalry*, ch. 2.

a final determination, after consultation with the Lord Chief Justices.[50] He then delivered a short homily on the place of the ancient nobility within society, which summed up his intentions as Earl Marshal.

The aristocracy, he insisted, in line with the recent writings on heraldry, were a race apart from ordinary mortals, with a distinctive blood line ordained by God and a prominent place in the natural order sanctioned by the Bible. They played an essential role in defending their country and sustaining the welfare of its people. 'England', he maintained, was 'most mighty when the nobility lead and commaunded in warre and weare great housekeepers at home and compounded causes amongst their neighbours'. They were also the main support for princely authority and government.

> In pollicey there should be an especiall regard of nobilitye, bothe in respect of the prince and the people: in respecte of the prince for they are the very subalterne parts of the prince and the very shoulders wherein the head resteth; when nobilitye is suppressed the magistrates are contemned and consequently all government subverted; distinctions of honnours have been in all civill kingdoms, onely neglected in states popular.

Upholding the status of the aristocracy, then, was fundamental to royal power and to the stability of a well-ordered, monarchical estate. This placed a heavy burden of responsibility on the prince who, as the fount of honour, was the source of all grants and titles. He or she must recognise that it was their duty to support the honour and reputation of noble families and promote their welfare. 'The favour of princes', Essex emphasised, 'should be regular, like the even ebb and flow of a river'. The prince was under an obligation 'to contyewe dignityes in heares capable thereof', and in making or withholding grants of title there should be an assurance that 'nether the prince nor the person is disgraced or dishonored'.[51] This was where the Earl Marshal and the officers of arms played a particularly important role. It was their responsibility to guide and counsel the prince in such matters and ensure that the honours system was properly regulated to protect the interests of both parties.

Essex was setting an ambitious agenda for himself and, in the event, he was unable to deliver it. His departure for Ireland in March 1599,

50 Beinecke Library, Yale University, Yale MS 370, unfoliated, sections headed 'Questions which I moved the LL Chief Justices 19 February at the command of the E. Marshall', '15 Feb 1598, att Essex House, Londinii'. This is a heraldic commonplace book belonging to William Camden, newly appointed Clarenceux, and the herald given responsibility for managing the proceedings in this case. I am grateful to Alex Gajda for informing me about this.

51 *Ibid.*

and his rebellion and execution in February 1601, put a temporary stop to reform, as much of the drive and energy that he had supplied to new initiatives drained away.[52] But his manifesto, and Howard's memorandum on abuses in the granting of arms, had highlighted the continuing importance of regulating the honours system. After nearly 50 years of proposals and initiatives the problem of how to deal with social 'upstarts' and protect the status of the noble elite still appeared intractable. The Earl Marshal and the heralds had extended their remit and developed new procedures for scrutinising titles and descents. The emergence of the new 'genealogical science' had fostered far greater awareness of the claims of those with pedigrees and coats of arms. But the numbers of 'upstart' gentlemen continued to rise, the corruption and venality of some of the heralds had been exposed and the status and prestige of the aristocratic order continued to be challenged. Addressing these problems appeared to be as urgent as ever.

The inflation of honours in early Stuart England

From the start of his reign James I was bent on reform. He encouraged petitioners to bring forward their grievances and then launched debate on a variety of topics including the church, the law courts, trade, monopolies, purveyance and taxation.[53] Reforming the honours system was part of this process. James took very seriously his obligations as the 'fount of honour', describing this role in 1611 as 'the chiefest calling' of monarchs and 'worthiest of their care', in which they 'doe most expresse the image of that imortall God which hath placed them in their thrones'.[54] As king of Scotland he had become accustomed to legislating on issues such as the regulation of precedence and the usurpation of coats of arms that were central to these concerns.[55] In England he entrusted reform of these problems to Henry Howard, now Earl of Northampton, who in February 1604 was made *de facto* head of the commission for the Earl Marshalship that had succeeded Essex.[56] After consulting Sir Robert Cotton and other leading members of the antiquarian community, Northampton drew up another substantial treatise setting out 'Certaine rules to be prescribed and ever observed for the reformation of all abuses that have crept into

52 'Robert Devereux, 2nd Earl of Essex (1565–1601)', *Oxf.DNB*.

53 R.C. Munden, 'James I and "the Growth of Mutual Distrust": king, Commons and Reform 1603–4', in *Faction and Parliament*, pp. 43–72.

54 BL, Lansdowne MS 152, fo. 38.

55 *The Acts of Parliament of Scotland*, 12 vols. (1814–75), iii.554–5; iv.164, 230, 246, 435–6.

56 'Henry Howard, Earl of Northampton (1540–1614)', *Oxf.DNB*; CA, I.25, Earl Marshal's Book of Orders, 1601–1683.

the office of armes, & for the prevention of all meanes which may bring in the like hereafter.'[57]

This identified two principal areas where action was required. One was the damage caused by James's reckless dubbing of over a thousand new knights in the first two years of his reign, 'the very stinke' from which 'hath poisoned an order of high reputacon over all the world and left a scandalous offence both to domesticall and forraine eares'. The other was 'the general contempte and skorne' with which the heralds were regarded 'in this carping age' as a result of persisting allegations of venality and corruption. To remedy the problems caused by the new knights he proposed that James use his prerogative to determine whether those who were found unworthy should be degraded from their new rank.[58] In the case of the heralds he suggested a tightening of entry qualifications, more regular visitations, the revival of the 1566 scheme to make the Earl Marshal's court a court of record and heavy fines for those acting as bogus heralds or unauthorised arms painters who, according to a report by William Smith, Rouge Dragon pursuivant, were becoming a major nuisance.[59]

In the event, Northampton's programme promised more than it delivered. There was a tailing off in grants of knighthoods, and in the 1610 Parliament the king apologised for his profligacy; but after 1610 the inflation of honours continued with the introduction of the order of baronets.[60] There was also a draft proclamation in 1606–7 'prohibiting all persons to invade the right of the heralds', which was directed towards preventing anyone painting arms or conducting funerals without the approval of the heralds. However, it was never issued, and other proposals, such as the extension of the remit for the Earl Marshal's court, remained dead letters.[61] Nonetheless, Northampton had picked up on the aspirations outlined in the heraldic literature of the Elizabethan era and put together a series of concrete proposals for tightening the regulation of

57 CA, Heralds, vol. II, fos. 972–1003. Howard's treatise was written at some point during 1605–6. For Cotton's involvement, see K. Sharpe, *Sir Robert Cotton 1586–1631* (Oxford: Oxford University Press, 1979), pp. 114–17.

58 CA, Heralds, vol. II, fos. 995–1003; Stone, *Crisis of the Aristocracy*, pp. 74–7. This policy had been proposed by Elizabeth in a draft proclamation of January 1600 to strip the titles of those who had been knighted by Essex in Ireland: P.E.J. Hammer, '"Base Rogues" and "gentlemen of quality": the Earl of Essex and his Irish knights in 1599' (forthcoming article). I am grateful to Paul Hammer for allowing me to read this prior to publication.

59 CA, Heralds, vol. II, fos. 979–81, 978–9; FSL, V.a.199; Wagner, *Heralds of England*, pp. 237–9.

60 Stone, *Crisis of the Aristocracy*, p. 78.

61 CA, Phillipps MS 13084, vol. 8, fo. 336. In a collection of Camden's papers this draft is attributed to Northampton: BL, Cotton MS Faustina E.1, fos. 182–4.

order and degree which was to provide a template for the reforms implemented under Arundel in the 1630s. He also succeeded in implementing a change of approach and attitude in another area that greatly exercised James: the problem of duelling.

Duelling had been one of the king's particular preoccupations in Scotland where endemic feuding among the aristocracy had offered a significant challenge to royal authority.[62] At the start of the reign, as a coda to Northampton's reform programme, James urged an inventive and far-reaching solution to the whole problem whereby 'a solide and sound definition' was to be 'set downe upon all the points of gentillmenn's honour', and 'a certayne number of persons' were to be chosen, 'being nobles by birth, of honourable reputation and of sounde judgement, who should, as the marshalls of France, have powaire and authoritie to interprete and compounde all questions of honour according to that written reule'.[63] However, he had not followed through on this. The whole issue was put on the back-burner until 1609 when Henry IV of France issued his famous anti-duelling edict, proscribing the practice as an offence against God and the king, and establishing a machinery to punish offenders.[64] Following a fatal duel between Sir George Wharton and Sir James Stuart at court in November 1609, James decided to follow suit. Northampton and Cotton began extensive research into the whole matter; and the lords commissioners for the Earl Marshalship started to pursue a more interventionist role in preventing challenges from developing into duels.[65] However, James's interest in the matter fizzled out amidst preparations for the 1610 Parliament, and it did not revive until 1613 when there was another spate of combats involving court noblemen, including the fatal encounter between Lord Bruce and Edward Sackville, brother to the Earl of Dorset.[66] On 15 October 1613 the king issued a proclamation that he himself had drafted against 'the publishing of any reports or writings of duels'. This made it an offence punishable in Star Chamber to publicise proceedings relating to a duel, and ordered that anyone insulted in such a way as to provoke a challenge should refer himself to the lords commissioners, 'who shall right him in his reputation'.[67] He then commissioned Northampton and the newly appointed Attorney General, Sir Francis Bacon, to devise a lasting solution to the problem.

62 K. Brown, *The Bloodfeud in Scotland 1573–1625* (Edinburgh: John Donald Publishers, 1986).
63 CA, Heralds, vol. II, fo. 972.
64 F. Billacois, *The Duel. Its Rise and Fall in Early Modern France* (New Haven, CT: Yale University Press, 1990), chp. 10.
65 BL, Cotton MS Titus C.1, fos. 164–7, 367, 372; CA, R. 19, fos. 123–4.
66 Peltonen, *The Duel*, pp. 83–5. 67 *Proclamations*, ii.295–7.

Bacon's remedy was to mobilise the force of Star Chamber to punish the preliminaries to combat as well as the actual fight. At the first sitting of the court in Hilary term 1614 he brought an exemplary prosecution against two Surrey gentlemen, William Priest and Richard Wright, for writing and sending a letter of challenge. After a brief hearing, the two men were sentenced to suffer imprisonment in the Fleet and make a public apology at the next assizes. It was also ordered that Bacon's lengthy speech on the subject be published and the court's decree be read out by the judges on circuit. This was the forerunner to a series of hearings during the 1610s in which it was made clear that Star Chamber would severely punish the act of giving or receiving a challenge to duel.[68]

Northampton and Cotton pursued a different approach. In a proclamation against 'private challenges and combats' issued in February 1614, and the accompanying 119 page *Edict and severe Censure against private Combats and Combatants*, the earl set out, in the king's name, to tackle the root causes of the problem. Like Bacon, he focused on preventing duels before they happened, and outlined a whole raft of new penalties for issuing challenges. But whereas the Attorney General sought only to punish the offence itself, Northampton set out to provide the gentry with a remedy for insulting words – 'the first foule word upon which a quarrel is begunne' – by following the example of Spain where, he claimed, the readiness to punish 'ill language' had led to the virtual eradication of the practice.[69] Under the terms of the royal edict, insults were to be reported to the lords commissioners and the Court of Chivalry if the parties lived in the vicinity of London, or to the Lord Lieutenant and his deputies if they lived elsewhere. It was their responsibility to inflict immediate punishment on the offender and provide reparation for the injured party. Punishment was normally to take the form of a spell in prison, banishment from court, removal from the commission of the peace (if the offender was a JP) and deprivation of 'that usual and ordinarie libertie (which all gentlemen enjoy as their birth right) to weare swords and daggers'.[70] Reparation would usually be by means of a public apology and submission, which would not only compensate the injured party, but also act as a deterrent to others. In devising these

[68] Sir Francis Bacon, *The Charge of Sir Francis Bacon, knight, his Majestie's Attorney General touching duels upon information in the Star Chamber against Priest and Wright* (London, 1614). The most high profile of these cases was *Darcy* v. *Markham*, in November 1616, after which, again, Bacon's speech was circulated, along with those of the leading judges, in this instance as separates: *Life and Letters of Francis Bacon*, ed. J.A. Spedding, 7 vols. (1861–74), vi.113; Beinecke Library, Yale University, Osborn file 6115.

[69] James I, *Edict and severe Censure against Private Combats* (London, 1614), pp. 47–8.

[70] *Ibid.*, pp. 22, 42, 48–58, 91–2.

remedies, Northampton was explicitly acknowledging the view that had become firmly established within the contemporary honour code, that if a gentleman allowed an insult to go unchallenged his reputation would suffer irreparable damage. 'Whether they be spoken to the partie's face that is depraved, or behinde his backe . . . nothing flies more swiftly, nothing sinckes more deeply, nothing spreades more widely then the slanders that emblemish any man's good name': 'by this meanes', the earl insisted, 'all men may bee robbed of their reputation which as a birth right they brought with them into the world'.[71] What the Edict proposed was that the repair of such injuries should now be in the hands of noblemen who 'in respect of their honour by birth' had both the experience and integrity to resolve 'all questions of honour'.[72] By offering the gentry an 'honour court' of unimpeachable authority it was hoped that they could be weaned off the temptation to duel. Once this system was in place, the February 1614 proclamation explained, it would no longer be possible to make the argument that a gentleman had no remedy other than the duel when he was insulted or given the lie.[73]

These remedies revealed a profound difference of philosophy between Northampton and Bacon. Both endorsed the view that the private combat was a direct challenge to the king's authority and that of the legal system; however, they differed in their assumptions about what was needed to correct this. Northampton accepted the premise of the Italianate conduct literature, that honour was reflexive and depended on the individual responding aggressively to the slightest challenge to his good name. He had to demonstrate repeatedly, in the arena of public opinion, that he was neither a coward nor a liar. Hence, his aim was to ensure that the Court of Chivalry – rather than gossip or hearsay – became the supreme arbiter of an individual's reputation. Bacon, on the other hand, was opposed to the whole principle of safeguarding reputation. As he recognised, one of the consequences of the elaboration of the duelling code was to make 'private combats' much more likely. The rigid stereotyping of the conventions had become so elaborate that a gentleman found himself under an obligation to challenge an opponent for the most trivial of slights: a loose word, the unintentional jostle in a passageway, a touch of bad temper, all could be interpreted as demeaning acts that required a gentleman to give the perpetrator the lie and thus invite a challenge to fight. To attempt to arbitrate in matters of personal honour would, Bacon argued, simply perpetuate the whole elaborate charade. Instead the gentry must realise that the duelling code was based on a false premise. Those who subscribed to it were equating honour with the 'vain opinion of the world',

[71] *Ibid.*, pp. 42–6. [72] *Ibid.*, pp. 20–1. [73] *Proclamations*, i.303–4.

whereas, in fact, it was the reward and acknowledgement of virtue, and therefore something altogether more robust and enduring. Drawing on an alternative literature of honour, he challenged the link made in the courtesy manuals between external comportment and inner virtue, and insisted that the latter had nothing to do with manners. 'True fortitude' was about mastering one's passions rather than reacting to every trifling discourtesy; about internalising the Christian message of forgiveness and charity; and about understanding that if one was to sacrifice one's life it should be done in the service of one's country rather than in pursuit of some private quarrel.[74]

Both Bacon and Northampton's proposals were intended as stop gaps, pending legislation to deal with the whole problem. James brought this forward at the start of the 1614 Parliament, but nothing was achieved as his programme was buried under other grievances.[75] After that the anti-duelling campaign ran out of steam. Northampton's death in June 1614 deprived it of much of its drive and energy; and the belief expressed by James in March 1616 that 'we have by the severitie of our Edict, put down and in good part mastered that audacious custome of duelles', appeared to remove the need for urgent action.[76] Star Chamber continued to punish the act of issuing a challenge to duel, as proposed in the 1613/14 proclamations; but the next concerted drive against duelling was delayed until the 1630s when Northampton's approach became the basis for Caroline practice.[77]

In the aftermath of the 1610 Parliament, James began to look again at other aspects of the honours system. He had promised parliament on 21 March 1610 that henceforth he would be much more circumspect in granting honours and he remained sensitive to the need to preserve the integrity of the system.[78] However, at the same time, because of the

74 Peltonen, *The Duel*, pp. 108–45; A. Stewart, 'Purging Troubled Humours: Bacon, Northampton and the anti-duelling campaign of 1613–1614', in *The Crisis of 1614 and the Addled Parliament*, eds. S. Clucas and R. Davies (Aldershot: Ashgate, 2003), pp. 81–91.

75 *Life and Letters of Bacon*, iv.397; James I, *Edict*, pp. 35–6, 41–2; Stewart, 'Purging Troubles Humours', pp. 81–91.

76 *Proclamations*, i.359–60; see also his speech in Star Chamber in February 1616/17: TNA, SP 14/90/65.

77 For some of the Star Chamber cases on duelling, see TNA STAC 8/22/4, 8/28/10, 8/62/20, 8/251/1. It is worth noting that Bacon himself was, on occasion, sensitive to the demand to protect reputation. In the high profile Star Chamber case of *Darcy* v. *Markham*, he acknowledged, when giving sentence in November 1616, that 'the matter of reparation of honour of the Lord Darcy' should be referred to the Court of Chivalry: *Life and Letters of Bacon*, vi. 113.

78 James VI and I, *Political Writings*, ed. J.P. Sommerville (Cambridge: Cambridge University Press, 1994), p. 197.

failure of the Great Contract, he was in urgent need of new sources of revenue. The result was the notorious scheme for the sale of honours that began with the creation of baronets in 1611 and became institutionalised with the wholesale marketing of titles and offices once Buckingham had established his ascendancy. Historians such as Charles Mayes, Linda Peck, Lawrence Stone and Katherine Van Erde have highlighted the ways in which these developments discredited the honours system and brought it to the verge of collapse. For the first time the monarch's prerogative powers as 'the fount of honour' were openly questioned in the House of Commons; and the fallout helped to create factions of discontented peers and to fuel the attempts to impeach Buckingham in 1626. Stone also emphasises its contribution to a disastrous decline in respect for the peerage.[79] The consequences of the sale of honours were undeniably profound and far reaching, but they are, in many respects, more complex and ambivalent than the existing literature implies. The imputation that the crown simply abandoned its earlier concern for upholding the integrity of the honours system and became engaged in a cynical exercise in exploitation needs to be examined afresh. So too does the suggestion that the weight of abuses was causing a disastrous decline in the prestige and reputation of honours.

At the heart of many of the problems relating to honour in the 1610s was the issue of precedence. In honour-based societies the ordering of precedence between individuals has always been of particular concern. This was emphatically the case in early modern England where precedence disputes arose at every level, from peers jockeying for position on ceremonial occasions, such as the procession to the opening of parliament, to parishioners challenging each other for the best church pews. The observation by Sir William Segar that 'the loss of worldly wealth is lesse grievous to men of generous minds then the privation of place' was borne out in a complaint picked up by the king, and later recycled in the 1614 and 1621 Parliaments, that 'gentlemen of great livelihood and estimation' had begun to boycott 'public assemblies for the administration of justice . . . because they scorn to give place unto many . . . whom they account their inferiors'.[80] Precedence highlighted issues of respect, deference and personal dignity that were invariably close to the hearts of members of the noble elite.

79 C.R. Mayes, 'The sale of peerages in early Stuart England', *JMH*, 29 (1957), 35–7; L.L. Peck, *Court Patronage and Corruption in Early Modern England* (London: Routledge, 1990); Stone, *Crisis of the Aristocracy*, pp. 119–28, 747–53; K.S. Van Erde, 'The Jacobean Baronets: an issue between king and Parliament', *JMH*, 33 (1961), 137–47.

80 Segar, *Honor Military & Civill*, p. 207; *Proceedings in Parliament 1614*, 328–9; Van Erde, 'Jacobean Baronets', 146.

Its regulation was an age-old concern and ordinances issued by the monarch or senior officials, such as the Earl Marshal or Lord Chamberlain, can be traced as far back as 1399. The basic premise that guided these was 'antientcy', the notion that peers, knights and others should be placed within their ranks according to the antiquity of their creation. This was the assumption commonly applied by the Earl Marshal and the heralds when they were required to adjudicate on such matters, and enshrined in the Precedence Act of 1539 which largely consolidated existing practice and related it to the House of Lords.[81] However, there were always anomalies and inconsistencies. One of the most vexing of these related to the precedence of the sons (and daughters) of peers. The principles relating to this had been restated in what came to be regarded as an authoritative decree by the lords commissioners in January 1595. The doctrine enunciated here was that because the eldest sons of peers would be the next to inherit their title they should take their place after the fully fledged senior peers in the rank one down from their fathers, and the younger sons two ranks down. As members of the *nobilitas maior*, and therefore superior in blood and breeding, they should always rank above knights or other members of the *nobilitas minor*.[82] This decree appeared to settle the matter in an unambiguous and straightforward fashion, but, as we shall see, in matters of precedence issues were often far from clear cut and the status of the sons of peers, particularly younger sons, was to cause continuing aggravation.

Elizabeth's parsimonious approach to the granting of honours had helped to ensure that precedence disputes were relatively limited and could generally be resolved on an *ad hoc* basis, although Essex's creations in 1599 did cause problems.[83] James's profligacy, however, introduced an entirely new dimension to the whole issue. As David Gelber has pointed out, for the first time the monarch was required to adjudicate the claims of whole ranks and orders among the elite.[84] The extent of the problem became apparent in the wake of the mass dubbing of new knights in 1603–4. Within a few months the size of the order had increased threefold by nearly 1000 and such large numbers were being created that it was virtually impossible to keep track of the order of creation. As an anonymous herald grimly remarked,

81 D. Gelber, '"Hark what discord": Precedency among the early Stuart gentry', *The Coat of Arms*, 3rd ser. III (2007), 125; Squibb, *Precedence in England*, pp. 15–17, 30. I am grateful to David Gelber for guidance on these matters. It should be noted that the 1539 Act also gave higher status to those holding offices of state.

82 Squibb, *Precedence*, 98–100.

83 Hammer, '"Base Rogues"'.

84 Gelber, '"Hark what Discord"', 117–44.

it pityeth me to se all the partes of this kingdom almost in flames of fyrie quarelles, only for goinge before, and no man more contentious for yt then suche as wear wonte to go behynde.[85]

The consequences of the 1603–4 creations were, however, minimal compared with the fallout from the inauguration of the new order of baronets in May 1611.

The crown's primary consideration in creating baronetcies was, of course, revenue raising; but there was also an intent to use the scheme to sort out the problems over precedence created by the mass dubbings of the early years of the reign. In a misguided attempt to answer those who complained that knights and esquires of 'reputation and approved integritie' were being forced to 'yield the upper hand to their inferiors', James authorised the commissioners for creating baronets to ignore pre-existing titles and the rule of 'antientcy' and allow those considered 'more remarkable' for their 'house, years or calling in the commonwealth' to take their place before others.[86] Predictably this attempt to introduce reputational – and therefore subjective – criteria into the process of ranking simply confused the whole issue. The commissioners were bombarded with requests from knights and esquires lobbying for their own particular merits to be recognised by being granted first place in their shire. In the end they had to fall back on 'antientcy' as the surest means of resolving the whole issue, with the proviso that the king could always backdate creations to recognise particular worth.[87]

A more persistent problem arose over the placing of the baronets in relation to the younger sons of peers. The original letters patent had specified that they should be accorded precedence immediately below the barons, as the apparent equivalent of the medieval 'bannerets' who in the 1595 settlement had been placed above the younger sons of viscounts and barons. But this was challenged on behalf of the younger sons, and when the matter came before the Privy Council and the king it was initially resolved in their favour. However, the baronets refused to take this lying down, sought advice from lawyers and antiquarians and let it be known that they felt they had been short changed on their investment. James agreed to allow the two parties to put their case before the Privy Council in a three-day hearing in April 1612.

85 Stone, *Crisis of the Aristocracy*, p. 65.

86 *Somers Tracts*, ii.256; K.S. Van Erde, 'The creation of the Baronetage in England, *Huntington Library Quarterly*, 22 (1959), 313–22. For the king's sensitivity to considerations of precedence see his response to the proposed scheme for 'Knights of the Crown' that anticipated complaints about the boycotting of public assemblies: Stone, *Crisis of the Aristocracy*, pp. 78–9; Queen's College, Oxford, MS 144, fo. 25.

87 Gelber, '"Hark what Discord"', 131–9; Stone, *Crisis of the Aristocracy*, p. 85.

This was a thoroughly bad-tempered affair as the baronets became embroiled in arguments with individual privy councillors and even the king himself. James acknowledged that the main question was whether baronets were, indeed, the equivalent of bannerets, but concluded that the whole matter was too obscure to admit any clear determination. He therefore stuck by his initial resolution in favour of the younger sons and attempted to fudge the issue by declaring that there were two sorts of bannerets: those created on the field of battle, following the royal standard, who did, indeed, take precedence over the younger sons; and the rest who were the equivalent of the baronets and did not enjoy this privilege. He then tried to appease the baronets by granting them additional privileges, such as the right to have their sons knighted when they reached the age of 21 and to display the red hand of Ulster on their coat of arms. Finally, he attempted to lay the whole matter to rest by publishing a 'Decree and Establishment' announcing his decision.[88]

James's 1612 decree was the first of a series of declarations by which he tried to bring about a final resolution of the conflicts over precedence. It was followed in June 1620 by an adjudication in favour of the younger sons of earls whose placing had been challenged by eight knights who were members of the Privy Council; then in April 1623 by a proclamation for registering knights according to their dates of creation; and in October of the same year by a further set of orders that sought to settle a long-running dispute over whether knights should take precedence over London aldermen. The disputes came on thick and fast, with each attempted resolution stirring up new problems as it created winners and losers. By the late 1610s the volume of precedence disputes, and the bitterness that they engendered, had reached extraordinary proportions and officeholders at every level, from churchwardens and local justices to the lords commissioners for the Earl Marshal and the Privy Council, were being involved in arbitration.[89] It was these disputes that initially challenged the integrity of the honours system and brought the king's exercise of his prerogative in such matters into question. But their effects were compounded by the accelerating momentum of the sale of titles.

During the early 1610s exploitation of the honours system to raise revenue was constrained by the prospect of having to answer to another parliament and also by the presence of Northampton, who after Salisbury's death in May 1612 effectively became first minister. But with the collapse of the 1614 assembly and Northampton's own death most of

88 HMC, *10th report, Appx.4, Earl of Westmoreland MSS*, pp. 8–11.
89 Gelber, '"Hark what Discord"', 117–44.

the checks were removed. The Earl of Somerset and his successor as royal favourite, George Villiers, later Duke of Buckingham, had fewer scruples, and from 1615 onwards the emphasis was on raising revenue by whatever means came to hand.[90] This made the honours system an easy target. New schemes emerged thick and fast, and naked profiteering became the order of the day. Cotton picked up the mood of the moment by reviving Northampton's 1599 scheme for calling in all grants of arms made since 1568 and threatening to invalidate those that did not meet the heralds' criteria.[91] When this was made public in February 1615, the king proposed that claimants be forced to compound for £20–£30 or they would be 'disarmed and ungentilised', which the newsletter writer John Chamberlain estimated would apply to at least 7000 armigerous gentry.[92] Sir Robert Knollys promoted a similar project to sift claims to the title of esquire and again force them to compound, which he suggested, implausibly, would raise £500 000.[93] There was also an attempt to restart the purchasing of baronetcies, by adding yet more privileges.[94] By the late 1610s, with Buckingham firmly installed as royal favourite, a free for all had developed in the distribution of honours. Concern about the merit of the recipient, or about using titles as a means of regulating precedence, took second place to their value as a source of patronage. Buckingham was prepared to sell to almost anyone who could meet the asking price, regardless of their credentials, and the process had largely degenerated into an unseemly scramble to fill the pockets of the rapacious Villiers clan.[95]

This institutionalisation of sale of titles produced a sea change in attitudes towards the honours system. The whole issue became politicised and linked to the wider concern about corruption and the abuse of

90 A. Thrush, 'The Personal Rule of James I, 1611–1620', in *Politics, Religion and Popularity*, eds. T.E. Cogswell, R.P. Cust and P.G. Lake (Cambridge: Cambridge University Press, 2002), pp. 86–95. According to Sir Robert Cotton, Somerset did adopt a more responsible approach than Buckingham, turning down some of the new projects that were put to him and attempting to restrict honours to persons 'of noble extraction'. The unrestricted sale of honours did not materialise until after his fall in late 1615: Sharpe *Sir Robert Cotton*, p. 129; 'Robert Carr, Earl of Somerset (1585/6–1645)', *Oxf.DNB*.

91 This project may have been first proposed by Cotton in August 1611 (Stone, *Crisis of the Aristocracy*, p. 69; BL, Cotton MS Faustina C.VIII, fos. 2–3); however Cotton's memo on this topic is undated and could also apply to 1615 when he was seen by York herald as the chief promoter of such a project (Cotton MS Faustina E.1, fo. 141).

92 BL, Cotton MS Titus C.1, fos. 422–3, 450; Chamberlain, i.584.

93 BL, Harleian MS 1323, fo. 278; Stone, *Crisis of the Aristocracy*, p. 70.

94 Van Erde, 'The Jacobean Baronets', 142–4; Stone, *Crisis of the Aristocracy*, pp. 92–4. It was not until 1618, when the crown abandoned direct sales and granted the right as a reward for needy courtiers, that large numbers of new baronets were created.

95 Mayes, 'Sale of peerages', 21–37; V. Treadwell, *Buckingham and Ireland 1616–1628* (Dublin: Four Courts Press, 1998), pp. 103–14.

patronage that came to the fore in James's reign.[96] Whereas previously discussion of problems and remedies had largely been confined to the circles of professional heralds and antiquarians, it now became a matter of general concern and in the 1614 Parliament for the first time the Commons directly questioned the king's exercise of his prerogative in matters of honour.

On 23 May Sir Edwin Sandys presented a memorandum of 'Motives to induce knights, citizens and burgesses of the Commons House to petition his Majesty for the revoking and abolishing of the degree of baronets' approved by a committee on the 'matter of baronets'. This rehearsed familiar arguments about usurping the precedence of more worthy or ancient knightly families and discouraging them from attending public assemblies, then widened the attack to an assault on the whole practice of sale of title. 'To purchase honor with money (as baronets have done) is a temporal simony, and dishonorable to the state.' It was bringing 'the honor of knighthood, which was wont to encourage generous myndes unto high exploytes . . . into contempte.' Moreover, it constituted a dangerous challenge to the traditions of custom and common law. The petition acknowledged that 'His Majesty by his prerogative royal creates barons, viscounts, earls and any other degrees of nobility, as other his ancestors and progenitors have done.' But it denied that the king had any right to introduce this 'new degree', complaining that 'the creation of this or any other in the commonalty is not warranted by any former precedent, usage or custom.'[97]

The memorandum was not only condemning sale of baronetcies as a particularly pernicious form of corruption; it was also directly questioning the king's right to create such a new order. This led to a heated debate about whether 'the Motives' should be 'openly read' that prompted the crown spokesmen, Sir Ralph Winwood and Sir Thomas Lake, to protest that the Commons was attempting to call 'into question the king's honour' and 'impeach the king's prerogative and discretion'. Nonetheless MPs ploughed on and established a select committee to give further consideration to the petition.[98] With the acrimonious dissolution of the parliament at the start of June, the debate, for the time being, got no further; however, it was now out in the open and it had been given a wider legitimacy. The king's prerogative right to create what amounted to a new species of hereditary property had been challenged and his

96 Peck, *Court Patronage and Corruption*, chs. 7–8.

97 *Proceedings in Parliament 1614*, pp. 328–9; *CJ*, i.494; Van Erde, 'Jacobean baronets', 140–1.

98 *CJ*, i.494.

actions were seen as threatening the ultimate purpose of the honours system, which was 'to advance virtue' and thus maintain 'a flourishing kingdom'.

These themes were picked up again in an important memorandum prepared in April 1615 by Sir John Holles, one of the MPs nominated to sit on the 1614 committee. This was probably intended as a contribution to an internal council debate about whether to summon another parliament, in which Holles' newly acquired patron the Earl of Somerset was a prime participant. Holles was answering the case being put by Cotton, another Somerset client, for relaunching the baronets' scheme as one of the ways of finding an alternative to parliamentary supply; but he also appears to have been voicing many of the concerns of his fellow 'parliament men'. His memorandum, picking up the wording of the 'Motives', described the sale of titles as a form of 'temporall simonie' allowing honours to become 'markitable' in a way that undermined the fundamental principle that they should be a reward and encouragement for virtuous service. The creation of the new order was pandering to the basest instincts and vanities of the people, for whom 'worldy estimation' had become simply an appealing commodity, and opening the way for unworthy upstarts to supplant the truly noble and deserving. The result could only bring 'confusion and prejudice . . . to the king and state'. It was also, he insisted, a dangerous 'extension of the praerogative', employing methods to raise money that because they were outside the scope of custom or law were 'allwaies distastefull and sumtimes dangerous as it appeareth by many examples enrolled in the scriptures, antient and modern histories, as well at home as abroad'. The sale of baronetcies could be compared to impositions and other 'projects' devised 'to supply their king's wants without questioning, or accounting with them their mispendings'. He therefore urged the king to wind it down, rely in the future on raising money through parliament and use his prerogative as the 'fount of honour' to make it clear that baronetcies would not be hereditary.[99]

Much of what was implicit in the Commons' attack on baronetcies in 1614 was made explicit by Holles. Familiar rhetoric about the rise of upstarts and the damage to social order if the honours system was not properly maintained were being recycled and directly connected to some of the most sensitive political issues of the day: impositions, projects and

[99] *Holles Letters*, iii.525–9; Peck, *Court Patronage and Corruption*, pp. 211–13. For Holles' connection with Somerset at this time and the debate within Somerset's entourage and the Privy Council to which the proposal probably relates, see *Holles Letters*, i.x–xli; Van Erde, 'Jacobean Baronets', 142–3; Sharpe, *Sir Robert Cotton*', pp. 129–30.

the corruption of patronage. The royal prerogative was being subjected to searching criticism and efforts were being made to limit its extent and application by invoking custom and common law. The effect of this was to turn anything connected with sale of honours into another potential flashpoint in exchanges between crown and subject.

The issue resurfaced in the 1621 Parliament in discussions within the committee of grievances in late April. However, in spite of the fact that in the meantime large numbers of new baronetcies had been sold, it had lost much of its impact. MPs were no longer so bent on confronting the question of James's use of his prerogative to create a new title and the complaints raised on this occasion were mainly about precedence.[100] When Secretary Calvert communicated the king's wish that they 'forbeare to meddle' – because 'all honor belongs to the king's prerogative' and therefore 'he may raise the meanest to the greatest honor' – the Commons accepted this and backed off, although, as the diarist John Pym observed, 'not without some mutteringe that it was a grievance to the gentry'.[101] The issue of the royal prerogative in such matters came up again in the 1624 and 1626 parliaments, but in rather different contexts. In 1624, as we shall see, it linked to the activities of patentees and became an element in the attack on the jurisdiction of the Earl Marshal and abuses by the heralds; in 1626 it was prominent in the attack on Buckingham for undermining the integrity of honours.[102] In neither case was the question of placing customary or legal limits on the king's authority as 'the fount of honour' addressed as directly as it had been in 1614–15. But it was clear that a powerful discourse had been established connecting abuses of the honours system with the wider corruptions that were undermining the foundations of the state.

Alongside this there was the re-emergence of the issue touched on by Essex in 1598: how far the monarch's exercise of his prerogative power was constrained by the rights and privileges claimed by the 'ancient nobility'. This came to the fore in the 1621 Parliament in a petition against the precedence accorded to Scottish and Irish peers. Since 1616 Buckingham had been selling these titles to Englishmen. As a result, the Irish peerage, in particular, was expanding rapidly, with an enlargement from 28 to 80 between 1616 and 1630 and the majority of new titles going to those who had little or no connection with Ireland. While Scottish and Irish titles had largely been confined to natives of the two countries who attended ceremonial and official events in England only

[100] Van Erde, 'Jacobean baronets', 145–7; *Commons Debates 1621*, iii.104, 113; v.169.
[101] *Commons Debates 1621*, iv.283; v.124.
[102] Peck, *Court Patronage and Corruption*, pp. 194–5.

occasionally, English peers had been content to afford them the privilege of 'noblemen strangers' and allow them to take their place in line with their rank, immediately behind their English equivalents. However, now that so many of these titles had been acquired by native Englishmen this began to cause tension and resentment.[103] After the favourable judgements in the cases relating to baronets and knights of the Privy Council, the English peers seem to have been confident that the king would again come down on their side. A group of them met together at the London houses of the Earls of Dorset and Salisbury and in February 1621 33 of them drew up a petition to James complaining that they and their children were being 'prejudiced' by the current arrangement of according the 'respect of place as to noblemen strangers'. They prefaced this with an apparently unconditional acknowledgement of the king's prerogative to grant titles to whoever he wished:

> it is far from us to meddle with, much less to limit or interpret the power of your sovereignty, knowing that your Majesty (being the root whence all honours receive sap under what title soever) may collate what you please, upon whom, when and how you please.

But at the same time they referred to their duty to 'preserve our birth rights', which was an unmistakable assertion that there were certain respects in which noblemen were obliged to defend their honour, regardless of the monarch's inclinations. They therefore petitioned that 'we may be excused if in civil courtesie we give them not the respect or place as to noblemen strangers, seinge that these being our countrymen.'[104]

James was normally very wary of denying his peers in anything pertaining to their honour. His first instinct, as he had shown in the precedence cases, was to take their part. But on this occasion the fact that Buckingham was closely involved in the creation of Irish peers, and that several of the signatories were implicated in opposition against him, meant that he would have none of it. He demanded that if they went ahead they should do so by petitioning the Privy Council rather than himself. This the peers refused to do and after further threats and a tongue-lashing from the king, the petition was dropped.[105] However, the issue of the precedence of Scottish and Irish peers would not go away and at the end of the decade it was to re-emerge to cause considerable problems for Charles.

103 C. Mayes, 'The early Stuarts and the Irish peerage', *EHR*, 58(1958), 227–51.

104 *Ibid.*, 248; A. Wilson, *The History of Great Britain Being the Life and Reign of King James the First* (London, 1653), p. 187.

105 R. Zaller, *The Parliament of 1621* (Berkeley: University of California Press, 1971), pp. 60–1; *APC 1619–21*, pp. 352–3.

In the meantime, the message behind the parliamentary protests against the sale of honours and the activities of the heralds was not lost on James and during the final 4 years of his reign he did make a significant effort to restore his reputation as 'the fount of honour'. His main ally in this was the Earl of Arundel who followed in the footsteps of his great uncle, the Earl of Northampton, and grandfather, the 4th Duke of Norfolk. Like other members of the Howard family, Arundel had a highly developed sense of his responsibility for upholding the integrity of the honours system. He was regarded as the premier member of the English aristocracy and worked hard at living up to this by deliberately cultivating an image as the epitome of ancient nobility.[106] In 1616 he was nominated as one of the lords commissioners for the Earl Marshalship and by 1618 he had acquired the services of Sir Robert Cotton as his chief antiquarian adviser.[107] On 29 August 1621, when he was at the height of his favour with Buckingham, he finally achieved the position that his great uncle had so long coveted and was appointed Earl Marshal.[108] The following month, in the court masque *The Gyspies Metamorphosed*, his friend Ben Jonson set out what was effectively his 'mission statement':

> Yours shal be to make true gentry known
> From the fictitious, not to prize blood
> So much by the greatness as by the good;
> To show and to open clear virtue the way
> Both whither she should and how far she may;
> And whilest you do judge twixt valour and noise
> To extinguish the race of the roaring boys.[109]

Jonson shared Arundel's desire to restore the pristine values of true nobility against the 'noise' of all those whose claims to honour and title were based on swaggering display and empty self-advertisement. But he had set the earl an extremely demanding task, particularly in the face of the institutionalised corruption of the Buckingham regime.

Arundel's main asset in the early stages of his Earl Marshalship was the support of the king. This was put to the test almost immediately in October 1621 when Ralph Brooke, York Herald, challenged the authority of the Court of Chivalry on the grounds that the Earl Marshal had no

106 Walker, 'Life of Arundel', in *Historical Discourses*, p. 221. For the earl's claims to be regarded as the premier member of the aristocracy, see Walker, *Historical Discourses*, pp. 209, 223 and the comments by the Venetian ambassador in 1612, cited in Sharpe, 'The Earl of Arundel', p. 211.

107 Sharpe, *Sir Robert Cotton*, pp. 136–7.

108 Sharpe, 'The Earl of Arundel', pp. 212–15.

109 M.F.S. Hervey, *The Life, Correspondence and Collection of Thomas Howard, Earl of Arundel* (Cambridge: Cambridge University Press, 1921), p. 197.

jurisdiction in the absence of a Lord High Constable. Brooke had a long history of crossing swords with the lords commissioners and his fellow heralds, and on this occasion he openly declared that he would overthrow the authority of the Earl Marshal and his court. Arundel referred the matter to James who vindicated the Earl Marshal's authority to convene the court and at the same time instructed Arundel 'to restore and settle the honourable proceedings of that court with addition of all the rights thereto belonging'.[110]

Over the following months Arundel did much to re-establish the Court of Chivalry's position as a forum for adjudicating all matters relating to honour. He laid down the basic procedures for hearing a case, secured a warrant from the attorney general to set a table of fees, and appointed Dr Arthur Duck as king's advocate to the court. This last move was particularly significant because Duck was one of the leading civil lawyers of the day, and, as we shall see, his appointment signalled that from now on the court's procedures were to be based firmly in Roman civil law.[111] Proceedings in the revived court finally commenced on 24 November 1623, with a formal opening in the Painted Chamber, set out according to the arrangements for the Essex House meeting in November 1598. The Earl Marshal and six leading peers sat on a raised platform under the king's arms, with the court register, heralds, counsel and officials arranged around a large table below them. Arundel himself made a speech, 'importing the long discontinuance of the said office, and his honor's intent to revive that which had long bin in the dust'. He also explained that he had made careful search of precedents to ensure that he 'might not incroach upon other courts, as his lordship hoped other courts would not incroach upon his'.[112] The court then turned to tackle its first case, *Leeke* v. *Harris*.

This was carefully chosen to demonstrate the king's determination to uphold the integrity of the order of baronets. In early 1623, Simon Leeke, a Shropshire esquire, had petitioned against Sir Thomas Harris claiming that the baronetcy he had purchased in December 1622 was invalid because his grandfather John Harris had been disclaimed in the Shropshire visitation of 1584. Arundel consulted the king who, in October 1623, gave him the authority to go ahead with a full-dress hearing in the Court of Chivalry, restating unequivocally his determination to abide by the principle that 'no person whatsoever should be advanced to that degree unlesse he were a person of undoubted gentrie & descent

110 Squibb, *High Court of Chivalry*, pp. 43–6, 129–30, 239; *APC 1621–3*, p. 99; AC, EM 1395.

111 Squibb, *High Court of Chivalry*, pp. 47–50.

112 *Ibid.*, pp. 48–9; CA, R. 19, fos. 370–3.

at the least from a grandfather that was a gentleman'. James also took the opportunity to confirm that no more than 200 baronets would be created, as stipulated in his original letters patent. The case quickly became a *cause célèbre*, attracting the attention of newsletter writers and the London gossip networks.[113] When it came to a hearing, Harris attempted to secure a prohibition to have it removed to a common law court and then used every device available to obstruct the proceedings, including procuring a certificate from Segar, Camden and several of the other heralds declaring that the 1584 disclaimer was in fact invalid.[114] There were at least 23 further sittings of the court before a verdict was reached on 19 November 1624. Harris was 'declared and denounced no gentleman'; but, in spite of James's request that if the court found him guilty they should proceed to 'actuall degradation', they discovered that they were unable to rescind a title granted under the great seal and, with the assistance of Buckingham's brother, the Earl of Anglesey, Harris and his family were able to go on enjoying their baronetcy.[115]

The inconclusive outcome of the Harris case was indicative of the problems faced by Arundel in trying to reform the honours system. Chief among these was the hostility of the royal favourite, both towards anything that threatened to reduce his lucrative income from the sale of titles and, increasingly, towards Arundel himself. Having initially supported him in securing the office of Earl Marshal, Buckingham turned against Arundel in 1623–4 as it became clear that he was opposed to the breach of treaties with Spain. The royal favourite probably encouraged attacks on the Earl Marshal's jurisdiction during the 1624 Parliament, which were led by two of his principal allies in the Commons, Sir Robert Phelips and Sir Edward Coke. These left the earl considerably weakened with the threat of a full-scale inquest into the powers of the Earl Marshal and the Court of Chivalry hanging over him.[116] His position was weakened still further by the death of James who had been his principal source of support. However, as we have seen, he remained committed to reform and at the start of the new reign decided to gamble that the new king would share his priorities.

113 CA, R. 19, fos. 303–4, 362, 364; TNA, SP14/153/54; Chamberlain, ii.532.

114 *Reports of Heraldic Cases in the Court of Chivalry 1623–1732*, ed. G.D. Squibb (Harleian Soc., 107, 1956), pp. 3–4; F. Heal and C. Holmes, *The Gentry in England and Wales 1500–1700* (Basingstoke: Macmillan, 1994), pp. 28–9.

115 *Reports of Heraldic Cases*, pp. 1–5; CA, R.19, fos. 306–79; Squibb, *High Court of Chivalry*, pp. 50–1; Chamberlain, ii.590; TNA, SP 14/153/54; 14/185/92; 16/8/9; 16/9/41.

116 Sharpe, 'The Earl of Arundel', pp. 219–7.

Arundel's intervention in April 1625 was only the latest in a long line of initiatives to reform the honours system. They were intended to fix in place the existing hierarchy, ensure that different ranks within it discharged their responsibilities and protect the status of the 'ancient nobility'. The success of these schemes, however, was mixed. During the 1560s and 1590s vigorous reforming proposals were brought forward, but never fully implemented. In the meantime the heralds had colluded with the social pressures pushing large numbers of commoners into the ranks of the gentry and, in the process, acquired an unsavoury reputation for venality. Perhaps the most significant innovation during Elizabeth's reign was the emergence of the new 'genealogical science' that equipped gentry and noble families to assert their distinctiveness and status. But the impact of this was gradual and it became just as open to abuse through the elaborate forged pedigrees designed to conceal the origins of 'upstarts'.[117] Under James the nature of the problems changed as the heraldic establishment sought to get to grips with the 'inflation of honours'. Here success was limited, with efforts to tackle the problem repeatedly stymied by James's financial needs and the pernicious influence of the royal favourite, Buckingham. But the king was at least aware of his responsibilities and, during the early 1620s, with the assistance of Arundel and the revival of the Court of Chivalry, the foundation was laid for positive action at the end of the decade.

In the meantime sale of titles and precedence disputes proved a combustible mix. Matters relating to honour became politicised and linked to wider concerns about corruption in a way that had not happened before. Politicians and social commentators ratcheted up the rhetoric, describing the abuses as a 'sicknesse', a 'temporall simonie' and an 'intollerable evill'.[118] Public opinion became highly sceptical of the motives of those engaged in the oversight of the honours system, especially the officers of arms. Parliament also became involved, with MPs queuing up to denounce the damage that was being done to the state's ability to reward the virtuous conduct of its servants. Two particular flashpoints emerged. The first was over the way in which sale of titles could be

117 Stone, *Crisis of the Aristocracy*, pp. 23–5.

118 For example, Thomas Scott, 'A Discourse of Polletique and Civill Honour', in G.D. Scull, *Dorothea Scott, also Gotherston and Hogben* (London, 1882), pp. 150–3, 156–9; Francis Markham, *The Book of Honour* (London, 1625), pp. 70–1. Even within the heraldic establishment there was an acknowledgement by the late 1620s that James had gone too far in granting baronetcies. According to Arundel's protégé John Borough, Norroy king of arms, in a memo of *c.* 1628 he had allowed it to become a device to 'gratify Scottishmen and other needy courtiers', which led to the admission of men of 'base birthe and meane estate': BL, Sloane MS 2904, fos. 33–4, memo by John Borough, Norroy king of arms, *c.* 1628.

seen as an abuse of the royal prerogative, creating new forms of saleable property that contravened law and custom and paralleled other 'projects' for raising revenue. The second was a result of the new titles upsetting established hierarchies and thus challenging the rights and privileges of the 'honour community'.

Historians have directed considerable attention to these developments, with Lawrence Stone, in particular, arguing that they brought the crown and aristocracy into disrepute and through the resulting faction and conflict ultimately contributed to the collapse of monarchy.[119] As we shall see, the linkage between abuses in the honours system and the rebellion of the 1640s was much less clear cut than this. Nonetheless, some of the fault lines revealed under James did persist and continued to cause problems for Charles. The discourse which connected abuses of honours with 'projects' and corruption more generally persisted to fuel opposition to Buckingham in 1626 and attacks on the Court of Chivalry in 1640. Alarm about royal interference threatening the rights of the 'honour community' flared up in the dispute over Irish peers in 1629 and hampered royal efforts to deal with the problem of duelling. Above all, the legacy of disrespect for the noble order was seen as a problem requiring urgent attention by the late 1620s.

Amidst all this, however, it is important not to exaggerate the effects of 'inflation of honours'. It does not appear to have resulted in any straightforward decline in the prestige and attractiveness of honours *per se*. Most commentators were certainly agreed that the orders of knighthood and nobility had been tarnished by the admission of many who were considered unworthy of their honours. But, as Holles had noted, 'worldly estimation' retained all the power of its appeal, and the social elite continued to chase after titles even when some of the gloss had been taken off by the adverse publicity. The existing system retained its vitality and relevance and under Charles and Arundel's considerable energy was devoted to ensuring that it once more functioned in such a way as to provide the traditional rewards and incentives.[120]

119 Stone, *Crisis of the Aristocracy*, pp. 120–8, 750–3; L. Stone, 'The inflation of honours 1558–1641', *P & P*, 14 (1958), 45–70; Mayes, 'Sale of peerages', 35–7.

120 For an interesting commentary on this, see the manuscript 'Discourse of Polletique and Civill Honour' penned by the Kentish puritan esquire, Thomas Scott in the late 1610s. Scott was an enthusiast for the new order of 'knights of the crown' proposed soon after 1610, in spite of being highly critical of the sale of honours generally: Scull, *Dorothea Scott*, pp. 163–4; P. Clark, 'Thomas Scott and the growth of urban opposition to the early Stuart regime', *HJ*, 21 (1978), 1–26.

2 Charles I and the defence of aristocracy, 1625–1639

'Ancient nobility'

In February 1627 George Mountain, Bishop of London wrote to Sir Edward Conway, secretary of state, to report a book that had recently been published without licence containing 'matter of state'.[1] The book was Sir Robert Cotton's *A Short View of the Long Life and Raigne of Henry the Third*, and the 'matter of state' that it contained was the account of the rise and fall of a royal favourite, Simon De Montfort. The contemporary relevance was readily appreciated by one of the *Short View*'s early readers, the Oxford fellow, Thomas Crosfield. He recorded in his dairy for 3 March 1627 that

> There is a litle booke published comprising severall passages of state historically related as they were carried in the long raigne of king Henry the 3rd with some observations or application to our state at this present which by reason of favourites & discontented peeres resembles in many thing that ancient government.[2]

The timing of the book's publication in the aftermath of the attempted impeachment of Buckingham in the 1626 Parliament appears to have ensured its commercial success and it immediately ran into three editions.[3] Because of the subject matter and the identity of the author, who in the recent past had been supplying precedents on the fall of favourites to Buckingham's parliamentary opponents, it has been read as an oppositionist tract, giving a voice to the 'discontented peeres'.[4] But this was not how it had been originally conceived. When questioned by Mountain, Cotton explained that he had written the book some 15 years earlier and denied having had any part in its publication. The inference

1 TNA, SP 16/54/4.

2 *The Diary of Thomas Crosfield*, ed. F.S. Boas (London, 1935), p. 12.

3 W.A. Jackson, 'Sir Robert Bruce Cotton's *A Short View of the Long Life and Raigne of Henry the Third*', *Harvard Library Bulletin*, 4 (1950), 31–2.

4 McCoy, 'Old English Honour', pp. 145–6. On Cotton's involvement with 'opposition' at this time, see Sharpe, *Sir Robert Cotton*, pp. 177–80.

to be drawn from his account was that an enterprising publisher, recognising its topicality, had taken one of the many manuscript copies in circulation and published the *Short View* without its author's consent.[5] This information makes a considerable difference to the implications of the book and the ways in which it can be understood.

The *Short View* is a classic example of what contemporaries called 'politic history'.[6] As Crosfield recognised, it used lessons from the past to provide guidance to the conduct of politics in the present, and, in keeping with this, Cotton's text was larded with numerous asides in the form of maxims and gobbets of distilled political wisdom. It presented a portrait of a monarchical state, recognisably similar to that of early Stuart England, in which order and stability were under threat from ambitious nobles, domineering favourites and a fickle popular multitude. Only a virtuous and benevolent monarch, guided by the wisdom of an experienced and disinterested 'ancient nobility' could overcome these challenges.[7]

In the early years of his reign the young Henry had to deal with a 'Commons... greedy of liberty', egged on by 'young and noble spirits' who were the 'darlings of the multitude'. But, with the guidance first of all of his uncle, the Earl Marshal, the Earl of Pembroke, and later the Earls of Norfolk and Kent, he had prospered:

> These vapours did ever and easily vanish so long as the helme was guided by temperate spirits and the king tied his actions to the rule of good councell and not to young, passionate or single advise.[8]

However, the disgrace and removal of Kent and the rise of Simon De Montfort destroyed all this. De Montfort was the supreme example of the overweening favourite: he drew 'all publike affayres into his owne hands, all favours must passe from him, all preferments by him, all suites addressed to him, the king but as a cipher set to add to this figure'.[9] With the aid of foreign-born 'minions' he had stripped the crown of its assets, ridden roughshod over the people's legal rights and excluded the 'great and gravest men' from office. To make matters worse he had formed an alliance with 'unquiet spirits' in the church who sought to 'frame to themselves some other forme of government... as that which with the giddy multitude winneth best opinion'.[10] In an attempt to retrieve

[5] Jackson, 'Cotton's *Short View*', 28–32; Sharpe, *Sir Robert Cotton*, p. 238.
[6] F.J. Levy, *Tudor Historical Thought* (San Marino, CA: Huntington Library, 1967), ch. 7.
[7] Sir Robert Cotton, *A Short View of the Long Life and Raigne of Henry the Third King of England* (London, 1627).
[8] *Ibid.*, pp. 3–8. [9] *Ibid.*, pp. 14–15. [10] *Ibid.*, pp. 15–20.

the situation Henry had summoned a parliament, but then found De Montfort's party using it to dictate his choice of councillors and establish themselves in power. 'Parliaments that before were ever a medicine to heale up any rupture in princes' fortunes are now growne worse then the malady, sith from thence more mallignant humors beganne to raigne in them then well composed tempers.'[11] At this point rebellion broke out and after their victory at Lewes, De Montfort and his allies were able to seize 'regall power', only to have the tables turned on them by a fluky royal victory at Evesham. Having been rescued by good fortune, however, Henry determined to learn the lessons of 'his former misery'. His main mistake he now recognised was 'referring all to base, greedy and unworthy ministers whose councells were ever more subtle than substantiall'.[12] He set about repairing the situation by purging the court of its vices and 'immoderate liberality', restoring the rule of law and filling 'the seates of judgement and counsel . . . with men nobly borne . . . [whose] abilities he measureth not by favour or by private information as before, but by the publike voyce'. Above all he took the direction of government into his own hands and ensured that his councillors fulfilled their proper role as advisers not directors of the monarch.

> He sitteth himselfe in councell daily and disposeth affaires of most weight in his owne person. For councellors be they never so wise or worthy are but as accessaries not principals, in sustentation of the state . . . [they] have ability to advise, not authority to resolve.[13]

It is not hard to see why the *Short View* has been read as an 'oppositionist' tract. With its commentary on the dangers of royal favourites and the need for the 'ancient nobility' to resume their rightful place in royal counsels it matched the agenda of those – including Cotton and, his patron, Arundel – who supported the impeachment proceedings of 1626. It also fits well with the analysis of recent historians, such as John Adamson and Richard McCoy, who have emphasised the hostility of members of the 'ancient nobility' towards the policies of the crown. Following the lead given by Arthur Wilson, in his history of James's reign, written in the 1630s and 1640s, they have stressed the commitment of the political legatees of the 2nd Earl of Essex – mainly comprising the circles around his son, the 3rd Earl, and the Earls of Southampton and Warwick – to upholding the notion of 'Old English Honour', which meant defending 'publick liberty' and preventing the rise of 'upstarts' at court. Their interpretation suggests that the interests of the 'ancient nobility' were generally at odds with those of the crown leading to the

[11] *Ibid.*, pp. 22–5. [12] *Ibid.*, pp. 43–4. [13] *Ibid.*, pp. 44–6.

attacks on Buckingham and eventually 'The Noble Revolt' of 1640–2.[14] If we return to the *Short View*, however, and gloss it in terms of the circumstances in which it was originally written, it offers a rather different perspective.

As with so much 'politic history', context is everything.[15] In 1612 the principal concern was not with royal favourites – the rise of Somerset was not yet regarded as a problem – but parliament's failure to address the king's financial needs and the threat to royal authority posed by 'popularity'.[16] In such circumstances the 'ancient nobility' were cast not as the crown's opponents, but its main bulwark and source of support. These were the 'great and gravest men' on whom the king could rely for loyalty and service in his hour of need, and whose guidance and counsel provided the surest recipe for order and stability. In this context, then, the *Short View* can be understood not so much as a manifesto of 'discontented peeres', but an account of the reasons why a monarch should cultivate the interests and allegiance of the 'old aristocracy'. In other words, it offers a valuable insight into the considerations behind the programme being advanced at this time by the Earl of Northampton and, later on, by Cotton's other principal patron, the Earl of Arundel.

According to a note on one of the surviving manuscript copies, Cotton presented James with the *Short View* in 1614.[17] It would, perhaps, have been even more appropriate had he presented Charles with a copy in 1628–9, because the situation it described closely paralleled the king's own.[18] The Caroline political world had been transformed by the assassination of Buckingham on 23 August 1628. This held out what for many the enticing prospect of the king taking over the reins of

[14] Adamson, *The Noble Revolt*, esp. pp. 31–2; James, *English Politics and the Concept of Honour*, pp. 84–8; McCoy, 'Old English Honour', pp. 135–46; N. Cuddy, 'The conflicting loyalties of a "vulgar counsellor": the third Earl of Southampton', in *Public Duty and Private Conscience in Seventeenth-Century England*, ed. J.S. Morrill, P. Slack and D. Woolf (Oxford: Oxford University Press, 1993), pp. 121–50; V.F. Snow, 'Essex and aristocratic opposition to the early Stuarts', *JMH*, 32 (1960), pp. 224–33. For valuable correctives to this emphasis on the 'oppositionist' associations of 'ancient nobility', see L.L. Peck, 'Peers, patronage and the politics of history', in *The Reign of Elizabeth*, pp. 98–108 and Hibbard, 'The Theatre of Dynasty', pp. 169–70.

[15] For an example of this see the discussion of the implications of Hayward's, *The First Part of the Life and Raigne of king Henrie IIII* in P. Hammer, 'The smiling crocodile: the Earl of Essex and late Elizabethan "popularity"', in *The Politics of the Public Sphere in Early Modern England*, ed. P. Lake and S.G. Pincus (Manchester: Manchester University Press, 2007), pp. 95–115.

[16] Thrush, 'The Personal Rule of James I', pp. 84–5, 242.

[17] Sharpe, *Sir Robert Cotton*, p. 238n.

[18] Cotton did provide advice to the Privy Council in January 1628 in 'The Danger Wherin the kingdom standeth', which harked on some of the same themes, warning of the need for 'prudent' and experienced counsellors, following the example of Lord Burghley, to 'constrain the humour of the heedless multitude that are full of jealousy and distrust': Rushworth, i.467–72.

government himself and, during the days that followed, Charles seemed intent on following Cotton's script. He let it be known that he intended 'not to discharge himself so much of affairs upon any one man, but to take the main direction to himself'.[19] He also began to place much greater reliance on the 'ancient nobility'. Among the senior politicians he now turned to for guidance were the two most prominent representatives of this group, and also two of the most notable casualties of Buckingham's ascendancy, the Earls of Arundel and Pembroke. Arundel re-established himself as Earl Marshal to become the king's most trusted counsellor on all matters relating to honour. Pembroke emerged from virtual retirement to take his place as the elder statesman of the Privy Council, performing a leading role in advising on foreign policy and preparations for the 1629 Parliament and being groomed to take over as Lord Admiral, and the nation's effective commander-in-chief, in the event of a resumption of hostilities with Spain.[20] But Charles was not just seeking to rehabilitate leading members of the 'ancient nobility', he also proposed a compact with the aristocracy as whole.

The king explained this in his closing speech to the 1629 Parliament. He and his councillors had approached the parliament with high hopes of settling the crown's differences with the people through a series of concessions on key issues such as religion and tonnage and poundage. But they were thwarted by the intransigence of a Commons leadership bent on punishing all those who were seen as threatening the liberties of the subject. The last straw was the famous incident on 2 March when the speaker was held down while Sir John Eliot read out the declaration condemning anyone who supported innovation in religion or the collection of tonnage and poundage as 'a capital enemy to kingdom and commonwealth'.[21] Charles moved quickly to dissolve the parliament and in his closing speech to the Lords on 10 March explained that he was now looking to them for loyal support and service. Initially, he told them, he had been prepared to rely on the good sense and moderation of the members of the Commons, of whom 'there are many there as dutiful subjects as any in the world'. But his faith had proved unfounded and instead 'some few vipers amongst them . . . did cast this mist of undutifulness over most of their eyes' and turned the loyal majority against him. In contrast, the Lords had stood by him as models of rectitude and dependability. The king roundly declared that 'I take as much comfort in

19 TNA, SP 16/114/17; R.P. Cust, *Charles I. A Political Life* (Harlow: Longman, 2005), pp. 76–8.

20 R.P. Cust, 'Was there an alternative to the Personal Rule? Charles I, the Privy Council and the Parliament of 1629', *Hist.*, 90(2005), 336–8.

21 *Ibid.*, 330–52; Cust, *Charles I*, pp. 105–18.

your dutiful demeanors, as I am justly distasted with their proceedings.' He therefore gave them an assurance that just as those responsible for the recent turmoil would receive 'their reward of punishment', 'so you, My Lords, must justly expect from me that favour and protection that a good king oweth to his loving and faithful nobility.'[22]

Charles was to prove as good as his word. During the Personal Rule he went out of his way to protect the welfare and nurture the interests of the established nobility. In return he expected them to uphold and reinforce royal authority and serve him in peace and war. He regarded them, as he explained in another parliamentary speech, as those 'persons in rank and degree nearest to the royal throne' who 'having received honour from him and his royal progenitors, he doubted not would for those and many other reasons be moved in honour and dutiful affection to his person and crown'.[23] This notion of bonds of reciprocal loyalty and obligation was also shared by the peers themselves. In a 1629 petition requesting that an 'adequate estate' be granted to Robert de Vere, Earl of Oxford, Arundel and a committee of the Lords emphasised the mutual benefits of sustaining members of the 'ancient nobility'. 'Those persons who have both the honour of their ancestors and good estates' were 'doubly engaged to give good and faithful [service] to your Majesty and the state'. It was therefore 'of great consequence, both to your own service and that of the publike' that the king take particular care to provide for such families and find employment for them 'before others of meaner birth and merit.'[24] Charles accepted this principle and looked to the peerage as his natural partners in government, standing alongside the bishops as one of the twin pillars on which rested the effective management of the state. If his monarchy was to prosper and flourish it was as important to promote the welfare and loyalty of his nobles, and respect for their honorific status, as it was to promote Laudian reform in the church.

The most pressing consideration that led Charles to draw his nobles into closer alliance with the crown was the imperative of building a body

22 *LJ*, iv.43. Lord Montagu's summary of the speech was that Charles had 'given us commendation for our carriage' and concluded with 'some protestation of favour and protection to us Lords': HMC, *Buccleuch*, iii.342.

23 Rushworth, iii.1163.

24 *LJ*, iv.34. Lord Clifford harped on a similar theme when petitioning Buckingham for renewal of the cloth export licence that had sustained his family's fortunes for more than a quarter of a century. The loss of the grant, he lamented, would be the 'underimininge of an ould house untainted in their loyalty towards the soveraines': cited in Stone, *Crisis of the Aristocracy*, p. 432. On the even greater benefits to the crown of securing the service of men who had 'estates' as well as 'blood', see Viscount Wentworth's comments to Archbishop Laud on the need to find suitable employment in 'the king's service' for the Earl of Northumberland in 1636: *The Earl of Strafforde's Letters*, ii.42.

of political support. Recent events had demonstrated that if his monarchy was to prosper he needed to be able to rely on the backing of his peers. During the 1626 Parliament they were thrust into the role of judges during the impeachment proceedings against Buckingham. In this capacity they eventually showed themselves amenable to royal persuasion, dropping the charges brought by the Commons after the king had given his personal assurance that the duke was innocent.[25] But on other matters they were less compliant. Early in the parliament a majority had voted to restrict the number of proxy votes held by each lord to two, which was interpreted as a gesture of hostility towards Buckingham. A majority of the house also insisted on pursuing the issue of the Earl of Arundel's exclusion and imprisonment, in spite of Charles's insistence that this had happened because of a private misdemeanour. Finally, they were less than helpful to the king over the Earl of Bristol's case, resisting efforts to put him on trial for treason and ensuring that he was allowed an impartial hearing.[26] It was a similar story in the 1628 Parliament, during the debates over the Petition of Right. Once again, as Conrad Russell has observed, the Lords did their best to steer a middle course and act as 'arbiter between the king and Commons'.[27] They respected the claim being made by the king that it was an intrinsic part of his prerogative to be able to imprison without showing cause, and they worked hard to devise a form of words that would accommodate this. However, when push came to shove and the Commons refused to back down on this issue a majority of the Lords went along with them and approved the Petition of Right.[28]

The responses of the Lords in parliament demonstrated to Charles that their loyalty could not be taken for granted. It was something that he had to work hard to cultivate and sustain. This was brought home even more powerfully during the collection of the forced loan in late 1626 and early 1627. Charles pulled out all the stops in rallying support among the peers. On 31 October 1626 he wrote personally to each of them, explaining that his honour was engaged in providing assistance to his uncle, Christian of Denmark, and that he expected them to promote the service by setting a personal example:

25 C.S.R. Russell, *Parliaments and English Politics 1621–1629* (Oxford: Oxford University Press, 1979), pp. 318–19.

26 *Ibid.*, pp. 285–6, 309–20.

27 *Ibid.*, pp. 369–70.

28 *Ibid.*, pp. 369–74; J.S. Flemion, 'The struggle for the Petition of Right in the House of Lords : the study of an opposition party victory', in *Peers, Politics and Power*, ed. C. Jones (London: Hambledon Press, 1986), pp. 31–48.

we making no doubt but you of our nobility (whom we have always found readiest to provide for the public), will be forward in this, not only to do as others have done, but so to advance and expedite the business in those counties where you are resident as that timely we may be enabled to give succour in those cases which, if they be not helped in time, will turn to the irreparable loss and dishonour of the state and us.[29]

He also engaged in extensive lobbying in which he let it be known that he regarded this as a crucial test of loyalty to his person and that any who refused would be consigned to 'the black book' of royal disfavour. In spite of this, at least 15 peers resisted and, as a consequence, most were removed from the commission of the peace and the Lord Lieutenancy.[30] This opposition left a deep impression on the king and for several years after he continued to regard it as the litmus test of personal loyalty.[31]

The events of 1626–8 exposed the range of political responses that he could expect from his peers in moments of crisis and brought home to him how hard he had to work to secure their loyalty. At one end of the spectrum he could rely on an ingrained sense of obligation and personal service that was often felt most strongly by members of the peerage. This was exemplified by Edward Lord Montagu, the Northamptonshire peer who had been ennobled by James in 1621. Montagu thought long and hard about whether to support the loan, having harboured serious misgivings about its legality and coming under strong pressure from his 'countrymen' to stand out against it. In the end he decided to pay up and stand alongside the council commissioners who came to his county to launch the service in January 1627. He set out his reasons for doing so in a statement drawn up to answer his detractors. First, he rehearsed the main features of the king's case, reiterated his promise that the loan would not be allowed to become a precedent and, in response to suspicions about his relationship to Buckingham, insisted that he had 'not been led by any by respects'. However, the heart of the matter, for him, appears to have been the king's personal request to each member of the peerage: 'Upon this letter and the causes therein alleged', he wrote,

I could not with an upright heart and good conscience deny this desire of the king's. For if it be the duty of one Christian brother, being able, to lend to another . . . how should I answer it before the tribunal seat if I should deny so amicable a desire of my sovereign lord the king.

29 HMC, *Buccleuch*, i.264.
30 R.P. Cust, *The Forced Loan and English Politics 1626–1628* (Oxford: Oxford University Press, 1987), pp. 55, 102–6.
31 TNA, SP 16/257/69i; 16/334/51.

For Montagu this combination of personal obligation and Christian duty probably represented bedrock. Throughout the 1620s his correspondence displayed a deep concern with the responsibilities implied by his rank; and in 1642, at the age of 80, he was to respond in very similar fashion when he again received what he felt was a personal summons to execute the Commission of Array.[32]

Charles could also draw considerable support from the notion that the *raison d'être* of the nobility was personal service to the monarch. Ironically, this was revealed most clearly by those who found themselves deprived of the opportunity to serve for opposing the loan. When the Earl of Essex was removed from the Lord Lieutenancy of Staffordshire in July 1627 he wrote to his friend the Earl of Monmouth to explain how deeply wounded he was by this:

> I am infinitely sorry for the opinion that his Majesty exprest to have of mee for I doe assure you I never framed to myself any other way of acquiring glorie or opinion then that by which I might with the most advantage do his Majesty the best service . . . And it is my hope that his Majesty wilbee pleased in his own tyme and according to the mesure of his owne royal heart to remove this cloud which now hangs over mee and to receive mee againe into his grace and favour which is the only glorie I doe and ever shall value in the world.[33]

Essex was not the only peer who felt the force of such a disgrace. During the 1628 Parliament a succession of lords who had received similar treatment, including Bristol, Huntingdon and Warwick, spoke up to plead that the passage of the Petition of Right be regarded as an amnesty for them. They had suffered loss of office, exile from the court and, most hurtful of all, 'the displeasure of my Prince' that Bristol described as 'fully equal to close imprisonment', 'being the debar of all promotion or imployment in the state'.[34] Their hope was that they could now make their peace with the king and enjoy the 'grace and favour' that they craved. For many peers this was the ultimate affirmation of their sense of status and identity, and it provided, perhaps, the most powerful of all incentives to remain loyal in moments of crisis.

At the other end of the spectrum, however, there were habits and beliefs drawing the peerage to the service of the commonwealth, or 'country'.

32 HMC, *Buccleuch*, i.265; Cust, *Forced Loan*, pp. 110–11; E.S. Cope, *The Life of a Public Man* (American Philosophical Soc., 142, 1981), pp. 119–22, 191–4.

33 Cust, *Forced Loan*, p. 109.

34 *Proceedings in Parliament 1628*, v.466–8. See also Arundel's comment when he was languishing in prison in April 1626 that 'I conceve myself to be barred of active virtue whylst I am restrained, until I be new qualified by the king's favour, which I desire to cum from himself': *Holles Letters*, ii.328.

These were grounded in a powerful sense of their 'birth rights' as members of an autonomous honour community that derived its status and privilege as much from lineage and inheritance as from royal 'grace and favour'. This brought with it a forceful recognition of their obligation to provide virtuous service to the state as a whole by striving to protect 'publick liberties' and the laws of the land, and offering the king wise and disinterested counsel. In certain contexts, this awareness of a wider obligation to the commonwealth and liberties – often in combination with a commitment to the 'godly cause' and/or a sense of personal grievance – could tip members of the peerage into opposition.[35] The most extreme example of this in the late 1620s was the stance taken by the Earl of Lincoln in opposing the forced loan. Not only did he attend the local meeting at Lincoln to challenge the loan commissioners' right to collect the levy in March 1627 – for which he was imprisoned in the Tower – he also appears to have been responsible for the distribution of an inflammatory tract 'To all English freeholders from a well-wisher of theirs' calling on 'honest men and wise men' to openly resist the loan because of the threat it offered to the liberties of the subject and the future of parliaments. Lincoln was a relatively young peer, driven by godly zeal.[36] Most members of the order adopted a more measured approach, seeking, as they saw it, to strike a balance between the interests of crown and subject in the manner described by Russell. Nonetheless, amid the stresses and strains of 1626–8, this meant that a significant number of them were drawn into opposing the king's wishes.

An insight into the considerations that lay behind their responses is provided by the correspondence of John Holles, now Earl of Clare. Clare had been thwarted in his ambition to become a member of the council of war during the early 1620s and was becoming increasingly disenchanted with Buckingham whom he blamed for blocking his preferment and attempting to destroy his two main court allies, Arundel and the recently dismissed Lord Keeper, Bishop Williams. He represented himself in his letters to his friends as a 'country peer' who wanted nothing more than to withdraw from the self-seeking and deception of the court to a moral high ground where he could preserve his honour and integrity. At the same time, however, as 'a good patriot', he felt drawn back in to the conflicts at the centre. It was this that persuaded him to take a leading role in the campaign against Buckingham in the 1626 Parliament and then, in December 1626, to resist the forced loan.[37] His justification for

[35] McCoy, 'Old English Honour', pp. 135–6, 141–5; James, *English Politics and the Concept of Honour*, pp. 72–92; Cust, *Forced Loan*, p. 108.

[36] Cust, *Forced Loan*, pp. 170–5. [37] *Holles Letters*, i.liv-lxiii.

his actions – which he presumed was shared by a range of correspondents, including the Earls of Arundel, Exeter and Somerset, Viscount Saye, Bishop Williams and his son-in-law, Sir Thomas Wentworth – was that the first duty of the peerage was to strike a balance between the royal prerogative and the laws and liberties of the subject. It was their responsibility to prevent one from becoming too powerful at the expense of the other. Explaining this, in the context of his concern at the prospects for the coming parliament in February 1626, Clare observed that 'it were muche better the king and people mett not at all till they both knew that neither the head can live without the boddy, nor the boddy without the head'.[38] What principally threatened this balance during 1626, he believed, was the combination of the overweening power of Buckingham and the threat from unparliamentary taxation. In the duke he saw an example of the selfishness, corruption and tyranny that characterised the classic favourite. Through unparliamentary taxation, he remarked, 'we gallop all to the overthrow of parlament and consequently to that of the state.'[39] To rectify the situation, the earl looked to the inherited wisdom and integrity of the peerage. He described this to the upper house on 19 May 1626, in the course of summarising the Commons' charges against Buckingham:

> The Lords are great judges, a court of last resort. They are great commanders of state, not only for the present but as lawmakers, counselors for the time to come. And this not by delegacy and commission but by birth and inheritance.[40]

This ingrained sense of responsibility, he explained, in a remarkable conversation with Buckingham himself, meant that the Lords could be relied on to act the part of 'honest men' and judge what needed to be done. He also looked to the leading members of the 'ancient nobility', chief among them Arundel and Pembroke, to provide what he called

[38] *Ibid.*, ii.320; see also his comments on 322, 330.

[39] *Ibid.*, ii.334. Another peer who was involved in the impeachment proceedings in 1626, Dudley Lord North, reflected on the counselling role of peers in a series of 'characters', which he composed around this time. They were those who 'nature, study and experience' had fitted for the role of the 'good counsellor' and it was their principal duty to act as a 'demi-God, placed between king and people, and must steare a course of justice indifferently betwixt both'. The noble counsellor's 'honour' lay not in titles and favours, but in the capacity 'to do good offices', and 'nothing shall be more prevalent with him than to maintaine his master in the love of his people.' The good king, conversely, sought to cultivate 'counsellors in their wisedomes and integritie', 'give a free eare to discreet persons about him that love him and his good' and acknowledge in full the value of 'a choice and great assembly', such as the House of Lords, which 'like a great streame can hardly be corrupt' and whose 'happinesse being involved with their king are likely to give him as good, honest, safe and wise counsel as any three or foure heads in his cabinet': Dudley Lord North, *A Forest of Varieties* (London, 1645), pt. 1, pp. 85–7.

[40] *Proceedings in Parliament 1626*, i.451.

'a prudent directing councell'. If the king would only rely on this, he confided to his friend Arundel, 'we should not have these complainings in our streets'.[41]

Clare firmly believed that the peerage were the key players if a political settlement was to be secured in the late 1620s. So too did Charles. By the time of his proposed compact in the 1629 Parliament he had come to recognise that, in the light of bitter experience, if his monarchy was to prosper it was crucial to get the peerage on his side. But he had also learned that achieving this was going to be far from straightforward. From this point onward, therefore, he made it a priority of his domestic policy to cultivate the support of his nobles. He would use appointments, crown patronage, personal contact and various other means at the disposal of the crown to try to ensure that they provided the body of loyal adherents that his monarchy needed. But this was more than just a matter of political calculation. It also reflected a series of beliefs and concerns that were deeply ingrained in his understanding of the nature of kingship.

The first of these was his conviction that generally the soundest course of action was to follow precedent and tradition. The notion that a loyal and prosperous established nobility would enhance the strength and authority of the crown, and that an effective ruler should, therefore, do everything in his power to promote their interests, was one of the commonplaces of contemporary politics. James clearly subscribed to this. One of his first actions on becoming king of England in 1603 was to issue a declaration increasing the size of his Privy Council so that he could add members of the 'ancient nobility whose birth and merit makes them more capable than others'.[42] In this he was following his own advice to his son in the *Basilicon Doron*. Good monarchs, he declared, should

> delight to be served with men of the noblest blood that may bee had: for besides that their service shall breed you great good-will and least envie, contrarie to that of start-ups, ye shall ofte finde virtue follow noble races.[43]

The message was clearly understood by Charles who repeatedly acknowledged that one of his principal functions as a monarch was to uphold the honour and welfare of established noble families and encourage their loyalty and service. 'As all honour hath its originall fountaine from us', he explained in a signet letter of 1632, 'soe shall it always be our

41 *Holles Letters*, ii.321, 329–30.

42 Peck, 'Peers, patronage and the politics of history', p. 107. James may well have been responding to recent complaints voiced by, among others, the Earl of Northumberland, 'that places of honor [and] offices of trust are not laid in their [the ancient nobility's] handes to manage as they were wont': Cuddy, 'Southampton', p. 124.

43 *James VI and I. Political Writings*, p. 37.

principall care to preserve it in such persons and to their posterity to whome those particular marks of merit and favour have ben bestowed either by us, or by our progenitors'.[44] He backed this up with declarations of his determination to restore their 'ancient luster', protect their reputations and privileges, and promote their 'virtuous education' and family interests.[45] Charles felt most secure when he believed that the policy he was following accorded with conventional political wisdom and in this case there was a comfortable fit.[46]

But there were also two further sets of imperatives that particularly disposed him to rely on the support of his nobility. One of these was fear of 'popularity'. The notion that there was a conspiracy of factious and self-interested troublemakers, seeking to play on the irrational and destructive impulses of the 'multitude' to advance their own ends and pull down the monarchy, had become a familiar discourse in late sixteenth century politics.[47] James explained how it worked in the *Basilicon Doron* written at the end of the 1590s. Analysing the origins of the opposition he had faced in Scotland, he described how

> Some fierie spirited men in the ministerie got such a guiding of the people . . . as finding the gust of gouvernment sweete they begouth to fantasie to themselves a democraticke forme of government . . . [and] fed themselves with the hope to become *tribuni plebis* and so in a popular gouvernment by leading the people by the nose to beare the sway of all the rule.

'Such puritanes', had they succeeded, would have spread 'paritie, the mother of confusion and enemie to unitie' and overwhelmed not only 'ecclesiasticall gouvernment', but also the 'politicke and civill estate'.[48] James continued to be highly sensitive to such concerns once he became king of England; and his experience of opposition there led him to extend his analysis to encompass common lawyers and 'free speakers' in parliament, and those who challenged his efforts to secure the 'Spanish Match', as well as the puritans.[49] The *Short View*, with its account of the people and parliament being duped into opposing the crown by a combination of demagogic nobles, corrupt favourites and self-serving church reformers spoke directly to many of these royal fears, as Cotton surely intended.

Charles shared his father's analysis of the dynamics of opposition. Refusals to pay royal taxes, puritan hostility to his government of the

44 TNA, SO 1/2, fo. 116.

45 BL, Add. MS 64,898, fos. 41–2; TNA, SO 1/1, fo. 208; SO 1/2, fos. 162–3; SO 1/3, fo. 8.

46 Cust, *Charles I*, pp. 137–8. 47 Cust, 'Charles I and popularity', pp. 238–40.

48 *King James VI and I. Political Writings*, pp. 26–7.

49 Cust, 'Charles I and popularity', pp. 241–2.

church, attacks on the royal favourite and the obstinacy and obstructiveness that he encountered in parliament, were all interpreted as manifestations of a wider popular conspiracy to overthrow monarchy. But there were particular moments when this threat seemed especially menacing, and one of these was the aftermath of the 1629 Parliament. In a lengthy declaration setting out his reasons for dissolving parliament he laid the blame squarely on the forces of 'popularity'. Those 'ill affected spirits' whose 'seditious carriage' had led astray the moderate majority in the Commons, he argued, had been acting in the same way as the '*tribuni plebis*' described by James. They had stirred up the people to resist tax payments, challenged the Privy Council and the judges, and undermined respect for law and authority, endeavouring 'to break, by this means, though all respects and ligaments of government and to erect an universal, over-swaying power to themselves'. Moreover, it had become apparent that they were part of a wider and more sinister conspiracy.

> Now it is manifest the duke was not alone the mark these men shot at but was only as a near minister of ours taken up on the by and in their passage to their more secret designs which were only to cast our affairs into a desperate condition, to abate the powers of our crown and to bring our government into obloquy that in the end all things may be overwhelmed with anarchy and confusion.[50]

The only viable response, Charles concluded, was a period of calm reflection and consolidation in which royal authority could be re-established by mobilising the forces of stability and order.[51]

Of these, perhaps the most obvious was the 'ancient nobility'. Political theorists had long recognised that within the tripartite model of classical forms of government (democracy, aristocracy and monarchy), the aristocracy played a crucial role in balancing the power of the people. The role of the Roman senate, representing the 'best and wisest' men, was regularly cited as an example of the way in which the established nobles acted as a brake on democracy and a force for stability.[52] The same attributes were generally ascribed to the 'ancient nobility'. This was the gist of Cotton's case in *The Short View*, and it can be found in other, less learned contexts such as a petition from the Cornish gentry in 1645 asking that the king entrust oversight of any settlement to the 'ancient nobility' as the personification of virtue, tradition and good

50 *Constitutional Documents*, pp. 83–99.

51 Cust, *Charles I. A Political Life*, pp. 119–21.

52 R. Tuck, *Philosophy and Government 1571–1651* (Cambridge: Cambridge University Press, 1993), p. 75; M. Peltonen, *Classical Humanism and Republicanism in English Political Thought 1570–1640* (Cambridge: Cambridge University Press, 1995), pp. 172–4, 179–80.

order.[53] This was why they were so attractive to Charles and why, particularly in 1629, they offered the obvious antidote to the 'popular' threat. As far as he was concerned, their interests were naturally aligned with those of the crown that had created them; they had recently demonstrated their loyalty in the face of the 'seditious carriage' of the Commons; and their values seemed comfortingly conservative.

For an insight into what the 'ancient nobility' stood for he needed to look no further than the reassuring figure of his Earl Marshal. Arundel, as depicted by contemporaries such as his secretary and biographer Edward Walker, was in virtually every respect the antithesis of 'popularity' (see Figure 2.1). Walker described him as 'not popular at all, nor cared for it as loving better by a just hand than flattery to let the common people to know their distance and due observance'.[54] Clarendon, whose verdicts on the earl tended to be rather less complimentary, interpreted this stance as a haughty aristocratic disdain for anything that he regarded as 'common'. But he acknowledged that Arundel had a reputation unparalleled among his contemporaries as 'the image and representation of the primitive nobility and native gravity of the nobles when they had been most venerable'.[55] The earl's pedigree was as ancient and distinguished as any peer in England and he embodied the virtues of 'integrity and courage' that his Howard ancestors had displayed on the nation's battlefields. Above all he was the model of the old-fashioned royal counsellor portrayed in Cotton's *Short View*:

> In council he was grave and succinct, rather discharging his conscience and honour than complying with particular interests . . . free from covetousness and so much above a bribe or gratuity as no person ever durst tempt him with one.[56]

He even looked the part. The earl had long been renowned for adopting the Spanish fashion of dressing all in black to emphasise a Stoical gravitas. Charles himself had copied this style as the Prince of Wales, although he had largely abandoned it by the 1630s.[57] Arundel, however, persisted, drawing attention to himself in 1633 on the journey north for the king's coronation in Scotland when he 'kept his old plainness' while all around him 'did outvie each other in the bravery and richness of their apparel and entertainment'. This prompted Walker to recall a 'common saying'

53 Bodl. L, Clarendon MS, vol. 27, 2105, fos. 22–3. For 'ancient nobility' combining the qualities of 'virtue' and 'descent' see also C.B. Herrup, '"To Pluck Bright Honour from the Pale-Faced Moon"; gender and honour in the Castlehaven story', *TRHS*, (6th ser, VI, 1996), 147.

54 Walker, *Historical Discourses*, p. 223.

55 Clarendon, *History*, i.69–70.

56 Walker, *Historical Discourses*, pp. 222–3.

57 Cust, *Charles I. A Political Life*, p. 150.

Figure 2.1 Sir Peter Paul Rubens, *Thomas Howard, Earl of Arundel, 1629–30.* Commissioned on Rubens' visit to England in 1629, this shows the Earl Marshal at the height of his powers, clad in his jousting armour and revelling in his status as the leader of the English nobility in war. (Reproduced by permission of the Bridgeman Art Library and the Isabella Stuart Gardner Museum Boston).

of the Earl of Carlisle: 'Here comes the Earl of Arundel in his plaine stuff and trunk hose, and his beard in his teeth, that looks more like a noble man than any of us.'[58] The Earl Marshal, and the values that he

[58] Walker, *Historical Discourses*, pp. 214, 221.

personified, then, appeared to offer the perfect riposte to the popular challenge.

There was also another set of considerations that inclined the king to put his trust in the 'ancient nobility': his 'Elizabethanism'. Charles shared to the full the conviction of most of his contemporaries that 'innovation' and 'novelty' were pernicious, and degenerated from the purity and integrity of the past.[59] As far as he was concerned, the high point of this past was represented by the Elizabethan age. He grew up with the myths and images of Elizabeth that were being perpetuated in the 1610s and 1620s and he sought to recreate her achievements within his own monarchy.[60] The two best-documented examples of this are the appeal of Elizabeth's 'chaste and virtuous' court, which was cited as the model for the household reforms of the early part of his reign, and the attraction of the Hookerian image of Elizabeth's church, supposedly embodying the best of 'primitive doctrine and discipline'.[61] The queen was held up to Charles's generation as the model of a 'wise and politic princess', and an important part of her wisdom and policy was seen as residing in her respect for, and cultivation of, her 'ancient nobility'. This was captured in a story told by Sir Fulke Greville in his *Life of Sir Philip Sidney*, which had become a definitive text on the essence of 'true nobility' following its composition in the 1610s. Greville recalled the solemn lecture that the queen had given to Sidney when he had the temerity to answer back after being insulted by the Earl of Oxford in a tennis match. He must recognise, she reminded him,

> the difference in degree between earls and gentlemen, the respect inferiors ow'd to their superiors and the necessity in princes to maintain their own creations, as degrees descending between the people's licentiousness and the anointed sovereignty of crowns; how the gentleman's neglect of the nobility taught the peasant to insult upon both.[62]

The lessons summed up here – about upholding royal authority and discouraging 'popularity' through preserving respect for noble rank – were reiterated in Sir Robert Naunton's *Fragmenta Regalia*, composed in the early 1630s. In a series of character sketches of leading Elizabethan courtiers and noblemen, Naunton analysed how Elizabeth had taken personal control of her government in much the same way as Charles

59 Stone, *Crisis of the Aristocracy*, p. 22.
60 S. Doran and T.S. Freeman ed., *The Myth of Elizabeth* (Basingstoke: Palgrave Macmillian, 2003), pp. 5–9.
61 *CSP Ven. 1625–6*, p. 21; Chamberlain, ii.609; *Constitutional Documents*, p. 89.
62 F. Greville, *The Prose Works of Fulke Greville, Lord Brooke*, ed. J. Gouws (Oxford: Clarendon Press, 1986), pp. xxi–iv, 40; Stone, *Crisis of the Aristocracy*, p. 747.

aspired to do. She had based her 'policy' on balancing the different interest groups and 'parties' among her courtiers and counselors 'as her own great judgement advised'. But she had also recognised that much of the ballast and continuity for her regime was provided by the loyalty and service of ancient noble families. The 'incurrence of old blood with fidelity', Naunton observed, was 'a mixture which ever sorted with the queen's nature . . . It was a part of her natural propensity to grace and support ancient nobility'.[63] Elizabeth's 'wise and politic' government provided an attractive model for Charles. But beyond this he was also drawn to a larger package of ideals and principles associated with the Elizabethan aristocracy. These can, perhaps, best be understood by exploring the values articulated by William Cavendish, Earl of Newcastle who was appointed by the king to act as governor to the young Prince Charles in 1638.

Newcastle's 'Elizabethanism' was at the core of a carefully constructed identity. It provided a set of standards and aspirations that he sought to live his life by; but, at the same time, it also underpinned a calculated pitch for political preferment. Newcastle himself was not a member of the 'ancient nobility', having been endowed with the recently created title by Buckingham in 1628. But he went out of his way to cultivate the image of the old-fashioned 'country peer'. In his biography, written by his second wife, Margaret Cavendish and published in the 1660s, he was portrayed as a nobleman who had 'lived for the most part in the country and pleased himself and his neighbours with hospitality and such delights as the country afforded'. When he was finally appointed as Prince Charles's governor, and then the following year as a privy councillor, she described how it was the king who had 'called him up to court', as if he was a Roman general or consul summoned from his plough to perform some service to the state.[64] Newcastle cultivated this image assiduously. He plied the Privy Council with a stream of letters detailing his conscientious service as a local governor, and repeatedly told his wife and friends that he aspired to do nothing more than 'rest quietly here in the country'.[65] It was also the profile that he presented to the king. When Charles stayed at his house at Welbeck in May 1633, Newcastle laid on a series of lavish entertainments prepared by his friend Ben Jonson, the main theme of which was the earl's embrace of country pastimes and obligations. The king was treated to a pageant in which the two

[63] Sir Robert Naunton, *Fragmenta Regalia*, ed. J.S. Cerovski (Washington DC: Folger Books, 1985), pp. 41, 69, 85.

[64] Cavendish, Margaret Duchess of Newcastle, *The Life of William Cavendish, Duke of Newcastle*, ed. C.H. Firth (London: Routledge & Sons, 1906), pp. 3–5.

[65] *Strafforde Letters*, i.101: BL, Add. MS 70,499, fos. 198–9.

central comic roles represented his overlordship of Nottinghamshire and Derbyshire; and the main spectacle involved various local 'characters' trying their hand at 'running at the quintain', a rustic version of the tilts traditionally performed at court.[66] This carefully nurtured image was, of course, somewhat at odds with the truth of the situation. In many respects, Newcastle was very much a court insider. He assiduously cultivated Buckingham and other 'great men' at court; he was a friend of the court painter, Anthony Van Dyck; a patron of scientists, literary figures and musicians; and, as his letters reveal, he was desperate for preferment.[67] In the end what appears to have particularly recommended him to Charles was the package of traditional knightly skills that he personified. He was famous as the leading English horseman of his day – again very much a theme of the Welbeck entertainments – and he was also renowned as a jouster and fencer.[68] These were regarded as essential accomplishments for a young prince or aristocrat – and Newcastle was to take personal charge of the prince's training in the manner of the great French riding masters of the day.[69]

Newcastle's projection of himself as an old-fashioned country peer was not just a pitch for courtly preferment, however; it also provided the cultural and ideological underpinning of a much broader agenda which intersected with the programme proposed by Arundel in April 1625 and adopted by Charles in 1629. This consisted of a series of prescriptions for achieving order and stability by turning back the clock to Elizabeth's reign and recreating the relationship that had supposedly existed between the queen and her nobility. The earl provided his fullest account of this in a remarkable and comprehensive letter of advice that he prepared for his former pupil, the soon-to-be restored Charles II, in 1658–9. One has, of course, to be particularly wary of reading back views expressed in the 1650s to the Personal Rule because of the intervening experience of civil war; but there is sufficient evidence of his attitudes during the 1620s

66 C.C. Brown, 'Courtesies of the place and the arts of diplomacy in Ben Jonson's last two entertainments for royalty', *The Seventeenth Century*, 9 (1994), pp. 150–7.

67 'William Cavendish, 1st Duke of Newcastle (1593–1676)', *Oxf.DNB*.

68 For his acknowledged mastery of the various aspects of riding and horsemanship on which even a leading court figure such as the Earl of Pembroke would defer to him, see BL, Add. MS 70,499, fos. 135, 143–4, 170.

69 L. Worsley, V. Harting and M. Keblusek, 'Horsemanship', in *Royalist Refugees. William and Margaret Cavendish in the Rubens House 1648–1660*, ed. B. Van Beneden and N. De Poorter (Antwerp: Rubenshuis and Rubenarium, 2006), pp. 37–41; 'William Cavendish', *Oxf.DNB*. This was similar to the way in which the French master, Monsieur De St Antoine had instructed the young Charles and, indeed, Newcastle in their youth: R. Strong, *Henry Prince of Wales and England's Lost Renaissance* (London: Pimlico, 2000), pp. 41–4.

and 1630s to indicate that, at least in this respect, Newcastle's thinking changed little.[70]

At the centre of his perspective was the belief shared by many in the 1630s that the partnership of crown and aristocracy could only work if the monarch was sparing and selective in the granting of honours. He or she must take great care to ensure that those preferred were those who displayed the requisite virtue and public service, and also had the wealth to sustain their titles.[71] The damage caused by inflation of honours was one of the principal themes of the advice to Charles II, but was also a prominent motif in his city-comedy *The Variety*, written at the end of the 1630s. In the play it helped to create a world-turned-upside-down in which the undeserving 'Simpleton' seemed about to secure honours, preferment and an advantageous marriage, while 'Manly', who represented old-fashioned Elizabethan values, was mocked and jeered.[72] In the advice it was seen as giving rise to a series of distortions and disorders that had helped to bring on civil war.

One of these was the introduction of 'faction' into the House of Lords. The plethora of new peers in parliament had, according to Newcastle, prompted eruptions of squabbling and in-fighting, as each competed for the preferment and recognition that they now believed was their due. It also encouraged them to make 'parties' with the Commons 'to disturb your Majesties government'. The result was the attacks on Buckingham in 1626 and later the attainder of Strafford.[73] With hindsight, this was a pattern that Newcastle could discern very clearly; but it was also a development that he had picked up at the time. In a letter to Secretary Conway in August 1626, he can be seen analysing 'faction, the dregges of the late parliament' that had endangered the duke, and identifying it with a more general malaise that was now threatening to infect county gentry and taxpayers and destroy loyalty to the crown.[74] All this was a marked contrast to the Lords in Elizabeth's day. Then, according to Newcastle, the highly selective attendance had ensured that the house

70 This is a view shared by other scholars working on Newcastle who have observed that much of what he said in the advice was foreshadowed in his dramatic works in the late 1630s: J. Knowles, 'From gentleman to prince', in *Royalist Refugees*, pp. 13–20; L. Hulse, 'William Cavendish', *Oxf.DNB*.

71 This was a view summed up in Thomas Fuller's observation that Elizabeth had 'honoured her honours by bestowing them sparingly': Stone, *Crisis of the Aristocracy*, p. 97.

72 M. Butler, *Theatre and Crisis 1632–1642* (Cambridge: Cambridge University Press, 1984), pp. 195–8.

73 *Ideology and Politics on the Eve of Restoration: Newcastle's Advice to Charles II*, ed. T.P. Slaughter (Philadelphia, PA: American Philosophical Soc. Memoirs, 159, 1984), pp. 50–1.

74 TNA, SP 16/33/126.

maintained a united front. There had been no faction, 'no joyneing with the Commons', and such reverence for monarchy that whenever Lord Burghley read out a message from the queen all the peers had stood up.[75]

Another component of government that had been undermined by the inflation of honours was what Newcastle called 'ceremony'. By this he meant the rituals of respect and reverence that sustained the authority of noblemen and monarchs. In an earlier set of advice to Prince Charles, drawn up soon after he became his governor in the late 1630s, he provided a perceptive account of how this operated.

> What preserves you kings more then ceremony? The cloth of estates, the distance people are with you, great officers, heralds, drums, trumpeters, rich coaches, rich furniture for horses, guards, martialls men making room . . . I know these masters the people sufficiently . . . Even the wisest though he knew it, and not accustomed to it, shall shake of[f] his wisdom and shake for fear of it: for this is the mist cast before us and masters the common wealth.[76]

The power and dignity of ceremony could best be maintained, he insisted, by ensuring that courtly rituals were performed by 'men of partes and power'.

> When they [the people] see this nobleman sarve as cupbearer on his kness, or suer or carver, upon great dayes or upon any day to kisse his hand upon his knee, or kneels to him, whilst his Majestie is sitting, sertenly sire this adds much to you and gives Magisty a great luster.[77]

Looking back from the vantage point of the 1650s, Newcastle insisted that one of the mistakes made by the early Stuarts had been to allow too many 'meane men' into the court. They lacked the wealth and status to command respect, which had not only diminished the traditional ceremonies but also opened the way to new fangled forms of address and the grosser absurdities of court etiquette. The latter provided one of the main comic themes of *The Variety*. In the course of a lengthy interlude Monsieur Galliard, the farcical French man of mode, set out to argue that the most important principle of good government was to teach the latest style of 'reverence'. ('Tis great matre to make a de lord, to make a de ladie . . . to make a de good reverence . . . den de reverence is obedience to monarchy and begar obedience is al de ting in de world.') No one, Galliard insisted, not even the most eminent privy councillor or

75 *Ideology and Politics on the Eve of Restoration*, p. 50.
76 H. Ellis, *Original Letters Illustrative of English Histories*, 1st ser., 3 vols. (1824), ii.290; see also *Ideology and Politics on the Eve of Restoration*, pp. 44–6.
77 *Ideology and Politics on the Eve of Restoration*, p. 48.

nobleman should be allowed into the royal presence until they had first mastered the niceties of posture and footwork. ('Dere is nobodie can be viseman, but does not make a de most excellent reverence.')[78] This scene was undoubtedly played to extract every ounce of comic potential, right down to the heavy handed French accent. But a serious point was intended. Looking back in his later advice, Newcastle claimed that 'meane people that were about the king and queene would jeer at the greatest noble man in England iff hee did not make the laste month's reverence à la mode that came with the last dancer from Paris'. He was drawing attention to the danger that the 'men of parts and power' were being driven from the court. Whereas Elizabeth, and also Prince Henry, had taken great care to ensure that they were waited on and served by such men, James and Charles had allowed too many impoverished nobles, 'favoritts' and 'grooms of the bedchamber' to steal the limelight.[79] 'Ceremony' had suffered as a consequence.

To retrieve the situation and 'sett things straight', Newcastle proposed detailed regulation of all matters relating to precedence and degree. The heralds were to publish a list of the ranking of the peerage, which would establish once and for all their seniority in relation to each other. This was to be accompanied by sumptuary regulation, which would govern not only 'degrees of apparell' but other luxury goods such as furnishings, carpets and numbers of coach horses. And these various provisions were to be enforced by the Court of Chivalry, which he described as 'a most excellent courte, for itt keeps upp seremony & order'.[80] Newcastle was making these proposals from the vantage point of the 1650s; but among the heraldic establishment and defenders of 'ancient nobility' there was no shortage of advocates for a similar approach during the 1630s.[81]

The earl's comments on ceremony and order also had implications for a third area of particular concern: the partnership of crown and nobles in governing the provinces. Here again his sense of the ideal was shaped by Elizabethan examples. He had grown up in the household of Gilbert Talbot, 7th Earl of Shrewsbury, and the techniques that Talbot used to establish his ascendancy in the north midlands were, according to Newcastle, a prescription for how to project royal and noble power. He recalled how at garter day processions Shrewsbury had been able

[78] William Cavendish, Earl of Newcastle, *The Country Captain and The Varietie. Two Comedies. . . .* (London, 1649), pp. 36, 17.

[79] *Ideology and Politics on the Eve of Restoration*, pp. 44–9, 58.

[80] *Ibid.*, p. 46.

[81] For example, see Charles's proclamation to regulate the wearing of jewellery, or Arundel's suggestions for sumptuary legislation: *Proclamations*, ii.507–8; 'Thomas Howard, 14th Earl of Arundel, 4th Earl of Surrey and 1st Earl of Norfolk (1585–1646)', *Oxf.DNB*.

to recruit the likes of Sir George Booth and Sir Vincent Corbett to accompany him, wearing the Talbot livery; then 'the next day they satt both at my lord's table nexte him and nothing but good coosen Corbett and good coosen Booth.' This 'did oblige my lord to bee their servant all the year after with his power to serve them both in courte and Westminster Hall, and to bee their solicitor – and agen my lord had no business in the country, but they did itt for him'. The consequence of this carefully nurtured framework of mutual obligation and service was to make the monarch's task in enforcing his authority at a local level relatively straightforward: 'for whatsoever busines his Majestie had in any county in England . . . itt was but speaking to Shrewsbury or Darby & such great men'. Moreover it could be accomplished without causing resentment or opposition: 'for the people doth not envey great men as they doe meaner men, and then all their kindred, friends, dependance, servants, tenantes are well pleased and your Majestie safe'.[82] Newcastle himself sought to apply these techniques in his oversight of Nottinghamshire and Derbyshire, displaying a combination of courtesy, hospitality and diplomacy to engage the leading gentry in the government of the two shires. According to the otherwise hostile Lucy Hutchinson this 'so endeared them to him . . . that no man was greater prince than he was in all that northern quarter'.[83]

Newcastle, then, envisaged royal government operating through a pyramid of power and authority which stretched downward and outwards, through nobles and gentry to the king's subjects. But the precondition to making this work was the king's ability to cultivate a sense of personal loyalty and obligation among the 'country lordes'. Guidance on how to do this was one of the main themes of his advice to the young Charles in the late 1630s. It was all about learning how to 'win' their affections with a gracious and civil manner: 'a hat or a smile in the right place . . . making a leg . . . will get their hearts'.[84] In the late 1650s, he developed this further, by outlining the ways in which he could institutionalise this personal contact and nurture a sense of obligation. First, he must ensure that they received the rewards their high position deserved: 'what doth it coste your Majesty, a blue riban [the Order of the Garter], a privye counsellorship, or such offices as your Majesty cannot bestow better than upon such great men.' A second way was to maintain the Lord Steward's dining establishment at court on a sufficiently lavish scale to ensure that 'all . . . lordes, knightes and gentlemen of worth that can serve your Majestie in the

82 *Ideology and Politics on the Eve of Restoration*, p. 47.
83 Lucy Hutchinson, cited in *Life of Newcastle*, p. 6n.
84 Ellis, *Original Letters*, pp. 289–90.

countery . . . may be invited to the severall tables . . . which gives a great satisfaction and pleases them infenitly'. Third, there was the need to involve as many noblemen as possible in the rites of court ceremonial. 'These countrey lordes' should be allowed 'to carry the sorde before your Majestie to the chapell in their turns . . . and your Majestie to speake to them sometimes as they goe & to thanke them for their attendance'. 'They would take it as it is for great dell of honor' and it 'would infenitly please and oblige them'.[85] This exercise of personal charisma, combined with effective use of the court as a 'point of contact', had, according to Newcastle done much to ensure the effectiveness of Elizabeth's rule.[86] He wanted to see the same techniques applied during the 1630s and, indeed, after the Restoration.

But restoring this quasi-Elizabethan partnership between crown and nobility was not just about institutional arrangements and regulation. It was also about reconstituting a lifestyle that for Newcastle and many of his contemporaries was indissolubly linked with the Elizabethan era. The essence of this, according to the earl, lay in accentuating the martial and chivalric elements of noble identity and reinstating the masculine qualities on display on occasions such as the garter feasts and accession day tilts. One of the reforms that he urged on the future Charles II was the revival of 'tilting by young lords and other great persons' that he had grown up with, but which had lapsed in 1622: 'I assure your Majestie [this] is the most glorious sight that can be seen and the most manlyeste.' This theme was developed further in *The Variety* which, as various commentators have observed, is full of references to the revival of Elizabethan values. The hero, 'Manly', appears on stage dressed in Elizabethan costume, as he explained, in order to highlight the contrast between the foppery of his own day and those 'honest days . . . when knights were gentlemen and proper men tooke the walls of dwarfes . . . when men of honour flourish't that tam'd the wealth of Spaine.' To emphasise the point, 'Manly' evoked the image of garter feast day processions that had displayed the sort of robust loyalty and sense of service manifest in Newcastle's portrayal of Shrewsbury.

Manly: To have seen but a St George's feast then!
Sir William: Why what difference, sir?
Manly: When they [the knights of the Garter] were install'd to see the twenty mile to Windsore strew'd with blew coates, feathers, and cognisances, as do county townes with boughs and flowers for Princes,

85 *Ideology and Politics on the Eve of Restoration*, pp. 47–59.
86 *Ibid.*, pp. 45, 47, 57–8.

> and not to go privately in a coach with a page and a barber to cut off the charges . . . Then you should have the best knighte of the countrey with the ragged staffe on their sleeves . . . Every knight had his hundreds, and these would take all the taverns in the towne, be drunke to the honor of their lordes and rather then not pay their reckoning pawne their chaines.[87]

This evocation of a hard-drinking, honest, masculine society, in pointed contrast to the timid effeminacy of the noblemen who travelled by coach with a page and barber, was a distillation of everything that Newcastle found appealing about 'Elizabethanism' and distasteful about the contemporary court. It summed up his agenda for reform.

In their commentaries on *The Variety* Martin Butler and John Adamson have both highlighted the elements of nostalgia for a lost past and opposition to the unpalatable realities of the present.[88] They depict Newcastle as an author profoundly at odds with the court culture of the 1630s. But there is a problem with reading the play, and indeed the earl's general pitch for an Elizabethan revival, in this way because it suggests an individual alienated from the regime. As we have seen, in spite of his careful cultivation of the image of a 'country peer', he was quintessentially a creature of the court. The critique that he delivered at the end of the 1630s, and again in the 1650s, was not so much a despairing lament for a vanished age, as the fleshing out of a serious programme for restoring order and tradition. Court culture in the 1630s was far from being monolithic. There certainly were those, notably in the circles around the queen, who embraced the Frenchified fashions and manners to which Newcastle took such exception. But equally there were senior figures close to the heart of the regime who embraced his project for restoring Elizabethan values and policies, not least the king himself. The measures prescribed by Newcastle – of carefully controlling grants of honours, increasing aristocratic participation in court ceremonial, using the heralds and the Court of Chivalry to regulate degree and precedence, and encouraging the service of 'country peers' – were all policies that the king did his best to promote.

The concept of 'ancient nobility' commanded widespread approval among the Caroline elite; but the meanings attached to it could differ

[87] *The Varietie*, pp. 39, 41. The reference to the bear and ragged staff was to the livery of the Earl of Leicester whose dress Manly had sought to replicate: J.S.A. Adamson, 'Chivalry and political culture in Caroline England', in *Culture and Politics in Early Stuart England*, ed. K. Sharpe and P. Lake (Basingstoke: Macmillan, 1994), p. 181.

[88] Butler, *Theatre and Crisis*, pp. 198–9; Adamson, 'Chivalry and political culture', pp. 180–1.

widely. It encompassed a whole range of values, ideals and rhetorics which were flexible, open ended and often, apparently, contradictory. In some contexts it was taken to describe those noble families who were literally 'ancient', with three or more generations of noble blood; in others it glided over these distinctions and its qualities could be appropriated by newly minted peers like Newcastle. It could be taken to sum up the ideals of the 'country peer', but also traditions of loyal service in court and council. It could be treated as almost synonymous with 'Elizabethanism', with both terms encompassing ideals of honour, patriotism, pedigree and loyalty, but it could also look significantly different, with 'Elizabethanism' conjuring up images of war against Spain and the mythology of the Protestant cause, while 'ancient nobility' alluded to the more ideologically neutral values of the golden age of chivalry in the fourteenth and fifteenth centuries.[89] From amongst this assortment of rhetorics, narratives and role models contemporaries were able to pick and choose when it came to constructing their cultural and political identities, or promoting a particular agenda. Sometimes these were deployed to legitimate opposition to royal favourites or crown policies, but more often to underpin notions of loyalty and service. Whatever the differences in the understanding of the term, however, few could challenge the notion that a loyal and prospering 'ancient nobility' would strengthen the monarchy and enhance social and political stability. For Charles this was to provide one of the guiding principles of the Personal Rule.

The aristocracy and the royal court

Charles's programme for restoring the 'ancient nobility', and promoting the interests of the peerage more generally, began in the opening weeks of his reign. As we have seen following Arundel's initiative in April 1625, he went down to the council and ordered a cessation of the sale of honours. At the same meeting he also gave Lord Lieutenants – most of whom were senior peers – power to appoint their own deputies, which, it was claimed had been the practice 'of ancient tymes was used'.[90] This was to be a mantra for the early months of the new reign. There was much talk of restoring 'ancient form' and reintroducing 'the rules and maxims of Elizabeth'. A start was made on reforming the royal household in keeping

[89] For the varying resonances of 'ancient nobility' see John Adamson's very perceptive and revealing discussion of the 'role models' and 'plurality of values' associated with the closely related concept of 'chivalry: Adamson, 'Chivalry and political culture', pp. 161–82.

[90] *APC 1625–6*, pp. 24–5; V.L. Stater, *Noble Government. The Stuart Lord Lieutenancy and the Transformation of English Politics* (Athens: University of Georgia Press, 1994), p. 19.

with ancient practice and an Elizabethan-style austerity was applied to the granting of honours. This lasted until the end of the 1625 Parliament. At the turn of the year the king was still telling the Lord Keeper that 'there being more kn[igh]ts in England already then are necessary' he was 'resolved' not to make any more, even though a coronation was in the offing.[91] Thomas Knyvett was also picking up reports of his opposition to new baronetcies: 'the king cannot induer to heer of the makeing of a baronett & thay say he will not allowe the title to discend to posterity of those which are made alredye.'[92] However, in the early months of 1626 this campaign stalled as Buckingham was able to re-establish his control over the distribution of honours.

There were two main reasons for this: first the eclipse of Arundel; and second the overwhelming need to fund the war effort. In the aftermath of the 1625 Parliament Buckingham had become convinced that the Earl Marshal was one of four senior court politicians (the others were the Earl of Pembroke, the Archbishop of Canterbury, George Abbott, and the Lord Keeper, Bishop Williams) who had been plotting to stir up opposition against him.[93] Over the following months he did everything he could to neutralise the Earl Marshal's political power. At the royal coronation in February 1626, which, in his official capacity, Arundel had played a leading part in organising, he was very openly snubbed. Buckingham had himself made High Constable for the day, so that he could take precedence before him, and Charles was persuaded to ignore the elaborate reception that he had prepared in the garden of Cotton's house in Westminster.[94] During the 1626 Parliament Arundel became more fully implicated in opposition to the duke and Charles used the excuse of his son's clandestine marriage to the daughter of the Duke of Lennox to have him imprisoned in the Tower and banished from court. He was again humiliated during the 1628 Parliament when he was prevented from taking his place as Earl Marshal at the head of the nobility in the opening procession.[95] Arundel's loss of status and authority was plain for all to see and, although he retained the office of Earl Marshal, this had a profound impact on his ability to manage the honours system.

The consequences were demonstrated in a confrontation that took place at the Office of Arms in June 1627, arising out of a previous decision to remove heralds' families from Derby House. Arundel insisted on strict enforcement of the order when he became Earl Marshal and all but one of the families moved out to ensure that the officers had enough

91 TNA, SP 16/522/81.
92 *The Knyvett Letters, 1620–1644*, ed. B Schofield (Norfolk Rec. Soc., 20, 1949), p. 69.
93 Sharpe, 'Arundel and opposition', pp. 228–9.
94 Sharpe, *Sir Robert Cotton*, p. 140.
95 Sharpe, 'Arundel and opposition', pp. 231–4; CA, Heralds, vol. VII, pp. 751–4.

room to carry out their duties. In 1626, however, they began to return, and he decided to reassert his authority, targeting Henry St George, Richmond Herald.[96] St George had long been an opponent of Arundel's protégé, John Borough, protesting against Borough's appointment as Norroy after Camden's death in November 1623 and continuing to snipe at him thereafter.[97] More significantly, he had also thrown in his lot with Buckingham and persuaded the favourite to lobby the king for him to succeed as the next Garter king of arms. Arundel came down to Derby House in person on 16 June 1627 and issued a decree ordering that all the heralds residing in the college, including St George, must move their families out immediately or face suspension. St George complained to Buckingham and, in spite of being about to depart on the Isle de Rhe expedition, the duke immediately took up the matter with the king, presenting it as an attack on one of his dependents. Arundel, he declared, must not be allowed to 'prejudice' St George's position 'out of spleen' against himself. The Earl Marshal was forced into a humiliating climbdown; and, to emphasise the weakness of his position, over the following months five more of the heralds moved their families back into Derby House.[98]

With Arundel effectively neutered Buckingham was able to persuade Charles that the needs of the war effort required a new round of sale of honours. The market reopened at his coronation in February 1626 when 59 knights of the bath were created and eight barons were raised to earldoms. The conferring of coronation honours was a long standing custom, but money had changed hands for some of the titles and once the precedent had been re-established Buckingham moved in to take full advantage. The sale of baronetcies, which had been put on hold when James's limit of 200 had been reached in 1622, was resumed. In December 1626 the duke was granted the right to dispose of 85 titles and these were soon changing hands in simple monetary transactions that made no pretence of honouring service or status. By this stage, however, the main focus of his attention was on the much more lucrative sale of peerages, some of which were rumoured to have a market value in excess of £10 000.[99] Buckingham gained from these transactions twice over. He was able to fill the Villiers family coffers and at the same time promote

96 Wagner, *Heralds of England*, pp. 230–1; CA, Heralds, vol. VII, pp. 15–16, 23–4, 168–73.

97 TNA, SP 16/68/12; CA, Heralds, vol. V, fo. 144. For St George's memorandum on why Borough was unfit to be Norroy, including his mean parentage, his acceptance of bribes from arms painters and his interference in the jurisdiction of St George's father, Sir Richard, as Clarenceux, see Heralds, vol. VII, pp. 83–4.

98 CA, Heralds, vol. VII, pp. 12–13, 58, 159–60, 163–73, 441–2; TNA, SP 16/68/12.

99 Mayes, 'The sale of peerages', 30–1; Stone, *Crisis of the Aristocracy*, pp. 94, 111–17. Even Irish peerages, which were very much a consolation prize, were bringing in £2000–£3000 a time: Mayes, 'The early Stuarts and the Irish peerage', 233, 238–48.

a phalanx of loyal clients to seats in the House of Lords, peers described by Sir Benjamin Rudyerd as 'Cardinals to carry the consistory'.[100] Parliament's articles of impeachment in 1626 included the charge that the duke was soiling 'the most beautiful flower' of the prerogative and stripping the Crown of the readiest means of rewarding loyal and virtuous servants; and the Venetian ambassador picked up a general perception that 'the number' of 'titled persons' had been 'so constantly multiplied that they are no longer distinguishable from common people'.[101] But such complaints cut little ice, and the only thing to put a stop to the sales was Buckingham's assassination.

In this, as in so many other respects, the death of the favourite marked a watershed. It brought an abrupt halt to the sale of titles and changed the whole tenor of the crown's management of the honours system. Only three baronetcies were sold between 1631 and 1641 and peerages were granted so sparingly that during the Personal Rule the total number of peers actually declined. Petitioners for baronetcies were told firmly that the king 'woulde not grant any more of that kind' and those hoping to be ennobled were generally disappointed.[102] Early in 1636 Sir Gervase Clifton was picking up hopefully on 'constant report that the list of nobility shall shortly be lengthened', with the king's newly elevated cousin, James Stuart, Duke of Lennox, having a particular say in the new creations; but, as with previous speculation on this score, it came to nothing.[103] Even the most loyal of crown servants, like Viscount Wentworth, was kept waiting years for a new title.

Just as significant as the curbing of the sale of honours was the reinstatement of Arundel. This had in fact begun shortly before the duke's assassination, as part of a charm offensive to win over former enemies. With the mediation of his old friend Sir Richard Weston, the earl was readmitted to court in July 1628 and allowed to kiss the king's hand. Over the following months he regained much of his former self-confidence and

100 TNA, SP 16/20/23; *47th Report of the Deputy Keeper of the Public Records* (1886), pp. 111–14.

101 *Proceedings in Parliament 1626*, i.446–7; *CSP Ven. 1626–8*, p. 607.

102 TNA, SP 16/120/59, 16/257/69; Stone, *Crisis of the Aristocracy*, pp. 108–9. The new mood of austerity was illustrated by the fate of George Viscount Chaworth, an Irish peer, who was driven to distraction in the early 1630s in pressing Charles for the English title he felt he deserved. He rather tactlessly tried to remind Charles that he had previously promised him such a title and even went to the lengths of sending him a list of seven peers who were recently deceased, one of whom he felt he should be allowed to replace. Charles was not impressed and after reading his letter 'saying nothing to it, called for a candle & with his owne hands burnt it': SHC, More of Loseley MSS, LM 1327/9, fos. 65–7.

103 NUL, Clifton MSS, Cl.C 660, 686.

assertiveness. With Spanish *mores* back in fashion on the back of pro-Spanish foreign policy he once again became a much-admired exemplar of noble *gravitas*.[104] He also benefited from the changed political mood following the 1629 Parliament, with the restoration of 'ancient forms' and 'ancient nobility' now a priority to counteract the pernicious influence of 'popularity'. The transformation in the earl's fortunes became very clear in March 1629, with the second instalment of the battle over the occupancy of Derby House.

Four days after the dissolution of the parliament, on 14 March, he visited the heralds accompanied by his son, Lord Maltravers, and the queen's chamberlain, the Earl of Dorset. He was equipped for a trial of strength and his target was Buckingham's erstwhile client, and the leader of the opposition to him in 1627, Sir Henry St George. Using the pretext of St George's failure to remove his family from the house in accordance with his previous order, he immediately suspended him. Sir Henry and his father Sir Richard St George (as Clarenceux the senior herald present), tried to argue that under the terms of the original college charter of 1555 it was up to the heralds to determine who resided in Derby House, which Arundel countered by asking them 'if they stood upon the Petition of Right'. This was tantamount to accusing them of embracing the legalist and 'popular' platforms that had caused so much trouble in the recent parliament. The St Georges quickly averred that they had no such intention, whereupon Arundel pressed home his advantage by asking the elder St George 'whether he thought as earl marshal it was not fitt his orders should be obeyed'. Sir Richard was forced back to his original line of defence, saying 'he was noe lawyer, but the charter would better satisfie him than he could', which the earl simply brushed aside declaring that 'he would be obeyed' and that the suspension should take effect immediately.[105]

This was a huge blow to Sir Henry St George. Not only was he deprived of his income and fees as Richmond herald, but he was exposed to some very public humiliations. The most painful of these occurred in September 1629 when, believing that he was about to be pardoned, he turned up at Windsor, attired in his heraldic surcoat, to join the other

104 Sharpe, 'Arundel and opposition', pp. 236–7. In contrast to his exclusion from the opening procession to parliament in 1628, at the start of the 1629 assembly it was reported that special preparations were being made for Arundel to 'ride in state from his house to Whitehall by virtue of his office of Earl Marshal': BL, Add. MS 35,331, fo. 26v. The Rubens portrait of the earl (*c.* 1629) provides striking visual testimony to the revival of his fortunes, depicting an Earl Marshal at the height of his powers: D. Howarth, *Lord Arundel and his Circle* (Yale University Press), pp. 152–3.

105 CA, Heralds, vol. VII, pp. 35, 47, 57–8, 81–2.

heralds for the formal signing of the peace treaty with France. With what was no doubt a certain amount of sadistic pleasure, Arundel 'sent him command' via his old adversary, Borough, that he was 'not to waite' and must leave immediately.[106] Over the following months, the luckless herald was made to squirm. He dutifully attempted to appease the Earl Marshal by removing his family from Derby House, even though six of the other heralds' families went on living there. When he anxiously inquired after the progress of one of his many petitions he was told by the earl's secretary, Humphrey Hagget, that it had simply been lost. In desperation he consulted several sergeants at law and contemplated trying to bring a suit against the Earl Marshal on the basis of the 1555 charter. But at a time when imprisoned MPs were drawing opprobrium at court for taking a stand on the provisions of Magna Carta and the Petition of Right this would have been suicidal. Eventually, after more than a year of this treatment, he swallowed his pride and made a grovelling apology. The terms, dictated to him by Hagget, involved asking pardon for having done anything that 'might offend your lordship', begging Arundel 'to settle such order therin as to your great wisdome and justice shall seeme fitt' and presenting a certificate of conformity from his fellow heralds.[107] The Earl Marshal's victory was complete and the heralds were effectively cowed for the remainder of the decade. Borough was made Garter in succession to Sir William Segar in 1633 with none of the opposition that had attended his previous appointment as Norroy, and most of the plum appointments thereafter went to his clients, such as William Le Neve, George Owen, Edward Walker and Edward Norgate.[108]

The revival of Arundel's political authority, the removal of the duke and the king's determination to exorcise the 'ill affected spirits' that had disrupted the parliament, led to a return to the agenda of April 1625. Restoring 'ancient forms' and reinstating the 'rules and maxims' of Elizabeth once more became the order of the day. This began when Charles picked up again on the reform of his household, which took the shape of introducing many of the features of the more disciplined and hierarchical Spanish court that he had observed at first hand on his trip to Madrid. Within a few weeks of the start of the reign the Venetian ambassador noted a marked difference of tone and style.

> The king observes a rule of great decorum. The nobles do not enter his apartments in confusion as heretofore, but each rank has its appointed place . . . The king has also drawn up rules for himself, dividing the day from his very early rising, for prayers, exercises, audiences, business, eating and sleeping.[109]

[106] *Ibid.*, pp. 63, 168–73. [107] *Ibid.*, pp. 25, 63, 65, 73, 117–18, 168–73.
[108] CA, Heralds, vol. V, fos. 214, 216, 226, 251. [109] *CSP Ven. 1625–6*, p. 21.

How far Charles was able sustain this initiative through the early part of his reign is unclear; but there is no doubt that he sought to reinvigorate it in 1629, this time with a marked emphasis on encouraging the attendance of his nobles.

This is apparent from an important memorandum prepared by a commission of privy councillors charged with exploring arrangements for the imminent 'lying-in' of the queen, on the occasion of her first pregnancy. The 'lords committee' reported back on 21 March 1629 and set out a series of principles which not only summed up the aims of his household reforms, but also Charles's policy towards his nobility more generally.

1. That the best way to restore the court to the auncient splendor is to resume the ancient formes both within dores & abroad.

2. These formes within dores consisted principally in distinguishing of roomes & persons, places of chiefe respect being frequented with persons of honor & ranke, & others with such as were of lesse quality, every distance & degree being then well knowne & strictly observed.

[. . .]

4. The tables were always kept which drewe recourse & attendance upon the court.

. . . Both within doors & abroad, according to occasions, warning was given to prime persons to attend the princes who receaving good countenance of them were therby encouraged to give attendance which they always did with chearfulnes & alacrity.[110]

With its emphasis on preserving due decorum and ceremony, and at the same time ensuring the personal attendance of his nobles, this accorded closely with Newcastle's recipe for the king's management of his entourage. It envisaged the re-establishment of what was taken to be an Elizabethan-style court that would serve as an essential 'point of contact' between the monarch and the leaders of the political elite.[111]

[110] BL, Add. MS 64,898, fos. 105–6.

[111] The advice of the 'lords committee' and, indeed, of Newcastle, echoed one of the commonplaces of early modern politics, that an impressive noble attendance was essential for the prestige of monarchy: R.M. Smuts, 'Art and the material culture of majesty in early Stuart England', in *The Stuart Court and Europe*, pp. 87–90. This principle was succinctly stated in Sir Henry Spelman's advice to James I on the Union: that the royal court was 'the theatre of the state' where 'the solemnityes . . . lifteth upp the hartes of the people and the frequent concourse of nobles and gentlemen . . . magnifies the government and confirmeth regalitye': *The Jacobean Union. Six Tracts of 1604*, ed. B.R. Galloway and B.P. Levack (Edinburgh: Scottish Hist. Soc., 4th ser, 21, 1985), p. 180.

Opinion, among both contemporaries and later historians, has been divided about how far Charles achieved this. Newcastle, at least by implication, suggested that the royal court of the 1630s was not a hospitable place for noblemen and that there was a tailing off of attendance, a view endorsed in Lawrence Stone' study of *The Crisis of the Aristocracy*.[112] Other contemporary observers, however, disagreed. Sir Philip Warwick, emphasised the size of the king's aristocratic entourage, particularly at services in the chapel royal, where 'he was invariably well attended by his court lords and chief attendants, and most usually waited on by many of the nobility in town.'[113] This view also receives support from the chorus of complaint during the 1630s about noblemen frittering away their time on the pleasures of the royal court and London instead of attending to their duties in the country.[114] The size of attendance on the king among peers is difficult to measure – although it is possible to offer some estimates, as will be demonstrated later. However, what is clear is that persuading noblemen to come to court – and treating them with due honour and respect once there – was one of the priorities of the king's household ordinances.

A good example of this is provided by ordinances relating to services in the chapel royal. These provided the most regular opportunity for large numbers of the political elite to attend on the king, and express their loyalty and devotion, in front of foreign dignitaries and court observers. Peter MacCullogh has described the service as 'one of the most important . . . political theatres in early modern England', 'a tableau vivant of the ideal . . . body politic'.[115] Charles attended chapel services with great regularity, and he looked to his nobles to display a similar dedication. One of the duties specified for the gentlemen ushers at court was 'to send warning to all noblemen wheresoever they be in towne' to

112 Stone, *Crisis of the Aristocracy*, pp. 463–4.

113 Warwick, Sir Phillip, *Memoirs of the Reign of Charles I* (Edinburgh, 1813).

114 See Lord Keeper Coventry's charge of 1632: *Reports of Cases in the Courts of Star Chamber and High Commission*, ed. S.R. Gardiner (Camden Soc., new ser., 39, 1886), p. 179. The king's policy on this score was contradictory. At the same time as wishing to ensure that they fulfilled the duty of hospitality in their shires he expected there to be a large reservoir of nobles on hand in London, to attend the various ceremonial occasions at court. He also regarded the nobility and gentry as an essential adornment of his capital city and supported various initiatives to improve London housing, which had among its objectives the creation of residential enclaves for nobles and gentlemen most notably in Covent Garden: R.M. Smuts, 'The court and its neighbourhood: royal policy and urban growth in the early Stuart West End', *JBS*, 30(1991), 117–49.

115 P.E. MacCullough, *Sermons at Court. Politics and Religion in Elizabethan and Jacobean Preaching* (Cambridge: Cambridge University Press, 1998), pp. 30, 42. See also A. Milton, '"That Sacred Oratory"; Religion and the Chapel Royal during the Personal Rule of Charles I', in *William Lawes (1602–1645): Essays on His Life, Times and Work*, ed. A. Ashbee (Aldershot: Ashgate, 1998), pp. 69–96.

remind them to attend chapel on 'high day or any other holyday'.[116] The ordinances governing the services during the 1630s drew heavily on precedent, copying almost verbatim a set of regulations issued by James in 1623 which themselves were an attempt to reinstate the ancient ordinances of our house.[117] However, they were applied with an attention to detail and readiness to set a personal example which was quite new. The conversations recorded by the master of ceremonies, Sir John Finet, reveal a king who was highly knowledgeable on the finer points of court protocol and a stickler for correct observance.[118] This led to what was, from start to finish, a highly regulated occasion.

The ceremonial began with the ordering of the opening procession, described in the ordinances as 'one of the most eminent and frequent occasions whereby mens' ranks and praecedencie are distinguished and discerned'.[119] Peers took pride of place in this, since they were the only ones permitted to sit in the chapel stalls. They would form up in ranking order in the king's presence chamber, with the sword of state being borne in front by an earl followed by senior nobles and visiting dignitaries. Once inside the chapel peers would take their places on the left hand side (the king's side), with the most senior seated in the upper stalls closest to the wall, and their wives and ladies similarly arrayed on the opposite side (the queen's side).[120] Throughout the service, the liturgy required close attendance on the king by selected noblemen. When he knelt to make his offertory, the peer 'greatest of estate' would hand it to him, with the next senior peer kneeling on the other side; and on Palm Sunday, having received his palm from the officiating cleric, he would hand it to the Lord Chamberlain who would then hand it to 'the most eminent earle of blood that day being present, to bear it before the king in procession'.[121] Order, decorum, attention to detail and scrupulous respect for precedence attended every stage of the proceedings.

Unfortunately we do not have regular attendance lists for the chapel royal services; but Finet's account of the christening of James Duke of York on 24 November 1633 indicates the turnout that might be expected at a full-dress ceremonial occasion. He describes a lengthy procession

116 BL, Sloane MS 1494, fos. 9–10.

117 MacCullough, *Sermons at Court*, p. 27; TNA, LC5/180; K. Sharpe, 'The image of virtue: the court and household of Charles I, 1625–1642', in *The English Court from the Wars of the Roses to the Civil War*, ed. D. Starkey (Harlow: Longman, 1987), p. 235.

118 J. Finet, *Finetti Philoxenis* (London, 1656), p. 197; *Ceremonies of Charles I, The Note Books of John Finet 1628–1641*, ed. A.J. Loomie (Bronx, NY: Fordham University Press), pp. 148, 160.

119 TNA, LC 5/180.

120 MacCullough, *Sermons at Court*, pp. 14–15, 38. BL, Sloane MS 1494, fos. 9–10.

121 BL, Sloane MS 1494, fos. 10, 22–3.

of heralds, London aldermen, judges, knights of the Privy Council and unnamed 'barons, viscounts and earles', followed by the queen's chamberlain, the Earl of Dorset, the Lord High Chamberlain, the Earl of Lindsey, and the Lord Chamberlain, Pembroke. Then came those allotted specific roles in the ceremony: Portland and Arundel acted as deputies to the godfathers, the Prince of Orange and the Palatine prince; the Earl of Hertford bore the basin, assisted by Viscount Wimbledon; the Countess of Kent, assisted by the Earl of Manchester and the Duke of Lennox carried the young prince; the train of his mantle was born by the Earl of Huntingdon, assisted by Bedford and Southampton; the canopy that covered him was supported by Lords Feilding, Willoughby of Parham, North, Seymour, Craven and Cottington; and finally the marchioness of Hamilton, acting as deputy godmother for the queen of Bohemia, was supported by the Earls of Kent and Rutland.[122] This may not have been a typical occasion; but it demonstrated the sort of attendance that the king could command when he pulled out the stops.

A similar degree of decorum and regulation attended the other rites of Charles's court, such as dining in state or receiving foreign ambassadors. The primary purpose of these was twofold: to celebrate the monarch's semi-divine status and perpetuate the aura of majesty that Newcastle saw as making such a powerful contribution to the power of kingship. But its additional, and undoubtedly intended, consequence was to draw noblemen into the king's presence and provide more opportunities for personal contact and the honouring of their own status and ranking. To these ends they invariably enjoyed privileged roles and positions. They were the only courtiers, apart from the gentlemen and attendants, who had the right to enter the privy chamber and converse there with the king. The Venetian ambassador described how Charles would come down to the chamber each morning where he 'detains' some of 'the lords and officials of that department . . . in conversation and salutes the others, and leaves them all happy and devoted'.[123] They also played a leading role in waiting on the king. When Charles dined in state they were allowed to approach him and set foot on 'the carpet of state' and they played an intimate and carefully choreographed role in rituals like the washing of the king's hands.[124] The implications of this were demonstrated in the attendance lists for the dinner for the annual garter feast, one of the most prestigious events in the round of court ceremonial, which reveal a rota of leading peers waiting on the king, besides the knights of the garter themselves. In 1638 the 'great bason' for washing the king's hands

122 *Ceremonies of Charles I*, pp. 144–5. 123 *CSP Ven. 1625–6*, p. 27.
124 TNA, LC5/180; BL, Sloane MS 1494. fos. 11–16.

was borne by the Earls of Bedford, Hertford, Clare and St Albans and Lord Herbert of Raglan, in 1639 by the Earls of Denbigh, Monmouth and Lords Herbert of Raglan and Cardiff, and in 1640 by Bedford, Bath, Hertford and Manchester. The Earl of Essex acted as cupbearer in 1638, Lord Herbert of Cardiff in 1639 and Essex again in 1640; Denbigh and Lord Sligo carried the ewer; the Earl of Carlisle and Lord Wharton acted as carvers; the Earls of Elgin and Clare, and Lord Edward Howard bore the royal napkin and the Earls of Dover, Northampton and Lord Grandison superintended the arrangements as 'sewers'.[125] These occasions, then, provided precisely the combination of 'ceremony' and personal contact that Newcastle so valued.

The ceremonies about which we know most were the receptions for visiting ambassadors organised by Sir John Finet under the direction of the Lord Chamberlain, the Earl of Pembroke. Again there was a well established set of protocols, originally devised in James's reign, but then refined and tightened up under Charles. Visiting ambassadors were greeted with a series of three 'welcomes' in which the host was carefully graded according to the ambassador's status and the dignity afforded to his predecessors. On first landing at Greenwich or Tower Wharf, they would be greeted by an earl or a baron according to whether they were representing a monarchy, republic or duchy. That evening they would be given a second 'welcome' by the son of a peer. Then a few days later they would be conducted to their first formal audience in the royal presence, again accompanied by an earl or baron. Because this involved a very public procession through London at the head of a cavalcade of coaches, particular care would be given to partnering the ambassador with an escort who would reflect precisely the degree of honour and status that the king wished to confer on his visitor; and much of Finet's work consisted of scouring the town to find the right nobleman to make the match.[126]

The demands of court ceremonial, then, required a large reservoir of peers to be available, often at short notice, to attend on the king. Substantial numbers of noblemen, in addition to those with specific court offices, were drawn into Charles's presence, either on a regular or occasional basis, and this helped to foster the sense of obligation and service that Newcastle saw as so essential to cultivating a loyal and supportive aristocracy. Historians have tended to underestimate the extent to which this was happening during the 1630s. Lawrence Stone, in particular, has argued that the ideological complexion of the royal court, combined with

[125] Bodl.L., Ashmole MS 1110, fo. 35; 1112, fos. 63–4.
[126] *Ceremonies of Charles I*, pp. 27–30.

the marked diminution in the volume of royal patronage, resulted in a rapid decline in attendance compared to James's reign. Whereas 'at least three quarters of the aristocracy were permanent or occasional courtiers between 1603 and 1615', he asserted, during the 1630s 'the number of court peers had been reduced to between a third and a half of the whole body'.[127] As Stone acknowledges, these figures are necessarily imprecise, and much depends on how one defines a 'court peer'; but the impression of a nobility alienated from the royal court during the Personal Rule has tended to stick.[128] However, a more detailed investigation of lists of attendance and such other sources as there are, suggests that this view needs to be revised.

Two of the assumptions made in Stone's analysis are particularly problematic. The first is that antipathy towards the ideological regime that was dominant at court necessarily precluded attendance on the king. As Conrad Russell, Caroline Hibbard and Kevin Sharpe have pointed out, a string of noblemen who have often been portrayed as 'disaffected' nonetheless waited regularly on the king on ceremonial occasions, Bedford, Essex, Hertford and Warwick prominent among them.[129] The second assumption is that what mainly drew peers to court were material rewards – in the form of grants, pensions, patents, offices and all the other myriad forms of royal patronage – and that therefore a fall in the value of such rewards produced a corresponding decline in attendance. Stone calculates this fall at over three-quarters (from an annual unit value of 105.4 down to 25.2 when one compares the period 1603–28 to 1629–40) and it is mainly from this that he deduces the decline in attendance to well under half.[130] There certainly were peers who went to court to further their financial interests. Thomas Cogswell's careful documenting of the fortunes of the 5th Earl of Huntingdon is a case in point. After years of living mainly in Leicestershire, the earl transferred his household to London for long periods during the early 1630s, in search of compensation for the loss of his rights and office in Leicester Forest.[131] But many more were drawn by the less tangible prospect of honour.

127 Stone, *Crisis of the Aristocracy*, pp. 463–4.

128 See, for example, *The Princely Courts of Europe 1500–1750*, ed. J. Adamson (London: Weidenfeld and Nicolson, 1999), pp. 112–13 and comments in the article on the 'Robert Devereux, 3rd Earl of Essex (1591–1646)' by John Morrill in *Oxf.DNB*.

129 C.S.R. Russell, *The Fall of the British Monarchies 1637–1642* (Oxford: Oxford University Press, 1991), pp. 3–5; Hibbard, 'Theatre of Dynasty', p. 174; Sharpe, *The Personal Rule of Charles I* (New Haven, CT: Yale University Press, 1992), pp. 741–2.

130 Stone, *Crisis of the Aristocracy*, pp. 471–6, 775.

131 T.E. Cogswell, *Home Divisions. Aristocracy, the State and Provincial Conflict* (Manchester: Manchester University Press, 1998), pp. 203–13, 239.

It was an essential part of the *raison d'être* of the aristocracy that they should serve, and be seen to serve, the king; and, because service at court was the most visible and the most personal form of service, it was also the most prestigious. There are numerous examples from this period of the financial, personal and, indeed, emotional sacrifices that noblemen made to serve at court. Newcastle, for example, regularly complained about how much he detested the backbiting and mockery that he had to face at court, and how much it was all costing him; nonetheless, he was still, compulsively, drawn to the royal presence. His main reward, at least in the early 1630s, appears to have the fleeting moments of royal favour and attention when he could confide to his friends that the king 'seemed to be pleased with me very well, and never used me better or more graciously'.[132] Even the weary old Earl of Huntingdon seems to have perked up when he was around at court, and was able to draw considerable satisfaction from escorting the Venetian ambassador to an audience at Whitehall in 1638 and from sitting alongside the Earl Marshal as one of the panel of noble judges in the Court of Chivalry.[133] Service at court was, as we have seen, the ultimate affirmation of the aristocracy's sense of status and identity, and it was this, above all, which drew them into the royal presence.

If one accepts that neither the ideological complexion of the court, nor the relative sparseness of the material rewards, were likely to deter peers from going to court, then the obstacles to attendance during the 1630s look much less significant. Noblemen had good reason for wanting to be in the presence of the king and he had every incentive to draw them in. These circumstances worked together to produce a much higher attendance than has generally been supposed. By combining the evidence about various types of attendance and service one can calculate that, in fact, nearly 65 per cent of the English peerage in 1640 can be regarded as Stone's 'permanent or occasional courtiers'.[134]

For the purposes of this analysis, the peerage can be divided into four categories. The first consisted of those who held significant posts at court or in the Privy Council, and who also, according to Stone's calculations, received the lion's share of the patronage available during the 1630s. This comprised the court and council heavyweights of the decade, such as Portland, Arundel, Pembroke, Carlisle, Holland, Hamilton, Lennox, Dorset and Cottington; but it also includes perennial courtiers, such as Lord Goring, who was lieutenant of the gentleman pensioners, vice

132 HMC, *Portland*, ii.127; *Strafforde Letters*, i.101; NUL, Clifton MS, CL.C 342.
133 Cogswell, *Home Divisions*, 238–9.
134 See below Appendix 1, 'English Peers at Court, 1625–40' for a full listing.

chamberlain of the queen's household and also the beneficiary of valuable patents and trade licences.[135]

The second category comprises those who waited regularly on the king, and often had aspirations to higher office, but who primarily valued the honour, prestige and influence that regular court service afforded. Henry Lord Clifford is a good example. In 1618 he had taken over from his elderly father as Lord Lieutenant of Cumberland, Westmoreland and Northumberland, and established himself as the premier peer in the northwest and north Yorkshire; but he had been bred up as a courtier in James's reign and the habit of attendance stayed with him. During the 1630s he spent much of his time shuttling back and forth between the two main family seats at Skipton and Londesborough and the court in London. He served at royal receptions, spent time in the company of senior courtiers such as Lindsey, Salisbury and Newcastle, and was regularly nominated as a prospective knight of the garter, which demonstrated the strength of his court connections. Like Newcastle, he invested considerable energy and emotion in making the right impression on the king and, again, it was with a sense of triumph that he was able to announce to his friends in June 1637 that 'the king never receaved me soe well in all his life (which all the court can witness and observe)'.[136] It was the peers in this category who provided the bulk of the regular attendance at services in the royal chapel and the reception of ambassadors. They included those, like Clifford, who divided their time between the court and their country estates, peers such as the Earls of Bedford, Stamford and St Albans, and Lord Howard of Escrick; those who served abroad as soldiers then in between times congregated at court, such as the Earls of Cleveland and Carnarvon, and Lords Craven and Wharton, and also the lesser fry among the perennial courtiers, such as Lord Herbert of Cherbury.

The third category consists of more occasional courtiers, like the Earl of Huntingdon, whose main sphere of interest was 'the country', but who nonetheless participated in enough of the court's ceremonial to fulfil the expectations of the king. In this category one can place a noblemen like Dudley Lord North, a former courtier again living mainly in the country, but nominated for the Order of the Garter, helping to bear the canopy at Prince James's christening and serving as one of the jury of noble judges at the trial of the Earl of Castlehaven[137]; or the 5th Earl of

135 Stone, *Crisis of the Aristocracy*, pp. 424–49; 'George Goring, 1st Earl of Norwich (1585–1663)', *Oxf.DNB*.

136 NUL, Clifton MS, Cl.C 689, 692, 704, 706; *Strafforde Letters*, ii.214–15.

137 'Dudley, 3rd Baron North (1582–1666), *Oxf.DNB*; *Ceremonies of Charles I*, pp. 144–5; C.B. Herrup, *A House in Gross Disorder* (Oxford: Oxford University Press, 1997), pp. 87, 124, 159.

Bath who, like Huntingdon, sat regularly in judgement in the Court of Chivalry[138]; or the Earl of Westmoreland who bore substantial responsibilities in the government of Northamptonshire, but also escorted the Savoyard ambassador in 1631 and entertained the king on his progresses to the east Midlands in 1634 and 1636.[139] The category also includes 'oppositionist' peers like Essex, Warwick and Hertford who were less well integrated into the structures of the court than their ally Bedford, but who, nonetheless, attended on a significant number of occasions. These were men that the king could call upon for those ceremonial events that demanded a particularly impressive turn out, such as the installation procession planned for his son's inauguration as a knight of the garter in May 1638.[140]

Finally, there was fourth category of those noblemen who, for a variety of reasons, did keep their distance from the royal court. Warwick and Essex's fellow 'oppositionist' peers, Viscount Saye and Sele and Lord Brooke, can be assigned to this category; so too can those who had been exiled from the court for political reasons, like Bristol and the Jacobean favourite, the Earl of Somerset, soldiers in foreign service, like Lords Cromwell and Gerard, those who were too old to attend (although they had often done so in the past), such as the Earls of Derby and Mulgrave, and those who suffered from ill health, like Buckingham's elder brother, Viscount Purbeck, or who were too young, like the royal favourite's nephew, the Earl of Anglesey.[141] But a significant proportion of this category comprised authentic 'country peers', who visited London only occasionally and when they did so generally steered well clear of the court. Typical of this group was the Earl of Kingston, the Nottinghamshire peer, whose extensive correspondence with his friend Sir Gervase Clifton indicates that he divided most of his time between his residences at Thoresby, Woodhouse and Holme Pierrepoint, with occasional visits to London to pursue business interests and litigation[142]; or Edward Lord Montagu, the Northamptonshire peer, who had been much in evidence in the House of Lords during the 1620s, but who had never been an enthusiastic courtier and during the 1630s continued to devote himself mainly to the government of his native county.[143]

Within this final category must also be included open and avowedly Catholic peers who, alone among the nobility, appear to have been

[138] *Cases in the Court of Chivalry*, pp. 26, 49.
[139] *Ceremonies of Charles I*, p. 103; TNA, SP 16/271/86; 16/329/2.
[140] Bodl.L, Ashmole MS 1113, fo. 212.
[141] For details on these peers, see *Oxf.DNB* and *GEC*.
[142] NUL, Cl.C 282–97, 647–87. [143] Cope, *Life of a Public Man*, ch. 3.

discouraged from involvement in court ceremonial.[144] This is, perhaps, somewhat surprising in view of the emphasis in recent work by historians such as Caroline Hibbard and Michael Questier on Charles's willingness to reach out to Catholics. Questier has highlighted the remarks regularly made by Charles about his willingness to extend friendship and favour to Catholics and has commented that this produced 'a climate of (potential) tolerance' during the 1630s. This was supported by a number of policy initiatives aimed at making life easier for Catholics, notably the proposals to modify the oath of allegiance and the institution of a formal system allowing Catholics to compound for their recusancy, thus releasing them from the full rigour of the law.[145] In spite of all this, and his acceptance of the queen's Catholicism, Charles, appears to have been determined that his court and his government should be clearly and publicly defined as 'Protestant'. He expressed fury at the well-publicised conversions to Catholicism of courtiers such as Wat Montague and the Countess of Newport; and he was notably less tolerant than his father had been of open Catholics occupying high offices such as the Lord Lieutenancy.[146] This appears to have extended to a deliberate policy of excluding Catholic peers from court ceremonial. There were exceptions. The Earl of St Albans, an Irish Catholic with an English title and large estates in Kent, was a regular attender at court, by dint of family connections with Buckingham and other leading courtiers. He was involved in the garter ceremonial, as was the Earl of Worcester's son, Lord Herbert of Raglan, another perennial courtier. But it is striking that, for the most part, Catholic peers, including those like Lord Brudenell who expressed their yearning to serve their monarch,[147] were omitted from the rosters of those summoned to court ceremonial. Of the 16 openly

[144] By 'open' Catholics is meant those who publicly continued to avow their faith, as opposed to those peers who were regarded by contemporaries, often with good reason, as being Catholic or crypto-Catholic, but who publicly conformed and took the oath of allegiance – such as the Earls of Arundel, Carnarvon and Portland, and Lords Cottington and Fauconberg (for their religion see the articles on them in *Oxf.DNB*). As Michael Questier has shown the 'open' Catholics can be most readily identified during the 1630s through the lobbying campaigns around the approbation of the English jurisdiction of Richard Smith, Bishop of Chalcedon in which the support of the Catholic peerage was heavily solicited by both sides: M. Questier, *Newsletters from the Caroline Court, 1631–1638: Catholicism and the Politics of the Personal Rule* (Camden Soc., 5th ser, 26, 2005), 1–8, 79–82, 119–23.

[145] C. Hibbard, *Charles I and the Popish Plot* (Chapel Hill: University of North Carolina Press, 1983), chs. 2–3; M. Questier, *Catholicism and Community in Early Modern England* (Cambridge: Cambridge University Press, 2006), ch. 14; *Newsletters from the Caroline Court*, pp. 1–31.

[146] Hibbard, *Charles I and the Popish Plot*, pp. 22–3, 62; for the lord lieutenancies, see p. 86.

[147] TNA, SP 16/412/141.

Catholic peers summoned to parliament in 1640 – including senior peers such as the Marquis of Winchester and the Earls of Shrewsbury and Worcester – only St Albans can be identified as a regular participant in court ceremonial.[148]

Using these various categories it is possible to classify some 94 per cent of the 111 members of the English parliamentary peerage summoned to the Short Parliament in April 1640. Of these 21 (20 per cent) can be ascribed to the first category of senior court insiders; 20 (19 per cent) to the second of regular attenders; 26 (25 per cent) to the third category of more occasional courtiers; and 37 (of whom 13 were Catholics) or 36 per cent can be described as 'country peers'.[149] There is, of course, overlap between these categories; and it may be the case that with more evidence some of those classified as 'country peers' could be placed in the 'occasional' category. Certainly a number of them presented New Year's gifts to the king in 1627 and 1638 (Saye and Sele, Brooke and the Earl of Lincoln among them), which implies that they wished to remain on good personal terms with the monarch and keep open the possibility of an entrée at court.[150] But, overall, this indicates that nearly 65 per cent of the English peerage was engaged with the court during the 1630s, in varying degrees of closeness. What the consequences of this were for political allegiance and how far it did, in fact, foster a sense of loyalty and obligation in the manner envisaged by Newcastle, is a separate issue – and one that will be discussed more fully in Chapters 4 and 5. But from this assessment it would appear that Charles was relatively successful in drawing his nobles to court and developing it as the 'point of contact' that conventional political wisdom suggested would ultimately benefit the crown.[151]

This analysis of noble attendance also reveals a further interesting conclusion: that attendance at court was higher among the more senior nobles – at 66 per cent among the 62 earls and above, compared to 50 per cent among the 49 barons and viscounts. This is as one might expect. Charles, with his strong sense of hierarchy and tradition particularly

148 See Appendix 1, 'English Peers and the Royal Court, 1625–40'. Shrewsbury and Lord Audley can be described as 'occasional courtiers'.

149 See Appendix 1, 'English Peers at the Royal court, 1625–40'.

150 BL, Egerton MS 2816; Harley, Roll T2. Over three-quarters of the peerage provided these gifts in the two years for which we have surviving rolls; however the interpretation of these rolls is problematic. In addition to the 'oppositionist' peers among the gift givers were 'country peers' with little apparent interest in gaining access to the court, such as the Earl of Kingston and Lord Montagu, and missing from the 1638 list were perennial courtiers, such as the Earl of Stamford and Lord Clifford.

151 G.R. Elton, 'Tudor government: the points of contact, III, the court', *TRHS* (5th ser., 26, 1976), 211–28.

valued the attendance of the senior group of peers, which included the bulk of the 'ancient nobility'. On important occasions – such as the ceremonies connected with the Order of the Garter – it was the earls whose attendance the Lord Chamberlain and master of ceremonies worked hardest to secure.[152] But there was a further dimension to this. Charles, to a greater extent than either Elizabeth or James, took pains to ensure that the most elevated positions in the service of the crown were filled by the more senior and established peers.

It has been demonstrated by Gerald Aylmer that the proportion of lay peers on the council increased from two-thirds in 1625 to over three-quarters in 1640. Among the 28 peers on the council in 1640, 21 were earls or dukes; but perhaps more strikingly it is also apparent that this group constituted the bulk of the 40 or so leading English and Scottish peers who the king might have considered eligible for a place on the council.[153] Of the senior English peers, 11 were disqualified from being on the council by age or adherence to the Catholic religion (or in the cases of Somerset and Middlesex by disgrace and exile from court) and a further four (Bath, Huntingdon, Lincoln and Nottingham) probably had little ambition to be councillors. This left only six leading English peers (Bedford, Essex, Hertford, Northampton, Southampton and Warwick) who were eligible and are likely to have sought a place on the council. Their omission can be accounted for by a variety of reasons: Essex, Warwick and Bedford were probably regarded by the king as politically disloyal; Hertford and Southampton were probably not consistent enough courtiers, and may have been tainted by association with Essex and Warwick; and Northampton was away on campaign in Europe in the late 1630s, at the time he was most likely to have been promoted.[154] The members of Bedford/Essex/Warwick circle may have blamed their exclusion on 'what was perceived as the ousting of the "ancient nobility" from its proper place in the king's counsels', as John Adamson has suggested.[155] But, if they did so, this was not based on an impartial assessment of Charles's policy. The king appears to have gone out of his way to follow his father's advice and ensure that he was counselled by men 'of the noblest blood'.

152 Contemporary observers took particular note of the number of earls and members of the 'ancient nobility' attending on ceremonial occasions: see, for example, *Strafforde Letters*, i.234.

153 G.E. Aylmer, *The King's Servants* (London: Routledge and Kegan Paul, 1974), p. 20. In 1640 of the 40 most senior English and Scottish peers 18 were privy councillors. This calculation is based on the list of privy councillors in October 1639 (TNA, PC2/51) and the list of peers summoned to the Short Parliament in April 1640 (*LJ*, iv.45).

154 See *Oxf.DNB* articles for these peers.

155 Adamson, *Noble Revolt*, pp. 31–2; Adamson, *Princely Courts of Europe*, p. 113.

The ways in which Charles sought to make use of his leading nobles in office is, perhaps, even more evident from his appointments to the Lord Lieutenancy, the most important and prestigious of the local offices. The king took a close personal interest in these appointments – and occasional dismissals – and used them in very deliberate fashion not only to signal his respect for the claims of senior peers to high office, but also to indicate the types of service that he wanted to encourage and was prepared to reward.[156] As we have seen, one of his first acts as monarch was to augment the prestige of Lord Lieutenants by giving them sole power to appoint their deputies. Like his father, all the appointments he made (except those to the Lord Lieutenancy of Durham, which was governed by the Bishop) were of peers, and with very few exceptions they were either earls, or the sons of earls. Charles recognised that holding a lieutenancy was an important mark of status and that certain noble families enjoyed what virtually amounted to a hereditary claim to occupy the office in their native shires. Some senior peers, like the Earl of Banbury, were allowed to continue in office long after the age at which they could usefully be of service and sons were regularly appointed alongside their fathers in the expectation that they would one day succeed them, as in the case of Lord Strange who joined the Earl of Derby on the commission for Lancashire and Cheshire in 1626, or Lord Hastings who was promoted to serve with the Earl of Huntingdon on the commission for Leicestershire and Rutland in 1638. In addition, as part of a policy of grooming young peers to serve the Crown, he would appoint 'caretaker' Lords Lieutenant until the intended appointees came of age. The Earl of Newcastle was chosen in this capacity to look after the lieutenancy of Derbyshire during the minority of the Earl of Devonshire, which came to an end in 1638; and Pembroke looked after Buckinghamshire, following Buckingham's death, until his ward, Robert Dormer, Earl of Carnarvon, was ready to assume the Lord Lieutenancy in 1633.[157] Charles's appointments and dismissals, however, also involved a much greater degree of partisan political calculation than his father's had done.

He initiated the first purge of Lord Lieutenants in the summer of 1627 to punish those peers who had refused to support the forced loan. The Earls of Bolingbroke, Essex and Kent were all dismissed at this time to join the Earl of Warwick who had been removed (probably for disloyalty to Buckingham) the previous autumn. Their places were filled by peers who had earned his personal trust, often regardless of whether they

156 Stater, *Noble Government*, p. 12

157 *Ibid.*, pp. 12–16; J.C. Sainty, *Lieutenants of the Counties 1585–1642* (Bulletin of the Institute of Historical Research, Supplement 8, 1970), pp. 12–13, 14, 17, 26, 30.

had appropriate local connections. For example, Robert Carey, Earl of Monmouth, former head of his household replaced the Earl of Essex in Staffordshire and Lord Weston, the Lord Treasurer, was yoked together with Warwick on his reappointment to Essex in 1629.[158] Less widely noticed, but just as significant, was the purge of Catholic Lord Lieutenants in late 1628–early 1629. This included three peers with virtually hereditary claims to the lieutenancies of their shires, the Earl of Rutland in Lincolnshire, Sussex in Essex and Worcester in Glamorgan and Monmouth, as well as the Lord President of the Council of the North, the Earl of Sunderland. The immediate cause of these dismissals was the preparations for the 1629 Parliament during which king and council were eager to demonstrate their readiness to remove the Catholic officeholders that the Commons had complained about in 1626 and 1628.[159] But once out of office these peers also ran up against Charles's determination that those who served him in high office should be conformable Protestants. When Worcester's son, Lord Herbert, pleaded for his father's restoration to office in 1636 – on the grounds that he had shown 'loyal, real and affectioned service' in supporting the forced loan, and that he was now suffering humiliation in his 'country' as a 'Jack out of Office' – he found the king sympathetic, but unyielding. Instead of reinstating Worcester, he wrote to the Earl of Bridgewater, president of the Council of Wales, with a very unusual instruction that he should allow Worcester to nominate the deputy lieutenants for Glamorgan and Monmouth and then let everyone know he had done this by circulating copies of the signet letter requesting him to do so. The king was insisting on this, he said, because he did not wish to see Worcester's 'power or reputation to be diminished' – although, on this occasion, he appears to have overlooked any damage that might have been done to Bridgewater's reputation.[160]

Charles's management of the Lord Lieutenancy, then, offers interesting pointers to the type of following that he was seeking to cultivate among the nobility. He looked primarily to his earls who had the strongest claims in terms of birth and estate, to take the lead in running the localities; and, among the earls, particularly to those with a strong record of service at court. He particularly valued political loyalty, especially at moments of crisis like the forced loan, and he was determined that those who served him in senior positions should, at least outwardly, be conformable to the

158 Stater, *Noble Government*, pp. 16–17; Sainty, *Lieutenants in the Counties*, pp. 11, 20, 24, 32.

159 Stater, *Noble Government*, pp. 16–17; Sainty, *Lieutenants in the Counties*, pp. 20, 26, 21, 37.

160 TNA, SP 16/334/51; 335/21.

Protestant religion. At the same time, however, he was very conscious of the honorific claims of noble families to particular offices and positions, and, generally, sensitive to the indignities they would suffer if these were not supported. He also acknowledged Newcastle's point that, other things being equal, the most effective way to govern the localities was to employ senior peers with the territorial connections and hereditary influence to work with the grain of local society. All of this indicates that, while the king was very respectful of the claims of 'ancient nobility', he was also working hard to build a court-based following among his senior peers. He was looking for his nobility to deliver the sort of loyal support and direction that the Laudian bishops were expected to provide in the church.

Reform of the aristocracy

So far the king's dealings with the peerage have been explored largely in terms of his efforts to secure political loyalty through attendance at court and preferment to high office. But his attitude towards his nobles was less instrumental than this focus might imply. Charles was also very ready to acknowledge that a good king had a moral duty to attend to their welfare. He was expected to help them when they ran into personal and financial difficulties, resolve their differences and take a fatherly responsibility for the order as a whole. His acceptance of this range of obligations is, perhaps, best illustrated in the personal letters that he wrote to individual members of the peerage under the royal signet. Typical of these was his letter to John Lord Roberts in 1629, in response to an appeal by his son-in-law, Charles Lord Lambert, to mediate over Robert's refusal to pay his daughter's marriage portion. Declaring his readiness 'to interpose in favour of a nobleman whome we respect both in his own person, and in memory of his father's many faithfull services', the king instructed Roberts to pay the portion and submit to arbitration over his other differences with his son-in-law.[161]

The range of issues in which Charles became involved was extensive. A number of his interventions related to matters of precedence. He repeatedly pronounced in favour of the children of peers who had had their claims disputed, such as Francis Ward, daughter to the prospective heir to Lord Dudley who, the king declared, was to be ranked as if her father had succeeded to the title.[162] He also showed a good deal of sensitivity to the plight of those nobles whose 'power or reputation' was slighted. As we have seen in the case of the Earl of Worcester, he would intervene to try to

[161] *Ibid.*, TNA, SO1/1, fo. 208. [162] *Ibid.*, SO1/2, fo. 226.

ensure that they were treated with proper respect. And marriage brokering among the nobility was another abiding concern. Caroline Hibbard has shown that, like most early modern rulers, Charles paid a good deal of attention to the marriages of those families who were favoured at court and went out of his way to foster a series of dynastic alliances between the Stuart, Villiers and Weston families, which offered mutual protection and also bound them more closely to the royal family.[163] But he also looked after the welfare of nobles less close to him. When the wife of the 4th Earl of Bath died in 1632, the king wrote to propose that he console himself by taking another bride, Mistress Dorothy Seymour, one of the queen's maids of honour. Bath turned this down, citing his continuing sense of grief at the loss of his first wife, but not before the king had engaged the good offices of Bath's 'kinsman', the Earl of Bedford, to try to make the arrangement work.[164]

Charles, then, was fully engaged with promoting the welfare of individual nobles and their families. He was also committed to furthering the interests of the order as a whole. He issued various declarations and proclamations to protect their privileges, such as the proclamation of April 1636 that prohibited the buying and wearing of counterfeit jewellery because this allowed lesser mortals to deck themselves out in the finery normally reserved for noblemen.[165] He forbade the killing and dressing of game by commoners out of his care 'to preserve the right apperteyninge to our nobility and gentrye in their lawful and commendable pleasures and recreacons'.[166] He even took care to stand up for their interests when they found themselves badgered by royal officialdom. Lord Brooke was able to draw on Charles's support in 1637 when he rejected a request by the master of ceremonies that he let his house in Holborn to the Spanish ambassador. Finet had the royal prerogative on his side (which allowed the 'taking up of houses' on such occasions); but Charles decided in Brooke's favour in spite of his standoffishness towards the royal court, declaring that 'he should be loath against his custome to force or perswade any of his nobility to quit his own conveniency'.[167]

Behind these initiatives to bolster the noble order, there was an awareness on Charles's part of the erosion of respect that was picked up by contemporary commentators, such as Spelman. His efforts to reverse this were particularly evident in the encouragement he gave to his Privy

[163] Hibbard, 'Theatre of Dynasty', pp. 171–4.

[164] TNA, SO1/2, fo. 116; HMC, *Cowper*, ii.14; TNA, SP16/239/9, 10, 54.

[165] *Proclamations*, ii.507–8. [166] TNA, SO1/2, fo. 248.

[167] *Ceremonies of Charles I*, pp. 86–7, 229. For the prerogative, see *ibid.*, p. 73. On Brooke's 'standoffishness', which probably included absenting himself when the king visited Warwick in 1636, see 'Robert Greville, 2nd Baron Brooke (1607–1643)', *Oxf.DNB*.

Council to tackle the problem of libellous words and other assaults on the honour of the nobility, described by Lord Cottington in Star Chamber as 'the vice of the time'.[168] The king's concern with the problem was apparent from a signet letter of December 1633 when he intervened to order that a Star Chamber case against the Lord Willoughby of Parham be abandoned. The case had been brought by a Lincolnshire plaintiff, John Burges, who was seeking redress for having been assaulted and beaten by Willoughby. The king's ruling was that

> although wee bee willing that all our subjects should finde our Courts of Justice open to all men alike, yet when a man of meane quality shall prosequte against a nobleman for an offence of passion or heate only, & that provoked by ill wordes & saucy carriadge as wee heare this was, it is not reasonable to give way to every man's will in such a case. Therefore wee will not that persons of place should be soe neglected.[169]

In other words, the king was saying that where a nobleman had been insulted, and had recourse to physical assault to redeem his honour, the person assaulted had no legal redress. The seriousness of the original insult against the nobleman overrode all other considerations. A similar attitude was apparent in July 1637 when two London draymen collided with the coach of the Earl of Exeter. A local jury acquitted the draymen of any offence, but the case was brought before a council session attended by the king and order was given that the two men be 'presently whipped publiquely through the towne, as well for theire bould and insolent carriage towards the said earle as also for an example to deter others from the like insolencies and misdemeanours'.[170]

This was an attitude that permeated the privy councillors' approach to cases involving noblemen. They were extremely sensitive to anything which might be construed as a challenge or an insult to a peer. From 1631 onwards there was a succession of Star Chamber actions involving slanders against the nobility in which the plaintiffs were awarded heavy damages and the offenders sentenced to make grovelling and humiliating submissions. In May 1631, in a case that was widely reported, Edward Eure was sentenced to pay £2500 in damages, £1000 in fines and stand in the pillory for having called the Earl of Danby 'a base cozening lord, a cheating lord [and] a base fellow'.[171] Similarly, in October 1637 the Earl of Marlborough was awarded £1000 in damages after Thomas Bennett, a Wiltshire gentleman, had 'taxed the earl with baseness and base dealing' and claimed 'that he was 'as good a gentleman as he was, for the Bennetts

168 TNA, SP 16/191/6.
169 *Ibid.*, SO1/2, fos. 162–3.
170 *Ibid.*, SP 16/363/82.
171 *Ibid.*, SP 16/191/6; BL, Harleian MS 390, fo. 526.

were as good as the Leys'.[172] Following an important Star Chamber ruling in February 1638 – after a case in which Lord Sherard had been libelled by Sir Henry Mynn at the Rutland assizes – most such actions were referred on to the reformed Court of Chivalry; but there they were prosecuted with similar severity.[173]

The king also took a more positive interest in the well being of his nobility. Philip Warwick described how whenever young noblemen came to take their leave of Charles before travelling abroad, he would give them a mini lecture on moral virtue and tell them that 'if he heard they kept good company abroad, he should reasonably expect they would return qualified to serve him and their country well at home'.[174] This concern prompted his sponsorship of a noble academy set up in Covent Garden in the mid 1630s, known as the *Musaeum Minervae*. In a signet letter of June 1636, soliciting contributions to support the *Musaeum*, he described it as bringing into effect

> that which wee have long most earnestly wished, namely . . . the virtuous educacon of our nobility and gentry . . . at home in safety, and their preservacon from the too frequent vices of the times by a diversion of their mindes from idlenes & vanity to noble and better imployments.[175]

Not only would it provide the ideal preparation for the service that the king had in mind; it would also avoid the moral hazards and temptations that young noblemen were exposed to, especially when they travelled on the continent. The *Musaeum*'s director was Sir Francis Kynaston, a longstanding courtier and also an author, experimenter, polymath and intellectual entrepreneur. Kynaston saw an opportunity to use his various connections to fill a significant gap in the educational market by providing young nobles and gentlemen with the type of finishing school that at the time was only available on the continent. However, the main promoter of the scheme was Charles himself.[176]

As the king indicated in his signet letter, the scheme had been a long time in gestation. The only previous such establishment in England had been Prince Henry's academy at Nonsuch. This was essentially a riding school at which Henry and, from around 1610, Charles were instructed in the latest style of Italian horsemanship by Monsieur De St Antoine, a French riding master sent over by Henry IV to help train James's young sons. However, like the French academies on which it was modelled, it

172 TNA, SP 16/369/58. For the proliferation of such cases, see Cogswell, *Home Divisions*, pp. 216, 221–9, 237–9.

173 R.P. Cust 'A Rutland Quarrel, the Court of Chivalry and the Irish Peerage during Charles I's Personal Rule', *Midland History*, 35 (2010), 149–73.

174 Warwick, *Memoirs of Charles I*, pp. 73–4.

175 TNA, SO1/3, fo. 8.

176 For what follows, see Cust, 'Charles I's Noble Academy' (forthcoming).

also aspired to equip young noblemen with the full range of skills needed to serve at court or in the army.[177] Henry's academy collapsed with his death; but the scheme was picked up by Buckingham and, during the 1621 Parliament, he introduced a proposal to the House of Lords for the 'erection and mayntenance of an Academy for breeding and bringing up the nobility and gentry of this kingdom'. This was received enthusiastically by their lordships, including Prince Charles. They immediately began to discuss 'the place where such an academie shall be seated and erected', 'what qualities, arts, sciences and exercises shall be taught and practised', who should attend and how the academy should be funded. The following year, James formally adopted the scheme and entrusted the responsibility for bringing it to fruition to his son.[178] For the remainder of the decade, however, it foundered on a lack of revenue and overambitious efforts – mainly sponsored by another educational entrepreneur, Edmund Bolton – to graft it on to an early version of the Royal Academy.[179] It was revived in the Lords by Arundel in 1629 and, again, there were strong expressions of support. But it was not until Kynaston came forward with his proposal in 1633 (probably while he was accompanying the king on the progress to Scotland), that a concrete and workable scheme was forthcoming.

With royal backing, the project quickly secured promises of support from a wide variety of noblemen and councillors, including Arundel, Pembroke, Lord Keeper Coventry and Archbishop Laud. By early 1635 it was up and running, with premises in Covent Garden and a prospectus advertising the services of Kynaston and a team of seven professors equipped to teach everything from the practical skills of heraldry, dancing and fencing to the latest discoveries in astronomy and medicine.[180] In June 1635 Charles gave it his official blessing, with a grant under the great seal, a formal constitution and a donation of £100.[181] During the latter part of 1635 and the early part of 1636 the academy was flourishing. It received a royal visitation in February 1636, when the young princes,

177 Strong, *Henry Prince of Wales*, pp. 8, 41–3, 215; M. Motley, *Becoming a French Aristocrat. The Education of the Court Nobility 1580–1715* (Princeton, NJ: Princeton University Press, 1990), ch. 3.

178 *LJ*, iii.36; TNA, SP 14/141/70.

179 BL, Add. MS 39, 177, fos. 2–7; Harleian MS 6103, fos. 13–15; Royal MS 18A.LXXI, fos. 1–10; E.M. Portal, 'The Academy Royal of King James I', *Proceedings of the British Academy*, 7 (1915–16), 189–208.

180 *The Constitutions of the Musaeum Minervae* (London, 1636); BL, Harl. MS 7571, fos. 2–3; G.H. Turnbull, 'Samuel Hartlib's connection with Sir Francis Kynaston's "Musaeum Minervae"', *Notes and Queries*, 97 (1952), 33–7.

181 T. Rymer, *Foedera* (1743 edn.), vol. 8, pt. 4, pp. 130–1; *Notes and Queries*, 3rd ser., vi (1964), 265.

Charles and James, attended a masque performed by the 'young schollers' in celebration of the fruits of Minerva, goddess of wisdom. Numerous 'worthy and bountifullie disposed persons' followed the king's example and promised their own contributions to the upkeep of the academy. The demand for places was such that by mid 1636 Kynaston was looking to move into larger premises.[182] But then suddenly London was hit by plague and, in June 1636, the establishment in Covent Garden was forced to shut down. Charles continued his support, furnishing Kynaston with the signet letter to help collect the promised subscriptions and ordering the warden of Chelsea College, Dr Featley, to provide temporary accommodation for the scholars and professors. But Featley was obstructive, the collection of subscriptions was disrupted, and rumours spread that one of the young scholars had picked up the infection. When the plague finally abated in 1637 the lack of a solid financial base and the parlous state of Kynaston's own finances left the *Musaeum* without sufficient resources to start up again.[183] This marked the end of the whole project. But during the brief period in which it had flourished, it provided striking testimony to Charles's ambition and commitment to young noblemen. He was determined to do what he could to prepare them for effective service to monarchy and state.

Alongside benevolence towards his nobles, however, Charles also showed a readiness to call them to account when they failed to meet the exacting standards required of them. Perhaps the most visible, and certainly the most striking, instance of this during the Personal Rule was the trial and execution of the Earl of Castlehaven.[184] The Castlehaven case linked together, and exemplified, several strands of Charles's policy towards his nobles. The earl was executed in May 1631 on charges of rape and sodomy; but the urgency and personal attention that the king gave to the proceedings suggests that he saw these as about much more than the sexual misdemeanours of a wayward peer. Members of the nobility, because of their privileged position and their high public visibility, were expected to set an example to the rest of society. 'A peer of the realme of a very ancient noble family... as he is great in his birth so should he have been good in his example', the Attorney General explained in Castlehaven's indictment.[185] Failure to fulfil these expectations not only undermined respect for the noble order, it also threatened the

182 *Corona Minvervae or A Masque presented before Prince Charles... at the Colledge of the Musaeum Minervae* (London, 1635); Bodl.L., Tanner MS 142, fo. 69.

183 TNA, SP 16/341/134, 134i; Bodl.L., Tanner MS 142, fos. 69, 71.

184 Herrup, *A House in Gross Disorder*.

185 C.B. Herrup, 'The patriarch at home; the trial of the 2nd Earl of Castlehaven for rape and sodomy', *History Workshop Journal*, 41 (1996), 13.

maintenance of social discipline across society as a whole. It was one of the commonplaces of contemporary social and political thought that control and order depended to a considerable extent on the elite setting standards of honourable behaviour as an example to those below them. Charles himself was a dedicated proponent of this view and it found its way into the constitution he approved for the *Musaeum Minervae*. One of the central purposes of the education of young nobles, it explained, was 'to excite' them

> to virtuous and heroick mindes, by the example of the most renowned, but especially to set before their eyes the images of the worthies of our own nation and of our own ancestours in their severall families; so that having taken impression in the *Musaeum* from the best ideas the whole kingdome of inferiour people, in those severall counties where they shall be distributed to live, and shine, may finde example, help, reason, and happinesse in being under them.[186]

It was this process that Castlehaven's misdemeanours threatened to undermine.

The investigation began in October 1630, when the earl's son, Lord Audley, petitioned the king complaining that his father was threatening to disinherit him through showing excessive favouritism to his servant, Henry Skipwith. Audley expressed the hope that he would find in the king 'a father' who would protect him. He probably anticipated, as was normal in such cases, that the king would reprimand the earl and order a mediation. However, for reasons which are unclear, Charles put the matter in the hands of a high-powered Privy Council commission, consisting of Arundel, Weston, Manchester, Coventry and Laud. They began questioning witnesses in November, and as soon as they did so started to uncover a sensational tale of depravity and corruption. Castlehaven had, allegedly, encouraged Skipwith to rape his wife while he stood by and watched. He also, supposedly, arranged for his daughter-in-law to commit adultery with Skipwith; and had, himself, sodomised two of the other servants. Arundel, who, according to Castlehaven, was the driving force behind the investigation, must have been shocked at this flagrant disregard of the standards expected of a member of the 'ancient nobility', and he may well have been instrumental in persuading Charles that such an offence required the severest punishment.[187] But the king probably did not need a great deal of convincing. Over recent months, as well

186 *Constitutions of the Musaeum Minervae*, p. 14; Herrup, 'Gender and honour in the Castlehaven story', 147.

187 Herrup, *A House in Gross Disorder*, pp. 38–52. An additional explanation for the king's action may have been further complaints from the Countess of Castlehaven who was entitled to feel even more aggrieved than her son. As a Stanley, and the daughter of the redoubtable Countess of Derby, she was able to draw on a powerful range of

as promoting the aristocracy as paragons of virtuous conduct, he had begun the campaign to reform the royal household so that it could stand as a model of order and moral integrity. Castlehaven must have appeared to be doing everything in his power to undermine this project. He was personally debauched; he had played favourites among his servants; he had disparaged the principles of lineage and hierarchy by encouraging his daughter-in-law to pollute the family blood; and, above all, he had failed to exercise the wise and benevolent direction of his household which was the prime responsibility of a noble patriarch. In short, he constituted, the virtual 'anti-type' of the ideals that the king was seeking to instil into his people.[188]

By mid December 1630 Castlehaven had been moved to the Tower and the charges against him were becoming public knowledge. Lurid and salacious tales began to circulate about what the newsletter writer Joseph Mead described as 'abominable & never heard of villainies'. Once this happened Charles had no alternative but to act decisively and, already, he was reported as saying that the earl 'should be hanged or howsoever dye for his villaines'.[189] Thereafter, the process moved forward rapidly. Lord Gorges was issued with a commission to hear the evidence locally, and on 6 April 1631 Castlehaven was indicted at Salisbury. Less than three weeks later, on 25 April, he stood trial in Westminster Hall before a specially convened court of 25 of his fellow peers, presided over by Lord Keeper Coventry, who had been appointed Lord High Steward for the occasion. The trial was over in a day and the verdict against Castlehaven was a foregone conclusion. However, contemporary observers still expected Charles to exercise the prerogative of mercy, as his father had done in cases where peers had been guilty of capital offences. That he did not do so was partly because Castlehaven himself refused to offer any submission or acknowledgement of guilt; but it was also because of the nature of the offences. These were such a blatant affront to the king's current policies that any pardon would have been interpreted as showing a lack of resolve. However, the king did not forget that he was dealing with a nobleman, and in deference, as he said, to his 'ancestors who had done good services to the crown', he allowed him to be beheaded rather than hanged. He also treated the family as generously as he could, restoring to his son the English barony and the bulk of the ancestral estates which had been forfeit at the earl's conviction.[190] The Castlehaven case

connections among the 'ancient nobility': *Ibid.*, pp. 12–13, 18. I am grateful to Thomas Cogswell for suggesting this possibility.

188 Herrup, 'The Patriarch at home', 9, 13.

189 BL, Harleian MS 390, fo. 529.

190 Herrup, *A House in Gross Disorder*, pp. 48–105.

was a remarkable demonstration of Charles's readiness to inflict exemplary punishment on those noblemen who failed to match up to the high standards expected of them; but it was not the only one.

Perhaps the most familiar example of this approach was the campaign to persuade noblemen and gentlemen living in London to return to their shires, to fulfil their traditional duty of hospitality. There was nothing new about such campaigns. Elizabeth had started issuing instructions to this effect in the 1590s and James had stepped up the crown's efforts from 1614 onwards, with repeated injunctions and proclamations which in 1622–3 appear to have had some success. The rationale for this policy, as James had explained it, was to promote good government and social harmony by following the principle that everyone should live 'in his own place' and discharge his proper calling, which meant that nobles and gentry were expected to maintain the 'old fashion' of hospitality.[191] Charles articulated this principle in the proclamation of June 1632, which marked the start of his offensive. By serving the king 'in severall places according to their degrees and rankes in ayde of the government, and by their house keeping in those partes', the proclamation declared, 'the realme was defended and the meaner sort of people were guided, directed and relieved'.[192] Like Charles's other policies relating to the nobility – and indeed Newcastle's recipe for managing his nobles – the aim was to restore a 'golden age' of order and stability. What made this particular campaign distinctive, however, was the king's willingness to give it teeth.

It began with the exemplary punishment of William Palmer in Star Chamber in the autumn of 1632 for remaining in town in contravention of the proclamation. This was followed by long lists of subpoenas against named individuals to initiate further prosecutions in February 1633 and April 1635.[193] Charles, himself, took a close interest in the enforcement of the policy. In October 1634, after it had been in force for over two years, it was being reported that he was still 'verie zealous in the persecution of his proclamation against towne dwellers and therefore hath often charged his attorney to prosecute against them'.[194] The Attorney General's proceedings did not run their course, but they appear to have had the desired effect in that significant numbers of nobles and gentry were persuaded to think again about travelling up to London. In March 1635, for example, Lord Poulett wanted to come to the capital to arrange

191 F. Heal, 'The crown the gentry and London: the enforcement of proclamation, 1596–1640', in *Law and Government Under the Tudors*, ed. C. Cross, D. Loades and J.J. Scarisbrick (Cambridge: Cambridge University Press, 1998), pp. 212–14, 218–19.

192 *Proclamations*, ii.350.

193 Heal, 'Crown, gentry and London', pp. 222–3; Rushworth, ii.288–93.

194 TNA, C115/8439.

credit for his son's tour abroad, but, as he told the secretary of state, Sir John Coke, he 'dare not adventure to, in regard of the proclamation'. Another of Coke's correspondents, Viscount Chaworth, confirmed that the message about the aristocracy's duty to keep hospitality was getting through. In petitioning for a dispensation for his wife to visit physicians in London he was quick to explain that 'in obedience to the proclamation we leave our son at one of my houses with a competent family for house keeping in the country'.[195] The campaign was kept going through 1635, and the procedure for punishing delinquents was still under active consideration in April 1636; but thereafter it ran out of steam.[196] In the meantime, however, it does appear to have had at least some impact on the behaviour of the elite. It may have made little long-term difference to their desire to reside in London, but Felicity Heal has concluded that, in combination with a good deal of writing about the subject, it encouraged contemporaries to think again about their management of social relations and make some serious gestures towards maintaining hospitality.[197]

The success or failure of the other principal campaign in which Charles sought to ensure that his nobles were fit to discharge the roles he had assigned to them is even harder to assess. This was the drive to curb duelling. The problems caused by duelling attracted much less concerted attention than under James because alarm over the number of fatalities never reached the levels of 1609 and 1613. They have, therefore, largely escaped the notice of later historians.[198] However, duels involving senior nobles and courtiers were a regular event during the 1630s and were a considerable challenge to the king's efforts to instil high standards of behaviour in his nobles. The main problem was that the whole duelling ethos was deeply embedded in the honour culture of the day.

Duels involving noblemen and courtiers were newsworthy events that aroused a mixture of fascination and admiration among contemporaries. In August 1631, for example, Viscount Scudamore, who was widely regarded as a paragon of noble virtue, and was also a trusted servant of the king, received a newsletter account of his brother slaying a Scotsman in a duel in the Netherlands. In the writer's opinion the news 'wilbe welcome to you: for as it is tould it is honourable to the gallant

195 Sharpe, *Personal Rule of Charles I*, p. 414; HMC, *Cowper*, i.485.
196 Heal, 'Crown, gentry and London', p. 223.
197 F. Heal, *Hospitality in Early Modern England* (Oxford: Oxford University Press, 1990), pp. 117–21.
198 They are not mentioned, for example, in R.B. Manning, *Swordsmen. The Martial Ethos in the Three Kingdoms* (Oxford: Oxford University Press, 2003), ch. 6 or in Sharpe, *Personal Rule of Charles I*. Hibbard, 'Theatre of Dynasty', pp. 162–6 is the main exception.

gentleman your brother and to his name'.[199] The assumption that Scudamore would look favourably on such an event was typical of the attitude of contemporary correspondents. Leading duellists of the day were celebrities who gained considerable public reputations for their displays of manhood and courage. The swordplay of George Goring, eldest son of Lord Goring, both home and abroad, was regularly reported, with one gentleman newsletter writer describing a subterfuge by which he had attempted to evade a royal prohibition on him fighting as 'a passage much commended . . . proceeding from sweetnesse and stoutnesse of spirit'.[200] The duels of Sir Kenelm Digby who made a particular name for himself in challenging foreigners who had impugned the honour of his king, were reported in similarly glowing terms.[201]

There was a powerful demonstration of the attraction of the duelling culture to leading noblemen and courtiers during the most celebrated court quarrel of the decade. In April 1633, the Earl of Holland, the king's master of the horse, but also a renowned duellist, challenged Lord Weston, the son of the king's leading minister. Weston had been returning from an embassy in France when he intercepted a suspicious looking packet, addressed to a councillor of Louis XIII. He opened it, discovered that it contained letters from Holland and the queen and on his return presented it to the king. Holland was affronted by the suggestion that he could not be trusted and sent Henry Jermyn, the queen's attendant, to present Weston with a demand for satisfaction. The king, however, had already expressed his approval of his ambassador's action, and, anticipating Holland's response, personally ordered both men not to take their quarrel any further. However, when Weston tried to deflect the earl's defiance by citing the king's command, Holland invoked the claims of the honour code by pointing out that this did not preclude him from 'meeting being a cavalier'. He also intimated that if Weston refused to give him satisfaction this 'left him at libertie to seek his remedie any other way he should choose', which appears to have included spreading the word that he had declined his challenge. This was an approach Weston found hard to withstand. He had no wish to be seen to be hiding behind the king's prohibition and returned a message, via Henry Percy, to say

199 TNA, C115/ 8137. On Scudamore's reputation, see I. Atherton, *Ambition and Failure in Stuart England* (Manchester: Manchester University Press, 1999), chs. 2–3.

200 BL, Add. MS 34,727, fo. 59. For other feats by Goring, see TNA, C115/ 8433, 8439; *Court and Times*, ii.270; Hibbard, 'Theatre of Dynasty', p. 164.

201 *Sir Kenelme Digby's Honour Maintained* (London, 1641); Hibbard, 'Theatre of Dynasty', p. 163. William Crofts and Henry Percy were other courtier-duellists whose names appeared regularly in the newsletters: TNA, C115/8429, 8554; *Court and Times*, ii.257, 270–1.

that the next time he walked abroad it would be armed with his sword, to which the earl replied that he himself would be out walking the next day in the Spring Garden at court.[202] Charles got wind of what was happening from Weston's father and immediately had Holland and Jermyn placed under house arrest. However, by now the quarrel had developed a wider momentum. Crowds of well-wishers flocked to Holland's house in Kensington to express their support and admiration; the queen's attendants began to spread it around that Weston was a coward for seeking to evade combat; and Lord Feilding, who was about to marry Weston's sister, stepped forward to challenge George Goring who had been the nosiest of those alleging Weston's 'want of courage'. The two men fought in Hyde Park, and it was reported that they were only prevented from killing each other by the intervention of workmen who dragged them apart.[203] Charles eventually brought the situation under control, then appointed a high-powered Privy Council committee to conduct an investigation and instructed the attorney general to prepare a prosecution in Star Chamber.[204] The whole episode, however, illustrated that when it came to a clash between obedience to the king and allegiance to the code of honour even senior councillors found it hard to resist the duelling ethos.

Charles was sufficiently concerned by the whole problem to have a proclamation drawn up in August 1631, after Peter Apsley, the son of the keeper of the Tower, had absconded when the Earl Marshal tried to detain him for fighting a duel. Declaring in its preamble that 'many of our subjects of the better qualitie' had 'obstinately embraced' the 'ungodly and barbarous maxims and conclusions' of the duelling code, 'contrary to the laws of God & man', this reminded the king's subjects that he had 'deputed' the power 'to compose & settle such differences and quarrelles' to the Earl Marshal and the 'Court Marshall', and that anyone who defied their authority would face 'our high displeasure & such further punishment as shall be fitting to so high a contempt'. This was a less vigorous and concerted response to the problem than James's proclamations and edict of 1613–14 – and, in the event, the proclamation does not appear to have been issued.[205] But it did reflect a concern that

202 TNA, SP 16/236/43 i–vi.

203 Bodl.L, Rawlinson MS D.392, p. 363.

204 TNA, SP 16/236/43, 43i–vi.

205 Queen's College, Oxford archives, Sel.b.229, item 63, 'A proclamation against such as willfully and presumptuously contemne his Majestie's Royall Authority used in prevention of the barabarous use of duels; particularly against Peter Apsely Esquire', given at Oatlands, 9 August 1631. Because the 'stile & phrase' of this draft had not been approved by the Privy Council, the Attorney General was instructed on 23 August to draw up a new version 'in substance according to this' and was instructed to present it

surfaced at intervals during the 1630s, that this was a problem that required urgent action.

Concentrations of such events were especially alarming. In March–May 1633 the Holland/Weston confrontation was accompanied by other quarrels at court. Mr Drumond, a gentleman usher, was sent to the Tower after challenging the Earl of Carlisle within earshot of the king for reprimanding him about not clearing the way as the royal couple approached; Mr Elliott, the king's cloak bearer, had fought with Mr Price, the queen's sewer, over one of the ladies in waiting; and Peter Apsley was again embroiled in a quarrel when he tried to provoke the Earl of Northumberland into issuing a challenge by accusing him of cowardice as he was about to join the king's progress to Scotland.[206] There was a similar cluster of quarrels during the summer and autumn of 1634. First of all, Lord Digby challenged the notoriously combative William Crofts and the two parties had to be separated by leading noblemen and temporarily incarcerated; then Henry Percy challenged Lord Denluce and the king himself had to intervene; finally there was a clash outside Blackfriars playhouse in which the courtier-poet Sir John Suckling killed a servant of Sir Kenelm Digby's brother. Each of these episodes was widely reported, often in lurid detail, and they prompted considerable alarm among social commentators.[207] In 1634, in his *Guide of Honour*, Anthony Stafford voiced a common lament of this 'wretched age . . . we live in that maketh effusion of bloud the only means for reparation of honour'.[208] A year later, in the anti-duelling tract, *Duel Ease*, G.F. warned – in terms reminiscent of James's reign – that this 'bloody fluxe wherewith the gallants of our age are too much distempered', this 'consumption or waste of bloud fatall to the noble bowels of your kingdome', would escalate uncontrollably unless the king took steps to cure it.[209] In the mid 1630s, then, the need for a concerted royal campaign to tackle the problem was coming to appear urgent. However, the scope for this was limited.

to the Lord Keeper to be issued. It seems likely that in the meantime Apsley had been apprehended, removing the immediate need for it: TNA, SP 16/198/55.

206 Bodl.L, Rawlinson MS D.392, p. 363.

207 TNA, C115/8429, 8440, 8442, 8554. There was a similar rash of challenges in May–June 1636 that again required royal intervention: C115/8607, 8800; *CSP Dom. 1636–7*, p. 66; *Court and Times*, ii.248; AC, Arundel letters, 362.

208 A. Stafford, *The Guide of Honour* (London, 1634), p. 77. Four years before this, in his best-selling *The English Gentleman, containing sundry excellent rules* (London, 1630), Richard Brathwait lamented 'how many of your ranke and quality have perished by standing upon these termes' (p. 206).

209 G.F., *Duell Ease. A Worde with Valiant Spiritts . . .* (London, 1635), 'Epistle dedicatory to . . . Prince Charles', 'To the courteous reader'.

Part of the problem was that the mechanisms for dealing with duels were relatively *ad hoc*. When the king or Earl Marshal found out that a duel had taken place – or was about to – they would often intervene personally, binding the parties over to good behaviour, providing arbitration and, sometimes, ordering the incarceration of the combatants. But such interventions depended on prompt and regular intelligence which was not always available.[210] There was the further problem that, in the early 1630s, there was no clearly defined legal mechanism for dealing with the issue. Privy councillors sitting in Star Chamber on a duelling case in 1632 reiterated the declaration in the 1631 draft proclamation, that this was, basically, the responsibility of the Earl Marshal.[211] But, in the absence of regular meetings of the Court of Chivalry, there were limited opportunities for him to intervene judicially. Most duelling cases continued to come before Star Chamber, following the cue provided in James' proclamations and edict of 1613–14. However, Star Chamber procedure was cumbersome and unwieldy. It tended to work best when delivering heavyweight judgments that could act as a deterrent rather than providing a forum for resolving day-to-day disputes. Councillors also tended to feel uncomfortable about using it to punish members of the aristocracy. The Star Chamber case against those involved in the Holland/Weston case was soon dropped; so too was the intended prosecution of Lord Digby and William Crofts.[212] It was not until the Court of Chivalry was established on a regular basis in 1634 that there was a prompt and flexible judicial mechanism for addressing the whole problem.

A more intractable issue was the ambivalence of attitudes among the elite. This is apparent in the advice and conduct literature of the decade in which gentlemen and noblemen applied a mixture of high-minded aspirations and practical wisdom to reflect on their personal experience. A central theme of much of this was the need for the man of honour to control his passions through the use of reason. The Gloucestershire gentleman William Higford echoed Sir Francis Bacon's approach when he told his heir that 'fortitude or courage' ultimately meant triumphing 'in the conquest of yourself', subjugating your 'affections and appetite to the government of reason', overcoming 'all fear' and, above all, displaying the virtues of patience and moderation. He must learn to pacify quarrels rather than inflame them and above all avoid duelling.[213] It was

[210] *Cases in the Court of Chivalry*, p. xxx.

[211] *Cases in the Courts of Star Chamber and High Commission*, p. 114.

[212] TNA, PC2/43, fos. 341, 342; PC2/44, fo. 27; PC2/46, fo. 118.

[213] *Harleian Miscellany*, ed. T. Park, 10 vols. (London, 1808–13), ix.594. For fuller discussion of these points, see R.P. Cust and A.J. Hopper, 'Duelling and the High Court of Chivalry in early Stuart England', in *Cultures of Violence*, ed. S. Carroll (Basingstoke: Palgrave Macmillan, 2007), pp. 156–71.

also acknowledged that it was the sign of a base spirit to pay too much attention to popular opinion. Stafford urged his young charge, George Lord Berkeley, that 'having the assurance of your owne conscience that your proceedings are faire and honest', he should ignore 'the censure of the merely vulgar'.[214] At the same time, however, these gentlemen recognised that in the real world such high-minded sentiments were not always practicable. In the best-selling conduct book of the decade, *The English Gentleman*, Richard Brathwait insisted that an insult to one's 'good name, being indeed the choicest and sweetest perfume', must not be allowed to pass without some 'labour to wipe off the staine'. In such circumstances it was appropriate for 'generous spirits' to act promptly and forcefully, because in 'actions of this nature the only meanes to gain opinion is to come off bravely in the beginning'.[215]

This meant that, in spite of the general recognition that duelling offended against ideals of virtue and godliness, and was in direct contravention of the king's commands, duels fought to protect one's good name could be regarded as permissible. Higford stressed that 'to defend yourself in a just cause . . . and to do it with judgement and resolution will marvellously redound to your honour and safety'.[216] Seeking out quarrels, or aggressively inciting violence could not be construed as legitimate; but fighting a duel in defence of one's honour and reputation was.[217] Indeed, a failure to respond forcefully when the situation required could be interpreted as displaying a want of the 'spirit' and 'courage' expected of a gentleman. When Sir Robert Shirley was struck in the face by an envoy of the king of Persia at an ambassadorial reception, it was Shirley who was thought to have demeaned himself. 'The greatest blot and fault of this adoe', according to John Finet and others present, fell on him, for 'weaknesse and want of spirit' in failing 'to return with blowes (or wordes at least) the affront done him'.[218]

All of this created a large grey area, depending on how precise circumstances were interpreted. This made it far from straightforward for the crown simply to condemn duelling. The king had to tread carefully if he was to carry noblemen and courtiers with him. His difficulties were illustrated in the contrasting outcomes of the Holland/Weston clash and the provocation of the Earl of Northumberland by Apsley a few weeks later. Both cases represented clear-cut challenges to royal authority, what the Attorney General described in the Apsley case as offences 'against God

[214] *Guide of Honour*, p. 75. [215] Brathwait, *English Gentleman*, pp. 208–9.
[216] *Harleian Miscellany*, ix.596.
[217] See also the gentry conduct books cited in A. Shepard, *Meanings of Manhood in Early Modern England* (Oxford: Oxford University Press, 2003), pp. 140–1.
[218] *Finetti Philoxenis*, pp. 174–6. On duelling and courage, see K. Thomas, *The Ends of Life* (Oxford: Oxford University Press, 2009), pp. 51–2.

and the king, and an affront to the justice both of heaven and earth'.[219] Moreover both had taken place in the vicinity of the royal court, 'to the disturbance of his Majestie's peace'.[220] However, the outcomes were very different.

In a Star Chamber judgement on 31 January 1634 Apsley was subjected to the full force of exemplary royal justice. He was fined £5000, banished from the royal court in perpetuity, forced to make submissions to the king, Privy Council and Northumberland and prohibited from ever again wearing his sword.[221] The judges also made use of the occasion to lay down the parameters of what the king expected for his subjects. The nature of the offence was roundly condemned, particularly by Secretary Windebank, who declared that 'hee that takes a sworde in his hand to revenge himselfe doth as much as in him lieth depose the kinge, att whose dispose the sworde of justice is.' Equal emphasis was given to Northumberland's response, which was presented as a model of how 'a person of a most noble familye' was expected to conduct himself. He had eschewed the 'vayne honor of . . . a mere bragadochia' and displayed true attributes of 'honour, courage [and] judgement' by refusing to rise to Apsley's challenge and putting the whole matter in the hands of the king.[222] In this instance, Charles was able to convey very clearly how he wanted, and expected, his nobles to behave. In the Holland/Weston case, however, the message was much more blurred.

In the council hearing of the case, which took place on 13 April 1633, the main disputants escaped relatively lightly, with submissions to the king. Partly this was a consequence of their connections and circumstances. Holland, Jemyn and Goring were favourites of the queen, who interceded on their behalf, while Apsley who was on the fringes of the court, had got off with a warning on a previous occasion and had the misfortune to offend soon after the king had expressed his determination to take a stand on the issue.[223] But there are also telling indications that in the Holland/Weston case the king felt constrained by the extent to which the duelling ethos had permeated his court. The submissions before the Privy Council represented a much less robust condemnation of the practice than had at first appeared likely. The text of these was carefully

[219] TNA, SP 16/259/71. For similar condemnations of the offence in the Holland/Weston case as a direct contravention of 'the lawes of God and the king', see the submissions of the offenders before the Privy Council: SP16/236/47.

[220] TNA, SP 16/236/53. [221] HMC, *Portland*, ii.124.

[222] Woburn Abbey, Bedford Estate Office, Item 240, 'Camera Stellata Hil 9 Car. Jan–Feb 1633/4', fos. 6–10.

[223] S.R. Gardiner, *The History of England 1603–1642*, 10 vols. (London: Longman, Green & Co) vii.218; HMC, *Cowper*, ii.5–6

vetted by the two secretaries of state, Coke and Windebank, who were managing the process, and also by Charles himself.[224] What emerged was a series of fudges. Windebank initially inserted a phrase into Holland's submission which referred to the 'falsely pretended rules of duell', but then undercut this by requiring Holland to acknowledge that his 'fault' was 'much encreased by questioning a noble man in combat for life & honor without alledging any particular cause of wrong'.[225] The king's own draft of Goring's submission included the Bacon-like assertion that far from it being courageous to accept a challenge, 'it was the dewtie of all good subjects to confess that it is the trew point of honnor and courage to obey your Majestie's commands'; but this was omitted from the version delivered before the council.[226] The most prominent theme of the submissions was the need to repair Weston's reputation after the imputations of cowardice. Goring was required to testify that 'I had noe intention to lay any blemish upon the Lo. Weston for his courage or otherwise: for his obedience to your Majestie's commands neither ought nor can be imputed unto him as want of courage.' Similarly Holland was made to acknowledge that Weston had every legitimate reason for rejecting his challenge and 'hathe not thereby in any degree trespassed against either honor or courage'.[227]

The final text of the submissions, then, considerably diluted the original message. Neither the king nor his secretaries of state felt able to impose the full-blown denunciations of duelling that their earlier statements suggested they would like to have done. After his initial burst of anger at the blatant disregard of his commands, Charles was forced to come to terms with the conventions of the duelling code. He appears to have allowed himself to be talked into accepting that unqualified condemnation was not a viable option. This was grounded in a pragmatic recognition that if good relations between his leading court nobles were to be restored he had to meet Weston's legitimate concern for his reputation and at the same time find a form of words that the protagonists could agree to. But it also reflected an ambivalence within his own mind, steeped as he was in the martial values of his contemporaries. He could readily appreciate that, for a nobleman, in such circumstances the most important consideration was to vindicate his honour. The agreed text of the submissions, then, showed considerable respect for the etiquette of 'combat for life and honour', and also represented an implicit acknowledgement that it was not going to be possible to simply eradicate this among the young nobles and men of 'spirit' in his entourage. What was

[224] TNA, SP 16/236/50–1, 53–4, 57. [225] *Ibid.*, SP 16/236/50.
[226] *Ibid.*, SP 16/236/57, 47. [227] *Ibid.*, SP 16/236/47.

required was a mechanism for reconciling differences and restoring reputations before quarrels reached the stage of combat. It was in this context, as we shall see, that Northampton's programme for the Court of Chivalry came to be revived.

Amid the concern to draw the nobles to court, provide for their welfare and promote higher standards of conduct, the king's principal objective was to cultivate a reliable body of loyal support. His experiences in the late 1620s had taught him the need to get the peerage on his side, so that they could be relied on to back up the crown both in parliament and 'out of doors'. This was a complex and many-sided process. It involved encouraging the attendance at court and personal contact that Newcastle set such store by. It was also about the use of patronage and grants of office to establish traditions of reward and service that would create habits of allegiance. It entailed persuading peers to identify with the crown and recognise a sense of common cause by demonstrating that they had identical interests and ideological agenda. But there was a further dimension to this process that appears to have interested Charles considerably more than his immediate royal predecessors: the development of formal oaths of allegiance.

In the medieval past bonds of loyalty had been enshrined in the formal oaths of fealty which tied dependants to love and serve their masters in return for protection and benefits. This tradition of oath taking still persisted in the early Stuart period. At the royal coronation each nobleman present performed 'liege homage' in which he took an oath 'to become the king's "liege man of life and limbe, and truth and earthly honour to you shall beare against all men that live, so help me God"';[228] and at the creation of knights of the bath or knights of the garter those being honoured would take formal oaths to 'love their soveraigne' and 'serve their countrie'.[229] But such practices were less frequent than they had been in the past. Acts of homage for holding land of the crown had largely disappeared, and for most peers the act of creation did not involve any formal oath taking, but simply the issue of letters patent and the receipt of a summons to sit in the House of Lords.[230] This was a development that

[228] Bodl.L., Bankes MS 5/1, fos. 43, 46; Rushworth, i.201.

[229] J. Nicols, *The Progresses of King James I*, 4 vols. (London, 1828), iii.217; E. Vallance, *Revolutionary England and the National Covenant* (Woodbridge: Boydell Press, 2005), pp. 26–7.

[230] J. Hurstfield, *The Queens Wards* (London: Longmans, Green & Co., 1958), pp. 175–7, 180; Stone, *Crisis of the Aristocracy*, pp. 53–4; Cope, *Life of a Public Man*, pp. 89–90; *A Calendar of the Docquets of Lord Keeper Coventry 1625–40*, ed. J. Broadway, R.P. Cust and S.K. Roberts, 4 parts (List and Index Soc, special ser., 34, 2004), i.23–6. There were, however, some occasions on which the act of creation took place at a personal audience with the king and this did provide an opportunity for some sort of loyalty

Charles considered regrettable and the indications are that he wanted to reinstate and, indeed, extend the practice of oath taking precisely in order to bind his leading subjects more closely to the crown.

The most familiar instance of this was the ill-conceived military oath that he sought to impose on those peers who attended him at York in April 1639. As we shall see, this attempt to bind them to fight for the king's cause 'to the utmost hazard of their life and fortunes' had to be toned down to avoid exacerbating divisions within the ranks of the nobility.[231] But there were precursors to the military oath that demonstrated the value the king attached to formal declarations of loyalty among his nobles. The papers of Sir John Bankes, Attorney General in the late 1630s, include a scheme to revive the regular performance of oaths of 'homage and fealtye' by 'archbishopps, dukes, marquesses, earls, bishops, viscounts barrons & other nobles'. Part of the motivation for this may have been to restore fees that the Lord High Chamberlain, the Earl of Lindsey, had been deprived of since respite of homage had become widespread; but the author of the proposal also stressed its implications for fostering loyalty. Its restoration, he argued, would help to reverse the processes by which most of the king's tenants 'have never used to sweare their fealties & allegiance to his Majesty, whereby noe small tye & meanes to bind them to there dutyfull & faythfull obedience is left unperformed & undone'.[232]

What became of this proposal is unclear; but we do know that considerable attention was given, at the highest level, to a scheme to establish a new 'Order Military' based on an 'oath of fidelitie'. Drawn up in 1639, probably by an anonymous civil lawyer, its essence was that in future all newly created noblemen or knights should be obliged to enrol in the equivalent of a medieval military order and register their titles in the Court of Chivalry. There they would be required to take a loyalty oath 'to the king and his heirs and successors' and make a voluntary pledge of regular service, or else compound for this with an annual monetary payment. In return, they would gain privileges comparable to many continental nobles, including freedom from taxation, freedom from arrest and exemption from having to serve in menial offices or being picked as sheriff. They would also receive a 'badge or cognisance' entitling them to take precedence over others of the same rank 'in all publique places'. Once established, the author anticipated that the scheme could

pledge. For example, when Viscount Wentworth was created Earl of Strafford in the royal presence chamber on 3 August 1639 he made a speech thanking Charles for his grace and favour and pledging himself 'here upon my knees humbly at your feet to attend the honour of your commandes': Bodl.L., Tanner MS 67, fo. 122.

231 Gardiner, *History*, ix.11–12. See pp. 189–90.

232 Bodl.L., Bankes 5/1, fo. 42.

be extended to include those holding existing titles who would thereby secure comparable benefits.[233] Charles was sufficiently impressed that in December 1639 he referred the proposal to a commission of council referees consisting of the Earl Marshal, the Lord Keeper and the Lord Treasurer. His interest was financial as well as political. As Lawrence Stone has pointed out, in many respects this was a thinly disguised programme to revive the sale of honours at a time when he was in desperate need of money to fight his Scottish war.[234] However, a very considerable attraction was the prospect of binding the social elite far more closely than hitherto to the royal service. As the author emphasised, it would provide a cadre of noblemen and knights bound by oaths of loyalty, which would enable the king to 'command their service wheresoever his occasions shall require . . . as a dutie they are obliged to performe to him'.[235] In the event the scheme went no further, probably because within a few days of being referred to the council referees a decision was taken to summon a new parliament. It could be anticipated that it would almost certainly encounter the sort of attacks that had greeted the new order of baronets in 1614 and 1621. Nonetheless, it does show that Charles was prepared to contemplate an ambitious programme that would have traded privileges from the crown for pledges of personal loyalty and led to the creation of an overtly 'royalist' party among the peers and upper gentry.

The various themes discussed in this section – relating to the privileges, loyalty, service and the welfare of the nobility – were brought together in, perhaps, the most testing of the problems that the king faced in dealing with his nobles during the Personal Rule: the 1629 dispute over the precedence of Scottish and Irish peers who were Englishmen. In some respects this was a rerun of the quarrel during the 1621 Parliament, when the English peers had petitioned James against allowing these 'forainers' to take their place as 'nobleman strangers'. But by the late 1620s the stakes were much higher. The number of Englishmen who had been sold Irish peerages had increased considerably, with approaching 50 Englishmen with Irish titles, 30 of whom had no other connection with Ireland.[236] The whole issue of sale of honours had also been given greater prominence by the impeachment proceedings against Buckingham in the 1626 Parliament.

Sale of 'titles of honour' formed the basis of the ninth article of the charges against the duke, which accused him of having 'perverted that

233 BL, Add. MS 12514, fos. 1–8. There is a response to this from the herald Edward Walker in BL, Lansdowne MS 255, fos. 198–201.
234 Stone, *Crisis of the Aristocracy*, pp. 117–19.
235 BL, Add. MS, 12514, fo. 8. 236 Mayes, 'Irish peerage', 233, 238–48.

ancent and most honourable' principle that honours should be conferred as 'rewards' for 'vertuous and 'faithful service'.[237] Buckingham's fault, according to his accusers, had been to seek to destroy the very essence of honour by setting a price on it then selling it to unworthy persons. 'Honour' was not a commodity to be bought and sold, Christopher Sherland argued when he presented the charge on behalf of the Commons, but 'an immediate beam of virtue, and therefore can no more by a price be fixed upon an unworthy person than fire can be struck out with a stick'.[238] As the reward of virtue, it provided the crown with one of its most precious assets: the capacity to recognise and celebrate worthy service by its subjects. 'Great deserving servants . . . will never be satisfied with that which they find so much slighted and so easily to be purchased', Sherfield insisted. Contaminating the reward system 'soils the most beautiful flower of the Crown and makes it vile and cheap in the eyes of the lookers on'.[239] But this was not just an affront to the power and prerogative of the monarch; it also struck at the root of 'ancient nobility'. One of the foremost principles enshrined in a grant of title was that it was 'perpetual', not ending with the person to whom it had been granted 'but descending upon their posterity'. However, this could only be justified, Clare explained in glossing Sherland's speech for the Lords, if there was 'in the first root of this honour some active merit to the commonwealth as may transmit a vigorous example to their successors to raise them to an imitation of the like'.[240] This was the rationale for the place and privilege afforded to the ancient nobility: that their inheritance of virtue gave them a greater propensity than ordinary mortals to act virtuously themselves. Undermining this by granting titles for money was a denial of their claim to eminence and a 'diminution of that high respect due to the ancient and virtuous nobility of this kingdom'.[241] While Buckingham had been alive such arguments were able to secure little purchase, and the impeachment charge fizzled out just as had the Earl Marshal's proposals of April 1625. But now that he was out of the way, and the momentum was with Arundel and proponents of the restoration of 'ancient nobility', there was an opportunity to bury the sale of honours and its toxic legacy once and for all.

The occasion for attempting to do this was provided by an ill-judged intervention in the House of Lords on 9 February 1629, when Lord Fauconberg, an English peer, raised the issue of precedence on behalf of his relative, Lord Fairfax of Cameron, a Yorkshireman with a Scottish title. The intervention led to a heated debate and the Lords set up a

[237] Rushworth, i.334. [238] *Proceedings in Parliament 1626*, i.446.
[239] *Ibid.*, i.447. [240] *Ibid.*, i.451. [241] *Ibid.*, i.446.

high-powered committee, headed by Arundel and Pembroke, to draft a petition to establish that 'no foreign nobility hath any right of precedency within the realm of England before any peer of England'.[242] Eight days later the petition was presented to Charles, along with six points elaborating on the Lords' grievances.

These documents provided a far more aggressive and self-confident statement of the English peers' case than the petition presented in 1621. They did not offer any overt acknowledgement of the king's right, as the fount of honour, to 'collate what you please, upon, who, when and how you please' as the earlier petition had. Instead they focussed on the king's obligation to uphold the honours system and protect the interests of the 'English nobility'. They expected him to act according to

> the example of the best princes and times, upon consideracon of the manifold inconveniences which practice and observacon of circumstances have brought to light, being represented unto your Majestie by the nearest body of honor unto you & nearest concerning you in this . . . & that thereby the inconveniences of your Majestie's service may be prevented, & the prejudice & disparagement of the peeres & nobility of this kingdome may be redressed.[243]

This remarkably confident assertion of the English nobility's right to counsel the king in matters of honour, and expect to receive his approval and support, was accompanied by a stinging denunciation of those Scottish and Irish peers resident in England. They argued that it was unprecedented for men to hold titles where they did not reside; that such men would have no stake in the defence of the kingdom; that those holding 'forraine tytles' were simply using them to escape burdens that then fell on others; and that their only 'ambition was to precede others without ground or merit or estate to warrant it'. They also reminded the king that in the eyes of the law of England, the holders of these titles were still regarded as commoners since they were 'subject to arrest of their persones and all other circumstances of disrespect which by your meanest subjects are undergone'. In short, the elevation of these Scottish and Irish peers, constituted a derogation of the guiding principle of titles of honour in that they were 'atcheived principally by virtue and desert'. To overturn this was a danger and 'discontentment to your realms & subjectes of all degree, in the nature of it contrary to the foundacon of the grounds of honour layd in this kingdome, & in the whole course of it

[242] *LJ*, iv.25–6; Atherton, *Ambition and Failure*, p. 148. The committee included Lord Montagu, who delivered a particularly trenchant speech denouncing the precedence of the Irish and Scots peers: HMC, *Buccleuch*, iii.335–6.

[243] Bodl.L., North MS b.1, fos. 65–6.

breeding ill effect to the service of your Majestie and the publique, & disvalue & contempt to nobility itselfe'.[244]

The petition and its supporting arguments, with their strong echoes of the attack on Buckingham in 1626, constituted the most powerful statement from this period of what the 'ancient nobility', and, more particularly, the English peers, took to be their right and entitlement in relation to the crown. It was the product of a House of Lords in which Arundel and Pembroke were in the ascendancy and which was determined to finally nail the grievance of sale of honours. It was also a direct and unmistakeable provocation to the Scottish and Irish peers. Not only were they being told that they had no just claim to their titles and had sought them simply to evade taxes or gain precedence, it was also being asserted that their elevation was a threat to the whole principle that honour was the reward of virtue and merit. Unsurprisingly, they responded with a furious and concerted lobbying campaign of their own.

This was orchestrated by George Viscount Chaworth, an Irish peer from Nottinghamshire, who already felt a powerful sense of grievance over being denied an English peerage at the time of his creation in March 1628. Chaworth swung into action at the first rumours of the Lords' petition in mid February and assembled an influential lobby of court-based Irish peers, including Thomas Viscount Savile, son of the controller of the royal household, and John Viscount Scudamore, friend and ally of Laud. What was at stake for them was what they regarded as the essence of their identity as peers: the right on all public occasions to take their place according to their rank. As Scudamore put it, 'hee that is not sensible in a case of this quality degenerateth verry farre from the spyrit of a man'. Chaworth's first move was 'to get his Majestie a little prepared . . . least he might be surprised or misled'. This he achieved through the good offices of Susan, Countess of Denbigh, head of the queen's household and mother to another Irish peer, the Earl of Desmond, who prevailed on the king to read what Chaworth called a 'long preparative'.[245]

This document, drafted by Chaworth himself, set the tone for the Irish peers' campaign. The central plank of their case was the argument that the Lords' petition was an attack not so much on their own rights as on the royal prerogative. This was partly born of a recognition that their strongest argument was that precedence was an issue that had already been 'settled' by James in 1621 and that to reopen it now would to imply that the king's authority in such matters was limited. But it was

244 *Ibid.*, fos. 55–6.
245 TNA, C115/7241, 7240. The lobby of Irish peers also included Richard Viscount Lumley and William Viscount Monson.

also based on an astute tactical calculation. The Irish peers understood that they were outgunned within the Privy Council (where most peers were English) and in the English parliament (from which Scottish and Irish peers were excluded), and that they therefore had no alternative but to rely on the king himself to protect their interests. Moreover, they appreciated that the best way to get Charles on their side was to present themselves as ultra-loyalists by clothing their appeals in the language of the prerogative. Amid the fraught proceedings of the 1629 Parliament, this was an approach that yielded significant political dividends.

In contrast to the petition of the English peers, the Irish emphasised from the start that they recognised the king's sole right to determine matters of honour: 'your Majesty onely is our fountaine of honour and the great distributer of places of degree, neyther parliaments nor councells haveing power therein.' The whole matter had been 'stirred in your never enough renowned father's tyme, and soe settled by him' that revisiting it would not only invite questions about the king's prerogative power, but also James's judgement. They also pointed out that to argue that it was a novelty for peers to hold titles where they did not reside was an affront to the king's capacity 'to place which of your subjects you list in this or in any other of your kingdomes in what degree your Majestie pleaseth, without limitation of your choice of the person'. All this was wrapped in a rhetoric that presented them as far more steadfast supporters of the crown. Their opponents' petition was identified with the Petition of Right and the 'parlement language', which had recently caused so much trouble, while they themselves pledged 'to spend our lives & fortunes to maintain . . . your royal and undoubted prerogative'. Above all, they declared, 'we vallew & trust to your Majesty's care to preserve your owne praerogative and the honour of your owne acts.'[246]

Charles read the 'preparative' and, on Chaworth's account, was sufficiently impressed that when the English lords presented their petition on 17 February he responded with 'but a breefe and no satisfactory answer', saying only that 'it was harder to remove an inconvenyence than to prevent it.'[247] The English peers were plainly rattled. They began lobbying the heralds to test the strength of their case and, in late February, convened their own meeting to coordinate tactics.[248] What particularly exercised the more senior among them was the vexed issue of the ranking

[246] TNA, C115/7246, p. 3; repeated in their counter petition on 24 February 1628/9: Bodleian, North b.1, fo. 67. For Charles' attitude to the Petition of Right, see R.P. Cust, 'Charles I, the Privy Council and the 1628 Parliament', *TRHS* (6th ser, 2, 1992), 45.

[247] TNA, C115/7241; Bodl.L., North b.1, fos. 65–6.

[248] CA, Chapter Bk I, fo. 19v.

of their sons that had caused so much discord in the precedence disputes of James's reign. The creation of large numbers of Irish viscounts during the 1620s had affected the ranking of the sons of earls more obviously than any other, because, according to the 1595 table of precedence, they were supposed to take their place immediately behind English viscounts. Feelings were running so high on the matter that, according to Chaworth, one earl said that 'he would disinherit his sonne should he yeild any of us his place'. The English lords also, reportedly, resolved 'to vote a protestation' against the Scottish and Irish on the day of the adjournment of the parliament. The king had received notice of this and, on Chaworth's account, it was one of the reasons why he had dissolved rather than adjourned the session. All of this left the English peers looking unruly and self-interested which, Chaworth smugly concluded, could only work in favour of the Scots and Irish.[249] However, just when everything seemed to be moving in their direction, they were thrown off course by an incident that summed up precisely what they were struggling for.

While attending a service at Westminster Abbey on 22 March, Viscount Monson was jostled out of his place by a number of English barons who 'did thrust before him'. Monson insisted that as a 'Vycount of Ireland [he] had by grant from his Majesty his honour and precedency of the Barons of England' and promptly challenged one of them, Lord Mandeville, to a duel. Chaworth, who reported the incident to Scudamore, applauded his action and doggedly insisted, that 'never . . . shall any of those ranks under us take place above us, howsoever they may disvallew my Lord Monson'. The viscount was talked out of going ahead with the combat by Mandeville's father-in-law, the Earl of Warwick, but promptly challenged another offending peer, Lord Poulett. He insisted to Poulett that the English barons had been acting 'uppon combination' and that their actions were an affront not only to him but also the king, because they brought into question the 'validity' of his royal grant of title and also served to 'trenche . . . upon the royall prerogative', which Monson was pledged to 'maintayn with his life'. Invoking the monarch forced Poulett, so he claimed, to inform the king of the challenge, whereupon the Earl Marshal stepped in, bound over both parties to keep the peace and arranged for an arbitration. Chaworth's verdict was that Monson had won the argument, and got the better of his opponents 'in point of manhoode', but that the whole affair had proved an unwelcome distraction.[250]

[249] TNA, C115/7241, 7248.
[250] NUL, Ne.C. 15, 406, pp. 78–81; TNA, C115/7241.

The Irish peers got their campaign back on course in early April. They set up a joint fund to cover their costs and secured the services of the Attorney General, Sir Robert Heath. Heath presented the king with a lengthy, point by point, refutation of the English peers' case following closely the arguments put forward in Chaworth's 'preparative'. The king's response was all that they could have hoped for. He summoned Lord Treasurer Weston and Lord Keeper Coventry and 'propounded the question to them'. They were hardly disinterested parties because, as Chaworth pointed out, their own sons stood to lose out if the Scots and Irish peers' ranking was confirmed and, predictably, 'they argued contra'. But Charles then showed his mettle and, as Chaworth, put it, 'with more art than was expected' took the Scots and Irish peers' side. When the Lord Keeper tried to 'intimate how necessarie it were to place the erles' sonnes above us because they must have their fathers' places, he responded that 'if the place was dew to us above those were peers it was fitt we shold have it of those were none.' Coventry then backtracked and urged that it was normal in such a case for the king to refer the matter to his Privy Council; but Charles, sensing that he had the upper hand, declared his intention to 'call two or three to me & determine it in my chamber and settle it by order'. Had the whole issue been decided at this point then, as Chaworth confidently predicted, it would probably have been resolved in favour of the Scots and Irish peers. But with Charles there was always the problem of getting him to follow through, especially when he was facing a difficult decision. As Heath observed, he was 'naturally slowe & loves not to be hastend'. This gave the English peers the opportunity to rally their forces.[251]

The key figure here was Arundel, who as Earl Marshal was the traditional arbiter of matters relating to precedence. He directed the English peers' line of argument to 'the point of novelty', concentrating on the strangeness of peers holding titles where they did not reside. Chaworth indignantly dismissed the argument as 'a false one', but he had to concede that Arundel was presenting his case 'with more art than others' and had put his finger on an issue that was likely to carry a good deal of weight with the king who, when he was uncertain how to proceed, tended to fall back on what he took to be precedent. Chaworth had a document drawn up naming 'those persons not having any landes in the kingdome of their tytles at the tyme of their creation', which ended with a pointed reference to the Earl of Oxford, on whose behalf the House of Lords had petitioned for the grant of lands to support his title.[252] However, it was

251 TNA, C115/7242.

252 *Ibid.*, C115/7242, 7247. Chaworth himself was a long-standing client and ally of Arundel (Sharpe, 'Arundel and the opposition', pp. 222–4), although on this issue, as he

to be another six weeks before the matter was finally settled, and then in a full meeting of the Privy Council at which the English lords had a distinct advantage.

Charles fully recognised the importance of the decision that he delivered on 28 June 1629. As he announced in his preamble, he felt keenly his responsibility to provide for the 'preservacon of the... English nobility in theyr ancient lustre without suffering the least diminucon of their due privileges and immunities'. At the same time, however, he acknowledged that the Scottish and Irish titles had been granted under the Great Seal and that the privileges accompanying them had been approved by his father. He therefore set out to achieve a compromise. In a carefully worded 'declaracion touching precedency', which he himself corrected at the drafting stage, and which was signed by 26 members of the Privy Council, he outlined his arguments and conclusions. He would not budge on the issue of precedence and declared that the existing system whereby Scottish and Irish peers were treated with the same 'courtesy' afforded to 'foreign nobility' and ranked immediately behind their English equivalents should continue. The main reason he gave for this decision was his determination to maintain 'the continued practice and usage of former times which is not suddenly to be invented or altered'. For Charles this was an argument that generally trumped all others. However, conscious of the need to do something to appease the English nobility, and 'encourage them with all alacritye to goe on with management of the affayres of the commonwealth', he also ordered the Lord Keeper to oversee the removal from 'all commissions concerning the publique service of this kingdome' of every Scottish and Irish peer above the degree of baron who did not hold land in the two kingdoms.[253] This sent out the unmistakeable message that the king valued the services of his English peerage above those of the 'foreign nobility'.

The king's declaration in June 1629 was to be his most significant statement about precedence and ranking within the nobility. It was carefully drafted following lengthy consideration and was clearly intended to be his final word on the matter. He concluded with a characteristically personalised warning that those who did not abide by the decision would be esteemed 'persons not worthie of the king's favour', together with an injunction to Arundel, as Earl Marshal, to oversee the execution of his

acknowledged to Scudamore, he was 'our mortal adversarie'. He also remarked of the earl, with more than a hint of sarcasm, that 'you knowe he is all for antiquity'. But then Chaworth himself promptly set about presenting his own case in terms of antiquarian precedent that was further testimony to its perceived power to shape royal policy.

253 Wording to the effect that he was determined 'not to alter... the course and practice hitherto used' and continue 'according to the precedent forms' was inserted into the draft by Charles himself: BL, Add MS 64,898, fos. 41–2; *APC 1629–30*, pp. 69–70.

orders. However, as an attempt to lay the whole matter to rest, it was a signal failure.

The Irish peers were clearly gratified by the pronouncement about precedence, but they were stunned by the order to remove them from commissions. This was not something they had seen coming. The removals took effect immediately and resulted in a more or less clean sweep of those ranked at viscount and above in various commissions. Loyalty and long service was no bar to removal. Chaworth complained bitterly to the king that after 24 years of service to the crown he was now put out of all commissions, as if he were a recusant or one of those 'who divide themselves from your Majestie's service, and opposed your commands' by refusing the forced loan.[254] The aggrieved peers organised themselves for another petition, this time focussing on the removals. Their main complaint now was that 'all the kingdome will conceive this your Majestie's acte to be a reproach & badge of your highness' displeasure always reserved for & laid on those onely who were publique offenders, either against lawe or against your Majestie.'[255] Their expressions of pain were not exaggerated. As we have seen from the responses of peers removed from commissions at the time of the forced loan, being deprived of the opportunity to serve the king in office was to divest them of one of the principal affirmations of their status and identity. But the king remained obdurate, and there was little more that they could do. However, their sense of grievance continued to fester and in 1635 they found a new reason for bringing their plight to the attention of the king.

The subsidy act passed by the Irish parliament in July 1634 specified that all Irish peers resident in England were liable to pay. Since these same peers had already been rated for subsidies for the English parliament in 1628 they were being taxed twice over and felt considerably aggrieved.[256] They also suffered a further indignity in December 1634 when Lord Fitzwilliam was cited by the Lord Lieutenant of Northamptonshire as a defaulter for failing to show his horse at musters and complained to the Privy Council. This was an obligation from which peers were normally exempt; but, after lengthy debate, the council ordered that the privilege of exemption should only apply to English peers.[257] This was a logical

[254] *Court and Times*, i.357 (This is misdated 20 May 1628, but the letter plainly refers to July 1629 since it also refers to the queen's miscarriage.); SHC, More of Loseley MS, LM 1327/9, fos. 65–7. Only Scudamore himself appears to have escaped, for reasons which are unclear: Atherton, *Ambition and Failure*, pp. 150–1. For the implications of the judgement for another Irish peer, William Lord Sherard, see Cust, 'A Rutland quarrel', 149–73.

[255] Bodl.L, North MS b.1, fo. 83.

[256] TNA, SP 16/295/2; C115/7237; LRO, DE1431/563.

[257] TNA, SP 16/303/17.

consequence of the Irish peers' legal position that excluded them from the exemption from prosecution in England enjoyed by English peers. But the decision still rankled as yet another example of the demeaning, second class, status to which they felt they were being subjected.

Once again, with Chaworth taking the lead, they swung into action. A petition was drawn up in early 1636, this time addressed to the chairman of the treasury commission, Archbishop Laud. It wrapped together a series of longstanding grievances, dwelling on the general inequity of their position which meant that 'in all payments & charges, fees & duties here we are lords; but in all suits, actions and questions we be made but common & meane persons and treated with all the reproach may be, & called forrainers which wee knowe wee ought not to be styled whilst the kinge is our soveraigne.' It also returned to the sore point of their exclusion from commissions: 'some of us are turned out, and all are kept out of the king's commissions which is a great reproach unto us, that beinge esteemed a punishment for Romanists and great offenders.' They then, rather dramatically, raised the stakes by begging 'his Majestie eyther to destroy the worke of his hand in us, or for his owne honour to maintaine us in our dignityes'. This request – in effect that the king either take away their titles or confirm them in the full privileges of members of the peerage – smacked of desperation; but it was a measure of the sense of injury the peers felt after years of being spurned, slighted and humiliated.[258]

Seventeen of the Irish peers then mounted a tax strike over the Irish subsidy, but caved in in June 1636 when the treasury commissioners issued writs for sheriffs to seize the persons and goods of defaulters.[259] However, this did not prevent Chaworth and some of the others from making a final appeal to the king. Again their petition rehearsed their sense of injury at being labelled 'forraine nobility' and deprived of legal privileges within the realm. 'Never any loyal subjects did suffer as we do', Chaworth complained, 'for not onely the subsedies both of England and Ireland are layd on us, but also all disestimations that may be are cast on us'. However, instead of the drastic proposal that the king either undo their grants or confirm their privileges the petition returned to the safer ground of arguing that their treatment was an affront to the royal prerogative and the king's claim to a united sovereignty over the three kingdoms of England, Ireland and Scotland. They therefore begged that 'the luster of . . . your acts under the great seale of England may not receive

[258] LRO, DE1431/585, 589. The wording may well have been Chaworth's who complained in very similar terms in late 1631: TNA, SP 16/201/45.

[259] LRO, DE1431/559, 569–72.

a wound of dishonour through our sides'. It was a powerful case well argued and supported by a raft of precedents. Chaworth lobbied vigorously for months, drawing on influential acquaintances such as Secretary Windebank. But the king, in spite of his earlier expressions of sympathy for their plight, did nothing.[260]

The issue of the precedence of Scottish and Irish peers was a very important test of Charles's overall policy towards the nobility. As we have seen, there is plentiful evidence that he was committed to doing his utmost to train up the nobility as the natural supporters of his monarchy. He was attempting to use his powers of patronage and the prerogative of the crown as the 'fount of honour' to create something akin to a royalist party, which would provide loyal and faithful service in peace and war. Within this scenario the precedence dispute provided a considerable opportunity. As the acknowledged arbiter of the whole matter, the king had scope for playing-off one side against the other, getting them to compete for their privileges with demonstrations of loyal service in a classic instance of divide and rule. There are hints in his Privy Council adjudication that Charles recognised this and attempted to draw advantage from the situation; but in the end it proved largely beyond him. The reasons for this are very instructive.

At a theoretical level the prerogative that the king enjoyed in matters of honour was as absolute as any he possessed; but in practice it was hedged around with qualifications and constraints. The most important of these was the claim made by the 'ancient nobility' that, by dint of tradition, inheritance and their prominence within the honour community, they were entitled to a principal place in the service of the crown. This meant that while the king's power to appoint whoever he wished to high office was in theory absolute, in practice he was constrained by a recognition that certain dynasties had hereditary claims to certain offices and that the promotion of 'upstarts' was likely to be regarded by the 'ancient nobility' as a slur on their ability to serve. Early modern rulers were generally wary of overriding such considerations and Charles was certainly no exception.[261] Claims for respect for the rights of established noble families invariably counted for a great deal in precedence disputes

260 TNA, SP 63/276/81; SP 16/325/50, 16/325/50. As a postscript to this dispute, when the Long Parliament passed the subsidy act in December 1640 there was a proposal to tack on to it legislation that would affirm that 'the lawe takes noe kind of notice of any forraine tytles of nobility, but that every one that is dignified with any forraine tytles shall take place onely here according to his quality, whether he be knight or esquire'. This would have denied holders of Scottish and Irish titles their courtesy rank and reversed the king's judgement in June 1629. However, nothing appears to have come of it: BL, Add. MS 11,045, fo. 147v.

261 Adamson, *The Princely Courts of Europe*, pp. 16–20.

and provided a very powerful argument in the hands of English peers in 1629. From the reminders in their petition of the dangers of a king ignoring the principle that honours should 'descend in the most deserving families' to subtler promptings by leading councillors – that to bring in 'novelty' and allow the claims of the Scottish and Irish peers was to open up a Pandora's box of challenges to the existing order – they pushed this line for all it was worth.[262] It was a case that Charles found hard to refute.

The other main constraint that the precedence dispute reveals was the monarch's obligation to preserve the integrity of the honours system. This was something that Charles again took extremely seriously. As we have seen, once Buckingham had been removed from the scene in August 1628 his instinct was to cut down on grants of honours and make them only sparingly. However, he still had to deal with the legacy of years of selling titles, which impaired the crown's ability to claim the moral high ground. The critique of this policy provided the other subtext for the English peers' petition in 1629. They did not mention specifically that most of the Scottish and Irish titles had been acquired by purchase; but their references to 'foraine tytles' and the 'ambition to precede others without ground or merit or estate to warrant it' were unmistakable reminders of the erosion of the honours system. The legacy of sale of honours, and admission of failings on the part of the crown, also explains why the Lords were able to use such forceful language which, as we have seen, went well beyond what was normally admissible in the upper house's dealing with the king. This was a grievance for which the king and his father bore considerable responsibility and, as a consequence he was forced to concede that he stood on shaky ground.

All of this helps to explain why Charles did not feel able to give more support to the interests of the Irish peerage. On the crucial issue of precedence he did come down on their side, and evidently felt able to do so because he believed he was following tradition and precedent. However, what he gave with one hand he took away with the other. The condition that all Scottish and Irish peers above the rank of baron be removed from commissions in England – which appears to have been introduced at the last moment as a result of pressure from Arundel and the English peers on the Privy Council – was a bitter pill for them to swallow, implying as it did that he valued the service of his English peers far more highly. When the Irish peers mounted a second petitioning campaign in 1635–6 it would have cost Charles relatively little to make some

262 For the English peers' petition, see Bodl.L., North MS b.1, fos. 55–6, 65–6; TNA, C115/7242.

minimal concession – perhaps granting them exemption from summons to musters – to show that he recognised their plight; but again he felt unable to do so. If Chaworth's reports of the behind-the-scenes manoeuvring in the first half of 1629 are to be believed, the king's instinct was to side with the Irish peers. In the aftermath of the 1629 Parliament, when the competing claims of the royal prerogative and the Petition of Right were very much under the spotlight, they had pitched their case very astutely, emphasising that unlike their opponents they stood, unambiguously, on the side of royal authority.[263] Charles seems to have recognised this and it represented precisely the sort of loyal support that he was looking for from his aristocracy. A more ruthless and pragmatic ruler could probably have made more of this opportunity to bind a powerful interest group to the crown; but Charles fell well short of doing so. The reasons for this were varied. They had to do with his respect for 'ancient nobility' and tradition, his scruples over interfering with the status quo, his sense that he lacked a certain amount of authority in matters pertaining to the honours system because he had helped to create the problem, and also a certain diffidence in forcing his views on senior councillors, which was characteristic of the early years of his reign.[264] But, perhaps, the most important element in all this was his understanding – again evident in his handling of the problem of duelling – that in questions relating to the claims of senior members of the honour community (most of whom had English titles), he had to proceed with tact, sensitivity and caution.

Charles's attempts to reform and strengthen his nobility had mixed results. This was not for want of trying. He made strenuous efforts to curb the inflation of honours, to promote the welfare of the aristocracy, to protect their reputations and improve their education – and, as we shall see in the next chapter, these were supported by radical reform of the Court of Chivalry. He also went out of his way to lay down what he regarded as proper and acceptable standards of behaviour, again intervening personally in episodes such as the Castlehaven case or the removal of peers from London. However, in all this he faced considerable obstacles, particularly when his initiatives contradicted the autonomous claims and rights of the honour community of the 'ancient nobility'. In the case of the Irish peers, these thwarted his efforts to recruit support from a group who were prepared to pledge the loyalty, obedience and respect for prerogative government that he craved. In the campaign against duelling, they persuaded him to water down his initial efforts to impose more restrained standards and acknowledge the ultimate privilege of nobles to

263 TNA, C 115/7241, 7242.

264 On Charles's early diffidence, see Cust, *Charles I. A Political Life*, pp. 183–4.

defend their honour by the sword. The result was a story familiar during the Personal Rule, of policies that were launched energetically but not sustained, and of partial success diluted by fudges and compromises. In one area, however, Charles was able to move forward with much less equivocation: the reform of the Order of the Garter.

The Order of the Garter

The Order of the Garter stood for everything that Charles valued about aristocracy and knighthood and he devoted a great deal of time and energy to reforming its rites and ceremonies. He took his role as garter sovereign extremely seriously. His first action on rising each morning was to put on the medal of St George and he was insistent that other members of the order wear the medal whenever they were in public. He promoted its celebration in painting and the decorative arts, most notably in the scheme for four tapestries intended to be hung in the Banqueting House illustrating the history and ceremonial of the order. He also had plans to enlarge the tomb house attached to St George's chapel to turn it into a mausoleum for himself and his successors.[265] Charles's devotion to the order is not in doubt; but what it meant to him has been the subject of considerable discussion among historians.

In a very influential interpretation, Roy Strong has argued that the order developed a less martial, more religious, aspect during the 1630s. There was 'a change of emphasis', as Charles abandoned the public spectacle of the St George's day processions at Whitehall, in which the knights marched with their retinues in a display of soldierly prowess, in favour of a more civil and spiritual celebration in the relative privacy of Windsor castle. The central focus became the type of procession depicted in a surviving oil sketch by Van Dyck in which the king paraded under a golden canopy, accompanied by choristers and canons from St George's chapel chanting the litany, with the knights walking two by two, without their retinues.[266] This theme has been picked up by others. In his

265 Sharpe, *Personal Rule of Charles I*, p. 219; C. Brown, *Van Dyck* (Oxford: Phaidon, 1982), 189–90; E. Ashmole, *The Institutions, Laws and Ceremonies of the Most Noble Order of the Garter* (London, 1672), p. 136.

266 R. Strong, *Van Dyck: Charles I on Horseback* (London: Allen Lane, 1972), pp. 59–63; R. Strong, 'Queen Elizabeth I and the Order of the Garter', *Archaeological Journal*, 119 (1962), 266–7. Van Dyck's oil sketch of *c.* 1638 probably represented not a drawing of an actual procession, but an idealised reconstruction employing a certain amount of artistic licence as Sir Oliver Millar has pointed out. The classical architectural setting appears to be fictionalised, members of the procession were missed out, the companions march bareheaded, whereas they would have been wearing their elaborate feathered head dress, and there were only four canopy bearers, whereas there would normally

commentary on the 1629 Rubens painting 'A landscape with St George and the dragon', Malcom Smuts has highlighted the way in which the 'martial ethos' of the garter tradition 'has undergone a symbolic transformation' and become Christianised.[267] Similarly, John Adamson, in his important account of the transformation of English chivalry during the 1630s, has argued that the order was emptied of much of its military significance and remodelled to highlight its sacerdotal and religious aspects. In a shift summed up in the requirement for knights to wear newly designed cloaks bearing the cross of St George surrounded by an aureole of silver rays, in emulation of the French Order of the Holy Spirit, 'the holiness of knighthood was re-emphasised . . . the historicity of St George was affirmed' and renewed stress was placed on 'sacred loyalty and idealised moral virtue'.[268] Others, however, have argued for a more open-ended interpretation. Kevin Sharpe, for example, has pointed to a range of multiple associations as varied as the ideals of knighthood itself. On his reading, the order symbolised, at one and the same time, 'manliness and chivalry, chastity, piety and self-regulation, honour and hierarchy'.[269]

This issue is worth exploring further. The rites and observances of the garter involved the king interacting with his leading nobles in ceremonial that harked back to the great era of English chivalry in the fourteenth century. Whether or not there was a shift in tone and emphasis during the 1630s, an investigation of how he understood it, and which aspects of chivalry he particularly valued, can tell us a good deal about how he imagined his relationship with his leading nobles.

Charles's devotion to the order can be traced back to his adolescent experience. He was elected as a knight companion on 24 April 1611 at the age of ten and, as Duke of York, took his place in the stalls of St George's chapel opposite his elder brother Prince Henry.[270] His presentation of 'the bezant' (the king's offertory) at the feast day service in April 1612 was probably the first occasion in which he played a significant role in court ceremonial.[271] When Henry died in November 1612 he

have been 12: O. Millar, *Van Dyck in England* (London: National Portrait Gallery, 1982), pp. 86–7. The themes of this section are explored more fully in my article 'Charles I and the Order of the Garter', *JBS*, 52 (2013), 1–27.

267 M. Smuts, *Court Culture and the Origins of a Royalist Tradition in Early Stuart England* (Philadelphia: University of Pennsylvania Press, 1987), pp. 247–9.

268 Adamson, 'Chivalry and political culture', pp. 174–5.

269 Sharpe, *Personal Rule of Charles I*, p. 220; see also Sharpe, 'The image of virtue', pp. 242–3.

270 Ashmole, *Order of the Garter*, p. 330; Bodl.L., Ashmole MS 1108, fos. 85–7; MS 1132, fos. 5–6.

271 Bodl.L., Ashmole MS 1108, fo. 87.

suddenly found himself thrust into the role of senior knight companion under the sovereign which meant that he was required to act as the king's lieutenant in the annual round of feast day services and rituals.[272] These experiences appear to have made a deep impression on the young prince and from an early age he took an avid interest in its history and customs.

The History of St George that Peter Heylyn presented him with in 1631 and then rewrote two years later, probably at his behest, provides a summary of the traditions and meanings of the order as they were understood by Charles and his contemporaries.[273] The themes highlighted were the three central themes of knighthood and chivalry itself: first, the importance of honouring men of courage and loyalty; second, the value of companionship and the equal standing of men of renown within the honour community; and third, the spiritual role of knighthood in defending true religion.[274] Heylyn's frontispiece emphasised that these were as relevant now as when the order was founded by Edward III. On one side was a picture of Edward on the other of Charles, each clasping a hand to the garter and underneath the motto 'Instituit Edwardus, Adornavit Carolus'.[275]

The order had been founded by Edward III as a society of fighting men, dedicated to the pursuit of martial valour and bound together by personal loyalty to their lord in deliberate imitation of King Arthur's foundation of the Round Table. The garter was introduced to distinguish the members of the order and to bind them together because it was a common device worn by knights dressing for combat.[276] The close identification of the order with courage and martial achievement was summed up in the garter investiture ceremony. When the young Prince Charles had the garter strapped to his left leg following his election to the order in May 1638 the acting chancellor solemnly declared that 'therby thou maiest be admonished to be curragious & having undertaken a just warre into which thou shalt be engaged thou maiest stand firme, valiantly fight & successfully conquer.' This courage and constancy was closely associated with loyalty and fidelity. The letter sent out to summon a new knight to be invested with the garter tied these two sets of qualities together, referring to the 'consideration of your approved truth and fidelity, as also

272 *Ibid.*, MS 1108, fo. 88.

273 A. Milton, *Laudian and Royalist Polemic in Stuart England: the career and writings of Peter Heylyn* (Manchester: Manchester University Press, 2007), pp. 29–32; P. Heylyn, *The History of that most Famous Saynt and Souldier of Christ Jesus, St George of Cappadocia* (1633, 2nd edn.), partic. pt. 3.

274 M. Keen, *Chivalry* (New Haven, CT: Yale University Press, 1984), partic. ch. 10.

275 'Edward established it, Charles has embellished it': Heylyn, *History of... St George* (1631, 1st edn.), frontispiece.

276 *Ibid.*, (1633 edn.), pp. 313–20, 323–4.

of your courageous and valiant acts of knighthood'.[277] And in the list of crimes for which a companion could be degraded from the order, treason and cowardice were the most heinous.[278]

Alongside courage and loyalty, the statutes and traditions of the order placed a heavy emphasis on what Maurice Keen has described as 'the bond of equal standing in chivalry'.[279] To qualify for entry to the order a candidate had to be of knightly status or above and able to demonstrate the three noble descents of blood and arms that had become established as the standard of true gentility. However, once elected all companions except the sovereign stood on an equal footing as in the original Round Table.[280] This was expressed in the process for electing new knights. Each knight companion present at the annual chapter would fill in a suffrage paper with nine nominations (three earls or 'those of higher degree', three barons and three knights), based on the tradition of the Nine Worthies, the heroes of chivalry. A summary of these would then be presented to the sovereign who after conducting a 'scrutiny' would make his election. The final choice of candidate was solely his prerogative, based on his understanding of the merits of those under consideration; but convention required that he should normally elect those who had received 'the greatest number of voices' and this was generally adhered to, through the simple device of letting the knights' companions know in advance which candidates the sovereign favoured so that they could include them in their suffrage papers.[281] The chapter, which took decisions relating to the governance of the order, worked in similar fashion. Again the sovereign had the final say, but he was expected to consult the companions and secure their consent. During the 1630s there was a nucleus of established companions, consisting of the Earls of Arundel, Salisbury, Dorset, Carlisle, Holland and Berkshire, and, in particular, the Earl of Pembroke, the lieutenant and 'ancientest knight' of the order, who attended the majority of feasts and chapters.[282] Charles felt comfortable working with such men and his respect for their advice was such that on occasion he would change course as a result of it. There was a good example of this in February 1641 when he proposed dispensing with the annual feast of the order because of 'the great and important affaires in parliament'. The knights' response was that while they 'did all confess an absolute power to dispense in the sovereign', they were unable to find any previous instance in which the celebration of the feast had

277 Bodl.L., Ashmole MS 1108, fos. 140, 120.
278 Keen, *Chivalry*, p. 176; Heylyn, *History of... St George* (1633 edn.), pp. 337–8, 343–4.
279 Keen, *Chivalry*, p. 197. 280 Heylyn, *History of... St George* (1633 edn.), p. 341.
281 Ashmole, *Order of the Garter*, pp. 265–83, 290.
282 WCLA, MS X.7, Annals of the Order of the Garter, passim.

been 'omitted', no matter how difficult the circumstances. They, therefore, 'humbly besought the sovereign not to begin to make a breach in the constant order'. The matter was debated, a vote was taken and it was decided to find time to celebrate the feast as normal.[283]

The Chapter's procedures provided a model of governance that Charles appears to have found highly congenial. In many respects, it matched the constitutional arrangements for the realm as a whole. As he readily acknowledged, a good monarch would consult with, and seek the consent of, both council and parliament and, where appropriate, follow their advice, although the final decision remained his, as the sovereign being endowed by the God with the kingly wisdom to discharge this role.[284] In the case of the garter, however, consultation did not involve the whole realm, but a small, select group of noble companions whose acknowledged virtue had earned them the right to have their say. It exemplified the traditional principle that a monarch should consult with his *consiliarii nati*, his natural counsellors, made up of the 'ancient nobility' whose innate wisdom and virtue equipped them to perform this role.[285]

The third prominent theme in the traditions and statutes of the order was the ideal of Christian knighthood. Central to this was the cult of St George which Heylyn himself had done much to revive.[286] The image of George slaying the dragon continued to be the central motif of the order, and nowhere was it more graphically or dramatically depicted than on the new seal of the order, introduced at Charles's behest in 1637.[287] It was an image which, as Heylyn explained, served to remind the companions that 'as their saint and patron was in his time a faithful champion of the church of Jesus Christ so should they also bee the guardians and defenders of the Christian faith . . . never to lay aside St George's resolution of dying, if need be, for the faith of Christ and in defence of his religion and the Holy Church'.[288] As the garter symbolised courage, fidelity and knightly companionship, so the George was a constant reminder of the Christian vocation of knighthood.

The traditions and ideals associated with the order, then, encompassed a wide range of references and allusions. In different contexts different

283 Bodl.L., Ashmole MS 1111, fo. 41r; MS 1108, fo. 146v.

284 Cust, *Charles I*, pp. 19–20, 469.

285 K. Sharpe, *Politics and Ideas in Early Stuart England* (London: Pinter Publishers, 1989), pp. 88–9.

286 Strong, 'Elizabeth I and the Order of the Garter', 262–6; Milton, *Heylyn*, pp. 30–2; Strong, *Charles I on Horseback*, p. 62; Heylyn, *History . . . of St George* (1633 edn.), passim.

287 P.J. Begent and H. Chesshyre, *The Most Noble Order of the Garter 650 Years* (London: Spink, 1999), pp. 157–70; Ashmole, *Order of the Garter*, pp. 246–7.

288 Heylyn, *History . . . of St George* (1633 edn.), p. 335.

themes were accentuated and symbolised. The question raised by recent writing about the order is which of these had the strongest resonance for Charles and which was being given most prominence during the 1630s. It is important to recognise that this was never a matter of either/or. It was not a case of one aspect being privileged to the exclusion of others. The order always retained its multifaceted identity. Nonetheless, within this, it is possible to detect changes of emphasis which, as has been suggested, could reveal much about how Charles conceived of his kingship and how he understood the role of his nobles within it.

The first point to stress is that there is no doubt that Charles was strongly committed to promoting the spiritual mission and welfare of the order. He gave powerful support to proposals to beautify and enhance the religious ceremonial of the garter chapel by purchasing a new set of silver church plate, which was consecrated by Laud in 1637. He also sought to promote what he regarded as proper liturgical practice in the services attached to the annual feast, setting an example by personally attending each of them and bringing to an end the practice of dividing the feast day services into two halves.[289] But, perhaps, the most significant of his reforms in this area was the change ordered in the companions' dress. This was one of his first acts as sovereign. At a chapter on 27 April 1626, he decreed that, 'out of his princely desire by all due means to advance the honour of the order', henceforth all companions and officers should wear the garter star on their 'cloaks, coats and riding cassocks' whenever they went abroad. Initially it was stipulated that the star should be a simple device, with the red cross of St George on a white background surrounded by the garter; but around 1629 it was transformed by the addition of the aureole of silver rays, a device commonly employed in paintings of the heads of Christ and the Apostles, to signify their heavenly associations, and generally thought to have been adopted 'in imitation' of 'the ensign' of the French Order of the Holy Ghost.[290] The purpose of this reform, as Charles explained it, was that 'the wearing thereof may be a testimony apert[open] to the world of the honour they hold from the said noble order.' It transformed the public appearance of the garter knights. The conspicuous silver star became the central motif of a whole genre of Van Dyck portraits during the 1630s. The most famous example is his 1637 portrait of Charles in his garter cloak, but, perhaps, the most interesting is the 1633–4 portrait of James Stuart, Duke of Lennox. It depicts the young duke, newly invested into the order,

289 Ashmole, *Order of the Garter*, pp. 491–5, 549–50.

290 *Ibid*, p. 216; WCLA, MS X.7, Annals of the Order of the Garter, fo. 156; Begent and Chesshyre, *Order of the Garter*, pp. 170–1.

resplendent in George, garter and decorated riding cloak, about to set out for the hunt.[291] This captures what must have become the everyday appearance of the garter knights in their new dress, with the distinctive garter star providing a striking reference to the spiritual associations of the order. This suggests, then, that recent historians are right to stress that this particular reform enhanced the religiosity of the garter. Its message was similar to the Rubens painting of Charles as St George, which was executed at about the same time as the aureole was introduced: this was a knightly order dedicated to the service of the church and true religion.

However, this theme was much less obvious in some of the other reforms. The intent behind these, as the reforming chancellor of the order, Sir Thomas Roe, explained in January 1638, was 'to restore' the order 'to the primitive institution, both in statutes, robes and all other honours degenerated and corrupted by tyme and observance'.[292] In Charles's lexicon, of course, 'primitive institution' could have a multitude of meanings evoking Elizabethan and medieval precedents. With respect to the garter, however, it was used to justify a campaign to revive ancient usage and emphasise the order's historical depth. Part of this was further reform of the robes in which Roe took the lead in ensuring that the mantles worn on ceremonial occasions were of 'a celestial blue' and the outer robes purple, in accordance with what was deemed to be early practice.[293] Attendance by companions at feast day celebrations was tightened up and those unable to make it were required to present formal petitions of excuse and then observe the feast day formalities in their own homes, as the ancient statutes decreed.[294] A new seal and signet was introduced, and formal measures were taken to regularise the pay of the officers' stipends out of a generous annuity of £1200 that Charles provided from 1634 onwards, all again under the auspices of Roe.[295] None of these measures had particularly religious connotations. They were about regularity, order and decorum. The imperative, as Roe had indicated, was to maintain hallowed traditions that would uphold the honour and sense of permanence associated with the order.

However, there was one reform that had rather different connotations and which looked more directly towards the order's military traditions.

291 S.J. Barnes, N. De Poorter, O. Millar, H. Vey (eds.), *Van Dyck. A Complete Catalogue of the Paintings*, (Paul Mellon Centre for Studies in British Art, 2004), pp. 475, 585.

292 Bodl.L., Ashmole MS 1108, fo. 113; HMC, *Salisbury MSS*, xxii.294.

293 Ashmole, *Order of the Garter*, p. 210.

294 Ashmole, *Order of the Garter*, pp. 485–6; Bodl.L., Ashmole MS 1108, fos. 98–9, 106; MS 1113, fos. 19–25.

295 Ashmole, *Order of the Garter*, pp. 247–8, 259; Bodl.L., Ashmole MS 1108, fos. 99–100, 109, 114, 116.

This was the effort to restore the original number of 'poor' or 'alms knights'. The order of 26 'poor knights' (one for each companion) had been established by Edward III, as Elias Ashmole the later historian of the order explained, to recompense 'valiant men, chiefly such as had behaved themselves bravely in war, yet afterwards hap'ned to fall into decay'. Originally conceived of as bedesmen to pray for the soul of the monarch, since the Reformation their duties had become largely ceremonial, attending at feast day processions and royal visits.[296] Nonetheless, the priority remained to provide relief for distinguished former soldiers who had fallen on hard times. Surviving petitions from those seeking admission to the order, and the accompanying testimonials from their commanding officers, make it clear that distinguished service in the recent wars, was the principal qualification for admission.[297] During the 1630s a good deal of attention was given to the plight of the 'poor knights'. Vetting of old soldiers for the next available place was part of the regular business at chapter meetings; Charles provided for them in the £1200 a year he allocated to the order; and Roe's predecessor as chancellor, Sir Francis Crane, set up an endowment in his will to provide lodging and stipends for a further five knights and Roe himself campaigned for the full complement of 26 to be restored.[298] In the event this was not achieved, but Charles's determination to increase the number of 'poor knights' was apparent in instructions he issued to the deputy chancellor, to pursue Crane's executor for the promised endowment.[299] This level of support for the 'poor knights' during the 1630s is instructive because it suggests a king and successive chancellors who understood the martial traditions of the order and were determined to maintain them as an essential expression of its identity.

Charles's determination to emphasise the continuing association of the garter with matters military needs to be viewed in the context of his wider efforts to promote chivalric values. In this respect, Charles has generally been contrasted with his elder brother, Henry, who is credited with fostering the Jacobean chivalric revival. Charles has been seen as more scholarly, less militaristic.[300] This appears to have been largely because he was more reserved than Henry, and less impressive when

296 Ashmole, *Order of the Garter*, pp. 158–65; Begent and Chesshyre, *Order of the Garter*, pp. 35–45.
297 Bodl.L., Ashmole MS 1132, fos. 186, 190–282.
298 Ashmole, *Order of the Garter*, pp. 164–5; Bodl.L., Ashmole MS 1108, fos. 95, 128; MS 1113, fos. 69, 176–7.
299 Bodl.L., Ashmole MS 1108, fo. 131.
300 Strong, *Henry Prince of Wales*, p. 9; A.B. Ferguson, *The Chivalric Tradition in Renaissance England* (Washington, DC: Folger Shakespeare Library, 1986), p. 140.

it came to projecting an image of martial vigour; but there is a good deal of evidence to suggest that he was keen to follow in his brother's footsteps. As a nine year old, he was complimented by the Venetian ambassador on his interest in war and matters military, and he told his father and the Earl of Salisbury that when he grew up he wanted to become a soldier in the service of the republic.[301] This was just the sort of high-spiritedness and martial enthusiasm that contemporaries looked for in young princes and noblemen for whom the supreme vocation was still seen as the performance of deeds of military prowess. Charles started the quasi-military training in which they were expected to engage at an early age, taking riding lessons alongside Henry, under Monsieur De St Antoine, and exercising with the pike as soon as he was strong enough to hold it.[302] When Frederick of the Palatinate visited England in 1613 to marry his elder sister Elizabeth he presented Charles with a New Year's gift of a rapier and spurs; and a few weeks later at the festivities to celebrate the wedding Charles greatly impressed onlookers with his prowess in the knightly exercise of 'running at the ring'. At the Accession Day Tilt in 1620, he accomplished a feat that his brother had never been old enough or practised enough to perform: he led the procession dressed in full armour and then jousted with various offspring of the aristocracy. Again this made a considerable impression on onlookers and confirmed the view of many that he had taken on the chivalric mantle that his brother had laid down.[303]

Charles also displayed the same admiration as his elder brother for military men. Perhaps the clearest indication of this was provided by the suffrage papers that he filled in between 1612 and 1615, nominating his candidates for the next vacant stall in the order. His choices were very evidently slanted towards those with martial connections. Among 'the earls', his two most regular 'picks' were Francis Earl of Rutland and Richard Earl of Dorset, both regular participants in the Jacobean tilts; among 'the barons' they included Lord Howard of Walden, another leading jouster who had seen service at the siege of Julich and was captain of the band of gentleman pensioners; and among 'the knights', Sir Horace Vere, Sir Edward Conway and Sir Edward Cecil, all veterans of the

301 *CSP Ven. 1610–13*, pp. 3, 115, 120.

302 Strong, *Henry Prince of Wales*, pp. 41–3; For a painting of the young Prince Charles in pike armour, see Government Art Collections, UK, A1.154 (I am grateful to Andrew Thrush for drawing this to my attention).

303 Chamberlain, i.403; A. Young, *Tudor and Jacobean Tournaments* (London: George Philip, 1987), pp. 38–40, 207. Newcastle himself was later to recall that the young Charles 'was the beste man at armes I vow to God that ever I saw, both for grace & sureness, eyther at running at the ring or running at tilte': *Newcastle's Advice*, p. 61.

English army in the Netherlands.[304] Charles evidently admired such men and believed that their rightful place was among the garter knights.

These early impressions did much to shape the king's attitude towards the garter through the 1630s, in spite of the military disappointments of the 1620s. Charles had embarked on war with Spain and France with high hopes of repeating the feats of the Black Prince and the young Henry V;[305] but his war effort had been a signal failure. This had prompted him to adopt a much more cautious and peaceable approach to foreign policy which was accompanied, as John Adamson has demonstrated, by efforts to distance himself from those aspects of the Elizabethan military tradition associated with hostility to Spain and support for the 'Protestant cause'.[306] Yet, at the same time, he was still very evidently drawn to the notion that the supreme expression of noble and princely honour lay in the performance of heroic feats of battle, and that his identity as a king was, ultimately, tied up with success in war. Van Dyck's 1633 portrait of him with his riding master, clad in jousting armour, wielding the baton of command and riding through a triumphal arch, was a powerful articulation of this ideal.[307] Such aspirations did much to define his attitude towards the Order of the Garter. The indications are that, while seeking to promote its religious and sacerdotal aspects, he continued to envisage it as a body of martial men, dedicated to celebrating military achievement.

This was, perhaps, most apparent in the choice of those elected to join the order while Charles was sovereign. Most elections were made either to woo foreign princes and influential noblemen, for diplomatic reasons, or as a reward for service at court or in civilian office. It was comparatively rare for an individual to be chosen because of his soldierly accomplishments and it would be difficult to identify any election made during James's reign primarily for this reason.[308] The majority of

304 WCLA, MS X.7, Annals of the Order of the Garter, fos. 120, 122v, 123v, 124v, 127. For those involved in Jacobean tilts, see Young, *Tudor and Jacobean Tournaments*, pp. 72–3; BL, Harleian MS 1368, pp. 44–6; Add. MS 14, 417, fos. 11, 23. For biographies of these individuals, see *Oxf.DNB*.

305 T.E. Cogswell, *The Blessed Revolution. English Politics and the Coming of War, 1621–1624* (Cambridge: Cambridge University Press, 1989), p. 194; Adamson, 'Chivalry and political culture', pp. 167–9.

306 Adamson, 'Chivalry and political culture', pp. 169–73.

307 Cust, *Charles I*, pp. 159–60.

308 For elections to the order during this period, see G.F. Beltz, *Memorials of the Most Noble Order of the Garter* (London, 1841), pp. clxxxiii–clxxxviii. Although some of James's choices went to regular jousters at the accession day tilts, such as Pembroke, Montgomery and Arundel, this does not appear to have been the principal reason for their election.

Charles's choices followed this pattern, with the appointment of office-holders, like Lord Treasurer Weston, courtiers and clients of Buckingham, like Dorset and Holland, and foreign princes, such as Gustavus Adolphus and his own nephew, Charles Louis, Elector Palatine.[309] But among Charles's appointees there were also some who were soldiers first and courtiers and councillors second. Robert Bertie, Earl of Lindsey, who belonged to one of the great military dynasties of late Tudor and early Stuart England, came into this category. He was commander of the English regiments in the Low Countries in the early 1620s and then took over as vice-admiral of the English fleet in the abortive efforts to relieve La Rochelle in the late 1620s, although when he was elected in April 1630 he had also recently been appointed Lord High Chamberlain.[310] Further clear cut examples were provided by Henry Danvers, Earl of Danby and William Douglas, Earl of Morton, both elected in November 1633. Among the press of senior courtiers and noblemen seeking the honour, neither had a particularly strong social or political claim, but both were distinguished soldiers. Danby was a veteran of the Elizabethan wars, and more recently a member of Charles's council of war, and his claim to distinction according to the annals later compiled by Edward Walker, garter king of arms, was that 'in his youth [he] had given evident proofes of his courage and conduct in the wars of Ireland.' Morton had been commander of the Scots regiments deployed during the wars of the 1620s and, to emphasise this connection, at his installation in April 1634 he paraded through London with 'all the Scottish Colonels' who had been fighting alongside the Swedes in the Thirty Years War.[311] But, perhaps, the most instructive example is the election of James, marquess of Hamilton. Hamilton was the king's cousin and a personal favourite so there is little doubt that sooner or later he would have been elected to the order. But his investiture and installation took place in a hurry, in October 1630, after a stall had become vacant with Northampton's death. This haste appears to have been closely connected to the fact that the previous month Charles had approved his command of a levy of 6 000 volunteers to serve Gustavus Adolphus in Germany. By conferring this honour on his cousin, as the Venetian ambassador noted, Charles could signal that although he was reluctant to support Gustavus with

309 Beltz, *Memorals*, clxxxvi–clxxxviii. For biographies of all these individuals (except the Earl of Northampton), see *Oxf.DNB*.

310 'Robert Bertie, Earl of Lindsey (1582–1642)', *Oxf DNB*; B. Donagan, *War in England 1642–1649* (Oxford: Oxford University Press, 2008), p. 47.

311 'Henry Danvers, Earl of Danby (1573–1644)', and 'William Douglas, Earl of Morton (1582–1648)', *Oxf.DNB*. For Walker's annals, see Bodl.L., Ashmole MS 1110, fo. 156; for Morton's installation cavalcade, see *Strafforde's Letters*, i.242.

subsidies, he thoroughly approved of Hamilton's expedition. He was also making it clear that this was the type of service that he associated with membership of the order.[312]

By the end of the 1630s the order had a markedly more military complexion than had been the case at the start of Charles's reign. It included two of the leading Scots commanders who had recently seen service on the continent, the current Lord Admiral (Northumberland, promoted to the position in April 1638) and former vice admiral, and a veteran of the Elizabethan wars in Ireland.[313] The growing pervasiveness of the military ethos was also evident in the suffrage papers filled in by the companions when they were called on to make their nominations to the sovereign. Many of the nominations were, predictably, of friends, relations and personal allies. Holland, for example, invariably nominated his brother, the Earl of Warwick, and Hamilton his brother-in-law, Lord Feilding. But over the period 1625–39 there was a nucleus of names that appeared again and again and which appear to have commanded general approval. Most of these were military men. In the category of 'earls', Essex and Warwick were the most frequent nominees, the former a commander in the Low Countries and on the Cadiz expedition during the 1620s and the latter an experienced naval commander. Head and shoulders above the other nominees in the 'barons' category, until his death in 1635, was Horace Lord Vere, the most revered English commander of his day. And among the 'knights' the three most frequently nominated candidates were Sir Charles Morgan, who commanded the expeditionary force to Denmark in 1627 and was still serving in Germany during the 1630s, Sir Robert Mansell, a veteran of naval campaigns back to the 1590s, and Sir John Ogle, another long-serving commander in the Netherlands.[314] The perception of the companions themselves appears to have been that the order they belonged to was one in which military distinction should continue to command the highest degree of honour and respect.

An interesting perspective on this is provided by the portrait paintings of the knights executed by Van Dyck and his studio during the 1630s. Twelve of these survive and the styles used can readily be categorised as either 'civilian' or 'military'. The 'civilian' version showed

[312] 'James Hamilton, 1st Duke of Hamilton (1606–49)', *Oxf. DNB*; Bodl.L., Ashmole MS 1108, fo. 179; WCLA, MS X.7, Annals of the Order of the Garter, fo. 171; Gardiner, *History of England*, vii.174–5; *CSP Ven. 1630–2*, p. 432; Bodl.L., Ashmole MS 1110, fo. 162.

[313] 'Algernon Percy, 10th Earl of Northumberland (1602–1668)', *Oxf. DNB*.

[314] This analysis is based on the suffrage papers 1625–39, in WCLA, MS X.7, Annals of the Order of the Garter, fos. 152, 157, 163, 169, 171, 185, 187, 192, 205 and Bodl.L., Ashmole MS 1108, fos. 101, 124–5, 130, 140.

the knights with the new robes designated in 1626 and the garter star prominently displayed, while the 'military' version depicted the companion wearing full tournament armour, or else the breastplate of the cavalry commander, and the George worn either on a ribbon or a chain. Charles was portrayed in both styles, as were Hamilton and Arundel. Lennox, Weston and Pembroke were portrayed as civilians, but Dorset, Holland, Northumberland, Charles Louis and the young Prince Charles were all depicted using the 'military' style, as ready for battle.[315] In Dorset's case this was remarkable because there is no indication otherwise that he had any military pretensions;[316] but this is surely testimony to the popularity of the genre. However, perhaps, the most striking portrait of all was that of Danby. He was painted in the blue and crimson robes of the order used as formal dress rather than in armour; but there was no mistaking the formidable battle scar high on his left cheek or the grizzled features which contrasted so markedly with the courtly elegance of the majority of Van Dyck's sitters.[317]

Martial values, then, played a prominent part in the ethos of the order during the 1630s. In part this was a function of the fact that by 1640 the proportion of the British peerage who had experience of some sort of military service stood at nearly 70 per cent, significantly higher than had been the case in 1600. But it was also a consequence of the shifting climate of ideas in which martial endeavour was once again coming to be seen as the most prestigious form of service for a member of the aristocracy, what Roger Manning calls a process of 'remilitarisation'.[318] There were various reasons for this. The upbringing of upper class boys still had a pronounced martial dimension, from the reading of chivalric romances and the brawls and mock battles of their schooldays, to the fencing and riding lessons, and study of fortification provided by noble academies. The English public was also fed a continuous diet of news about wars and feats of arms on the continent, particularly after the outbreak of the Thirty Years War.[319] But, perhaps, the most important reason for the strength of the martial ethos was the growing prestige which attached to

315 Barnes et al., *Van Dyck*, pp. 436–7 (Arundel), pp. 461–75 (Charles I), p. 483 (Prince Charles), p. 485 (Charles Louis), p. 517 (Hamilton), p. 535 (Holland), pp. 566–7 (Northumberland), pp. 569–72 (Pembroke and Montgomery), p. 585 (Lennox), p. 632 (Dorset), p. 633 (Hamilton), p. 639 (Weston).

316 Walker described him in his annals as 'fitter for councell than action' and beyond a visit to the European war zone in 1613 there is no mention of military involvement in his biography: Bodl.L., Ashmole MS 1110, fo. 165; 'Edward Sackville, 4th Earl of Dorset (1590–1652)', *Oxf.DNB*.

317 Millar, *Van Dyck in England*, pp. 62–3.

318 Manning, *Swordsmen*, pp. 17–19.

319 Thomas, *The Ends of Life*, pp. 44–62; Donagan, *War in England*, pp. 33–40.

serving the state as a soldier, rather than as a courtier or governor. Influenced by the ongoing debate in France about the merits of the *noblesse d'épée* and the *noblesse du robe*, favourable comparisons were increasingly drawn between 'swordsmen' and 'gownmen'.[320] Going to war in defence of one's country or in support of one's sovereign was claimed to be the most demanding, and also the most honourable, service a nobleman could perform; courage in combat was acclaimed as the supreme validation of his status; and soldierly 'honesty' was increasingly contrasted with courtly artifice and trickery.[321] After the challenge presented by sixteenth century humanist critiques of the ignorant, over-militarised aristocracy, soldiering was being rehabilitated as the supreme vocation of the nobleman and this had a significant impact on the Order of the Garter.

It would, however, be misleading to suggest that these martial values dominated to the exclusion of other elements – just as it is misleading to argue that there was a shift away from them to a more peaceable and spiritualised version of the order. Like any cultural activity, the ceremonies and traditions of the order could signify different things to different participants on different occasions. During the 1630s all three of the central themes of knighthood and chivalry – the honouring of men of courage and loyalty, the companionship of men of honour and the responsibility to uphold true religion – were kept in play, and indeed were given renewed vigour by Charles's enthusiasm and commitment to the order.

But what part was played in all this by 'Elizabethanism'? As we have seen, Newcastle associated the order with the tilts and tournaments, and old-fashioned, noble processions of the heyday of the Elizabethan chivalric revival. However, he also implied in *The Variety* that these were a thing of the past, and this view has been shared by modern scholars who point to a withdrawal from the spectacle of knights companions parading through the streets of London with their retinues to processions in the more private surroundings of Windsor Castle without their retinues, which stressed the more civil and spiritual aspects of the order.[322] On closer examination, however, it turns out that many of the features associated with the Elizabethan rites of the order were retained and indeed that under Charles there was a self-conscious effort to revive what were

320 R. Mettam, 'The French Nobility, 1610–1715', in *The European Nobilities in the Seventeenth and Eighteenth Centuries*, ed. H.M. Scott, 2 vols. (Harlow: Longmans, 1995), i.114–20.

321 Manning, *Swordsmen*, pp. 28–9. See, for example, Naunton, *Fragmenta Regalia*, pp. 48, 52, 55, 61–2, written in the 1630s, which contrasted the 'militia' and 'togati' among Elizabeth's leading nobles to the advantage of the former.

322 See pp. 119–20.

seen as some of the features of an earlier era as part of the reforms to restore the 'primitive institution'.

The centrepiece of the garter celebrations was the three-day feast of St George, which normally took place on 22–24 April. This constituted the main annual event in the court's ceremonial calendar.[323] The venue varied. Traditionally the feast had taken place at Windsor Castle, but Elizabeth abandoned this and preferred to hold it at Whitehall, or sometimes Greenwich.[324] In 1603, however, James moved it back to Windsor and thereafter it was celebrated at either of the main locations.[325] Under Charles eight of the traceable feasts were held at Windsor, six at Whitehall and one (in April 1642) at York.[326] The central elements of the ceremonial and celebrations accompanying the feast appear to have altered little from Elizabeth's to Charles's reign in spite of Strong's suggestion of a shift of emphasis. Charles was more punctilious in his attendance at services and some of the trappings had become more elaborate, with the introduction of a canopy and more standardised dress. But the attendance of 'poor knights', canons, heralds and officers, the chanting choristers and musical accompaniment, the solemn procession of the pairs of companions and, for nearly half the feasts the Whitehall setting, remained constant.[327]

This element of continuity was also apparent in another aspect of the garter ceremonial where Strong and others have detected change: the processions that accompanied the feast and other rites of the order. To understand what was happening it is important to recognise that there were three different types of ceremonial procession associated with the order. The Grand Procession on St George's day was a decorous and restrained affair; but the other two – the procession of knights companions at the beginning and end of the feast, and the cavalcade of elect knight companions as they set out from London for Windsor on the occasion of their installation – were much more showy and public. These took place on the streets of London before large crowds, with the companions decked out in all their finery and accompanied by entourages

323 The feast was sometimes prorogued to a later date because of plague or the sovereign's other commitments.

324 Ashmole, *Order of the Garter*, pp. 474–5; Strong, 'Elizabeth I and the Order of the Garter', 249.

325 Ashmole, *Order of the Garter*, pp. 475, 549; Bodl.L., Ashmole MS 1108, fos. 64–5; WCLA, MS X.7, Annals of the Order of the Garter, fos. 104–5.

326 Bodl.L., Ashmole MS 1108, *passim*; WCLA, X.7, Annals of the Order of the Garter, *passim*.

327 Strong, 'Elizabeth I and the Order of the Garter', 249–52, 255; Ashmole, *Order of the Garter*, pp. 508–602, 629–36. For a fuller discussion of the ceremonial of the feast celebrations, see Cust, 'Charles I and the Order of the Garter', 18–20.

of servants, retainers and friends.[328] A contemporary description of the opening of Whitehall feast in April 1629 conveyed the theatricality of the occasion:

> Upon the morning of the feast day the Earl of Dorset came from Dorset house with a brave show of men very rich in jewels, chains and clothes, being directed by Somerset herald and Rouge Dragon. And soe at Arundel house took up my Lord of Arundell and went along the Strand, took up the Earl of Rutland and his men, and the Earl of Northampton and Salisbury and Suffolk and their men who rode in this manner unto court: first the Earl of Northampton's servants and himself after, as the youngest knight; next [to] him the Earl of Suffolk with his trayne before him and Rouge Dragon; then the Earl of Dorset with his company, [and] Lancaster [herald]; last came Rutland and Arundel together; before them rode Chester, Somerset and York heralds. They alighted at the court gate. They wore robes of the garter.[329]

With its heralds, its rich costumes, its bands of liveried retainers and its sheer size, as it snowballed on its way down the Strand, this procession resembled the great noble entries of a bygone age.[330]

There was a strong element of competition on such occasions, particularly at the installation cavalcades. Ashmole describes how the companions elect would take up lodgings in the Strand 'to the end [their procession] might pass through some of the eminent streets to the people's satisfaction'. On the day of the procession they would pull out all the stops, recruiting friends and allies to join them, decking out their servants and retainers in the costliest dress they could afford and providing sumptuously decorated coaches. The whole event would generally take place in the presence of the sovereign who would take up a house on the Strand for the day so that he and the queen and Prince Charles could watch the procession from the balcony.[331] George Garrarde, the London correspondent of Viscount Wentworth, compared the installation cavalcades of Danby and Morton in April 1634 to a celebrated occasion nearly 20 years earlier when Lord Knollys and Viscount Fenton had 'a secret vy' to see who could put on the more spectacular show. This time Garrarde reckoned that Danby had won the day. By clothing 'fifty men in tissue doublets and scarlet hose thick laced', providing two coaches, 'set out bravely' and recruiting 'all the ancient nobility of England that were not of the garter' to ride alongside him, he trumped Morton's parade

[328] Ashmole, *Order of the Garter*, pp. 338–40, 509–10; Strong, 'Elizabeth I and the Order of the Garter', 253.

[329] Bodl.L., Ashmole MS 1110, fo. 106.

[330] Stone, *Crisis of the Aristocracy*, pp. 211–14.

[331] Ashmole, *Order of the Garter*, pp. 338–9; *Strafforde Letters*, i.242, 427; *CSP Ven. 1633–6*, p. 389.

of Scottish colonels and nobles.[332] A year later Garrarde was able to report that the installation cavalcade of the Earl of Northumberland had surpassed even these.[333] But of all the cavalcades of the 1630s the most impressive was the one planned for the installation of Prince Charles in May 1638 (see Figure 2.2).

Arundel, as Earl Marshal, drew up plans for an elaborate round of ceremonial that would first involve Charles being dubbed a knight of the bath with 26 companions, before setting out from Somerset House for Windsor.[334] To ensure that the procession was as majestic as possible, Pembroke, as lieutenant of the Order of the Garter, wrote to a number of peers signifying that the king, 'having formerly taken notice of some slacknes among the lords in giving their attendance upon his royall person in the place of publique solemnity, and expecting to have it more frequently observed in the future', specifically desired their attendance.[335] In the event, a decision was taken late in the day to move the feast to Windsor and, as a result, the installation cavalcade was cancelled. But the scale of the preparations demonstrated Charles's commitment to these processions.[336]

The size and opulence of the processions provide further indications of how Charles viewed the garter and saw it as enhancing the prestige of his kingship. In many respects they bucked the contemporary trend, identified by Lawrence Stone and others, of a decline in the scale and showiness of aristocratic pageants. Reductions in the size of noble households, a decline in the attendance of young gentleman and a taste for greater privacy and less public ostentation had led to the passing of the grand noble entry.[337] However, as Malcolm Smuts has pointed out, such costly and lavish display was still very much a feature of crown-sponsored processions, as both James and Charles sought to channel the power of magnificence and display to amplify the majesty of their kingship.[338] The

332 *Strafforde Letters*, i.242. For the Knollys/Fenton cavalcade, see Chamberlain, i.597.

333 *Strafforde Letters*, i.427; Bodl.L., Ashmole MS 1110, fos. 109–10.

334 CA, Phillips MS 13084, vol. 14, unpaginated, 'Earl Marshal's order of 13 Feb 1637/8'; Ashmole, *Order of the Garter*, pp. 341–2.

335 Bodl.L., Ashmole MS 1113, fo. 212.

336 For the ceremony that did take place, see CA, Phillips MS 13084, vol. 14, unpaginated; Heralds, vol. VI, fos. 305–6. The reasons for the cancellation are unclear. Kevin Sharpe has suggested that it was due to the onset of the Scottish crisis (*Personal Rule of Charles I*, p. 222); but this seems unlikely as the preparations to meet this were not yet having an impact on other areas of government.

337 Stone, *Crisis of the Aristocracy*, pp. 209–14, 583–4; R.M. Smuts, 'Public Ceremony and Royal Charisma: The English Royal Entry in London', in *The First Modern Society*, ed. A.L. Beier, D. Cannadine and J.M. Rosenheim (Cambridge: Cambridge University Press, 1989), pp. 82–7.

338 Smuts, 'Art and the material culture of majesty', pp. 90, 93–6.

Figure 2.2 Sir Anthony Van Dyck, *Charles Prince of Wales (1630–1685), later Charles II.* Painted soon after Prince Charles's inauguration into the Order of the Garter in May 1638, this portrait emphasises the martial associations of the order. The young prince wears a suit of jousting armour, which had formerly belonged to his uncle Prince Henry, with a cocked wheelock pistol in his right hand, his left hand resting on a plumed cavalry helmet and round his neck a chain bearing the lesser George, the insignia of the order. (Reproduced by permission of the National Portrait Gallery, London).

garter processions are a good example of this as they show both kings making conscious efforts to harness the possibilities offered by the installation cavalcade. Ashmole records a 1606 decree by which James ensured that 'the ancient custom, which for some years have been intermitted, wherein at the solemnity of this feast all the knights companions were wont to go attended each with a large train, was recalled and brought back again into use.'[339] This resulted in some spectacular Jacobean processions.[340] However, in 1616, prior to the installation of Sir George Villiers, James issued another decree 'for saving of charge and avoiding of emulation' that forbade the wearing of livery coats. It may initially have been intended to spare his young protégé the embarrassment of having to compete with the Earl of Rutland who was installed at the same time; but the economy drive caught on and two years later the knight companions' attendance was limited to 50.[341] This relatively austere approach appears to have lasted until 1629 when the Earl of Northampton mounted a cavalcade with well over a hundred attendants, including a full complement of household servants dressed in blue livery coats, chaplains, officers, heralds, 80 gentlemen and yeomen and an array of senior nobles. The annals record that at the next chapter Northampton was 'thanked for his gallant attendance and a decree issued that knights elect should doe the like'.[342] This was the cue for the spectacular processions of the 1630s.

The reasoning behind this decree, and the extravaganza planned for his son in 1638, was not recorded; but a clue lies in Pembroke's remark that the king wished to ensure more frequent 'attendance upon his royal person in place of publique solemnityes'. As we have seen, Charles was seeking to enhance the elements of 'ceremony' by which Newcastle set such store, and one aspect of this to which he paid close attention was expanding noble involvement in the garter rites. Under Elizabeth most of the feast day duties had been assigned to officers of the order or gentlemen pensioners; but Charles deliberately drew in the larger body of the peerage.[343] These public pageants in which monarchs and noblemen paraded before the people with all the trapping of wealth, power and status were an additional means of cultivating an appropriate sense of respect, reverence and support for those in authority. Charles has been depicted as rather neglectful of this aspect of his kingship, shying away from the ceremonial entries that Elizabeth used so successfully to enhance the power and attractiveness of her monarchy.[344] But the evidence

339 Ashmole, *Order of the Garter*, p. 509.

340 Jefferson, 'A Garter Installation Ceremony in 1606', *Court Historian*, 6 (2001), pp. 141–50; Bodl.L., Ashmole MS 1108, fos. 81–2.

341 Bodl.L., Ashmole MS 1108, fo. 91; Ashmole, *Order of the Garter*, p. 339.

342 Bodl.L., Ashmole MS 1109, fos. 7–9; Ashmole, *Order of the Garter*, pp. 339–40; WCLA, MS X.7, Annals of the Order of the Garter, fos. 166.

343 Ashmole, *Order of the Garter*, pp. 589, 593, 596–7. See pp. 76–7 for the peers in attendance.

344 Smuts, 'Public Ceremony and Royal Charisma', pp. 65–93.

presented here suggests that he could readily embrace such occasions. He may not have participated directly in the parade but, as principal spectators, he and his family would have become almost as much a focus of attention for the crowds as the noble entourage passing before them; and the whole march past could be seen as a powerful affirmation of the loyalty and companionship of his leading nobles which was such a central component of the ethos of the order.

In 1620 when Edmund Bolton, the antiquarian, was seeking support for an 'Academ Royal', which would celebrate the heroic achievements of the English nation, both military and civil, he proposed siting it at Windsor Castle, under the auspices of the Order of the Garter. Windsor would become, he declared 'an English Olympus', dedicated to preserving 'all the lights of honour in the firmament of heroick virtue and discipline' and 'inflaming the will of men with the love of glorie'.[345] Although nothing came of Bolton's project, this association of the Order of the Garter with a pantheon of English heroes was an indication of its massive prestige and reputation. It was seen as bringing together everything that was most noble and most honourable about England's elite, and, indeed, the nation as a whole. This was a view shared by Charles. As we have seen, he invested considerable energy and enthusiasm – not to mention significant sums of money – in restoring the order to its 'primitive institution' and setting a strong personal example to the other knights. Charles's reverence and admiration for the order cannot be doubted; but this still leaves open the question of what it meant for him.

The argument presented here is that Charles readily embraced the full range of ideals and traditions associated with the garter. Far from demonstrating an unambiguous concern to refashion the order in a more peaceable and spiritual direction, as some historians have implied, Charles remained wedded to the martial ideals and noble companionship that played such a prominent role in its ethos and observances. An analysis of the order's central rites and ceremonies, and of those he elected to it and the reforms he introduced, suggests that while he was certainly open to enhancing its relationship with ideals of Christian knighthood, this was not to be done at the expense of downplaying the military dimension, which was more prominent by the late 1630s than at any other point in the early Stuart period. The order stood for everything that Charles valued about knighthood and aristocracy. He visualised the knights companions as a brotherhood in arms, bound to him by ties of fidelity, offering him 'good counsel' and political support, exemplifying

345 BL, Harleian MS 6103, fos. 11–15.

the old fashioned, 'Elizabethan', martial virtues of courage and steadfastness, and at the same time responsive to the knightly obligation to defend the church and true religion. In short, it perfectly articulated the variety of concerns that motivated his campaign to reform and resurrect the aristocracy.

3 The Court of Chivalry and the defence of honour

The reform of the Court of Chivalry

One of the most striking developments in the honours system during the 1630s was the reform of the Court of Chivalry. The court had not met on a regular basis since the fifteenth century, but in March 1634 it was re-established so that it became open for business in the same way as other Westminster courts, with frequent sittings, a set of routine procedures based on the civil law and a full staff of lawyers and officials. It existed in this form until December 1640 when it was suspended pending investigation by the Long Parliament. But in the meantime it had proved very popular with litigants, processing up to 70 cases a day at its peak in 1638 and drawing in business from gentleman plaintiffs far and wide. The court continued to deal with the type of business that had prompted its initial foundation in the mid fourteenth century and the effort to re-establish it in the 1560s: disputed titles, contested claims to gentility, rights to display particular coats of arms and the regulation of heraldic funerals. But during the 1630s, in the face of considerable opposition from common lawyers, it also secured jurisdiction over the offence of 'slanderous words likely to provoke a duel'; and this came to account for around 90 per cent of its business by the end of the decade.[1] An investigation of the processes that led to the court's reform, and the scope of its activities during the decade, provides another important perspective on the Caroline project to restore the status of the peerage and regenerate the honours system. Once the court had been re-established in 1634 it provided Charles and Arundel with a potentially powerful instrument to regulate matters of honour, title and status. Its failure to fulfil this potential reveals a good deal about the constraints and limitations under which they were operating.

[1] For a fuller account of developments in the Court of Chivalry, see *Cases in the Court of Chivalry*, pp. xi–xxxi; Squibb, *Court of Chivalry*, chs. iii, x–xiv.

The king initially showed little interest in the court's proceedings or its potential to bring about reform. As we have seen in Chapter 1, James and Arundel had taken the first steps towards re-establishing it on a permanent basis by fending off challenges to the Earl Marshal's right to oversee its proceedings, putting in place civil law procedures for its regulation and conducting a major hearing in the *Leeke* v. *Harris* case. But this was not followed up. A combination of Charles's lack of interest and Arundel's loss of authority ensured that it was operating at a very low ebb during the late 1620s. It continued to meet occasionally, but hearings were generally small, informal affairs held before Arundel or his deputy. In one important respect, however, the court was moving forwards. This was in working its way towards a more interventionist role in dealing with the problem of duelling by claiming jurisdiction over the insulting words that provoked a challenge in the first place, as had been envisaged in Northampton's proposal of 1614. This was leading the court into an area that was fraught with difficulty. The growth of litigation over 'plea of words' and defamation has been described by one historian as 'a phenomenon of the age'; but it was a very tricky area for the judicial system, with common lawyers traditionally very reluctant to allow such suits for fear of opening the way to a flood of litigation over every dubious insult.[2] In spite of this, some of the cases dealt with by the Court of Chivalry in the latter part of James's reign show that it was prepared to tackle such issues, using as its justification James's proclamations and duelling edict of 1613–14. For example, a complaint by Sir Samuel Argall in 1625 referred to having been 'disgracefully affronted' and given 'the lye, which uncivill behaviour was . . . in breach and contempt of his Majesties' proclamacon and ordinances'.[3] There is evidence, then, of a growing understanding that the Court of Chivalry was willing to provide reparation for gentlemen who had been slandered or defamed and this was to have important consequences for its development during the 1630s.

What eventually prompted Charles to take a significant interest in the court as an arbiter in matters of honour was a very different type of case involving an allegation of treason. This was *Reay* v. *Ramsey*, the

[2] J.H. Baker, *An Introduction to English Legal History* (London: Butterworth, 2nd edn., 1979), pp. 364–70; M. Ingram, *Church Courts, Sex and Marriage in England, 1570–1640* (Cambridge: Cambridge University Press, 1987), pp. 292–300; *Select Cases on Defamation to 1600*, ed. R.H. Helmholz, (Selden Soc., 101, 1985), pp. lxxxvi–cxi. I am grateful to Clive Holmes for advice on this point. For further discussion of the issue, see his article on 'The strange case of a misplaced tomb: family honour and law in late seventeenth century England', *Midland History*, 31(2006), 18–36.

[3] AC, Earl Marshal's Papers, 26–7, 290.

most high profile Court of Chivalry case of the decade. It arose when Charles's favourite, the Marquis of Hamilton, was accused of preparing to use the army he was commanding in the service of Gustavus Adolphus to set himself up as king of Scotland. Hamilton begged Charles to put him on trial for treason so that he could clear himself of the charge. The king declined to do this; but he was determined to get to the bottom of the matter and vindicate his favourite's honour. The charge was traced back to a Scottish army officer, Donald Mackay, Lord Reay, who claimed that Hamilton's lieutenant, David Ramsay, who was also a groom of the bedchamber, had revealed the plan to him. This Ramsay vehemently denied and, because the accusation rested solely on Reay's word, both men appealed to the ancient custom of trial by combat to test its veracity.[4]

Trial by combat had been more or less obsolete in England since the late fourteenth century, but it remained a legal possibility in trial of treason so long as it was supervised by the Court of Chivalry.[5] Charles, no doubt prompted by Arundel, was evidently intrigued by the possibility that appealed to his instinctive respect for the chivalric ethos. When the judges returned from their summer circuit on 22 August 1631, he consulted them about the feasibility of such a process and they confirmed that it was, indeed, justified as an appeal of treason, but that it would have to be authorised by a Court of Chivalry, with both the High Constable and Earl Marshal sitting. Undeterred by the fact that the office of constable had been vacant since 1521, Charles proceeded to appoint the Earl of Lindsey for the duration of the case. The court convened for its first hearing on 28 November 1631, with the constable and marshal joined by eight senior English and Scottish peers, most of whom were knights of the garter. Arundel took charge and, after careful observation of the formalities for a full session, last used for the Harris case, he explained the court's legal authority to try such an action and emphasised that combat would only take place as a last resort. Reay and Ramsay were then called on to explain themselves. The dramatic high point of the day's proceedings came when Reay threw down his glove in court as a pledge that he was telling the truth, whereupon Ramsay responded by declaring that he was 'a liar, a barbarous villain, and threw down his glove, protesting, to gar him dy for it, if he had had him in place for that purpose'.[6] Arundel sought to calm things down by insisting that both sides take counsel and deliver their answers in writing, and proceedings

[4] 'Donald Mackay, 1st Lord Reay (1591–1649)' and 'David Ramsay (d.1642)', *Oxf.DNB*; Gardiner, *History of England*, vii.182–3; *Court and Times*, ii.126–7.

[5] Peltonen, *The Duel*, pp. 98–9.

[6] *State Trials*, ed. W. Cobbett and T. Howell, 33 vols. (1809–26), iii. cols. 486–8; *Court and Times*, ii.145–7; 'to gar' meant 'to cause'.

were adjourned. There were further hearings in December and January 1632, but it proved impossible to determine the validity of the charge one way or the other; so the matter was referred back to the king, and in February it was decided that the combat should go ahead. The constable drew up various regulations about the weapons to be used, the date was set for 12 April 1632, at Tothill Fields, Westminster, in the presence of the king, and the combatants began to practise their fencing.[7] The whole event aroused enormous public interest and opinion was divided over whether such proceedings were valid. The newsletter writer John Pory reported in late January 1632 that

> the judges and common lawyers say, in case a combatt bee awarded, whosoever killes the other is by their law guilty of murther. And I have heard bishops and divines say it is a heathenish [act] to seek truth that waye, and that all duells and combats whatsoever are condemned by generall councills.[8]

Perhaps because of these objections, and the danger of appearing to sanction duelling, Charles eventually decided to call the whole thing off. In a letter to Hamilton in May 1632, he declared that he was now satisfied that there had been no grounds for the treason accusation and that the marquis would suffer 'no dishonour in this business'.[9] The trial fizzled out. But the king's willingness to approve such a cumbersome and antiquated procedure demonstrated the lengths to which he was prepared to go to protect the reputation of his leading nobles and his readiness to entrust the oversight of such matters to the Earl Marshal and his court.

This provided the context for regularising meetings of the Court of Chivalry in 1634. The decision to go ahead with this was not one that was clearly defined or traceable to any specific royal instruction equivalent to James's command to 'restore and settle' the court in 1622. Rather it was something that developed out of a series of opportunities, which the civil lawyers who supervised the court's business were able to seize upon and exploit. The first of these was provided by Charles's desire to do something about the problem of duelling.

As we have seen, duelling was a growing cause for concern in 1633–4. The Holland/Weston quarrel prompted the king to issue a statement in the Privy Council on 13 April 1633, the day on which the protagonists made their submissions, to the effect that he was 'resolved hereafter to prosequte all delinquents in this kind with all severity'. Henceforth, if any privy councillor issued or accepted a challenge he would be removed from

7 *State Trials*, iii. cols. 483–514; CA, Curia Militaris 8/16; Squibb, *Court of Chivalry*, pp. 52–3; *Court and Times*, ii.169; W.S. Powell, *John Pory, 1572–1636: the Life and Letters of a Man of Many Parts* (Chapel Hill: University of North Carolina Press, 1977), p. 219.

8 Powell, *Pory*, p. 202.

9 *State Trials*, iii. cols. 513–14.

his position immediately, and anyone challenging a councillor should be reported at once. His intention, he explained, was to ensure that those 'neerest' to him 'might serve for a patterne for all others'. He added that he had directed the Attorney General to draw up 'a publique proclamation' that would take particular notice of those 'quarrels which should ensue upon discourse of other quarrels'.[10] In other words, he appears to have envisaged a reissue of James's proclamations of 1613–14, which condemned both challenges to duel and the publishing of reports. What happened to this proclamation is unclear. It probably got lost in the rush of preparations for Charles's departure on his progress to Scotland in mid May. By the end of the month, however, the need for it was once again apparent with the Apsley case.

Apsley challenged the Earl of Northumberland while he was travelling northwards with the king and in direct contravention of the recent royal pronouncement. What made this even more serious was that the former had been pardoned for his offence in 1631, at Northumberland's behest. Charles was livid and Arundel, before whom Apsley had previously pledged his good behaviour in the Court of Chivalry, was hugely embarrassed. Apsley fled abroad, but was apprehended and, as we have seen, tried in Star Chamber in January 1634, with Attorney General Noy and the judges queuing up to vilify him for his blatant affront to royal authority. The trial and sentence were widely reported and this no doubt helped to encourage Arundel and the civil lawyers to press ahead with advocating a more lasting solution to the problem of duelling early in 1634.

The second circumstance that prepared the way for regularising the Court of Chivalry's procedures was a campaign by the king and council to bolster the career prospects of civil lawyers. For much of the early seventeenth century their profession was in decline. Attacks on civil law jurisdiction by common lawyers, and the aggressive use of prohibitions, had begun to produce a shortage of jobs which, as Brian Levack has demonstrated, fed through into a decline in the numbers of Doctors of Civil Law graduating from the universities and a fall in the membership of Doctors' Commons, the professional body representing those who practiced in London. James professed concern over the trend, but did little to try to reverse it. Charles, however, saw the civil lawyers as natural allies of the crown and the Laudian clergy, and inaugurated a series of measures to help them. As early as December 1625 he ordered Archbishop Abbott to work with the Privy Council to ensure that senior diocesan positions were reserved for Doctors of Civil Law. In February 1633 the

[10] TNA, SP 16/236/47.

Privy Council addressed the damage done to admiralty court jurisdiction by prohibitions – which were issued to remove proceedings from the civil law courts so that they could be tried at common law – and directed that in future these were not to be issued against cases that concerned matters taking place abroad or on the high seas.[11] Finally, in December 1633, Charles met with his councillors to discuss measures 'for the breeding up of able and sufficient professors of the Civil and Canon Laws' and to 'incite a sufficient number of men of eminent parts and abilities to apply their industry to the said studies and professions'. They came up with the solution of ensuring that henceforth all vacant masterships of the Court of Requests, together with eight out of the eleven masterships of Chancery, should be reserved for civilians.[12] These measures would take time to have an effect; but meanwhile they helped to create a climate of opinion that was markedly receptive to initiatives to improve the lot of civil lawyers. It was probably around this time that Arundel – as he later recalled for the benefit of Edward Hyde – received advice from 'Sir Henry Martin and other civilians who were held men of great learning' that the trial of cases for 'plea of words' in the Court of Chivalry was 'just and lawful'.[13]

In these circumstances the civilians were well placed to make the most of the opportunity offered by another high profile case, *Hooker* v. *Holmes*. This arose out of a murder committed during a duel, which had taken place overseas in Newfoundland, and which therefore fell under purview of the Court of Chivalry. Because it was a capital offence it again required the attendance of the High Constable, and once more Lindsey was temporarily appointed to the position. Hearings commenced on 26 February 1634 and continued through March and April until, on 26 April, Holmes was sentenced to hang and then, subsequently, pardoned.[14] On this occasion, however, the opportunity provided by the revival of formal sittings of the court was not allowed to slip away. With the encouragement of Martin and Dr Arthur Duck, who had been managing *Hooker* v. *Holmes*, other plaintiffs started to bring cases. At the session on 1 March, which Hyde identified as the first for which records of the 'new' court survived, another action was added in which Abraham Bowne complained that Henry Throckmorton had accused him of being 'cowardly, petty minded and a liar', and challenged him to duel. Dr Duck, acting as counsel to Bowne, argued that these words were 'punishable to prevent

[11] B.P. Levack, *The Civil Lawyers in England 1603–1641* (Oxford: Clarendon Press, 1973), pp. 64–5, 80.

[12] *Ibid.*, pp. 62–3; BL, Add. MS 34, 324, fo. 282.

[13] Clarendon, *Life*, i.85–6.

[14] Squibb, *Court of Chivalry*, pp. 53–6; *Cases in the Court of Chivalry*, pp. 129–30.

the effusion of blood' and the judges agreed, fining Throckmorton £6 13s 4d (with £10 costs) on 24 May 1634.[15] This appears to have been the first instance of a case in a full court hearing being determined on the charge of 'scandalous words likely to provoke a duel'. Others soon followed and by June 1634 ten cases were in progress.[16] What appears to have happened is that once word spread that the court was open for business this rapidly generated suits and the court's proceedings developed their own momentum, fed by the gentry's desire for cheap and rapid redress in cases involving defamation, and by the civilians' appetite for fees.

The reform of the Court of Chivalry, then, took place against the background of the king's awareness of its potential value in protecting the reputation of his leading nobles and determination to do something about the problem of duelling. Civil lawyers on the lookout for ways of boosting their income and career prospects, and encouraged by the Earl Marshal, quickly moved in to make the most of the opportunity. Within a matter of months the court had become established as a regular fixture and by the time of its suspension in December 1640 it had handled well over 1000 cases.[17] But how effective was it in addressing the agenda set for it by Charles and Arundel?

The main purpose of the reformed court was to curb the practice of duelling. But success and failure in this regard is very hard to measure because of the difficulty in making any sort of estimate of the amount of duelling that was taking place in early Stuart England. Historians have tended to rely on stray references in newsletters when it is clear from other sources that these are heavily biased towards combats involving courtiers and leading noblemen. Star Chamber and Court of Chivalry cases offer a better guide to the extent of the problem, certainly beyond the royal court, but again it is apparent that the combats resulting in litigation were only a small fraction of the total. Given these limitations, however, it is still possible to assess some of the ways in which the Court of Chivalry did have an impact.[18]

Numerous litigants appealed to the court after receiving a challenge, often specifically citing Jame's edict and proclamations. In such cases the Earl Marshal's usual response was to send a messenger to detain the parties involved and then bind them over to good behaviour for substantial sums in the order of £500–£1000. This put an immediate

[15] CA., Curia Militaris, 7/15; *Cases in the Court of Chivalry*, pp. 26–7.

[16] CA, Curia Militaris, 8/23. [17] *Cases in the Court of Chivalry*, pp. xi–xii.

[18] For a fuller discussion of the issues raised here, see Cust and Hopper, 'Duelling and the Court of Chivalry', pp. 156–71.

stop to some duelling – mainly around the fringes of the royal court or at the Inns of Court, which were two of the main trouble spots – but it is doubtful whether it had much impact as a longer term deterrent. Bonds of £500 apiece did not stop Guy Moulsworth and William Gartfoote from continuing to taunt and provoke the two fellow Inns of Court students who had appealed against them to the Earl Marshal; and Robert Walsh, one of the habitual duellists who crop up in the court's records, mocked and challenged Edward Gibbes, the son of a Warwickshire gentleman, in Westminster Hall in May 1639, in spite of having been bound over for 1000 marks the previous year to stop a duel over a horseracing bet.[19]

Where the court played a much more effective role was in providing disputants with an alternative means of settling their differences. There are numerous instances where gentlemen were able to sidestep challenges, or draw aside from quarrels likely to lead to a challenge, because they were confident that the court would vindicate their honour. In February 1640 William, Viscount Monson, who had challenged Lord Poulett and others over precedence in Westminster Abbey in 1629, caught Robert Welch cheating at cards. When Welch tried to cover up by giving him the lie and challenging him to fight, Monson felt able to hold back and the next day to launch a Court of Chivalry suit. Similarly Thomas Whatman was able to deflect a challenge to his son by Thomas Lunsford, the notorious royalist swordsman, by reporting him to Arundel for 'countertfeyting and publishing the challenge, and going to the field to fight without making the challenge known to your lordship, as by lawe and dutie he ought'. In such cases there was often a risk of being branded a coward for refusing to fight; but plaintiffs calculated that the benefits of being vindicated by the king's representative, the Earl Marshal, and of inflicting a humiliating submission on their opponents outweighed this. In some cases wily disputants can be seen leading on opponents to the point at which they would provide a *prima facie* case for the prosecution. There was more than an element of this in the Monson case where the viscount baited Welch to the point at which he lost all self-control and, in front of witnesses, tried to force a fight. In *Billiard* v. *Robinson*, two Northamptonshire gentlemen quarrelling in a Peterborough tavern appear to have known exactly what was at stake as each tried to manoeuvre the other into issuing a challenge. Billiard eventually came out on top, in spite of being the first to draw his sword. He was able to report to the court his sanctimonious response to the challenge that Robinson was eventually provoked into making: 'I will not meete you in the bushy

[19] *Cases in the Court of Chivalry*, pp. xxx–xxxi, 25, 198, 297.

close, but I will meet you in the Star Chamber, or some other Court of Justice, where the lawe shall right mee, and I will not right my selfe.'[20]

This was precisely the sort of conduct that the scheme devised by James and the Earl of Northampton was designed to elicit; and, to the extent that gentleman could feel that litigation was an acceptable substitute for violence when it came to vindicating their honour, the regularisation of the Court of Chivalry procedures can be said to have been a success. It did not eradicate duelling, as James rather fancifully supposed it might; but it did play a part in containing the problem, and ensuring that England never had to face the wholesale slaughter of young noblemen, which occurred in early seventeenth century France.[21]

What then of the other consideration that initially prompted the king to take an interest in the proceedings of the court: its potential for providing redress for noblemen whose reputation had been slighted. Initially the court was quite slow to develop this aspect of its business because it depended on the nobles themselves being willing to bring complaints before the court. But from late 1636 it was beginning to handle a series of cases in which noblemen had been insulted in ways that appeared to demand exemplary punishment, and in each case it dealt with the matter with notable severity. This was best demonstrated in another well-publicised case, the action brought by Henry Carey, Earl of Dover, against a London merchant, Humphrey Fox, for insulting his livery in November 1638. Fox had an exchange of words with a London waterman who was wearing the earl's livery coat in which he let slip the remark, 'You fellow with the goose on your sleeve, you are too saucy and peremptorie.' Despite Fox's protests that, as soon as he discovered that the goose was, in fact, the earl's insignia of a swan, he had apologised and declared that Dover was an honourable man, the court found that this remark amounted to defaming the earl himself and he was fined 200 marks. This case was later picked up by Edward Hyde as an example of the court's arbitrary proceedings; but it also shows its determination to develop its remit to protect the interests of members of the aristocracy.[22]

This process was considerably advanced by a landmark ruling by privy councillors sitting in Star Chamber in February 1638, in the case of *Sherard* v. *Mynne*. This involved a local gentleman slandering an Irish peer at the Oakham assizes. The court opted for a hefty fine of £1500 to the king, removal from office as a Justice of the Peace and the requirement that he apologise publicly to Sherard at the assizes. However, on the

[20] Cust and Hopper, 'Duelling and the Court of Chivalry', pp. 156, 160–6; *Cases in the Court of Chivalry*, pp. 19–20, 190, 308–9.
[21] Billacois, *The Duel.* [22] *Cases in the Court of Chivalry*, pp. 74–5.

matter of reparation for Sherard himself councillors were uncertain how to proceed. They therefore followed a precedent established in James' reign in the case of *Darcy* v. *Markham* (1616) and

> houldinge it most just that Lord Sherard should receive due reparacon for those insolent and scandalous speeches used against him . . . have therefore commended the same to the order and judgement of the right honourable the Earl Marshall (now here present) in the Court of Honour . . . where the same is most properly to be determined and where he maye be repaired.[23]

This ruling by what was regarded as the senior court in the land provided a considerable boost to the authority and jurisdictional self-confidence of the civil lawyers in the Court of Chivalry. It was later to be cited as supporting the presumption that the court was entitled to take 'co[g]n[i]sans of words tending to the dishonour of a gentleman', because if no remedy of this sort was offered by the courts 'every man will endeavour to be his owne judge and . . . right himselfe by duells and the like'.[24] It also encouraged the court to ramp up the fines on those who insulted or challenged the honour of a peer. The normal sanction in the Court of Chivalry was to enforce a public submission, or degrade a man from his honorific status, supported by modest fines and damages in the order of £20–£50. But in cases that involved members of the peerage fines and damages were often ten times these amounts. The precedent had been established in another high-profile case in late 1636, *De La Ware* v. *West*, in which George West was fined £500 for seeking to impersonate a member of the nobility. The following March Christopher Copley was again fined £500 for insulting the Earl of Kingston and claiming to be his equal. Thereafter the norm for cases involving members of the peerage was fines or damages in the order of £200–£500, and for members of the knightly class often around £100–£200.[25] Although these were sentences that fell well short of the thousands of pounds being awarded in Star Chamber during the 1630s, they still demonstrated the determination of the court to 'get tough' with anyone challenging a peer and provide a ready means of repairing his honour. However, significant as these proceedings were the number of cases involving peers that came before the court was relatively small. Their deterrent effect may well have been considerable, although by its

23 TNA, SP 16/381/65; CA, *Sherard* v. *Mynne*, 'A breife of the proofes on the parte and behalfe of William Lord Sherard against Sir Henrie Myn, knight', fo. 4. For fuller discussion of the ramifications of this case, see Cust, 'A Rutland quarrel', 149–73.

24 Cambridge University Library, MS Dd.3.64, fos. 30–1. I am grateful to Clive Holmes for this reference.

25 *Cases in the Court of Chivalry*, p. xxv. For cases involving peers, *ibid.*, pp. 66–9, 74–5, 138–9, 153–5, 158, 257–8; for knights, *ibid.*, pp. 117, 135–6, 164–6.

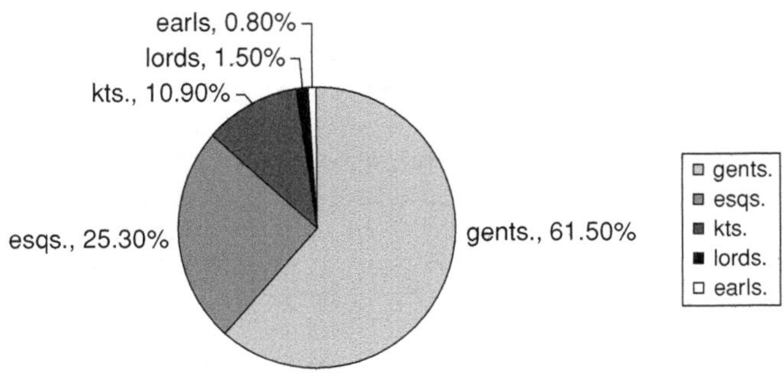

Figure 3.1 Social status of plaintiffs in the Court of Chivalry, 1634–1640
Source: *Cases in the Court of Chivalry*

nature this is hard to quantify. But as a regular forum for promoting the honour of the peerage the court's impact was relatively limited.

A third area where the Court of Chivalry had the potential to exert a considerable influence in matters of honour and reputation was in bolstering the authority of the heralds. Here once again, as we shall see in the next section, its impact was mixed. Ultimately rather than addressing the concerns originally identified by the king and the Earl Marshal most of the court's time and energy was taken up with cases involving defamation. In this regard, its development provides an object lesson in how the original intention of policy makers and judicial authorities could be superseded by the social and financial priorities of lawyers and litigants.

As its jurisdiction developed in the late 1630s, the Court of Chivalry became primarily a gentleman's court. This had not been James I's intention when he had authorised an extension of its remit in 1613–14 and it is not the reputation that the court has had among historians. As the cases that have attracted most attention are those involving aristocrats or senior gentry, such as *Rea* v. *Ramsey* or the inquest into Sir Thomas Harris's baronetcy, there has been a tendency to view it as a forum for noblemen, with a relatively rarefied jurisdiction. But this is misleading. Its role in catering for clients at the level of 'mere gentry' is apparent from the identity of plaintiffs. Of those bringing cases in the court 61.5 per cent designated themselves simply as 'gent.', with a further 25.3 per cent esquires, 10.9 per cent knights and only 2.3 per cent peers (see Figure 3.1). Once the court was established on a regular basis it came to be open to anyone who could demonstrate gentle status and who could plausibly claim that their honour had been impugned. The majority of cases (60.5 per cent) involved gentlemen who had been insulted by

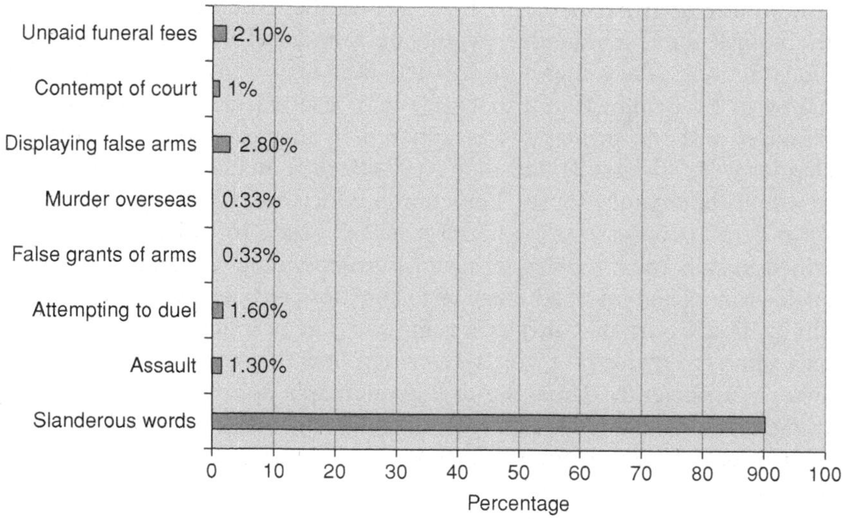

Figure 3.2 Types of offence in the Court of Chivalry, 1634–1640
Source: *Cases in the Court of Chivalry*

commoners, with the bulk of these actions (39.8 per cent) being brought by 'parish gentry'. There was something of a contradiction here in that one of the principal precepts of the honour code was that an insult should only be answered by a challenge to duel if it had been administered by a social equal. Where one was dealing with those of a lower status, the recommended course was either to administer corporal punishment on the spot or else ignore them. Yet the vast majority of cases that proceeded in the court (70.7 per cent) involved gentlemen or noblemen proceeding against social inferiors.[26] What had happened was that the original intention behind the proceeding became distorted as the civil lawyers adapted process to meet the seemingly insatiable appetite for action over defamation.

The great majority of actions that came before the Court of Chivalry in the late 1630s (91.4%) were related to defamation in which the nature of the offence was defined as 'scandalous words likely to provoke a duel'. This opened the way to admitting action on a much wider range of slanders than was the case for either the common law or church courts (see Figure 3.2). Since Elizabeth's reign, the common law judges had

[26] The figures are gentlemen/noblemen actions against social inferiors, 70.7 per cent, gentlemen/noblemen against social equals, 21 per cent, gentlemen/noblemen against superiors, 5.2 per cent, office cases 3.1 per cent: *Court of Chivalry Cases, passim.*

been doing their best to limit the number of such cases coming before the courts for fear that they would be inundated by trivial and malicious actions. They therefore insisted that for words to be actionable it had to be demonstrated that they had resulted in some quantifiable damage; and the principle was adhered to that only certain forms of slander were admissible and that every effort be made to construe these in a non-defamatory sense. The church courts were less restrictive, but for a defamation case to be heard it had to relate to 'spiritual matters', which usually meant a slander against an individual's sexual reputation, such as an allegation of adultery or fornication, or bearing an illegitimate child. The Court of Chivalry's remit was, in practice, much broader, extending to any form of words or written libel that the court might construe as sufficiently damaging to a gentleman's honour to provoke him to fight. This meant, for example, that the accusation of being a knave, a cheat or a rogue, which the common law courts tended to dismiss as general terms of abuse, uttered without a specific intent to damage reputation, was regularly admitted as grounds for process in the Court of Chivalry.[27]

The court's ability to cater for the great upsurge in defamation business was the main source of its appeal to litigants; but it was also attractive because it offered relatively cheap and speedy 'justice'. Brian Levack has made the point that there was a need within the legal system for civil law courts that could decide cases relatively quickly, based on summary process and written testimony, rather than having to rely on the cumbersome trial by jury.[28] These considerations applied to the Court of Chivalry. It offered a new form of relatively cheap and speedy redress before judges whose authority was unimpeachable. For a gentleman who had been insulted in a manner likely to provoke a duel the principal avenue for litigation prior to the 1630s was the Court of Star Chamber. But Star Chamber process was notoriously slow and expensive. T.G. Barnes has calculated that most cases took years to reach a resolution – with the preliminary proceedings lasting anything from 8 to 21 months, and then a further three months to two years before there was a final verdict. The average Court of Chivalry case, on the other hand, took just over a year from start to finish. The cost of Star Chamber suits is harder to calculate, but it appears that most plaintiffs could expect to pay several hundred pounds, whereas the mean costs in a Court of Chivalry case were £43, a sum which most plaintiffs could expect to recoup with a favourable verdict. Overall the experience of litigation in the Court of

27 Ingram, *Church Courts*, pp. 296–7; *Cases in the Court of Chivalry*, *passim*.
28 Levack, *Civil Lawyers*, pp. 154–6.

Chivalry compared favourably with the Court of Requests, which was renowned for providing prompt and reasonably priced justice.[29]

There was the added attraction that the odds were stacked in favour of the gentlemen plaintiff, with a tendency here, as in other civil courts where the judge assumed the roles of prosecutor, judge and jury, to make an initial presumption of guilt rather than innocence.[30] This is evident from those cases where we have a record of the final verdict and sentence. Of the 127 cases where the outcome is known 94 (74%) resulted in conviction, 19 (15%) were settled by arbitration and only 14 (11%) resulted in acquittal.[31] For the most part, comparable data does not exist for other courts of the period; so it is hard to know how conviction rates compare with these. But a situation where virtually three-quarters of all cases were won by the plaintiff does indicate a set of procedures heavily stacked in his favour. This is confirmed by the detailed record. In practice, if a case ran to its full term it was extremely difficult for a defendant to secure an acquittal, particularly where he was a plebeian. For knights and members of the peerage it was sometimes still worth the investment of a Star Chamber case which, if successful, brought a higher profile judgment and damages running into hundreds or thousands of pounds. But for litigants lower down the pecking order there is every indication that the procedures and outcomes offered by the Court of Chivalry were well suited to their requirements. Fines for damages tended to be low – in the order of £20–£40 in most cases – but, for the majority, what probably mattered more than any financial benefit was confirmation of their status and reputation, and the humiliation of their opponents. The former was provided for by the nature of trial process. Because only gentlemen were permitted to bring a prosecution, the grant of process (which was often made only after the heralds had investigated an individual's descent) provided valuable affirmation of gentility. Corroboration for those whose status might otherwise be questioned was also provided by the procedure for examining witnesses, which generally took place at a public venue in front of local worthies appointed by the court to act as commissioners. These hearings frequently constituted mini local courts of honour in their own right. Plaintiffs would line up witnesses, regularly drawn from the gentry and knightly classes, who would attest

[29] *Cases in the Court of Chivalry*, p. xxvii. For the duration of Star Chamber cases, see T.G. Barnes, 'Star chamber litigants and their counsel, 1596–1641', in *Legal Records and the Historian*, ed. J.H. Baker, (Royal Historical Society, 1978), pp. 16–18, 306, 309. In the Court of Requests the length of suits ranged from two months to three years and costs were usually in the order of £5–£20: T. Stretton, *Waging Law in Elizabethan England* (Cambridge: Cambridge University Press, 1998), pp. 83–4, 86.

[30] Levack, *Civil Lawyers*, pp. 154–7.

[31] *Cases in the Court of Chivalry*, p. xxvi.

their standing and worth within the local community.[32] And the effect of these hearings was reinforced by the submission. This was an integral part of the sentence given for plaintiffs, providing the element of reparation that James's duelling edict had set such store by. The submission usually required a defendant to apologise fulsomely to the plaintiff for the original offence, acknowledge his honourable status and undertake never again to insult him, or any other gentleman or noblemen. Performed at a public venue, such as quarter sessions, the local parish church or the site of the offence, often before an invited audience, this was an event that was both immensely gratifying for the plaintiff and deeply degrading for the defendant. George Searle, former mayor and future MP for Taunton, for example, had to make his submission in September 1639 at the Mayor's Feast before those who had witnessed his original insult to Robert Browne, the son of a Dorset knight; and the experience was still painful in January 1641 when he petitioned the Long Parliament for redress for this 'unworthie submission'.[33] Submission was evidently a disagreeable process, but, then, as far as the plaintiff was concerned, that was the whole point.

The indications are that the Court of Chivalry was meeting a widely felt need and plugging an obvious gap in the market for litigation. The speed with which suits multiplied once it was known that the court was open for business suggests as much. By 1637–8, when cases were running at over 70 per sitting, there were signs that the amount of work was becoming too much for the court to cope with. Plaintiffs were having to queue up to be assigned court days, witnesses were kept waiting in London for weeks on end and Dr Duck was pleading pressure of business as a reason for delaying hearings. In spite of the costs and delays, however, there is no indication of potential litigants being put off, and even after adverse publicity in the Short Parliament large numbers of new actions were still being started. Knowledge of the court's existence and procedures spread far and wide. The counties where cases originated were spread relatively evenly across England and Wales. London and Middlesex were well out in front, as one might expect given the advantage of geographical proximity, but the other leading providers of plaintiffs were the more far-flung counties of Devon, Cornwall and Yorkshire. Distance and difficulty of communication do not appear to have been any hindrance to the court's activities. Up and down the country potential litigants knew of its existence and understood the forms of redress that it could offer.[34]

32 *Ibid.*, xxvii–iii.

33 *Cases in the Court of Chivalry*, pp. xxvi–xxviii, 83–4; *D'Ewes Journal*, pp. 226–7.

34 *Cases in the Court of Chivalry*, pp. xxviii–xxx.

When the Long Parliament met in November 1640 the Court of Chivalry was subjected to widespread and searching criticism. On 23 November the Commons established a committee to receive petitions relating to Court of Chivalry proceedings, and 4 December was the last time the court met in full session. Edward Hyde was able to remark somewhat smugly that 'the very entrance upon this inquisition put an end to that upstart court'.[35] This raises the question of whether its rapid demise was a true reflection of its popularity and effectiveness during the 1630s. Put another way, did the Court of Chivalry collapse because of a groundswell of opposition to its actions and procedures; or was it a victim of changed political circumstance, trapped between the juggernaut of a reforming Long Parliament and the self-interest of common lawyers?

The criticisms of the court made by Hyde and his colleagues in parliament can be summarised under two main headings : first, that it was another innovation of the 1630s, 'sett upp when there was noe more hope of parliaments', designed to serve the interests of an increasingly arbitrary regime and ambitious, self-seeking, civil lawyers; and second, that once established it took powers to fine and imprison on 'plea of words', which represented all that was tyrannical and unjust about the 'imperial law' practiced by the civilians.[36] The first charge was, as we have seen, only partially justified. The rationale and basis for the newly established court had been set out in James's duelling edict and proclamations, and the initial steps towards its creation had been taken in the late 1610s and early 1620s. Moreover, responsibility for the form it took during the 1630s belonged at least as much to Arundel as to the civilians, even though, for political reasons, both Hyde and Sir Simonds D'Ewes took pains to deflect blame away from him. The second set of charges had more substance. Some of its proceedings were distinctly biased and arbitrary, and the high proportion of convictions suggests that the judges often failed the test of impartiality.[37] However, from the perspective of both civil lawyers and gentlemen litigants these features were probably not that unwelcome. What plaintiffs sought, above all, and what the court appears to have delivered, was relatively speedy and affordable justice that would vindicate their good name and put social inferiors firmly

35 Clarendon, *Life*, i.85.

36 These criticism were made in Hyde's speech of 18 April 1640 (*Proceedings of the Short Parliament*, pp. 260–2), the speeches by Selden and others on 23 November 1640 (*D'Ewes Journal*, p. 54; *Proceedings in the Long Parliament*, i.254), committee proceedings on the Court of Chivalry on 2 December and 6 January 1641 (*D'Ewes Journal*, pp. 96–8, 226–7) and the report from the committee on 19 February 1641 at which Hyde, D'Ewes and others spoke (*D'Ewes Journal*, pp. 375–9; *Proceedings in the Long Parliament*, ii. 491).

37 *Cases in the Court of Chivalry*, pp. xxiv–xxx.

in their place. For the civilians, the court offered a means of salvation which, temporarily, helped to rescue their profession from the decline and despondency of the early years of the seventeenth century.

The Court of Chivalry, then, became a relatively popular and effective court, although not in the way that Charles and Arundel had envisaged. Their original intent had been to use the court to vindicate the honour and reputation of peers and solve the problem of duelling; but these priorities were largely submerged in the torrent of defamation cases. The court's status and the high profile that it quickly established certainly helped to bolster the self-belief and assertiveness of the aristocracy because they could now be confident that a judicial forum existed in which their interests would be upheld. The court also offered potential duellists another means of sidestepping actual combat and emerging with their honour intact. But what it did not provide was the sort of permanent framework for resolving issues of elite honour on a day-to-day basis that its proponents had long envisaged. It was simply too busy dealing with the minor gentry and their litigation over 'slanderous words'.

Heralds and the Court of Chivalry

The other main dimension to the Court of Chivalry's activities during this period was its supervision of the honours system. The reform of the court offered a notable opportunity to deliver on the agenda that Arundel had set out in 1625. A Court of Chivalry meeting on a regular basis, acting under the auspices of a resurgent Earl Marshal and a supportive monarch that was sympathetic to the heralds' viewpoint and prepared to back them up, had the potential to make a significant difference in tackling the problems that had beset previous generations. There was the opportunity for the court to establish itself as the definitive arbiter in matters of honour. But once again the results were very mixed.

Much depended on the heralds and the Office of Arms with whom the Court of Chivalry needed to collaborate if it was to make progress. At the start of Charles's reign, however, the heralds were operating at a very low ebb after facing an attack in the House of Commons in 1624 that threatened their very existence. The origins of this could be traced back to a series of reforms in 1617–18 when their authority had been strengthened by new orders and a proclamation from the lords commissioners. Picking up on some of the recommendations made by Northampton early in James's reign, it was stipulated that grants of arms and gentlemen's funerals should be much more tightly regulated, fees payable to heralds should be increased and proper record keeping established through the appointment of a registrar.[38] These measures provided the impetus for the heralds to expand their activities; but also encouraged them to overreach themselves.

Beginning in 1619, there was a fresh round of visitations of the southern counties, led by Henry St George, Richmond herald, who adopted a highly aggressive tone in dealing with those who would not comply. His warrants for summoning those who failed to appear described them as having 'shewed themselves obstinate and contemptuous against the king's Majesties commissioners & authoritie', and bound them over for the sum of £50 to answer before the Earl Marshal in London and 'shewe the cause of this your disobedience and contempte'. This was the language of the high prerogative, liable to arouse all sorts of fears associated with the activities of projectors and threats to the subjects' liberties.[39] The sense that the heralds were now engaged in a form of licensed extortion was compounded by a concerted drive to collect funeral fees. Again beginning in 1619, local deputies were appointed to badger the relatives of deceased gentlemen and non-payers were again threatened with a summons to London.[40] This campaign achieved some success, but at the cost of antagonising gentry who were broadly sympathetic to the heralds' function of keeping a proper record of their descents and pedigrees. There were mutterings and talk of curbing the heralds' activities in the 1621 Parliament and then in 1624 the full-scale backlash that led to the most potent challenge to their continued existence since their incorporation.

The heralds became caught up in the House of Commons' witch hunt against patentees and monopolists. The attack began on 28 April when William Mallory, a familiar spokesman for the grievances of 'the country', protested about the recent drive to collect funeral fees. This had been complained about in 1621, when it was expected that the right to exact fees would be 'called in by the parliament' along with other 'pattents' and 'impositions'.[41] But on this occasion the grievance gathered momentum when another Commons' heavyweight, Sir Francis Seymour, raised the

[38] Bodl.L., Ashmole MS 835, fos. 383–98; CA, Phillipps MS 13084, vol. 4, p. 129; Wagner, *Heralds of England*, p. 236; *Munimenta Heraldica*, pp. 106–9.

[39] CA, Heralds, vol. III, fo. 1505, a warrant of Oct 1623 relating to the Wiltshire visitation which was the source of much of the trouble in parliament.

[40] 'Letters on the claims of the College of Arms in Lancashire', ed. F.R. Raines, in *Chetham Miscellany* 5 (Chetham Soc., 96, 1875), pp. 1–38.

[41] HoP, Yale transcripts of Parliamentary Diaries, Holland 28 April 1624: Bodl.L., Ashmole MS 836, fos. 507, 511.

issue of the heralds' proceedings on their visitation of his native county, Wiltshire, in 1623. He was particularly aggrieved at the way in which a local justice, Robert Hyde, had been summoned before the Earl Marshal for his 'contemptuous proceeding' after objecting to the heralds issuing warrants requiring the assistance of JPs. This was symptomatic, Seymour insisted, of a high-handed attitude that had led to the heralds demanding unwarranted fees for registering descents and also issuing punitive summonses for non-attenders to appear before the Earl Marshal.[42] The next speaker, Sir Robert Phelips, widened the issue still further into a matter of fundamental liberties. 'All the proceedings were unjust, disorderly and unreasonable', he insisted: 'they come into the country disorderly, for their own ends and gathered in time of much want when there was not money to commerce in markets, and got in some countries a £1000 or £1500'. Their actions were no different from those of the notorious alehouse patentee, Sir Giles Mompesson, and they were bolstered by a recently revived Earl Marshal's court 'where there was no law but arbitrary'. 'If this be suffered,' he argued, 'the subject's liberty is worth nothing', all of which prompted Sir Edward Coke to call for the house to limit the Court of Chivalry's jurisdiction.[43]

The whole matter was referred to a Commons' committee, which questioned the heralds closely about funeral fees and the conduct of visitations. This revealed what from the Commons' perspective was the extremely flimsy basis for most of their activities. When the heralds cited the proclamation by the lords commissioners in 1618 as justification for collecting their funeral fees, the committee rejected this as 'a mere novelty, unwarrantable by law, and a grievance'. They also condemned the warrants for summoning non-attenders at their visitations as 'a grievance and wrong to the gentry'.[44] The heralds recognised the danger. 'If the execucon of their offices and proporcon of their fees be left uncertain, and exposed to clamor and complaint', they pleaded, 'their whole corporacon will be utterly overthrowne'.[45] But this cut little ice with the Commons who regarded their activities as simply a cynical device to

42 *CJ*, i.692, 777; HoP, Pym and Holland diaries 28 April 1624; CA, Heralds, vol. II, fo. 866.

43 HoP, Pym and Holland diaries 28 April 1624. For Mompesson's infamous reputation, see Russell, *Parliaments and English Politics*, pp. 105–8.

44 *CJ*, i.786; HoP, Pym diary 8 May 1624.

45 Two petitions, which were apparently presented before this committee, have survived: one general petition signed by John Borough, Norroy King of Arms and MP for Hastings, who was acting as spokesman for the heralds (Bodl.L., Ashmole MS 857, pp. 545–6) and one defending their collection of funeral fees (Ashmole MS 857, pp. 528–9). The general petition was read out in the Commons on 8 May: HoP, Pym and Nicholas diaries.

extort money. When the heralds threw themselves on the mercy of the house and begged them 'to settle such things as they shall hold to be out of frame in some constant rule and order', their petition was ignored. On 8 May the Commons resolved that 'these visitations by these heralds as now used, by these warrants now presented to the house, a grievance'.[46]

In the event little came of the Commons' vote. James prorogued the parliament before he had time to give an answer to their list of formal grievances; and when the list was revived in Charles's first parliament in 1625, the complaint against the heralds had been dropped.[47] There was no follow up, either, on the proposal to investigate the jurisdiction of the Earl Marshal's court. Nonetheless the proceedings in 1624 were a thoroughly uncomfortable experience for the heralds, demonstrating widespread public disapproval of their recent activities and the fragile basis for the power on which these rested. This was compounded by Arundel's loss of authority in the early part of Charles's reign, and for the remainder of the 1620s, and during the early part of the 1630s, morale among the heralds was very low and their operations were scaled down. There were no more visitations to the counties until 1634; the collection of funeral fees was partially discontinued; any notion of expanding the remit of the Earl Marshal's court to support their activities was abandoned; and, as had happened in Elizabeth's reign when there was an absence of clear direction, the heralds began squabbling among themselves.[48] This situation did not change until 1633–4, when the more favourable climate of opinion created by the king's interest in matters of honour and the death of the ageing, and largely supine, senior herald, Sir William Segar, Garter King of Arms, led to an upturn in their fortunes.

The revival of the heralds' activities coincided with the attention given to the Court of Chivalry and the problem of duelling. The evidence of a changing outlook gave the heralds a fresh sense of purpose. They were encouraged to bring a test case over their right to collect funeral fees from the gentry, and on 30 March and 10 October 1633 they secured judgements in their favour from the Court of Chancery.[49] They also began to anticipate ways in which the reformed Court of Chivalry might support their activities. In August 1634, in response to a letter from an Oxfordshire gentleman seeking advice on how to display his arms, Somerset herald John Philipot and Bluemantle pursuivant William Ryley

46 Bodl.L., Ashmole MS 857, pp. 545–6; *CJ*, i.701.

47 *Proceedings in Parliament 1625*, pp. 215n, 302–5, 307–9.

48 For the squabbles of the 1590s, see Wagner, *Heralds of England*, ch. 6.

49 CA, Phillipps MS 13084, vol. 12, unfoliated, 'The state of the business concerning the fees of the Officers of Armes', prepared for the Long Parliament committee to investigate the heralds' fees.

confidently asserted their belief that the court had given them a fresh start:

the priviledges of generous bloud are nowe more to be cared for then heretofore, since his Majestie hath appointed my Lord Marshall to keepe his court & juditially to punish such as offer injury to gentlemen in any kind.

They then went on to reassure him that 'we that are sworne officers of honor & armes will have care to proced uprightly', and that his 'arms and pedigree' would be recorded in 'our books . . . which will ever preserve the right of all your father's issue'. This was how the heralds liked to see themselves, as custodians of the honours system, applying their expertise to preserve the honour of gentry families and uphold order and degree.[50] The advances of 1633–4 gave them a renewed sense of purpose.

This was assisted by the promotion of Sir John Borough to Garter on 27 December 1633. Borough was far more forceful and dynamic than Segar and he used his credit with Arundel and the king to boost his own fortunes and those of the heralds as a whole. During 1633–4 he was at the height of his powers. In spite of being born a commoner, he had worked his way up from the position of research assistant to Lord Chancellor Bacon and clerk to the records in the Tower of London, to become Arundel's secretary and then, in 1623, his nominee as Norroy King of Arms. As MP for the Arundel seat of Hastings in 1624, he had tried to defend the heralds against the Commons attacks. He was also considered an expert on antiquarian precedents and, after the death of his mentor, Sir Robert Cotton, in 1631 carved out a niche for himself as principal adviser to the Privy Council on matters relating to the historic rights of the crown and fiscal feudalism.[51] His greatest service in this regard was to draw up the collection of precedents showing how past kings of England had asserted claims for the dominion of the seas surrounding their shores, which was later published as the *Sovereignty of the Seas*. He wrote this treatise in late 1633–early 1634, after accompanying the king and Arundel on the summer progress to Scotland;[52] and over the same period, he was able to use his favour and connections to secure several valuable grants. The first of these, on 10 November 1633, was a royal commission for himself and his fellow provincial king of arms, Sir Richard St George, Clarenceux, 'to reform the abuses' of the office of arms, if necessary bypassing Garter Segar. The immediate result was a new commission on

50 TNA, SP 16/271/80, p. 27.

51 'Sir John Borough (d.1643)', *Oxf.DNB*. For his collaboration with Cotton, see Sharpe, *Sir Robert Cotton*, p. 209. See Sharpe, *The Personal Rule*, p. 13 for his important January 1628 memo on fiscal precedents.

52 Gardiner, *History*, vii.358.

25 December authorising the two heralds to resume provincial visitations. Two days later, at Arundel's behest, Borough himself was appointed Garter, and, in a remarkable display of royal favour, he retained the right to oversee the visitation process, a right that past garters had been struggling to secure since Henry VIII's reign.[53] Borough was riding high and, although his success aroused a good deal of resentment among his fellow heralds, the reforms he helped to introduce ultimately bolstered their fortunes as well.

The opening of a fresh round of visitations was central to the heralds' renewed sense of purpose. These began in the spring of 1634, with visitations by Philipot and George Owen, York herald, in Sussex and the first phase of Sir Henry St George's visitation of London as Richmond herald. During the summer months the heralds criss-crossed the southern counties, visiting as far west as Hampshire and as far east as Essex, and also venturing into the midlands. Their responsibility on these occasions, according to the royal commission that empowered them, was nothing less than the oversight and preservation of the existing social order:

> that the nobility and gentry of this realme may be preserved in every degree, as appeteyneth as well in honour as in worshippe, and that every personne or persons, bodies politique, corporate and others, may be the better knowne in his and their estate, degree and mistery, without confusion and disorder.[54]

It was a duty that they took very seriously. John Raven, Richmond herald, had explained what was involved when he addressed the knights and gentlemen of Norfolk, prior to the visitation in 1613. The heralds were charged with ensuring that 'that which is now amisse be reduced agayne to the first beawtie and decencye, and all offence and complaynte be hereafter moved with a uniforme observation of the rules of all antiquitye'. It was their responsibility to oversee 'the conservacon of peace and all good order, without the which all things goe to havocke & confusion'. To these ends, they had to perform two principal tasks: first, to maintain the distinctions between noblemen, gentlemen and commoners by identifying those who 'beinge ignoble and without deserte doe assume unto themselves the state and titles of gentility'; and second, to guarantee the accuracy of displays of coat armour, by correcting abuses, such as the failure of younger branches of a family to register due changes and

[53] Wagner, *Records and Collections*, p. 73; AC, Earl Marshal's Papers, 682. For these struggles, see A.R. Wagner, *Heralds and Heraldry in the Middle Ages* (Oxford: Oxford University Press, 2nd edn., 1956), pp. 9–12, 83–99; Wagner, *Heralds of England*, pp. 179–80, 185–6, 197, 202–3.

[54] AC, Earl Marshal's Papers, 682.

differences. The heralds were required to meet with all those claiming to be gentlemen, examine their pedigrees and coat armour, and then either record the details in their office books or else require them to disclaim their gentility.[55]

The value and importance of the visitation process was readily appreciated in heraldic and antiquarian circles[56] but many of the gentry remained to be convinced, as the complaints in the 1624 Parliament had demonstrated. Edward Walker, who, as Blanch-Lyon pursuivant and later Chester herald, was able to observe reactions to the 1630s visitation process at close quarters, complained that

> when the provintiall kinges of armes, once in 20 or 30 yeares . . . make any visitation whereby the memory not only of the gent[leman's] ancestors, but of all the descendants and collaterals are preserved, men disclaymed that are no gent[lemen] and usurpation and false erection of arms defaced, yet you shall find many gent that for the payinge of the ancient fee of 27s. shall wilfully omit the opportunity of preserving their rights, pretendinge they are well enough knowen and this can doe them noe good.[57]

Walker was exaggerating. There were plenty of gentlemen who did care greatly about such things and who attended before the heralds clutching armfuls of evidences and eager to have their descents registered.[58] But there was also a widespread cynicism, which made the heralds' task much harder.

The visitation process was complicated and required the cooperation of local gentry and officials, as well as back-up from the Earl Marshal in London. The first step was to draw up lists of those who were to be summoned to prove their gentility and right to bear arms. For this the heralds used records of past visitations, lists of local justices available in the crown office and the freeholders books drawn up by county sheriffs to identify all those aged between 21 and 70 who were liable for jury service. These were supplemented by local information about grand jurors and borough aldermen (who were formally designated as 'gentlemen' by dint of their office) and the personal knowledge of the hundred bailiffs who

55 BL, Harleian MS 1154, fos. 65v-61v (reverse pagination). I am grateful to Adrian Ailes for this reference.

56 See, for example, Thomas Habington, *A Survey of Worcestershire*, ed. J. Amphlett, 2 vols. (Worcestershire Historical Soc., 1895–99), i.192.

57 BL, Lansdowne MS 255, fo. 201.

58 See, for example, the determination of John Hampden and others to have their lengthy pedigrees recorded by the heralds in their office books for the visitation of Buckinghamshire in 1634: CA, C26, fos. 13–14, 70–1. For a fuller account of this round of visitations, see R.P. Cust, 'The failure of the Heralds' Visitations of 1634' (forthcoming).

assisted the heralds.[59] The visitation was formally launched at a sitting of the county assizes when the king's commission was read out in the presence of the heralds. On occasion this would then be accompanied by a charge from the heralds, after which warrants would be issued by the hundred bailiffs, summoning all those claiming to be gentlemen to attend a meeting at the local market town.[60] It was at these meetings that the main work of the visitation took place, with the heralds inspecting the arms and pedigrees brought before them, entering them in the office book that they carried with them and then getting the entries signed by the claimants. Those who failed to prove their title were required to sign disclaimers and later had their names publicly disclaimed, usually at the local market cross.[61] The main problem faced by the heralds was trying to ensure attendance at these meetings, with as few as 30 per cent of those summoned turning up on some occasions. Those who did not appear were supposed to be called to a later meeting, or else bound over to answer before the Earl Marshal in London. But these procedures were rarely applied systematically and, even when they were it was difficult to secure compliance. Sir Richard St George, Norroy, a veteran of earlier rounds of visitations complained that

> Upon our warrants for the gentlemens' appearance at a certain time & place, many will peremptorilye and contemptuouslye refuse, which being againe by a second warrant commanded to answear that contempt before the earl marshal upon a day certaine and upon a penaltie, all which we are by the commission warranted to doe, they, notwithstandinge, upon the second warninge come not at all, doubling their contempt to the king and to the Marshalls.[62]

These problems continued during the 1630s. However much St George might wish it otherwise, in the final analysis, the visitation was essentially a voluntary process, which the local gentry could participate in or ignore as they saw fit.[63]

In 1634, however, there was an opportunity to change the dynamics of the process. This was provided by the newly established Court of Chivalry

[59] Ailes, 'Elias Ashmole's "Heraldicall Visitacion"', pp. 87–97. The survival of the Essex freeholders book, used by Owen and Lilley for their visitation of the county in 1634, shows that all those identified as 'bart.', 'mil.', 'esq.' and 'gen.' were issued with warrants to appear before them: BL, Harl. MS 2240.

[60] Ailes,'Ashmole's "Heraldicall Visitacion"', pp. 121–6.

[61] Ailes, 'Ashmole's "Heraldicall Visitacion"', ch. 4. For details for Buckingham, CA, C26, fos. 141–2.

[62] CA, Phillipps MS 13084, vol. 8, fos. 339.

[63] This is the conclusion of Dr Adrian Ailes in his definitive study of the visitation process. He describes visitations as 'a dialogue between visiting herald and local gentry in which, at the end of the day, the latter could choose to enter or ignore the whole process': 'Ashmole's "Heraldicall Visitacion"', p. 264.

which, as Philipot and Ryley hinted in their letter cited earlier, offered the potential for much more effective policing of visitations. It is one of the more surprising features of the 1630s round of county inquests that this potential was not seriously exploited. Only five of the surviving cases between 1634 and 1640 involved heralds bringing actions connected with the visitations. One of these – in which George Owen brought an action against a Gloucestershire gentleman for having said that 'You goe upp and downe the country sharking and cheating' – related to precisely the sort of episode in which the court could have provided invaluable back up for the heralds' actions. Two of the remaining four were brought by the king's advocate, Dr Duck, on behalf of Sir Henry St George who was conducting the visitation of London. These concerned two London traders who were accused of displaying coats of arms to which they were not entitled. The other two related to disclaimers from past visitations that had not been adhered to. Following the Derbyshire visitation of 1634 Henry Chitting, Chester herald, and Thomas Thompson, Rouge Dragon pursuivant, brought an action against Robert Willymott who was continuing to style himself 'gentleman', in spite of having disclaimed in 1611; and the kings of arms brought an action against Thomas Tuckfield, a Devon justice, who had described his father as 'esq.' on his funeral monument after he had been required to disclaim this following the Devon visitation of 1620. In each of these cases the heralds were successful and the culprits were forced to pay fines, remedy the abuses and make their submissions.[64] The court's proceedings had worked very effectively to assist and support the heralds, which raises the obvious question of why they were not used more often.

The answer would appear to lie in the nature of the reformed court's jurisdiction. In some of the previous schemes to reform the Court of Chivalry, it had been anticipated that it would become in effect a heralds' court, acting as a 'court of record' for registering descents and coats of arms, and bolstering their normal range of activities, including visitations. But this was not how it developed during the 1630s. The civil lawyers who staffed the court in its new incarnation had little interest in providing support for the heralds. They would often work closely with them, drawing on their expertise to assess the validity of coats of arms or descents, and generally affording them a favourable hearing. But their priority was to process the growing volume of defamation business coming from the gentry, and to secure the fees that went with this. The heralds had to pay the costs of bringing an action like any other litigant,

64 *Cases in the Court of Chivalry*, pp. 78, 80, 152–3, 209–11; R.P. Cust, 'Sir Henry Spelman investigates', *Coat of Arms*, 3rd ser., III (2007), 25–34.

and these were often considerable. For example, it cost Chitting and Thompson £21 4s 2d to bring their action against Willymott and they were able to recoup only £10 of this in their award of expenses.[65] This was a considerable outlay since the overall income from a county visitation was generally in the order of only £200–£300.[66] Thus, however effective court proceedings might have been in making an example of defaulters and deterring others, they did not make sense as a financial proposition. The two actions brought by Duck on St George's behalf in May 1634 appear to have been test cases, launched to establish the effectiveness of using court proceedings to assist the heralds in their visitations. If so, the experiment was abandoned and thereafter such actions only arose where the heralds had a particular reason for pursuing the defendant: for example, to secure reparation for a personal affront, as in the Owen case.

The commission for the 1634 visitations also set out the provincial kings' responsibilities for funerals and arms painters. They were to ensure that the heralds attended and supervised heraldic funerals and licensed painters or engravers before they were allowed to provide any 'armes, creastes, cognisances, pedigrees'. This, along with the Chancery judgements of 1633 and the re-establishment of the Court of Chivalry, gave the heralds the opportunity to make an important contribution towards restoring the integrity of the honours system and recover much of the ground lost since 1624. As they explained in their response to the Long Parliament committee inquiring into their fees, ensuring that formal heraldic funerals were held where possible, and that otherwise nobles and gentlemen registered funeral certificates recording their descents, were essential to 'preservinge the discents of the nobility & gentry'. If this did not happen 'every man may usupe . . . the title and the badges of gentry, and so everyone that pleaseth may make himselfe equall to the auncient gentry of this kingdome and invest himselfe in their blood and familie'.[67]

The newly established Court of Chivalry encouraged them to look again at ways in which they could regulate gentlemen's funerals and exert control over the unlicensed arms painters. This time it did make financial sense to bring actions in the court. The fees from funeral certificates laid

65 CA, Curia Militaris 9/4/20; *Cases in the Court of Chivalry*, p. 209.

66 Ailes, 'Ashmole's "Heraldicall Visitacion"', p. 128n.

67 The only copy I have found of this important document is in CA, Phillipps MS 13084, vol. 12, unfol., headed 'The state of the business concerninge the fees of the Officers of Arms'. The document is undated but the subject matter, the references to precedents from the 1630s and the appeals it makes to the interests of nobility and gentry suggest that it almost certainly relates to the proceedings of this committee.

down in the 1618 proclamation were considerable, starting at 40s for a gentleman, going up to £6 13s 4d for an esquire, £10 for a knight and then on to £45 for a duke or marquis. In 1637 when John Philipot, Somerset herald, was challenged over how much the fees would yield if the bulk of them were collected, he accepted that it would be in the order of £3000–£4000 a year.[68] If the heralds could use the court to deter arms painters and ensure proper conduct of funerals, or registration of certificates, then, this would represent a sound financial investment.

They began with a concerted effort to target the Painters and Stainers Company in London and by bringing them under control set the pattern for arms painters elsewhere. In May 1634, under Borough's direction, the heralds set out once and for all to enforce earlier agreements that no arms painter should depict armouries or pedigrees without the consent and supervision of the heralds. There was a lengthy and wide-ranging inquest into the painters' activities, with large numbers of witnesses being interrogated. After 18 months of hearings, however, the action was inconclusive. The heralds were able to pick off individuals, but the company managed to defend its position and continued to make the case that if gentlemen had to seek the heralds' approval every time they wanted a coat of arms painted this would be an enormous expense and inconvenience.[69] Thereafter the heralds concentrated on making intermittent examples of those who were caught reproducing coats of arms without their consent. In December 1638, for example, Sir Henry St George, Norroy, secured an award of 200 marks in damages from Edward Moseley, after he had displayed unauthorised shields and banners at the funeral of his uncle, the former attorney of the Duchy of Lancaster. Such proceedings could be very profitable, as well as making an effective example.[70] But, like the actions brought in support of visitations, they were too irregular to have a sustained impact. In the case of funeral fees, however, their efforts yielded much more positive results.

In May 1635, after bringing an action against John Twistleton esq., executor to a Kentish gentleman whose funeral fees were long overdue, they secured a ruling from the Earl Marshal that Twistleton should 'attend the Court of Honour and make a recognisans of this default'.[71]

[68] F.W. Jessup, *Sir Roger Twysden 1597–1672* (London: Cresset Press, 1965), pp. 22–6.

[69] CA, Curia Militaris, 7/1, 39, 40, 57; Heralds, vol. II, fos. 779, 789–92, 796–814; TNA, SP 16/307/82; W.D. Englefield, *The History of the Painters and Stainers Company of London* (London, 1923), pp. 82–3, 102–4.

[70] *Cases in the Court of Chivalry*, p. 150. The Moseley award was later compounded for 100 marks; but this still meant payments of £30 to Norroy, £8 15s to each of the other heralds and £4 7s 6d to the pursuivants: CA, Partition Bk.3, fo. 253.

[71] CA, Partition Bk. 3, fo. 188.

This ruling encouraged the heralds to launch a systematic campaign to collect arrears of fees and over the following 12 months at least 13 cases of this type came before the Court of Chivalry.[72] One of the best documented of these, the case of *Officers of Arms* v. *Rose Rivers*, illustrates the determination of the heralds to press home their claims. Rivers was a wealthy widow who was called on to pay £16 13s 4d following the deaths of her husband and her uncle. She consulted the Middle Temple barrister, William Say, who told John Philipot that 'no such fees as were demanded of her were due by any lawe of this kingedome'. Philipot took out a summons for Say to make his answer in the Court of Chivalry and when the barrister was presented with this he delivered a further tirade. Thomas Thompson, Rouge Dragon pursuivant was told that he

> refused absolutelie to paie the fees and returne the certificates, and said he knew well that our constitution was of no validitie, and said if he might be counsell for us he would wish us to be quiet and stirre no further in the the business: for . . . it will prove worse for you.

This thinly veiled threat of counter action at a future parliament was reported to the court and the following day when Say appeared before Sir Henry Martin and Arundel's son, and deputy Earl Marshal, Lord Maltravers, he was subjected to an intensive grilling and made to enter bonds to answer for a charge of contempt 'for publishing both by word and writing that my Lord Marshall's decrees and constitutions were contrary to lawe'.[73] According to Edward Hyde, his Middle Temple colleague who took up the case in the Short Parliament, Say refused to retract his opinion and was 'fined, imprisoned and not discharged in a long tyme'.[74] Say already had 'form', having been fined earlier during the Personal Rule for acting as ringleader to a group of students drinking toasts to a future parliament;[75] but his prompt and exemplary punishment was an impressive demonstration of the court's determination to brook no defiance on this matter.

The evidence of the Partition Books, which recorded the fees paid to heralds, suggests that their campaign had a considerable impact. From the late 1620s through 1633, there were entries recording individual payments for funerals, but no reference to money being collected for certificates where no heralds were in attendance. This altered in May 1633, in the wake of the Chancery judgement, and thereafter regular monthly sums for 'certificate fees' began to appear again, as in the

[72] *Cases in the Court of Chivalry*, pp. 204–10.
[73] CA, Curia Militaris 1631–42, fos. 21–2, 23–4.
[74] *Proceedings of the Short Parliament*, p. 158. [75] 'William Say (1604–1666)', *Oxf.DNB*.

early 1620s. From early 1636 to the end of 1639 these accounted for around three-quarters of all the payments recorded, and from the start of 1637 the amounts rose markedly, with £50–£60 per month (and in some months well over £100) being regularly recorded. In all around £6000 was recorded as being paid for funeral fees between 1619 and 1641, the bulk of it in the late 1630s.[76] In their response to the Long Parliament the heralds pointed out that these were now the principal means by which they were able to supplement the relatively meagre salaries furnished by the crown.

The success of the heralds' campaign was borne out from another perspective by Edward Hyde's complaints to the Short Parliament. In the tirade against the Court of Chivalry that he delivered on 18 April 1640, it was the powers that the heralds had acquired to force all persons to pay at their funerals such 'several sums according to their several degrees' that he singled out as the most offensive aspect of its authority. With heavy irony, he described this as unique among the impositions of the 1630s in that it was 'a grievance that lasts longer than life'.

> In the grave ther used to be all peace, but heare is a tax outlived and an imposicon upon our carcasses. Some, Mr Speaker, of the knights of this house when they entered into that order thought they might happily be engaged to lyve at a higher rate, yet they might dy as good cheape as other men. They cannot, Mr Speaker. It will cost them £5 more at court and yet a gentleman cannot dy for nothing nether.[77]

Hyde's artful depiction of these fees as an early version of death duties, struck a chord with his fellow MPs. When he returned to the theme at the start of the Long Parliament a committee was appointed to receive complaints about the Earl Marshal's court and also, specifically, about the heralds' fees.[78] The fact that this was now fit to be considered alongside other grievances of the Personal Rule was a back-handed compliment to their success in persuading the gentry that they could not simply ignore these demands. Finally, after years of trying, the heralds had found a mechanism for getting their funeral fees to bite.

The heralds' relative success in using the Court of Chivalry to enforce the collection of funeral fees begs the question of why they were not able to do more to deliver the agenda set out by Arundel in 1625 for regenerating the honours system. The 1630s provided the best opportunity available during the late Tudor and early Stuart period for achieving this. The heraldic/antiquarian establishment had a leader in Arundel who enjoyed

76 CA, Partition Bk. 3, fos. 1–147, 191–268; Wagner, *Heralds of England*, p. 111.
77 *Proceedings of the Short Parliament*, pp. 260–2.
78 *Proceedings in the Long Parliament*, i.247, 254.

the favour of the king, and who was committed and willing to take risks in pursuit of what he saw as his mission to revive the 'ancient nobility' and restore the prestige of grants of honours. He was supported by powerful and ambitious professional interest groups in the form of the heralds and civil lawyers, both of them led by energetic and proactive individuals, like the Garter King of Arms, Sir John Borough, who as adviser to the Privy Council was the chief promoter of fiscal feudalism during the 1630s, or the leading civil lawyers, Sir Henry Martin and Sir Arthur Duck, who were the architects of the reform in the Court of Chivalry. And the reformed Court of Chivalry itself, for the first time, provided an institution that could add coercive muscle to the whole process. Philipot and Ryley's optimism that the new court would promote 'the privileges of generous bloud' was well placed. The fact that the Earl Marshal, or his deputy, sat in judgement in the majority of cases ensured the heralds would receive a sympathetic hearing and encouraged them to take on challenges to their authority, as in the Say case. The atmosphere was very different from the mid 1620s when they had felt beleaguered and powerless. There was now the potential to implement the reforms that Earl Marshals and heralds had been pushing for generations. At last it seemed they could make significant headway with registering grants of arms, regulating heraldic funerals, sorting out disputes over precedence and moving towards the fixity and stability that contemporaries craved. So what held them back?

Part of it had to do with specific circumstances that on occasion worked against them. Had the visitation process lasted longer, then, the benefits of pursuing defaulters through the court might have been more apparent. As it was the process started to run into difficulties after the death of Sir Richard St George in May 1635 that destroyed the temporary accord between garter and the provincial kings over the right to conduct visitations and ensured that there were no further county inquests.[79] Hard-headed financial calculation was another factor. In pecuniary terms there was little to be gained from bringing a case in the Court of Chivalry over a fraudulent claim to title or an incorrect display of arms. Even when the heralds won, the cost outweighed the benefits. In the case of funeral fees, however, the whole equation was very different. Philipot's back-of-the-envelope estimate of potential income was an indication of what the heralds thought they might be able to accomplish and the hefty fine in the Moseley case demonstrated the immediate dividend. If the heralds could establish these fees as a normal expectation among the gentry they would enjoy a bonanza. This is not to argue that their motives were purely

[79] Wagner, *Records and Collections*, pp. 73–4, 82–3.

mercenary. The lengths to which individual heralds were prepared to go to vet coats of arms and pedigrees, indicates that fees were often not the only, or the main, consideration. In spite of the criticisms made by their many detractors, most were responsible professionals, committed to upholding the integrity of the honours system.[80] However, when it came to conducting litigation in the Court of Chivalry they faced the same costs as any other plaintiff operating under the civilians' money-making regime and this deterred them from pushing their opportunity harder.

This indicates a third element working against effective reform: the division of interests between the heralds and the civilians. At the start of Charles's reign both professional groups were at a very low ebb, out of favour and largely friendless. It was very much in their interests to work in support of the project to restore the honours system, which would give both of them a sense of purpose and opportunities to enhance their status. By the mid 1630s, however, thanks to the backing of Charles and his Earl Marshal, their professional prospects had improved immeasurably and the need to cooperate was much less pressing. This was evident in the civilians' hard-headed approach to cases in the Court of Chivalry involving grants of arms and titles where, in spite of the obvious overall benefits, they failed to make it worth the while of heralds to bring suits against offenders. It was also apparent in the project for the new 'Order Military' in 1639 that appears to have originated with the civilians, who would have been the main financial beneficiaries, and opposed by the heralds. The 'Order Military' was sold to the king on the grounds that it would provide him with a dedicated cadre of noble followers, bound to service of the crown by an oath of fealty. But, in many respects, as was pointed out by Edward Walker, Chester herald, who wrote a tract denouncing the scheme, it could be seen as a reversion to sale of honours, with membership of the order and its privileges being sold in return for regular payments to the Court of Chivalry. Far from restoring the prestige and integrity of honours as its proponents claimed, Walker insisted that it would revive all the problems associated with baronetcies, disrupting existing hierarchies, generating disputes over precedence and tarnishing the whole system for granting honours.[81] The 'Order Military' was shelved largely, it would seem, for political reasons. But the squabbling that it led to between heralds and civilian lawyers was symptomatic of the divisions that prevented the potential for reform in the 1630s being realised.

80 See, for example, the Tuckfield case discussed in Cust, 'Sir Henry Spelman', 25–34 and the careful inquest into William Paston's arms, supervised by Philipot and Sir Richard St George: CA, Phillips MS 13084, vol. 5, fos. 130–1.

81 BL, Add. MS 12514, fos. 1–8; Lansdowne MS 255, fos. 198–201.

Of course, in the final analysis, the prospect of sorting out and regulating honours and titles in the ways that had been envisaged since the 1560s was largely illusory. A structure and hierarchy that was so open ended and competitive, and which allowed for so many different avenues of advancement, largely defied the sort of systematisation and regulation that Earl Marshals and heralds were seeking to impose. The best that they could hope for, in practice, was to curtail the grossest forms of abuse, reduce the level of disputes over precedence, ensure that honours and titles maintained their vitality and relevance for contemporaries and uphold respect for their role as arbiters of the existing system. By these standards some progress was made during the 1630s and the heraldic establishment was able to reverse much of the damage done by sale of honours and the assaults of the 1624 Parliament. But, given the opportunities, a good deal more could have been achieved. As with other royal projects of the Personal Rule, the whole programme promised more than it was able to deliver and its success was, at best, partial and fragmented.[82]

[82] Cust, *Charles I. A Political Life*, pp. 185–8.

4 The aristocracy and the Bishops Wars, 1639–1640

The first Bishops War and the military mobilisation of the peerage

In the early summer of 1638, as the Scottish crisis escalated towards armed confrontation, Charles announced to the world that he was moving into martial mode. After years of commissioning Van Dyck to paint him in a variety of civilian roles – as loving husband, father to his family, courtier prince and stately monarch – he authorised a series of portraits, of himself, his deceased brother and his son, as warriors, in full armour, weapons at the ready.[1] The basic 'type' for this, painted in full and three-quarter length versions, was a portrait of the king in jousting armour, the lesser George hanging round his neck from a chain (as distinct from the ribbon used with civilian dress), his left hand resting on the hilt of his sword, his mailed right hand clasping the baton of command and on a table his cavalry helm alongside his imperial crown.[2] The stance was considerably more purposeful and aggressive than any previous portrait by Van Dyck. Precisely the same stance and props were used for a posthumous matching portrait of his brother Henry, the only difference being that Henry was shown wearing his own jousting armour, which had remained in the king's collection. The two portraits appear to have been painted as a pair, and they may have originally been intended to hang alongside each other in the recently refurbished Cross Gallery at Somerset House where they would have spelt out the unmistakeable message that Charles was his brother's partner in maintaining England's chivalric tradition.[3] The same motif was used in the pair of portraits of his seven-year-old son, with and without his garter medal, which were painted either side of his inauguration into the order on 21 May 1638. Wearing a scaled down version of the king's armour, a cocked cavalry pistol in his right hand and his left hand resting on his helm, the child

[1] Barnes et al., *Van Dyck*, pp. 460–75, 482–4, 531. [2] *Ibid.*, pp. 472–4.
[3] *Ibid.*, p. 531. The full-length portrait of Charles was, however, given to Lord Wharton not long after it was painted.

Figure 4.1 Sir Anthony Van Dyck, *Charles I (1600–1649) on Horseback*. Probably painted in 1638, this shows the king preparing to go to war against the Scots. The king is wearing jousting armour, wielding the baton of command and mounted on a cavalry charger, with the cartouche bearing the inscription '*Carolus Rex Magnae Britanniae*' a reminder of his status as king of Great Britain. (Reproduced with permission of the trustees of the National Gallery, London.)

prince exudes a steady determination.[4] The most striking, and the most famous, portrait of this series is *Charles I on Horseback* (see Figure 4.1). With identical arms and armour, again clasping the baton of command

[4] *Ibid.*, pp. 481–3. Also see Figure 2.2, p. 136, this volume.

in his mailed fist, he gazes resolutely ahead as his dun-coloured cavalry charger breaks into a trot. The depiction of the king on horseback deliberately echoed the Roman tradition, in which this form of representation was reserved for Emperors, and at the same time conveyed the impression of his command over nature, by showing his skill in horsemanship. It also included a cartouche with the inscription '*Carolus Rex Magnae Britanniae*', a reminder of his status as king of Great Britain just when this was being contested by the rebellious Scots. This was the king as commander-in-chief and military leader of the nation.[5]

The assurance and conviction with which Charles assumed his martial role in the 1638 portraits is a reminder that soldierly accomplishments and ideals remained an integral part of the princely and aristocratic lifestyle. Military prowess and courage in battle were the supreme affirmations of the status accorded to a nobleman or a monarch.[6] It is important to stress this because the traditional view of the English aristocracy is that it became progressively demilitarised during the late sixteenth and early seventeenth century. Lawrence Stone has estimated that from a high point during the Wars of The Roses and the wars of Henry VIII's reign, when over three-quarters of the English nobility had some experience of war, the numbers declined sharply during the Elizabethan peace to around a quarter by the 1570s and less than a fifth in the early Stuart period. On this account, the English ruling class was becoming an aristocracy of courtiers and governors, increasingly unfamiliar with the weapons, training and feats of arms that had played such a prominent role

[5] Strong, *Charles I on Horseback*. The precise dating of these portraits, as with many of Van Dyck's works, is problematic. The most securely dateable are the two versions of the portrait of Prince Charles, which must have been painted either side of his inauguration into the Order of the Garter. The similarities in the style, the pose and the props suggest that the portrait of the young prince was painted around the same time as the martial portraits of his father, and, indeed, it appears alongside the painting of Prince Henry and one of 'Le Roy en armes donne au Baron Wharton' (the full-length version of Charles in armour) among a list of recent paintings for which van Dyck was seeking payment drawn up late in 1638: TNA, SP 16/406/4; Barnes et al., *Van Dyck*, pp. 10, 473, 483, 531. The most problematic dating is of *Charles I on Horseback*, which has been ascribed by some art historians to 1636–7 (Barnes et al., *Van Dyck*, p. 468) on the basis of the facial style that was being used for portraits which can be dated to 1636; however, it has also been noted that this same facial style was still being used for the '*c.* 1637–8' portraits. A more reliable guide to dating, as Roy Strong (*Charles I on Horseback*, p. 20) has pointed out, is the king's 'abbreviated collar', a fashion of the late 1630s, used for the other 1638 martial portraits, but not in the earlier painting ascribed to *c.* 1635–1636, which show a much fuller lace collar (Barnes et al., *Van Dyck*, pp. 465, 467, 471, 475). Strong therefore ascribes it to 1638, as does Christopher Brown (*Van Dyck*, p. 168). This dating is supported by the similarities in armour, sword, boots and collar with the other martial portraits ascribed to 1638 and also by the inscribed cartouche, which has obvious relevance to the Scottish crisis.

[6] Thomas, *Ends of Life*, ch. 2.

in its chivalric past. This was accompanied, Mervyn James has argued, by a diminution in the honour accorded to 'military renown'. The 'personal code' of military men came increasingly to be portrayed as a 'vain-glory' and touchiness that was contrasted unfavourably with the wisdom and *gravitas* of the civilian governor and servant of the state.[7] The emphasis was increasingly on a nobleman's civility rather than his valour.

However, it has become apparent from recent work that the extent of this demilitarisation has been overstated. In a striking reversal of the conventional view, Roger Manning has argued that in fact the 1620s, and, to an even greater extent, the 1630s witnessed a 'remilitarisation' of England's elite. He calculates that among the aristocracy the proportion 'who had experience of battle, sought military experience or pursued military careers' was in fact rising: from 40 per cent in 1585, to 45 per cent in 1605 to 65 per cent in 1635, and 69 per cent in 1640. Taking into account the Irish and Scottish nobilities as well – where the proportions in 1640 were slightly higher – he concludes that the British aristocracy had become 'more thoroughly militarised than many of those of Western Europe and at least as martial as those of France'. This is a striking claim, which should be treated with a certain amount of caution. The extent and significance of the military experience covered by Manning's estimates was very varied. Clearly, there was a considerable contrast between the degree of involvement of the Earl of Holland, who made a brief visit to the European front in the early 1610s before settling down to a career at court, and that of the 3rd Earl of Essex who spent much of the 1620s and 1630s commanding regiments in the Low Countries.[8] Nonetheless, the basic point still stands; and it is borne out in Ian Roy's account of the profession of arms and Barbara Donagan's study of the large and growing body of military publications in this period.[9] The martial ethos and the practice of warfare commanded continuing and, in some respects, increasing esteem among the English elite.

7 Stone, *Crisis of the Aristocracy*, pp. 265–6; J.S. Morrill, *The Nature of the English Revolution* (Harlow: Longman, 1993), pp. 4–5; James, *English Politics and the Concept of Honour*, pp. 87–9.

8 Manning, *Swordsmen*, pp. 17–18, 49–50. It is worth noting that the king and other contemporaries evidently regarded Holland, and others like Newcastle whose military experience was confined to tilts and tournaments, as 'martial men' and therefore worthy of senior commands in the Bishops Wars. For a European perspective on this phenomenon, also emphasising the remilitarisation of the aristocracy, albeit later in the seventeenth century, see C. Storrs and H.M. Scott, 'The Military Revolution and the European Nobility, *c.* 1600–1800', *War in History*, 3(1996), 1–41.

9 I. Roy, 'The profession of arms', in *The Professions in Early Modern England*, ed. W.R. Prest (Beckenham: Croom Helm, 1987), 181–219; B. Donagan, 'Halcyon days and the literature of war: England's military education before 1642', *P & P*, 147 (1995), 65–100.

There were various reasons for this. As we have seen, the upbringing of upper-class boys still had a pronounced martial dimension and going to war in defence of one's country, or in support of one's sovereign, was viewed as the most honourable service one could perform.[10] The growing, and avidly consumed, literature on military matters provided a series of role models that reinforced the image of the aristocratic soldier as the epitome of honest, masculine virtue. Men like Sir Philip Sidney, Sir Francis de Vere and the 3rd Earl of Essex were depicted as inspiring leaders, exposing themselves to immense risks, motivating their men by personal example and selflessly serving their country and the protestant cause.[11] At the same time opportunities for service in arms were becoming more frequent. The Dutch Revolt and the Thirty Years War provided the possibility of long periods of continental soldiering, which had not existed for much of the sixteenth century. Significant numbers of Englishmen began to make their careers as professional soldiers, among which were several noble dynasties where generations of the same family followed the same path: the Conways, the Sidneys, the Sheffields and the Willoughbys and, most famously, the Veres, with Horace Lord Vere, the most respected soldier of his day.[12] The 3rd Earl of Essex described the Netherlands during the 1620s and 1630s as 'the schoole of honour for the nobility of England in their exercise of arms'. This was borne out by events like the siege of Breda in the autumn of 1637 that became a virtual spectator sport for the English aristocracy, as the young Palatine princes, Rupert and Maurice, led 'a great train of English noblemen and gentlemen' to witness the siegeworks at first hand.[13]

Opportunities to engage in martial pursuits were also growing at home. Charles's programme to create 'an Exact Militia' may not have achieved the reforms that were intended, but it did provide an opening for local nobles and gentlemen to channel their military enthusiasms. The often lavish expenditure on uniforms and military accessories indicated how much they valued the opportunity to parade before their neighbours as militia colonels and captains on muster days. The movement to establish voluntary artillery companies, both in London and in the provinces, where the gentry and citizenry could train and show off their weapons skills was also at its height in the 1630s.[14] And there were several projects

[10] See pp. 131–2. [11] Manning, *Swordsmen*, pp. 35–40, 67, 247.

[12] *Ibid.*, 35, 37–9; Roy, 'Profession of Arms', 190–1; 'Horace, Lord Vere (1565–1635)', *Oxf.DNB*.

[13] Hibbard, 'Theatre of Dynasty', p. 161; Henry Hexham, *A True and Briefe Relation of the Famous Siege of Breda* (Delft, 1637), pp. 7, 14.

[14] Stater, *Noble Government*, p. 23; L. Boynton, *The Elizabethan Militia 1558–1638* (London: Routledge and Kegan Paul, 1976), pp. 215–16, 262–5; Donagan, *War in England*, pp. 56–8.

to form gentry and nobles into a 'refined militia' of cavalry contingents, 'comparable', one proposer claimed, 'to the bands of gendarmerie in France'. Finally, there were recurring schemes to create a Royal Regiment, the most notable of which was the 1638 proposal by the Marquis of Hamilton and Lord Wilmot, both veterans of the continental wars, to form a regiment of a hundred cavalry, selected from the cream of the young nobility, who would serve, as the king's lifeguards, in peace and war.[15] The prestige of soldiering had rarely been higher in England than it was in the late 1630s. This re-emphasis on the nobility's traditional martial role was to play an important part in the reassertion of their authority and status during the Bishops Wars. It also provides an important, and often overlooked, context for the recruitment of an army to face the Scots.

Planning for war began in April 1638 soon after news reached England of the signing of the National Covenant. It gathered momentum in June when the king declared his intention to invade Scotland with an army of 16 000 men, supported by a train of artillery and the royal fleet. The time needed to collect together men and munitions meant that it was too late to launch a campaign in 1638; but planning continued apace during the second half of the year and a new council committee was established to act as a council of war.[16] From an early stage Charles was looking to the nobility to furnish the backbone of his forces. He received advice from the Attorney General in July that, under the 'ancient laws' and terms of their tenures, he could command all those holding lands and offices in the north to take up arms and provide men to face the Scots. More significantly, he gave the main role in planning the war effort to Arundel who was put in charge of the council of war and dispatched to the north to prepare the defences of the border counties.[17]

Arundel's role in directing the campaign, and his eventual appointment as Lord General, dismayed Sir Edward Hyde, and has been heavily criticised by later historians.[18] Unlike some of the alternative candidates, he had never been on campaign and had never led men in battle. But from the king's point of view the earl had two vital qualifications. First, in an era when appointments to senior commands generally had more to do with political than military suitability, he was consistently identified as the most 'hawkish' of Charles's councillors. The advice that Sir Edmund

[15] Bodl.L., Ashmole MS 862, pp. 100–2; *Strafforde Letters*, ii.148, 181. See also, Endymion Porter's scheme of 1631: TNA, SP 16/203/38, 38i.

[16] Gardiner, *History*, viii.344–5; M.C. Fissel, *The Bishops Wars* (Cambridge: Cambridge University Press, 1994), pp. 10–13; TNA, SP 16/396 (The Council Committee Order Book).

[17] HMC, *Cowper*, ii.187; *CSP Dom. 1637–8*, p. 584.

[18] Clarendon, *History*, i.150; Gardiner, *History*, viii.385–6.

Verney credited him with giving in May 1639 – 'dayly urging the king how nearly it concerns him in honner to punish the rebells, telling [him] that they are weake and not able to encounter him' – probably represented the line that he was taking throughout, and it appears to have chimed in closely with the king's views.[19] Charles was determined to chastise the Covenanters in a way that would repair his wounded honour and the earl was the councillor most inclined to urge this approach.

Second, and of, perhaps, greater significance, was Arundel's position as Earl Marshal and heir to the Howard inheritance. The approach to the war was shaped, as were so many of Charles's other policies during the 1630s, by a search for precedent and a determination to abide by tradition. The Earl Marshal was customarily regarded as the leader of the English nobility in war, as well as peace. The treatises on the office drawn up by members of the Society of Antiquaries around the turn of the century had all emphasised that, in the absence of a Lord High Constable, it was the role of the Earl Marshal to lead the royal army in the field. Rubens alluded to this in the powerful 1629 portrait of Arundel, which depicted him as the warrior Earl Marshal, using many of the motifs that reappeared in the 1638 portraits of the king.[20] If Charles was to rally the landowning classes to face the Scots his Earl Marshal was the obvious person to give a lead. There was also the significant fact of his Howard ancestry. It was one of the family's proudest claims, familiar to his fellow nobles and, no doubt, to the king, that Arundel's great, great grandfather, the 2nd Duke of Norfolk, had triumphed over the Scots in the great victory at Flodden in 1513.[21] Since military prowess, like other aristocratic virtues, was presumed to run within particular families, this was another powerful recommendation for the earl. Not only did he possess the office, but also the pedigree, to lead a campaign in which the English nobility were to be cast in a leading role.

The mobilisation of the nobility began in earnest on 19 January 1639 when the king announced that he intended to march north to York and lead his army in person. The same day the council of war decided to put into the field a force of 30 000 men, with 24 000 foot to be drawn mainly from the trained bands and 6 000 horse, to be raised

[19] *Letters and Papers of the Verney Family*, ed. J. Bruce (Camden Society, 56, 1853), 228–9; *Strafforde Letters*, ii.186.

[20] T. Hearne, *A Collection of Curious Discourses*, 2 vols. (1775), ii.90–129. See Figure 2.1, p. 57, this volume.

[21] For the importance of military achievements generally, and the victory at Flodden in particular, in constructing the identity of the Howard family, see S.J. Gunn, D. Grummitt and H. Cools, *War, State and Society in England and the Netherlands 1477–1559* (Oxford: Oxford University Press, 2007), pp. 196–7, 215–22, 230; Walker, *Historical Discourses*, p. 216; HMC, *Various VII. MSS of Sir Hervey Bruce*, pp. 420–1.

primarily from noble and gentry volunteers.[22] This put a very different complexion on the preparations. Hitherto efforts to rally the landowning classes had concentrated on the northern nobility who, in late January, received specific instructions to leave London, return to their estates and 'attend the service and defence of their countrey'.[23] The king's decision to take the field in person, the first monarch to do so since Henry VIII on the expedition to Boulogne in 1544, placed a heavy onus on the nobility to accompany him. With Arundel to the fore, the council of war instructed Lord Privy Seal Manchester and Secretary Windebank to 'peruse the precedents of letters written in the tyme of H8 & Queene Eliz' and draft letters to all noblemen and principal landowners 'to acquaint them with the king's intenccon to goe to York with an army' and 'invite them to shew their particular affeccons'.[24] The two councillors turned to Arundel's protégé, Sir John Borough, for advice and he was able to instruct them that 'kings had usually when they went to make war in their own persons called as many of the nobility to attend upon them as they thought fit'. Borough also provided precedents from Henry VIII's expedition to Calais in 1520. These showed that dukes could each be expected to furnish 26 horse, earls 20 and barons 12, on which basis it was calculated that 'att least 1200 horse' could be raised, 'with no charge at all to his Majestie'.[25]

Signet letters were sent out to each member of the English nobility on 26 January 1639. These established that the Scots were in a state of rebellion, that the king, with the advice of his Privy Council, was about to travel north to confront them and that there was a serious threat of invasion. But the heart of the message was an individual appeal to each nobleman to fulfil his obligation of personal service to his monarch:

> Wee have though fit hereby to give you notice of this our resolucon . . . and . . . to require you to attend our Royall person and standard at our citty of Yorke by the first day of Aprill next ensuing in such equipage and with such forces of horse as your birth, your honor and your interest in the publique safety doe oblidge you unto and as wee doe have reason to expect from you.[26]

The king was reverting to 'ancient' practice and issuing a 'quasi-feudal' summons to the nobility to join him on the field of battle accompanied by their retinues.[27] This was to give his peerage a very prominent role

22 TNA, SP 16/396, pp. 59–61; SP 16/409/106, 107.

23 *Proclamations*, ii.648–50.

24 TNA, SP 16/409/116.

25 Clarendon, *History*, i.153; BL, Add. MS 64,918, fos. 23–4; TNA, SP 16/410/80.

26 TNA, SO1/3, fos. 114–15.

27 Gunn et al., *War State and Society*, pp. 20, 138–42; Stone, *Crisis of the Aristocracy*, pp. 203–4.

in the 1639 campaign, which would go some way towards restoring their battered prestige. But its immediate significance was political rather than military.

The most controversial aspect of the forthcoming campaign was that the king was intending to go to war without having summoned a parliament, for the first time since 1323.[28] Discussion of the matter in the inner circles of government had been somewhat muted. It was raised at the council of war in November 1638 when, according to Cottington, some of the members had warned the king that there was 'no other way'; but he had declared that 'he will not hear of a parliament'.[29] It surfaced again in late January 1639, after the decision had been taken to raise 30 000 men, with no visible means of support. According to Giovanni Giustinian, the Venetian ambassador, councillors had 'jointly urged upon the king, with free and weighty arguments, that amid all these difficulties he ought not to delay any longer to summon a parliament . . . to defend the necessity for the steps taken to his subjects and to obtain from them the necessary contributions'. Charles, however, had 'expressed sharply his displeasure at such advice and showed that by pledging the royal revenues for two years he would obtain enough money to support the army for six months without laying fresh charges on the people'.[30] Northumberland, who was probably one of those urging a summons, remained unconvinced by the king's assurances about supply; but Charles had stuck to his guns and a parliament had been ruled out. However, this still left the problem, identified by Giustinian, that the king lacked a clear mandate for going to war. In the absence of this the response of the peers to the request to attend on the king became a proxy for the votes of parliament. As Hyde later recalled, 'it was thought the drawing all the nobility together in that maner would look more like a union of this nation in the quarrel'.[31]

The linkage between the king's request and a mandate for war put huge pressure on the peers. This was the first time since the forced loan that Charles had appealed to nobles individually to give him their political support. As on the earlier occasion, his request prompted enormous public interest and a good deal of personal soul searching. The crown rallied its forces and used every means at its disposal to secure compliance. Threats were made and assurances were given. The Earl of Manchester warned his son, Lord Mandeville, that he would disinherit him if he did not cooperate and Catholic peers were promised that a display of support now would ensure favour in the future. Holland, Cottington, Goring and other leading courtiers set an example by pledging themselves to attend

[28] Russell, *Fall of the British Monarchies*, p. 82. [29] *Strafforde Letters*, ii.246.
[30] *CSP Ven. 1636–9*, pp. 496–7. [31] TNA, SP 16/410/80; Clarendon, *History*, i.99.

the king at York, accompanied in each case by 20 or more horse. And, as with the loan, Charles himself was closely involved, assuring those who cooperated of his goodwill, but making clear his 'jealousy' of any who refused.[32]

In spite of the pressures, during early February it appeared that the opposition would come out on top. On the 7th Sir John Temple reported that 'it is thought many will refuse to engage themselves in this service', and identified the Earl of Hertford as someone whose response was being particularly closely monitored: 'many eyes are upon him and his example as is conceived will either keep out or drawe in many with him'.[33] A week later it looked as if the whole scheme was about to collapse. News had got out that Viscount Saye and Lord Brooke had refused to cooperate, and there was speculation that 'others have returned in their letters to the king that they find no law for it, and therefore they cannot in conscience do it, and advise the king to take a parliamentary way.'[34] But then, suddenly, within a few days the prospects for the service were turned around. The pressures and assurances from the court began to have an effect, and the king was helped by a change of tactic. After initially letting it be known that he would welcome monetary compositions for performing the service, in order to relieve his hard pressed exchequer, he decided that pledges of personal attendance would have a more positive impact. When the Earl of Bridgewater inquired of his friend Secretary Coke on 13 February which the king would find more acceptable he was told that Charles 'conceiveth that it will suite better both his honour and your lordship's that you should serve him with your men and horses rather than the other way'.[35] Letters of support started to come in significant numbers, promising 10, 12 or 20 horse, in line with the numbers suggested by Borough. Several peers who had been expected to refuse – Hertford, Bedford, Lord Mandeville and the Earl of Warwick among them – pledged their assistance. And Saye and Brooke changed their minds, withdrawing their earlier refusals and undertaking 'to attend his Majesty in any part of this kingdom of England as ordered'. By 19 February Charles was reported to be 'very well pleased'.[36]

The recipients of Charles's letters faced difficult and uncomfortable decisions and, as in the case of the forced loan, the process of working out their responses tells us a good deal about the considerations and assumptions that shaped their political loyalties. Once again the peer about whom

[32] HMC, *Buccleuch*, i.283; TNA, SP 16/410/80; NUL, Clifton MSS, Cl.C 342, 346.
[33] Collins, *Letters*, ii.592–3. [34] TNA, SP 16/412/134; *CSP Ven. 1636–9*, p. 500.
[35] Hunt. L., Ellesmere MS 6600.
[36] *CSP Dom. 1638–9*, pp. 427–79; TNA, SP 16/413/117; HMC, *Buccleuch*, iii.381.

we know most was Edward Lord Montagu. His first instinct, as before, was that as a nobleman he was honour bound to respond loyally to a personal request from the king. He fervently hoped that when it came to it Charles and the Scots would be able to bury their differences and avoid fighting. He was also unhappy about particular aspects of the service. He worried that the early efforts to extract monetary compositions were reminiscent of benevolences and forced loans and 'may be of future ill consequence'; and, as a staunch protestant, he was disturbed by the encouragement being given to Catholics to arm themselves, make special voluntary contributions and demonstrate that they were the king's most loyal subjects.[37] However, like his brother, the Earl of Manchester, who he consulted with every step of the way, Montagu believed that 'if a king command it, wherever his person goes our allegiance ties us to follow him.' Even if the whole exercise eventually proved to be unnecessary, it was important, he insisted, that the king should 'see the readiness and forwardness of his peers and commons to attend [him]'.[38] After much deliberation and consultation – and having fended off his brother's suggestions that he should offer a monetary composition or send one of his sons in his place – on 18 February Montagu wrote to Secretary Coke with a trenchant declaration of his loyalty. 'I am ready to lay down my life and all I have,' he proclaimed, in the name of his allegiance to his monarch and 'birth, honour and interest in the public service'.

> And though I am 76 years old and have some great infirmities upon me, yet (God inabling me) I will rather venture my life then deny to serve his Majesty upon those occasions; and for assistance in this war to serve his Majesty with six horses armed in all points.[39]

Montagu could be fairly confident that Charles would excuse his personal attendance on the grounds of age and health – although he was evidently prepared to go if required, which caused considerable consternation among his children. But, even so, this was ringing affirmation of personal loyalty, which greatly pleased the king when it was communicated to him.[40]

Montagu was excused personal attendance, but he still had to send the six horse he had promised. Here he considered it very important not to be outdone by his fellow peers. There were reports that the king would inspect the horse contingents when they reached York and, as his brother

[37] C. Hibbard, *Charles I and the Popish Plot*, pp. 95, 99–103.
[38] HMC, *Buccleuch*, i.276–9, iii.379–83.
[39] TNA, SP 16/413/22; HMC, *Buccleuch*, i.277, iii.379–80.
[40] For an alternative reading of Montagu's response, see Cope, *Life of a Public Man*, pp. 158–62.

advised him, 'in that show' it was important that he appeared 'as brave and noble as the rest of your dignity'. He therefore spared no expense, equipping his troops with the appropriate uniforms and weapons, in spite of the difficulties in obtaining them because of the sudden demand. The men were duly delivered to York to take their place under the command of his son-in-law, the Earl of Lindsey's son, Lord Willoughby.[41]

The sense of obligation that Montagu displayed when he received a personal summons from the king, and the desire to demonstrate to his fellow nobles that he could dispense the largesse appropriate to his rank, were two of the central considerations that shaped the peers' responses. The wording of his pledge to the king may have been more fulsome than most, but the tenor of his overall response was much more typical of his fellow peers than has generally been supposed. The traditional account emphasises the opposition of Saye and Brooke and the obstructiveness of the majority. Conrad Russell has argued that although the peers' responses, 'with two exceptions, stop short of outright refusal... they indicate a marked lack of enthusiasm'; and Mark Fissel concluded that 'the display of loyalty and unity that Charles hoped for failed to materialize'.[42] However, such conclusions are at odds with the bulk of the replies sent in by the peers and the reaction of the king.

Charles evidently regarded the service as a great success. One of the measures originally contemplated to put pressure on the peers appears to have been an in investigation of noble privileges; but it was made clear in a memorandum in April 1639 that he felt he had been 'so affectionately served by the affections of his nobles' that now was not the time to undertake this. The accepted view in government circles was that 'all the nobility and many other persons of qualitie' had undertaken, 'readily and dutifully to assist'.[43] More to the point this was also a general perception among newsletter writers and commentators. Once the positive responses started to arrive in mid February it was acknowledged, as the Yorkshire diarist Sir Henry Slingsby recorded, that 'the greatest part of the nobility and gentry of this kingdom was personally engaged'.[44] The political elite was apparently united behind the king and Charles had secured the mandate he needed to go to war.

41 HMC, *Buccleuch*, i.278–81, iii.382–4.

42 Russell, *Fall of the British Monarchies*, p. 87; Fissel, *Bishop's Wars*, p. 158. See also M. Schwarz, 'Viscount Saye and Sele, Lord Brooke and aristocratic protest to the First Bishops War', *Canadian Journal of History*, 7 (1972), 19; Gardiner, *History*, ix.11.

43 TNA, SP 16/418/114; PC2/50, fos. 139–40.

44 *The Diary of Sir Henry Slingsby*, ed. D. Parsons (London, 1836), p. 31; HMC, *Various VII*, p. 421; HMC, *Buccleuch*, i.278–9.

Perhaps even more striking than the breadth of cooperation was the level of commitment expressed in the peers' responses. Many of them probably harboured reservations about the service. Like Montagu, they may have felt uneasy about the monetary compositions, the failure to summon parliament and the high profile of the Catholic peers; and such concerns would have reminded them that peers had an obligation to serve their 'country', as well as the king. They probably also felt ill equipped for the service, and had qualms about fighting their northern neighbours. In these circumstances, it was open to them to plead all sorts of excuses as get outs. Yet the majority expressed a readiness to serve, and often did so very enthusiastically. Of the 116 peers who were sent letters, there is a record of the responses of 93. Of these 31 pledged personal attendance on the king at York; a further 50 offered horsemen and/or money; 12 made excuses that ranged from illness, old age, minority, and service abroad to lack of means; and only Saye and Brooke refused outright, although they quickly changed their minds.[45] The high proportion of positive responses can be put down in part to the strength of the lobbying and pressure being applied by the court. It was also widely understood that there was a legal obligation on peers to attend the king when he took the field in person to encounter an invasion, as the second thoughts of Saye and Brooke indicated.[46] But many of the responses went well beyond what was strictly required. The king's plea for personal assistance appears to have unlocked a whole range of deeply felt reflections on what it meant to be a nobleman and what this implied in terms of loyalty to the monarch.

The peers were very conscious that the eyes of the public were upon them and their declarations were carefully crafted, often, apparently, after a period of soul searching and consultation similar to Montagu's. Lord Fauconberg drew up what he described as 'a free declaration of my fidelity and dewty', implicitly responding to those who might suggest that he was acting in response to pressure from court. He then delivered a fulsome declaration that there was 'not a subject more forward to draw his sword and spend his best bloode in his Majesty's defence'.[47] Lord Eure, aged 60, lame and bereft of means, nonetheless 'freely' offered his 'estate, howse and life to serve and be commanded by his Majestie . . . consideringe all that I am or have is his Majestie's due'. And Lord Vaux, one of the Catholic peers of whose participation Montagu

45 See Appendix 1, based mainly on TNA, SP 16/413/117. For the list of peers to whom letters were sent, see TNA, SO1, fos. 114–15; SP16/396, fos. 76–7.

46 Schwarz, 'Aristocratic protest', 32; see also the responses of the Earl of Cleveland and Lord Eure: TNA, SP 16/412/98, 127i.

47 TNA, SP 16/412/126.

so disapproved, announced his 'ready and forward heart to lay down my life and fortune at his sacred feet'.[48] For some peers the king's request called to mind the martial achievements of their forbears. Lord Clifford – whose summons to serve had come the previous July when the king was preparing the defence of the northern borders – presented his 'vows of loyalty and obedience' and declared that 'the same loyal blood of my ancestors runs still in my veins which they were never sparing of when their sovereigns commanded them to fight for them'; while Lord Abergavenny voiced his regret at the physical incapacity that meant he was not able 'to follow the steps of my ancestors'.[49] Others simply expressed their gratitude at being given the opportunity to serve. The Earl of Huntingdon esteemed it 'a great favoure', and for the Northamptonshire Catholic Lord Brudenell it offered a rare and precious chance to gain the king's approval, which he described as 'a thing I ayme at most in this world's occasions'.[50] Others, like Lord Herbert of Cherbury, hoped that they would not just be able to attend and provide horse, but also take on a military command.[51]

In the event the majority of these peers were not required to deliver on their promises of attendance. Some of them ended up paying compositions; others found substitutes or negotiated alternative ways to secure get outs. In the end it appears that only 15 of the so-called 'voluntary lords' eventually turned up to the muster at York.[52] However, this did not detract from the success of the service. The peers had furnished him with a series of powerful, semi-public, testaments of their loyalty at the moment when he most needed their political support. They had also gone at least two-thirds of the way toward providing the 1200 horse that was expected of them.[53] And, along with the noble councillors and commanders, and numerous gentleman 'volunteers' who travelled north, they provided sufficient attendance to enable the king to maintain something approaching a 'full court' while he was at York and Newcastle, which gave his cause the legitimacy that he was seeking.[54] Charles was suitably appreciative. He thanked the 'voluntary lords' fulsomely on several

[48] *Ibid.*, SP 16/412/127,116. See also the responses of Abergavenny, St Albans and Baltimore and the pledge by Lord Audley to return immediately from Italy to attend the king at York: SP16/412/78, 128; 16/415/80; for emphasis on the 'free hearte and willing minde', see Worcester's letter: SP 16/412/117.

[49] *Strafforde Letters*, ii.214–15; TNA, SP 16/412/59.

[50] TNA, SP 16/412/125, 141. [51] TNA, SP 16/412/77.

[52] HMC, *Rutland*, i.504–8; R. Warner. *Epistolary Curiosities . . . Illustrative of the Herbert family* (London, 1818), 199. The 'voluntary lords' were Berkshire, Bristol, Brooke, Devonshire, Dunsmore, Howard of Charlton, North, Northampton, Poulett, Rutland, St John, Saye, Savile, Strange and Westmoreland.

[53] Fissel, *Bishops Wars*, p. 160. [54] Clarendon, *History*, i.153–4.

occasions and also granted them the privilege of determining for themselves which commanders their troops of cavalry should serve under.[55]

The emphasis on noble service and loyalty continued throughout the preparations for the First Bishops War and the campaign itself. In many respects this was a throwback to the expeditions of Henry VIII's reign. The recruiting of cavalry contingents took place in much the same way as it had done 100 years earlier, with noblemen drawing on personal authority and ties of clientage to summon tenants, household servants and local gentry.[56] Lord Clifford's regiment was enlisted in this fashion, calling on the manpower of his northern estates and the prestige of the Clifford connection among local gentry.[57] The Earl of Newcastle's troop, drawn from his neighbours in Nottinghamshire and Derbyshire, was said to have been made up entirely of 'gentlemen of quality, many of great estates who provide some 6 and 3 horses a peece att their owne charge, such is their love and respecte they beare unto his lordship'.[58] These were classic demonstrations of what a loyal and dutiful 'ancient nobility' could achieve for their king, in the manner that the earl prescribed in his advices.

The prospect of serving alongside their monarch in battle stirred in many an anticipation of the chivalric adventures that they had grown up with. Lord Clifford went on campaign wearing the gilded jousting armour that he had inherited from his uncle, the redoubtable 3rd Earl of Cumberland, one of the leading lights of the Elizabethan chivalric revival. A number of 'Cavalier' poets wrote verses for the occasion, highlighting the sense of 'companionship in arms', which was such a prominent feature of chivalric culture;[59] while several nobles followed the king's example and had their portraits painted in martial style by Van Dyck. These provide a striking visual realisation of the excitement of going on campaign, particularly a pair of portraits of Mountjoy Blount, Earl of Newport, one showing him purposeful and composed against the background of a military encampment, the other with his companion in arms, George Goring, being dressed by a page prior to taking the field.[60] The sense

[55] Warner, *Epistolary Curiosities*, p. 199; HMC, *Rutland*, i.511.

[56] Gunn et al., *War, State and Society*, pp. 138–42, 200–3.

[57] R.T. Spence, 'Henry Lord Clifford and the First Bishops War', *Northern History*, 31 (1995), 142–8.

[58] Bodl.L., Rawlinson MS B 210, fos. 37–8. For further insights into the honour transactions that accompanied the formation of Newcastle's regiment, see BL, Add. MS, 70,499, fo. 239; HMC, *Various VII*, pp. 421–2; NUL, Cl.C. 342–3.

[59] Spence, 'Lord Clifford', 148; R. Wilcher, *The Writing of Royalism 1628–1660* (Cambridge: Cambridge University Press, 2001), pp. 29–32.

[60] Those painted, all, it appears, *c.* 1639, included Henry Lord Maltravers, Arundel's son, Philip Lord Herbert, Pembroke's son, Thomas Lord Wentworth, Cleveland's son,

of embarking on a great and noble enterprise was enhanced by the presence of the Earl Marshal, who travelled north with a staff drawn from the College of Heralds. Borough accompanied him as Garter King of Arms, to advise on noble etiquette and precedence, and ended up acting as clerk to the Privy Council when Thomas Meautys fell ill; Edward Walker, Chester herald, acted as secretary to the council of war; Edward Norgate, another Arundel protégé and Windsor herald, filled the post of clerk to the signet; and Sir William Le Neve, Clarenceux, and George Owen, York herald, were there to perform the traditional heralds' duties of recording promotions to knighthood, carrying messages between the combatants, arranging safe passage and exchange of prisoners and keeping a record of deeds of martial prowess.[61]

The actual campaign in the First Bishops War was largely an inglorious failure. After a standoff with the Scots army near Kelso in early June, Charles withdrew, believing that he was facing a superior force, and agreed to negotiate. But the 'voluntary lords' and gentleman 'volunteers' stuck by him to the close of the campaign. They pitched their tents alongside the royal pavilion when the king set up his camp at Birks, near Berwick, on the 30 May; several of their troops of horse served under Holland and Goring in the limited skirmishing that did take place; they rushed to arm themselves early on the morning of 5 June when the Scots arrayed themselves within sight of the English camp; and they did not finally depart until Charles ordered the disbanding of the army on 22 June.[62]

The English peerage may have achieved little in military terms on the 1639 campaign; but their high profile and the readiness with which they had adapted to the martial roles expected of members of the 'ancient nobility', went some way towards restoring the prestige and self-confidence of the order. The fact that for the first time in nearly 100 years they were taking the field alongside their king, led by their Earl Marshal, and accompanied by their retinues, in the manner of a quasi-feudal royal host, was a powerful demonstration of their continuing military and political relevance. This had been obscured for much of the 1620s

Philip Lord Wharton and the Earl of Holland. The Newport & Goring portraits were executed soon after the two of them received their cavalry commissions: Barnes et al., *Van Dyck*, pp. 422, 438, 535, 561–3, 574, 612, 613.

61 *CSP Dom. 1639*, pp. 116, 172, 222–3, 242–4; CA, Heralds, vol. II, fos. 600, 733.

62 Cust, *Charles I. A Political Life*, pp. 244–7; Bodl.L., Rawlinson B.210, fos. 40, 47; HMC, *Rutland*, i.515; *Six North Country Diaries*, ed. J.C. Hodgson (Surtees Soc., 118, 1910), pp. 27–8. When the Scots appeared on 5 June, Charles, again following a traditional chivalric 'script', was said to have taken out his telescope, surveyed the Scottish forces, then coolly declared 'come let us goe to supper [i.e. breakfast]; the number is not considerable': Rawlinson B.210, fo. 47.

and 1630s amid the scandals of sale of honours and predictions of noble decline. Now the peerage was being pushed to the fore, once again, and made highly visible as the natural leaders of the political nation.

Amid all these demonstrations of noble loyalty and authority, however, there was one episode that pointed to continuing divisions within the order. This was the application of the 'Military Oath', devised by Charles and Arundel as a loyalty oath for the nobles and the army. The aim was probably twofold. The king, as we have seen, set considerable store by oaths as pledges of fealty and obedience, and the 'Military Oath' appeared to offer reassurance as he was about to embark on a campaign in which the support of many of his subjects was still uncertain. In an affirmation of virtually unconditional loyalty, the oath taker was required to swear,

> constantly and cheerfully, even to the uttermost hazard of my lyfe and fortunes, [to] constantly oppose all seditions, rebellions, consperacyes, covenants, conjurations, treasons whatsoever against his Royall dignity, crowne or person, raysed or sett up under what pretence or culler whatsoever.[63]

The other objective of the oath was to close off a legal loophole in the king's letter of summons to his nobles, which clearly specified that he was seeking their attendance in a defensive war, against the threat of a Scots invasion. Should he require them to cross the border and march with him into Scotland, as was anticipated by some, then the oath appeared to offer the means of commanding their support.[64]

The limitations on the nobles' pledges of service had been highlighted in the responses of Saye and Brooke. These two peers were among the leaders of what was being referred to in court circles as the 'puritan party' who were already engaged in potentially treasonous contacts with the Covenanters and were looking for opportunities to disrupt the war effort. Their chosen tactic, as with the forced loan and ship money was to try to provoke legal challenges.[65] Initially they had attempted to question the king's summons to peers on the grounds that it was illegal except with the consent of parliament; but this proved unsustainable. As Saye was forced to acknowledge, the king did have a legal right to command his nobles' attendance when he was leading an army to counter the threat of invasion. What he did not have the right to do – according to the precedents from the twelfth and thirteenth centuries with which Saye armed himself – was to demand attendance beyond the borders of the kingdom in what could be construed as an offensive war.[66] The undertaking 'to attend

63 HMC, *Rutland*, i.508. 64 Schwarz, 'Aristocratic protest', 31–2.
65 TNA, SP 16/413/120; Adamson, *The Noble Revolt*, pp. 36–9; Cust, *The Forced Loan*, p. 334.
66 Schwarz, 'Aristocratic protest', 32.

his Majestie's person within any part of the kingdom of England' that the two peers eventually gave was carefully formulated to highlight this distinction; and they were still drawing attention to it in April when they arrived at York with the other 'voluntary lords'. The Earl of Rutland recorded being approached by them and told that 'they would goe so farr as the confynes of England upon the king's command to defend the realme from invasion. But to invade Scotland ther lordships knew no law for to warrant the sam'.[67]

Charles and Arundel were well aware of the opposition they faced and the 'Military Oath' was designed to flush out 'Puritan party' sympathisers and counteract their efforts to disrupt the service.[68] It was presented to the 'voluntary lords', without warning, at a council meeting at York on 21 April. Rutland and Northampton took the oath promptly, but when it came to Saye's turn he refused, once again declaring that while he was willing 'to adventure his lyfe and fortunes for the defence of this kindome of England . . . to goe and kill a man in Scotland he was not satisfyed of the lawfulness thereof'. The oath was then taken by Lords North, Poulett, Howard of Charlton and Savile, but refused by Brooke. Charles was furious. The two peers were kept behind and interrogated, then imprisoned at York and finally sent back to their counties under house arrest.[69] Reports of their defiance spread quickly and several commentators predicted that this would provoke widespread opposition.[70] But this did not materialise. The impact of the protest was diluted, partly because the public's interest came to focus almost entirely on the military preparations for the coming campaign,[71] but also because Charles and Arundel moved quickly to isolate the two lords and ensure the loyalty of the majority.

On the evening of the 21 April Arundel had an interview with the Earl of Bristol, who had been excused from the oath taking on the grounds of illness. Bristol fended off the Lord General's requests to take the oath now and, at the same time, was able to give what was described as 'good satisfaction' for doing so. What this involved was not specified, but it is likely that it was based on the arguments pressed by the Earl of Northampton, 'in the name of divers lords', a day or two later. These focussed on the 'ambiguity in the words of the oath', and the implications of the

67 HMC, *Rutland*, i.507.

68 See the discussions in council during February and March 1639 about how best to deal with them: TNA, SP 16/413/120.

69 HMC, *Rutland*, i.507; HMC, *4th Report, House of Lords MSS* (1874), p. 23; TNA, SP 16/418/114; *Lismore Papers*, iv.21.

70 *CSP Ven. 1636–9*, p. 536; TNA, SP16/418/30.

71 *Strafforde Letters*, ii.351; *CSP Dom. 1639*, pp. 96–9.

undertaking 'to mayntayne the war with the uttermost hazard of life and fortune . . . whether the king be in person or not.[72] Whatever 'free' and voluntary undertakings the peers had been prepared to make in their declarations of allegiance, they were evidently wary of subscribing to legally binding oaths that might oblige them to sacrifice their lives and fortunes in circumstances that went beyond the king's original plea for assistance. Charles and Arundel were quick to acknowledge the legitimacy of their concerns and the next day the earl announced that the king would offer a fuller 'explanation' of the oath. Two days later it was amended to remove the words 'uttermost' and 'fortunes'.[73] This new wording was incorporated into an official account of the proceedings on the 21st drawn up by the council clerk and alongside was recorded the king's gloss: that 'he took . . . in very good part their cheerfulness and readyness in taking the said oath' and that it was intended

> to extend and relate only to their faithfull and loyal serving of him in this present action as they had expressed upon his Majestye's letters of summons to them requiring their attendance.[74]

This represented a very significant climb down on the part of the king and his Lord General. They had watered down the unconditional support implied in the original oath and abandoned the attempt to get the peers to commit themselves to service outside England. Such was the importance of the 'voluntary lords', and all that they represented, that they evidently felt it was a concession that had to be made; and it served its purpose in maintaining a largely united front among the peerage for the duration of the First Bishops War.

The support, or at least acquiescence, that Charles enjoyed from the nobility over this period was impressive. Saye and Brooke had defied him openly; but others associated with the 'Puritan party', such as Warwick, Mandeville, Bedford and Hertford, had kept their heads down and, in public at least, cooperated with the king.

He had obtained his political mandate for going to war, recruited large numbers of cavalry volunteers and secured an ample attendance at his northern courts and camps, which had remained loyal and largely united up to the end of the campaign. The failure of the First Bishops War was not due to a lack of support from the peerage, but the king's own military

[72] HMC, *Rutland*, i.508; *Lismore Papers*, iv.21; Warner, *Epistolary Curiosities*, p. 198; HMC, *Buccleuch*, iii.386.

[73] TNA, SP 16/415/116.

[74] Schwarz, 'Aristocratic protest', 29–30; TNA, SP 16/420/141. A decision was later taken to omit this account from the council register; but it was still communicated quickly and widely via the news networks: SP16/420/109.

inexperience and loss of nerve when he confronted the Scots army outside Berwick. The support he commanded among the nobles was a striking contrast to the last occasion on which he had made a personal appeal to them, at the outset of the forced loan. On that occasion, as we have seen, the opposition to the service by some 15 peers set an example that proved to be a continuous obstacle to successful collection among gentry and freeholders. This time, through a combination of courtly pressures and well-calculated concessions when it appeared that the opposition might gain the upper hand, the appearance of a nobility largely united behind their king was maintained. The first substantive test since Charles had set out, in 1629, to cultivate the loyalty and support of his nobility had been passed.

The sense of obligation and allegiance displayed by the peerage in 1639 offers an interesting perspective on the effectiveness of the king's efforts to cultivate political loyalty through encouraging attendance of peers at court. Expressions of support for the king's cause were spread across the spectrum. Among those who can be classified as leading courtiers and regular courtiers 29 out of the 30 whose responses are known either attended on the king in the north or pledged money or horse; for occasional courtiers the figure was 20 out of 23; and even for 'country' peers it stood at 32 out of 40 (80 per cent). This proportion was boosted by Catholic peers who responded with alacrity to all the talk of a once-in-a-generation opportunity to demonstrate their loyalty to the king.[75] Out of 17 of the openly Catholic peers 14 either pledged their support or attended the expedition in person, a number of them delivering fulsome pledges of their loyalty and desire to serve along the lines of Lord Brudenell's.[76] The conspicuous loyalty displayed by those associated with the court, both regular and occasional courtiers, does suggest that Charles's policy had had a positive impact. However, the favourable response by 'country' peers also demonstrates that it was not the only reason for peers coming out and demonstrating their loyalty. Coupled with this – and arguably of even greater importance – was the force of Charles's appeal to individuals to serve him in person. This touched on the peerage's sense of the way in which their own honour and reputation was bound up with personal service to their monarch, often almost regardless, it would seem, of whether or not they were regular courtiers. Certainly this is what the responses of the Catholic peers, and individuals

75 For these figures, see Appendix 1, 'English Peers at Court, 1625–40'; Hibbard, *Popish Plot*, pp. 95, 99–103.

76 See the letters from Abergavenny, Vaux, Worcester, Fauconberg, Eure and St Albans: TNA, SP 16/412/78, 116, 117, 126, 127, 127i, 128.

like Lord Montagu, implies. As we shall see this was to continue to be the king's strongest card when it came to drawing on the political support of the peerage in 1642.

The Great Council of Peers

The military setback of the First Bishops War did not diminish Charles's determination to defeat the Scots and he signalled his desire to continue the war with the decision to summon the Short Parliament in December 1639. Wentworth (now made Earl of Strafford) had been recalled from Ireland in September and with the council of war set about planning a new campaign. This required a force of 35 000 men which it was estimated would cost well over £1 000 000. In the absence of alternative sources of supply, the council advised the king to call a parliament and this time he agreed.[77]

The meeting of the Short Parliament brought out into the open the political fault lines within the peerage in a way that had threatened to happen, but been narrowly avoided, in early 1639. On this earlier occasion, as we have seen, Charles was able to avert the threat of non-cooperation by reminding the peers of their duty of military service and focusing on their personal allegiance to their monarch. This was much harder to do while a parliament was in session. Here they were constantly reminded of their obligations to the 'public' and the expectation that they would work with the Commons to promote the welfare of the 'country'. In these circumstances, it was more difficult for Charles to maintain the united front that he sought.

The main source of contention in the Short Parliament was supply. From the opening of the assembly on 13 April 1640 the crown spokesmen pressed the Commons to give priority to the grant of subsidies; but they offered little in the way of concrete concessions in return and the bulk of the house insisted on pursuing the grievances that had mounted up during the 1630s. On the evening of 23 April Charles summoned a council meeting at which it was widely anticipated that he would dissolve the parliament. But instead he was persuaded by Strafford to keep it going and to take his case directly to the Lords. This was a risky strategy because the Commons was always likely to regard any attempt to initiate supply in the upper house as a breach of privilege. But it was a measure of the urgency of the situation and the king's confidence in the loyalty of his peers.[78]

77 Collins, *Letters*, ii.623; Cust, *Charles I. A Political Life*, pp. 250–1.
78 Cust, *Charles I. A Political Life*, pp. 252–6; Russell, *Fall of the British Monarchies*, p. 111.

Charles appeared in the upper house 'unexpected' on the morning of 24 April and delivered a short speech picking up where he had left off in 1629. The peers were informed of the urgency of the need for supply and the obstructiveness of the Commons, and then reminded of the promise he had made to the two houses to meet again in the winter to debate grievances. He urged them 'to consider your owne honour and mine' and indicated that they should take the initiative on supply. This tactic of appealing to the Lords' sense of honour – not only his and theirs, but also the honour of the nation – was to become a regular refrain in the following months. It was a line of argument to which they were very responsive.[79]

The king's sudden request was introduced into a house where the atmosphere was already tense because of disagreements between the lay peers and bishops. It led to the liveliest and most fractious debate since the proceedings over the Petition of Right in 1628. The privy councillors proposed that 'his Majesty's supply should have precedency', with Strafford homing in on the issue of their 'trust' in the king's promise of another session and Dorset warning that the Scots were about to take the field and that 'if we should disagree it will double their armie'. This was quickly countered by a proposal from Saye, Hertford and Mandeville that before going any further they should 'meete in conference' with the Commons. The debate then resolved itself into an argument between those supporting the council proposal – who highlighted the emergency and the need to respect the king's honour and take him at his word – and those who first wanted a conference with the Commons, on the grounds that the most important consideration was to preserve unity. Eventually the house divided and voted by 57 to 25 to give priority to the resolution on supply.[80]

For once it is possible to get a clear idea of how the Lords voted. A list was compiled – presumably for Charles's perusal – naming the 25 peers who 'wear against the kinge' in this debate and this can be set alongside the record of attendance to reveal the alignments.[81] Leading the opposition to the resolution on supply were 12 peers who were associated with the 'Puritan party' in their opposition to the Scottish war, or else had formerly opposed the forced loan: Bedford, Hertford, Essex, Lincoln, Warwick, Bolingbroke, Saye and Sele, Mandeville, Brooke, Saville, Howard of Escrick and Wharton. But supporting them were a further

[79] *LJ*, iv.67.

[80] *Proceedings of the Short Parliament*, pp. 71–9; Russell, *Fall of the British Monarchies*, pp. 103–4, 111–13.

[81] TNA, SP 16/451/39; *LJ*, iv.65–6.

13 peers, including several who were far from being natural opponents of the crown, notably the Earls of Rutland, Southampton, Clare and Bath and Lords Dunsmore, Lovelace, North and Montagu.[82] Montagu spoke up in the debate to urge that 'the question is the manner of the carriage lest there be a breach with the House [of] C.' and this concern may well have been what counted for most among the others in this group.[83] Their readiness to oppose the king on this issue was an indication of how seriously members of the peerage took their responsibility to maintain the unity and welfare of the 'country' and the 'public'.

Just as informative was the line up in favour of the resolution. The remaining attendance on this day consisted of 17 bishops, 16 privy councillors and a further 26 lay peers, of whom all but two voted to give precedence to supply. Several of the lay peers – notably Huntingdon, Northampton, Maynard and Herbert of Cherbury – were to emerge later in the year, at the time of the Great Council of Peers, as particularly staunch supporters of the maintenance of the king's honour and the continuation of the Scottish war; and in the longer term they were to provide the basis for a royalist party in the Lords. But, perhaps, the most interesting of this group was Bristol. In the debates he had followed the line of those opposing the resolution, warning that 'it is not only monie will doe, but the harts must be had to with the mony'; however, in the division he either abstained or voted with the king. This was indicative of the tacking back and forth which had been evident at York in April 1639 and which was to make the earl a particularly effective intermediary in the coming months.[84]

The king won his vote in the upper house, but it did him little good. As had been anticipated, the Commons took offence at the Lords' meddling in supply and declared it a breach of the privilege. The peers in turn reacted angrily and insisted that they were simply discharging their responsibility as 'the Great Counsell of the Kingdome' to warn of impending danger. This time they voted almost unanimously that they had not breached parliamentary privilege.[85] Meanwhile the Commons ploughed on with grievances and the crown's eventual concession, in the form of the abolition of ship money, came too late to effect a change of course.

82 The others were Deincourt, Nottingham, Paget, Roberts and Willoughby of Parham.
83 *Proceedings of the Short Parliament*, p. 72.
84 *Ibid.*, p. 77. The earl had made a remarkable comeback since being forced into political exile after opposing Buckingham in 1626. During the northern campaign in 1639 he was also to the fore in advising the king of the need for a parliament and promoting the Treaty of Berwick: 'John Digby, 1st Earl of Bristol (1580–1653)', *Oxf.DNB*.
85 *Proceedings of the Short Parliament*, pp. 84–9.

On 5 May Charles moved to a dissolution and addressed the Lords in very similar terms to 1629. Once again he laid the blame at the door of 'some few cunning and ill-affectioned men' who had persuaded the Commons to ignore his warnings and pleas. For the lords he had only praise and gratitude. He acknowledged their 'affection' in supporting the resolution on supply, then thanked them for 'the care you have had of my honour and affairs, desiring you to go on to assist for the maintaining of government and the liberties of the people'.[86] This theme of an implicit compact between the king and his peers was spelt out further in the declaration he issued after the dissolution. He regarded them, he explained,

> as persons in rank and degree nearest to the royal throne, and who, having received honour from him and his royal progenitors, he doubted not would, for those and many other reasons, be moved in honour and dutiful affection to his person and crown.[87]

Charles was just as desirous as he had been in 1629 of keeping his peers on-side and continued to emphasise that he regarded them as the principal supporters of his monarchy. But he could not overlook the fact that on a crucial test of loyalty 25 of them had voted against him. The fault lines of the late 1620s were re-emerging and it was once more becoming clear how seriously nobles took their obligations to the 'public' and the 'country'. Where the issues were about honour and personal service, the king could be confident of their support; but where the unity and welfare of the nation was involved peers felt much more torn. An important part of the political struggle over the coming months, then, as Charles readily appreciated, was to keep the issue of honour at the top of the agenda.

The peers played a much more limited role in the Second Bishops War than they had done in 1639. The Scots army crossed the border into England on 17 August 1640 and defeated the advance guard of the English army at Newburn on the 28 August, before the peers could be mobilised. Charles only announced his intention to travel to York on 16 August and the summons to northern nobles to repair to their estates and take up arms under the terms of their ancient tenures was not issued until the 20th. For the 1640 campaign, then, most nobles stayed at home.[88] However, in the aftermath the Privy Council and the king turned to them to rescue the crown from political disaster.

The news of the defeat at Newburn plunged London into political turmoil. Secretary Windebank described the 'danger' as 'the greatest

[86] *LJ*, iv.81. [87] Rushworth, ii.1163.
[88] Fissel, *Bishops Wars*, pp. 50–61, 212–13; *Proclamations*, ii.731.

that hath threatened this state ever since the Conquest'. There were fears that the rioting that had accompanied the dissolution of the Short Parliament in May would now escalate into full-scale insurrection. It was reported that a 'knot' of 'ill-affected' peers was meeting in the capital to demand a recall of parliament. There was even talk, as John Adamson has emphasised, of these dissident peers mounting a military coup, with the support of the city's trained bands who were about to hold their annual muster. Steps were taken to fortify Whitehall and evacuate the queen and the royal children. On top of all this, the king required the Privy Council to raise £40 000 immediately to enable him to hold back the Scots. Councillors were on the verge of panic, but they managed to keep functioning and on 2 September came up with a proposal for regaining the political initiative.[89]

They were asked to advise on raising money and manpower to counter the Scots and reconcile the king to his people. The obvious solution was a summons of parliament, and this was what several councillors initially advised. But then Lord Privy Seal Manchester – probably after consulting Sir John Borough about precedents – came up with the novel proposal of summoning a 'Great Council of Peers'.[90] This had happened on numerous occasions in the early Tudor period, when Henry VII and Henry VIII had summoned great councils as precursors to a meeting of parliament or a decision to go to war.[91] But the precedent Manchester had in mind was from Edward III's reign, in 1337, when, he argued it had 'raised great sums of money without a parliament and assisted the king'. The deliberations of such an assembly could also be regarded as a proxy for a parliament. They constituted 'the council of the kingdom, *consiliarii nati*', whose collective wisdom and experience was such, Manchester claimed, that 'the kingdom will follow'. Once on the table, the Lord Privy Seal's proposal became the favoured course of action. Several councillors seized on it as a way of escaping a whole range of problems. Arundel was predictably enthusiastic, describing it as 'the only way, the best way and the shortest way'. Others, notably Laud, were convinced that a parliament would have to be summoned in the end; but, in the meantime, they accepted that the Council of Peers could be an effective stopgap. Their collective advice was that a 'generall

89 Bodl.L., Clarendon State Papers, vol. 19, 1418; Adamson, *Noble Revolt*, pp. 51–72; Russell, *Fall of the British Monarchies*, p. 147; TNA, SP 16/466/28.

90 *Hardwicke SP*, ii.168. Manchester had consulted Borough in January 1639 on the summons of nobles to York and the herald was one of those deputed to travel north immediately after the meeting to explain the proposal to the king.

91 P. Holmes, 'The Great Council in the reign of Henry VII', *EHR*, 101 (1986), 840–862; P. Holmes, 'The last Tudor Great Councils', *HJ*, 33 (1990), 1–22.

counsell' was the most likely means of 'resisting this dangerous invasion and uniting of your Majesty and your subjects'. At the very least, they explained, it would allow the king to regain some of the political initiative by ensuring that credit for summoning a parliament was given 'to your owne lords, or rather to yourself by their common advice', rather than to 'the rebels'. Borough, and the council clerk, Edward Nicholas, were then dispatched to York to explain the scheme to the king.[92]

In the meantime, the 'ill-affected' lords were drawing up a direct challenge to the king's authority in the form of what came to be known as the Twelve Peers Petition. Drafted on the advice of Bedford's cousin and leading adviser, Oliver St John, with the intention of forcing Charles to summon a parliament, this was put together in a series of meetings in the last week of August after it became known that the Scots had crossed the border. The bulk of the petition rehearsed a familiar litany of complaint: the grievances of the 1630s, the increase of popery, the threat of an Irish army being brought to England and, above all, the dangers to which the king and kingdom were exposed by the whole misguided enterprise of the Scottish campaign. It then called for parliament to meet, not only to remedy 'the great grievances of your people', but also to bring to justice the 'authors and counsellors' of the present policy and ensure that 'the present war may be composed by your majesty's wisdom, without bloodshed'. The language was suitably deferential, but there was an implicit ultimatum. St John had discovered that, according to a precedent provided by the Oxford Parliament of 1258, a body of 12 peers could summon a parliament of their own volition if the monarch refused to do so. This was the threat that now hung over the king.[93]

The petition was signed at Bedford House on the 28 August, but was kept under wraps until it was presented to Charles in York on 3–4 September. Its timing was highly opportune. It reached the king as he and his councillors there were still trying to come to terms with the defeat at Newburn. To judge by the pessimistic tone of the despatches being sent to Windebank by Sir Henry Vane, the secretary of state attending on Charles at York, there were already those in the royal entourage who were contemplating having to summon parliament and reach a compromise settlement with the Scots.[94] The king was facing the prospect of a humiliating and dishonourable climb down when he was rescued, quite suddenly, by the arrival of the council's advice from London.

92 *Hardwicke SP*, ii.168–70; *Clarendon SP*, ii.97–8; TNA, SP 16/466/11, 12.
93 Adamson, *Noble Revolt*, pp. 46–8, 56–8; Russell, *Fall of the British Monarchies*, pp. 49–1.
94 TNA, SP 16/465/50; 466/2, 30, 54; C.S.R. Russell, *Unrevolutionary England* (London: Hambledon Press, 1990), p. 254.

As he and his immediate advisers were sitting down to contemplate their response to the Twelve Peers Petition on 5 September, the council delegation appeared and was quickly ushered in to explain the proposal for the 'Council of Peers'. The king adopted it immediately. The crucial matter of where and when it should assemble was quickly decided. The Privy Council had advised a meeting in London, but Charles plumped for York, and convening it as soon as possible (in less than three weeks) so that he could more effectively confront his peers with the danger presented by the Scots.[95] This was a dramatic, and highly effective, riposte to the Twelve Peers Petition. With one bound it appeared that he had freed himself from the threat to his authority and regained the political initiative. In the reply to the petition, drafted on the same day, he could barely conceal a note of triumph.

> Before the receipt of this petition his Majesty well foresaw the danger that threatens himself and crowns; and therefore resolved by the 24th of this month at York to summon all the peers, and with them to consult what in this case is fittest to be done for his own honour and safety of the kingdom, where they with the rest may offer anything that may conduce to these ends.[96]

The 'petitioner peers' were wrong footed by Charles's initiative, but they were far from defeated. At first there was a rumour that they were planning to organise a boycott of the Council of Peers. This was abandoned as it became apparent that they were divided on the issue of whether or not to support it; but pressure for a parliament continued. Copies of the Twelve Peers Petition were widely circulated and the number of signatories rose to 23. This took their support well beyond the ranks of those who were normally regarded as the 'ill-affected' to include Rutland, Bath, North and Lovelace who had joined them in the vote against the resolution on supply. They even achieved the considerable coup of getting a privy councillor to sign, in the person of the Earl of Pembroke, the Lord Chamberlain.[97]

The Privy Council counterattacked by lobbying assiduously. Bedford and Hertford, two of the ringleaders of the petition, were summoned before them and persuaded – as a matter of personal service to the king – to cooperate with the Great Council.[98] The Privy Council also urged Charles to 'declare the calling of a parliament that he may have the honour of it himself'. Charles appears to have recognised the force of

[95] TNA, SP 16/466/28, 28i, 54.
[96] *Ibid.*, SP 16/465/16. [97] Adamson, *Noble Revolt*, pp. 520–1.
[98] *Clarendon SP*, ii.110–12, 115, 120. Bristol gave a characteristically evasive response, reportedly saying that 'he likes not the petition, nor will meddle', but signing it nonetheless: Adamson, *Noble Revolt*, p. 567, n. 188.

this advice; but he refused to be rushed. He wanted to make it absolutely clear that he, and he alone, was in control of the decision by announcing it at the last possible moment.[99]

Meanwhile, with the encouragement of Strafford, the king was coming to believe that the defeat at Newburn was no more than a temporary setback. With the backing of the still growing army at York he believed that he could carry the fight to the Scots and defeat them. The key was securing enough money to prevent the army from disbanding, and he had high hopes that this would be provided by the peers.[100] He also looked to them to rally political opinion in support of the war. There were already indications that, in some quarters, the Twelve Peers Petition was regarded as 'a stab in the back', undermining the war effort and exposing the nation to humiliation at the hands of the Covenanters.[101] The crucial consideration here was 'honour' – both the king's own and the nation's – and this was something that was always likely to command sympathy in an assembly of peers. Hyde later speculated that one of the main motives for calling the assembly was that 'it was conceived that the honour of the king and kingdom being so visibly upon the stage those branches of honour which could not outlive the root would undoubtedly rescue and preserve it'.[102] Charles appears to have been banking on just such a response.

For the duration of its proceedings, which lasted from 24 September to 27 October, the Great Council at York became the main focus of attention for the political nation. In spite of the attempted boycott, some 63 lay peers attended the first day of proceedings and most of them appear to have remained in attendance to the end. This compared favourably with the 70 to 80 peers who were in regular attendance in the House of Lords during the Short Parliament.[103] Newsletter writers and commentators covered the proceedings as if they were a parliament, and Sir John Borough, in his capacity as Garter King of Arms, kept an extensive, if sometimes rather impenetrable, record of the debates.[104] In spite of this,

99 TNA, SP 16/467/75, 101, 135. 100 Gardiner, *History*, ix.202–4.

101 *Clarendon SP*, ii.115; Russell, *Fall of the British Monarchies*, p. 150; Adamson, *Noble Revolt*, p. 87; TNA, SP 16/470/17.

102 Clarendon, *History*, i.193.

103 TNA, SP 16/466/42, pp. 37–8; J.B. Crummett, 'The Lay Peers in Parliament 1640–1644' (University of Manchester PhD, 1970), p. 147; *LJ*, iv.*passim*. For a letter signed by 59 peers on 25 September, see Devon Record Office, Drake of Colyton MSS, 1700/M/C/P/17. For the pressures on the Earl of Bridgewater to stay to the end, see Hunt.L., Ellesmere MS, EL 6582–3.

104 Borough's record of proceedings is BL, Harleian MS 456, transcribed, although with some notable inaccuracies in *Hardwicke SP*, ii.208–98. I have referenced the Hardwicke version where this is accurate, but otherwise referred back to the original. For newsletter

the proceedings have received relatively limited coverage from historians, and those who have studied them have come up with very mixed verdicts.

Hyde, in his *History of the Rebellion* saw the council as a disaster, deflecting the king from what should have been his policy after Newburn, which was to fight on. The presence of large numbers of peers at York, 'who had no mind to the war and as little devotion to the court', simply produced confusion and disaffection. Given 'liberty to consult and advise', they undermined efforts to restart the war and then launched attacks on the king's ministers.[105] S.R. Gardiner and Conrad Russell have attributed to the peers a much more responsible and constructive role. They see them as using the council to talk the king out of a war that he could not win. But, from Charles's perspective, these historians regard the meeting as a failure, stymieing his efforts to achieve his principal objective, which was to rally the nation behind the forcible 'repulsion of the Scots'.[106] John Adamson goes further and describes the council meetings as a 'capitulation' because the king allowed it to set up a commission to negotiate with the Scots which contained 12 'petitioner peers' and only two privy councillors. This 'effectively conceded management of the forthcoming treaty to the petitioner Lords' and 'was arguably the first and most significant of a series of usurpations of royal authority that were to occur during the following months'.[107] Peter Donald, however, offers a more even-handed judgement. He acknowledges that Charles was prevented from pursuing a military solution to the crisis, but emphasises that this was largely of his own volition. He describes a king who was torn between a desire to uphold his honour by driving out the Scots and a realistic recognition that he probably lacked the military capacity to achieve this. He also points out that the king did gain a good deal from the council, notably in the promise of the supply he needed to keep his army together and avoid a humiliating capitulation. Overall, as Donald describes it, Charles gained as much as he had conceded.[108] These are very diverse assessments, but they have in common a recognition that the Great Council's deliberations played a crucial role in shaping the political legacy of the Bishops Wars.

One of the most significant features of these proceedings is that, unlike meetings of the House of Lords, the king attended throughout and

accounts, see Hunt.L., Ellesmere MS, EL 7740; *Lismore Papers*, iv.123–40, 143–9; SRO, D661/11/1/5.

105 Clarendon, *History*, i.210, 212.

106 Gardiner, *History*, ix.215–16; Russell, *Fall of the British Monarchies*, pp. 157–63.

107 Adamson, *Noble Revolt*, pp. 82–4.

108 P. Donald, *An Uncounselled King. Charles I and the Scottish Troubles, 1637–1641* (Cambridge: Cambridge University Press, 1990), pp. 261–72.

participated in the debates on a daily basis. They therefore provide a unique opportunity to observe Charles interacting with his peers over an extended period. On the opening day of the council he 'made offer of himselfe to be a dayly assistant amongst them, and as willingly to advise as he would advised by them'. At first the Earl of Bristol tried to dissuade him from this, urging him not to 'trouble himselfe' and suggesting 'that his presence might be an abridgement of their liberty of speech'. But this appears to have been at odds with the general feeling. When Charles offered to absent himself, the Earl of Bedford, embracing the notion that the peers were there to work in partnership with the king in resolving the nation's problems, urged that 'we may have the honour and comfort of your presence', and declared, 'I shall hold him unworthy to live whoe in your presence will be afraid to speake anythinge in reason for the advantage of his country.'[109]

The debates had a very different complexion from those in the upper house. As Bristol observed, they were sitting not as 'a court' (the 'High Court of Parliament'), where their role could be seen as one of adjudicating between different points of view and determining questions by 'number of voices', but as 'a council' expected to provide advice, backed by 'weight of reasons, which they must lay down at his Majestie's feete to balance'.[110] In many respects they were acting as an enlarged version of the Privy Council, but the tone of their proceedings was rather different because the king allowed them much more latitude than was normally the case in the Privy Council. After setting out his priorities in his opening speech, he gave an assurance that 'he would not at all abridge their freedom of debateing matters' and was 'wholely relying upon their discretion and fidelities'. He largely stuck to this, stressing repeatedly that he was there to defer to the lords and seek their counsel, and presenting himself in the role of a chairman or 'moderator'. He would raise issues, sum up the direction of debate, draw conclusions and sometimes try to nudge discussion in a particular direction; but he did not try to prejudge or rule out particular courses of action as tended to happen in Privy Council meetings. When he wanted to make what he regarded as a personal intervention he cast himself as one of their number and announced that he was speaking as the Duke of York.[111] This approach helped to define the dynamic of the proceedings in such a way as to open up more space

109 Hunt.L., Ellesmere MS, EL 7740; *Lismore Papers*, iv.125–6; SRO, D661/11/1/5.
110 *Lismore Papers*, iv.125–6.
111 *Ibid*, iv.125, 138; Hunt.L., Ellesmere, EL 7740; *Hardwicke SP*, ii.229–30, 243, 272, 281.

than was usually available for the king to be persuaded or talked round from his initial viewpoint.[112]

Proceedings opened on 24 September with a speech from Charles announcing his determination to carry the fight to the Scots Covenanters. He began by proclaiming that 'I have of myself resolved to call a parliament', which not only established that he was in control of the process of summons, but also cleared out of the way what would, inevitably, have been the first topic for debate. He then defined the two questions on which he required advice: first how to 'treat with' the Scots and second how to keep together his army. And finally, he attempted to secure a definitive condemnation of the Covenanters by asking the peers 'to declare their opinions, that his warre against the Scotts was justly grounded'. He apparently hoped that they would provide him with an immediate mandate to fight on; but, instead, 'for a pretty while', there was 'a great silence'.[113]

This was eventually broken by the Earl of Bristol, showing the leadership he was to display throughout the council. He suggested that, in view of the significance of what they were being asked to decide, they should be allowed to take time to consider and consult with the Covenanter 'lords' to understand their point of view. This was 'well relished' by the assembly and, put in such terms, it was a motion that the king found hard to resist. The principle of appointing commissioners to 'treat with' the Scots was quickly approved. It was picked up again in the afternoon when it provided the first indication of a division in the assembly between hard liners and moderates. When Bristol moved that they appoint a committee to meet with 'the Scotch lords', Strafford responded forcefully that 'he conceaved it was not for the king's honour to treat in such sort with rebels'. Bristol's reply – in the first of many efforts to spell out the realities of their situation – was that 'in the formes of treating they are not to be looked on as rebels since his Majestie hath not the power to punish them as such'.[114] The mood of the meeting was with Bristol and, again with the king's approval, they proceeded to appoint a commission of 16 peers to open negotiations. Crucially for what followed, the assembly accepted the earl's stipulation that the nominees should be such as the Scots 'could not except against'. This produced a commission heavily weighted in favour of accommodation, with 12 of the 'petitioner peers', including Brooke and Mandeville whom Charles had long regarded as two of the

112 On Charles's relations with his privy council, see Cust, *Charles I*, pp. 64, 66–7, 127, 195.
113 Rushworth, ii.1275; *Lismore Papers*, iv.130–1.
114 *Lismore Papers*, iv.131, 126–7; TNA, SP 16/468/23.

most obstreperous.[115] The king's readiness to allow these appointments without openly objecting was a measure of his recognition that he had staked his political fortunes on the success of the assembly and had to make concessions to ensure that it worked. For the time being this was a price worth paying. But he expected something in return, and on the second day of proceedings he got it.

After his recent experience of dealing with the House of Commons, the peers' willingness to underwrite the funds needed to keep together his army must have seemed like the realisation of all the hopes that he had invested in their loyalty and support. Strafford opened the discussion by spelling out the need for £200 000 over the next three months to avoid the 'infamy' of having to disband the army and surrender to the Scots. Mandeville and Saville briefly threatened to divert discussion on to the potentially damaging question of who was to blame for the current shortfall in the king's revenue. But Charles himself was able to head this off by urging them to 'rather looke forwards then backwards', and intimating that the main cause was the 'late distractions' in parliament.[116] The lords then got down to business. Lord North and the Earl of Berkshire proposed a benevolence from the peers as the quickest and most straightforward means of funding the army. The majority jibbed at this, perhaps because several of them had already lent large sums to the king. They preferred Bristol's suggestion that the money be raised from the City of London in the form of a loan which would be underwritten by a guarantee from the lords. The whole matter was settled within the morning and Charles was said to be so pleased that he 'broke out into most noble and brave expressions of kindness to them and his people'.[117]

The afternoon was spent drawing up a letter on behalf of the peers setting out the reasons for supporting the levy. This carefully balanced the different concerns that had been expressed on the previous day. It declared that they were seeking 'such an accommodation as may tend to the honour of his Majestie and the perfect union of both kingdoms'. If the Scots' demands were 'just and reasonable' they were assured that the king would 'listen' to them; but if they were to 'insist upon termes dishonnerable for his Majestie and the English nation . . . wee should all hold ourselves obliged in honner and duty to preserve and defend this kingdome . . . '.[118]

115 Russell, *Fall of the British Monarchies*, p. 158.
116 *Lismore Papers*, iv.131–2; BL, Harleian MS 456, fo. 1; *Hardwicke SP*, ii.209–10.
117 *Hardwicke SP*, ii.210–13; *Lismore Papers*, iv.132–4; Russell, *Fall of the British Monarchies*, p. 159.
118 Russell, *Unrevolutionary England*, p. 256; Devon Record Office, Drake of Colyton MSS, 1700/M/C/P/17.

Conrad Russell has described the statement as 'a fudge', which evaded the main issue of whether or not the lords were prepared to support a resumption of the war.[119] But it is arguable that this was as much as Charles could have hoped for. As he well knew, the peerage was divided in its attitudes to the Scots and on the previous day had pointedly declined to endorse his war policy. Yet here they were providing security for the funds that he had been scrabbling around to obtain since the defeat at Newburn. Moreover, they were making a point of acknowledging their readiness to defend his 'honour'. It was as yet unclear – to Charles as much as anyone else – whether the current break in the fighting would hold or whether the circumstances would tip back into open conflict. But he could now engage with the Scots from a position of relative strength, with a viable army and with his peerage united behind him. The letter that Secretary Windebank dispatched to the ambassador in Spain on 1 October summed up how things looked from the king's perspective. 'The nobility' had shown itself 'firme to his Majesty for the expulsion of the Scotts', either with 'reasonable and fayr conditions', or if they refused these, 'to be pursued by force as traytors'.[120]

Proceedings from 26–29 September were mostly taken up with defining the terms on which the lords commissioners would begin to treat with the Scots and this revealed a fundamental division over what was meant by the 'just and reasonable' demands alluded to in the peers' letter to London. The main issue was at what point would they be prepared to break off negotiations and assume a more aggressive stance? On this Strafford stuck to his hard line. He reiterated the advice given by the Privy Council the previous winter, that if the Scots challenged the 'rights' of the king they 'should be reduced to obedience by force'. He would not, he declared, 'advise positively to break a treaty; it is of too high a nature. But not to agree to all they demand, but to stand upon honour and justice'. Bristol responded with another dose of realism. If the king had been strong enough, he acknowledged, 'it were best to bring them to their knees. But . . . considering their strength . . . we must now speake of the business as to men that have gotten these advantages'. He then pressed Strafford on the English army's preparedness to fight and extracted a rather lame admission that they were not yet ready, but that, at least, the Scots were as 'unfit to fight . . . as we'.[121] Charles, mindful of this and conscious of his responsibility to the inhabitants of his northern shires, pursued a more measured line than his commander-in-chief. He

119 Russell, *Fall of the British Monarchies*, p. 160.
120 Bodl.L., Clarendon MS, vol. 19, 1437; Russell, *Unrevolutionary England*, pp. 256–7.
121 *Hardwicke SP*, ii.220–2, 225, 229–31.

made it clear that the Scots were still to be regarded as 'rebels' and that he did not 'fear to break [the negotiations] because they are stronger'. However, he also emphasised that he would 'refuse nothing that is reasonable' and gave his assent to the instructions that opened the way to the first round of negotiations at Ripon.[122]

The king could look back on the first session of the Great Council (which ended on 29 September) with considerable satisfaction. He had obtained the all-important promise of supply and successfully outmanoeuvred the 'petitioner peers'. Just a week earlier his prospects had appeared far more gloomy. The threatened boycott of the assembly had not materialised, but the 'petitioner peers' had mounted an impressive show of strength on the eve of the council, arriving at York *en masse*, in a cavalcade of coaches. It was anticipated that they would do their best to disrupt the council. But this had not happened.[123] Apart from the attempt by Mandeville and Saville to raise the issue of the state of the king's finances, they had kept their heads down or made interventions that fitted in with the generally constructive tone of the proceedings.[124] They may also have hoped to secure the disbandment of the English army that would have removed the main obstacle to their political influence – and both Charles and Strafford indicated their nervousness at this prospect in their opening speeches. But again this had not happened. The king was probably assisted by the absence of the 'petitioner peers' most effective debater, Lord Saye who according to Hyde was too ill to attend.[125] But he had also achieved a tactical coup by announcing the meeting of parliament right at the start of the session, which removed the main issue around which the 'petitioner peers' had united. And he made his own considerable contribution to the harmony of proceedings by repeatedly stating that he would do nothing without the advice of the lords and playing what Sir Kenelm Digby, who had closely observed the debates, described as 'the part of an excellent moderator'.[126]

With the leaders of the 'petitioner peers' relatively subdued, centre stage was taken by the Earl of Bristol. In a newsletter summing up the opening debates, Digby, his kinsman, described him as 'the first and governing wheele' of the council, 'and what he speakes may rather be tearmed the assemblye's resolucon then his particular opinion; for hitherto nothing hath been dissented from that his lordship hath moved'. There was an element of family pride in this verdict, but it accurately represented the tenor of proceedings. Bristol appears to have judged the

122 *Ibid.*, 230, 238, 241. 123 Adamson, *Noble Revolt*, p. 81.
124 See, for example, the contribution by Hertford on 28 September: *Hardwicke SP*, ii.233.
125 Clarendon, *History*, i.203. 126 *Lismore Papers*, iv.138.

mood of the council very skilfully and performed a difficult balancing act. He was prepared, as Digby said, to be 'very plaine in stating all things to the king'. But, at the same time, he was able to retain Charles's confidence by acknowledging the importance of being seen to uphold his honour and giving the impression that when push came to shove he would be 'stiffe and rigide . . . for the king's greatnesse and authority'.[127] This accomplished performance did much to steer the king and assembly on to a common course in which loyalty and deference to royal concerns were allied to a realistic recognition that the most viable course of action was to negotiate.

There was a week's break in the Great Council's proceedings as negotiations opened with the Covenanter leaders at Ripon on 2 October. When debate resumed on 6 October the central issue was the Scots demand that the English pay £40 000 a month 'maintenance' while their army was occupying the northern shires. This was a huge sum that even the more pro-Scots of the lords commissioners were said to have regarded as exorbitant and it brought into the open divisions within the assembly which had, hitherto, been largely submerged.[128] Opinion was now divided, according to newsletter reports, between those 'who talked very high how they would never yield their consents to any accommodations that were not passing honorable to our side' and those who 'saw that our affaires are in every circumstance upon such terms that we must expect, if we will have peace, to swallow and digest some very bitter pilles'.[129] These two viewpoints crystallised around the issue of how to respond to the Scots demand for maintenance. The question was succinctly stated by the Earl of Hertford, one of the commissioners at Ripon: 'Either we must drive them out, or a competency to be allowed for maintaining their army.'[130] Leading the hardliners was Strafford who argued that the scale of the Scots' demands 'hath opened our eyes' to their determination to throw off royal authority. He therefore urged the king to draw inspiration from 'the Londoners' example' and refuse to compromise. He was strongly supported by two non-councillor peers, the Earl of Huntingdon, who insisted they should give no money to the Scots and Lord Herbert of Cherbury who warned of upsetting the city. Against them Bristol continued to remind the assembly of the the weakness of English forces and warned of the 'ruin' of the northern counties if they did not pay up.[131] Most speakers, including several of the 'petitioner peers', shared this perspective, but they were very conscious that the Scots' demands constituted just the sort of 'terms dishonerable' that they had set themselves

127 *Ibid.*, 129–30, 139. 128 Gardiner, *History*, ix.209–11; TNA, SP 16/469/44.
129 *Lismore Papers*, iv.138. 130 *Hardwicke SP*, ii.242. 131 *Ibid.*, 244–8, 250–1.

against in their letter of 25 September.[132] Charles himself showed every indication of reverting to his more belligerent stance. At one point in the debate he expressed his desire 'to speake as duke of York' and pointed out that it would be a considerable 'shock' to both the Londoners and the coming parliament if they were to discover that their money had been used 'to give invaders or rebels money'. He also asked them to remember that the loan from the city was enough to maintain his army for three months and, indeed, to 'raise greater forces'. He refrained from telling the lords what conclusion they should come to; but they could have been left in little doubt about his opinion when he posed the question in terms of 'Whether better to give rebels money or to stop them?'[133]

The debate on 6 October, however, was inconclusive and when discussion was resumed on the 9th the situation was beginning to change. Reports were starting to filter through that the city's initial preparedness to provide the £200 000 was being watered down and that the English army was still in no state to take on the Scots.[134] This gloomier outlook dominated the latter stages of the debate on maintenance. Hard-line positions became more entrenched. Strafford amplified his rhetoric to declare that 'to grant' the Scots 'any dishonourable terms, he will first die', and Herbert of Cherbury urged the council to prepare to defend the barrier of the River Tees and start fortifying York. More peers started to come out in support of this line. Lord Maynard reminded them that 'giving them any thing a hard morsel to digest by any Englishman'; and the Earl of Northampton declared 'he neither can nor dare answer to the parliament if he gave the Scots assistance'. Taking their cue from the king's remarks on 6 October, there was a growing belief among hardliners that parliament would be more determined than the Great Council to resist the Scots.[135] The moderates, on the other hand, continued to warn of the devastation that would ensue if the Scots could not be paid, and the danger of derailing the whole treaty negotiation over this one issue.[136] Charles oscillated. At the end of the debate on 9 October he appeared to concede that compensation should be paid and the commissioners should be empowered to negotiate the lowest amount possible. But by the 12th he had backtracked to a more bellicose line, insisting that he would not allow the Scots to be paid out of the city loan, and drawing attention to their latest statement 'more insolent than the first'. He also appeared to be coming round to the view that he would be able to rally anti-Scots feeling in the coming parliament and urged that 'Nothing to be done

132 *Ibid.*, 242–3, 245. 133 *Ibid.*, 243–4, 246, 253. 134 TNA, SP 16/469/63, 85.
135 *Hardwicke SP*, ii.251, 253, 255–6, 258, 261, 264–6; Rushworth, ii.1293–4.
136 *Hardwicke SP*, ii.259–63.

without a parliament for uniting the affections of the people' and 'To send the rebels word that they will do nothing but with a Parliament.'[137]

The deadlock was finally broken on 13 October when the assembly adopted a proposal that the burden of paying maintenance should fall on the northern counties on the understanding that they would be reimbursed by parliament. This avoided the dishonour of the king being seen to give in to rebels – and even Strafford, seeing which way the wind was blowing, acknowledged that such an 'accommodation' could 'go on with . . . honour'.[138] Charles was now prepared to focus mainly on the practical details of how the money was to be paid and how the shires could be helped to provide it. He still harboured a deep seated hostility to the Scots, but increasingly this was tempered by doubts about his army's capacity to fight them and his recognition that there were advantages in a rapid conclusion to the treaty since this was the quickest way to remove the Scots from further interference in English politics. At the end of the morning he concluded the debate by accepting a resolution for the lords commissioners to go ahead and arrange the accommodation on the most advantageous terms that they could negotiate.[139]

The resolution of the debate on maintenance was a watershed in the discussions at York. Thereafter proceedings gradually wound down in preparation for the opening of parliament that was set for 3 November. Charles received confirmation from London that the City had undertaken to pay only £50 000 and on 17 October pressed the assembly to send another delegation to lobby for the full sum. The following day a dispute flared up between Bristol and Strafford over the preparedness of the English army. Strafford was finally forced to concede that 'the king's army not able to encounter the gross of their army'; but this was simply a confirmation of what most in the assembly already knew.[140] The final session on 27 October was mainly taken up with the ratification of the terms for a cessation of arms agreed by the commissioners at Ripon on the 22nd that involved paying the Scots maintenance of £850 a day. The lords commissioners were particularly concerned to secure the assembly's ratification of these terms because they did not want to be saddled with sole responsibility for what Bristol described as 'a treaty of the greatest disadvantage that hath happened since the conquest'. They therefore prepared a lengthy justification in which they explained that while they were painfully aware that it was 'derogatorie both to the honour of the king & kingdome to treat at all with subjects & such as had already actually

137 *Ibid.*, 253, 256, 262–3. 138 *Ibid.*, 267–73; Donald, *An Uncounselled King*, pp. 266–9.
139 *Hardwicke SP*, ii.268–9, 276.
140 *Clarendon SP*, ii.129–31; *Hardwicke SP*, ii.284–90.

possessed themselves of several provinces of this kingdome', the desperate condition of the northern shires and the acknowledged inability of their own army to repel the Scots, left them with no choice.[141] Charles, with the advice of the assembly, agreed. However, given the fulsomeness of the commissioners' expressions of regret, it was perhaps not surprising that he appears to have come away from these proceedings with the belief that they shared his sense of humiliation and would welcome an opportunity to carry the fight back to the Scots.

The proceedings at York have generally been presented as a 'failure' or 'capitulation' on the king's part. But, on the evidence of the proceedings cited here this is questionable. Charles certainly had to make significant concessions, notably over the appointment of the lords commissioners and his acceptance of a policy of negotiation rather than force. Over the following months this would enable 'the Junto' of leading opposition peers and their Scots allies to dominate the political agenda. But he also gained a good deal in return. The Great Council was what enabled him to extricate himself from the crisis of late August–early September 1640 when, as John Adamson has emphasised, he faced the possibility of a collapse of royal authority, or at the very least a humiliating climb down, as he was forced to abandon the war on terms dictated by his enemies and sacrifice trusted counsellors. Through the summoning of the council he was able to regain much of the political initiative from the 'petitioner peers'. As a result of its proceedings, he succeeded in removing the threat that his army would be disbanded and gave himself the opportunity to engage with the Scots from a much stronger position than at one stage seemed likely.

There was a considerable element of risk involved in entrusting his political fortunes to the Great Council at York; but, in the event, it proved to be one of Charles's more successful political gambits. Both king and peers were on their best behaviour for the duration of the assembly and this was made to work to the king's advantage. The peers took their role as *consiliarii nati* very seriously and bent over backwards to show that they were responsible custodians of the welfare of monarchy and nation. This made it difficult for them to refuse Charles's offer to give them the benefit of his wisdom by attending throughout. As Bristol had anticipated, this considerably restricted freedom of debate, compelling the council to give priority to his particular concerns and sensitivities, and forcing the 'petitioner peers' to keep their heads down and back-off for

141 *Hardwicke SP*, ii.290–8; BL, Harleian MS 457, fos. 117–19. The final day of the council sitting was 27 October, not the 28th as given in *Hardwicke SP*, ii.290 & Gardiner, *History*, ix.215; see Harleian MS 456, fos. 57–61.

the time being from their demand that ministers be bought to account. It also ensured that the issue of the king's 'honour' was kept at the forefront of their deliberations; and throughout the peers showed themselves to be particularly careful about this, in part, as they were repeatedly reminded, because it related so closely to their own. The proceedings at York, then, were in many respects a model of how Charles envisaged dealings with his peers, and the management of political assemblies more generally. The council was operating very much on his terms, in deference to an agenda that he had set and with the purpose – as stated by Bristol – of providing counsel and guidance that it was, ultimately, his prerogative to accept or reject. It also came as close to realising the ideals of unity and cooperation that he set out in his addresses to parliament as any assembly of his reign.

From the perspective of the peers, the Great Council did much to reaffirm their honour, reputation and self-confidence. After decades of being told that they were in decline and in danger of being marginalised, the experience of being placed centre stage and entrusted with important decisions had a revitalising effect. Newsletter coverage and commentary on the events presented the nobles as acting in a responsible, non-partisan, fashion to moderate between the crown and people and guide them towards a settlement of the whole Scottish crisis. Their prestige in the eyes of the public had rarely been higher in the early Stuart period.

A key consideration in all this was that they gave the appearance of operating as a united entity. In spite of the efforts of the 'puritan party' to divide them, the bulk of the peerage demonstrated a remarkable degree of loyalty and moderation. Most had responded positively in early 1639 when called on to participate in the muster at York and they again responded positively when summoned to the Great Council. In part, as we have seen, this was due to intensive lobbying and some quite skilful manoeuvring by Charles and his councillors. But, more than this, it was a consequence of their deeply ingrained sense of service and obligation to both crown and commonwealth that encouraged them to unite and cooperate even when there were intense political pressures pulling them apart. This was something to which even the 'puritan party' peers were susceptible, as the conduct of their more moderate members such as Bedford and Hertford demonstrated. The capacity to act collectively was essential to the recovery of their prestige and authority, but it is something that historians who have emphasised the decline of the aristocracy, such as Lawrence Stone, have tended to overlook. The focus has generally been on noblemen as individuals, exercising dominance through wealth, territorial influence and military force. In this respect, it is undeniable that their power was not what it had been 100, or even 50, years earlier. But events in 1639–40 served to highlight their collective capacity, fulfilling many of the expectations that contemporaries had of the 'ancient nobility', first of all in resuming their traditional martial role by taking the field alongside their monarch and then performing their function as *consiliarii nati*. From this perspective their power and influence remained enormous and they had vindicated their role as the natural leaders of the political nation.

5 The aristocracy and the outbreak of civil war, 1640–1642

The Long Parliament

As Charles headed south towards his meeting with parliament on 3 November two courses of action were open to him. The one that appealed most was to rally anti-Scots feeling and find a way of reopening hostilities so that he could redeem his slighted honour. Whether or not, as Hyde suggested, Charles had become disenchanted with the accommodating tone of the Great Council's dealings with the Scots, he certainly appears to have believed that the parliament would share his sense of indignation at having to submit to rebels and invaders and would support him in driving the Scots back across the border.[1] There remained the problem of his own army's poor state of preparedness and lack of funding; but he appears to have anticipated that this would be resolved with a grant of supply and a firm declaration in favour of renewing the war.

The alternative was to build on the accord established at York and work with the House of Lords to salvage the best settlement possible from the defeat by the Scots. This would involve compromises and concessions that Charles found painful; but it offered his best hope of retaining some political leverage in a situation that was threatening to slide beyond his control. The combination of a meeting of parliament in which the House of Commons was likely to be dominated by his critics and the occupation of the northern shires by a triumphant Covenanter army left him with few options. The terms of the truce with the Scots had, for the time being, removed the possibility of dissolving parliament if he did not like the direction in which it was going; and the alliance between the Covenanters and the instigators of the Twelve Peers Petition left him beleaguered and on the verge of becoming a political irrelevance. Reaching out to work with the body of peers, as on past occasions, offered his best prospect of exerting effective influence. It was also, for him, a relatively palatable

[1] Clarendon, *History*, i.208.

option. He may not have felt that the Great Council had been firm enough with the Scots, but at least, he believed, he could rely on them to do what was needed to protect his honour and uphold his authority.

In his opening speech to the Lords and Commons on 3 November Charles tried the first option, putting to the test his belief that parliament would be willing to support aggressive action. 'Had I been believed at the time of the last assembly', he told them, 'things had not fallen out as now we see. But it is no wonder that men are so slow to believe that so great a sedition should be raised on so little ground.' There were just two issues that he now wanted them to consider: 'First, the chasing out of rebels; and secondly, that other, in satisfying your just grievances.'[2] The king seems to have anticipated that confronted by clear proof of the Scots' seditious intent and encouraged by a firm promise to settle their grievances, parliament would unite behind the use of force. But he seriously misjudged the mood.

The following day, hoping to rally the peers, he summoned them to a meeting in the Whitehall Banqueting House. There he asked them once again to 'advise' him on how to raise the cash needed to keep his army together. This was picking up on unfinished business from York where a decision had been made on 17 October to send another delegation to petition London, but had not been followed up.[3] The peers were initially uncertain how to proceed. One of them asked 'in what capacity we stood there: as Lords of the Great Council at Yorke, or as Lords of Parliament', to which Charles replied, 'in both, as peers to advise him'. This prompted some forthright discussion as the peers reverted to their role as counsellors. The king's reference to the Scots as 'rebels' on the previous day 'excited some ill feeling' and it was made clear to him that the Lords were not about to support a resumption of the war. But eventually, again following the lead of the Earl of Bristol, they settled on a proposal to send another delegation to the Lord Mayor, to thank him for the £50 000 already provided, and ask for the same amount again, backed by the security of the peers' pledges.[4] It seemed that the relationship established at York was being continued now that they were back in London and, once more, the king was getting the financial help he needed via his peers. As a *quid pro quo* the next day, Charles returned to the upper house to clarify what he had meant by his speech of 3 November. He explained that 'he must needs call them [rebels] so long as they have an army that doth invade us', but also acknowledged that he was now 'under treaty' with the Scots and that the immediate priority was to proceed with

[2] Rushworth, iii.11–12. [3] *Hardwicke SP*, ii.282.
[4] HMC, *Buccleuch*, iii.387–8; *CSP Ven. 1640–2*, p. 95.

the negotiations as quickly as possible. He also assured the Lords that 'I shall conclude nothing without your knowledge and, I doubt not, but by your approbation.'[5] For the time being he seemed prepared to follow the script hammered out in the Great Council.

What this involved had been spelt out in more detail in an important speech by the Lord Keeper immediately following that of the king on 3 November. Traditionally this was an occasion for glossing and expanding on the monarch's words, and Finch had evidently sought royal and conciliar approval for what he said. Nonetheless the message he presented was very different from that of the king. It amounted to a manifesto for continuing the accord with the Great Council of Peers. His speech was mainly an account of proceedings at York, which presented these as a model for the approach needed to resolve the current crisis. He began with a eulogy of the king, the royal family and the peerage. The lords were depicted as the ideal moderating force, building bridges between monarch and people, but always remaining respectful of royal authority:

> Was there, or is there, in any part of the world a nobility so numerous, so magnanimous and yet with such a temper that they neither eclipse the throne nor over top the people, but keep in a distance fit for the greatnes of the throne?[6]

He then went on to outline how the debates at York offered a template for what should follow at Westminster. The king had demonstrated his respect for the lords' status as his *consiliarii nati* by allowing them full 'freedom of debate' and professing, repeatedly, that he sought 'to be wholly ruled, guided and directed by their advice'. This had produced a series of model exchanges:

> with such freedom of discourse did every man deliver himself, with such grace and sweetness did his Majesty hear them, and such content did they take in his moderating, guiding and directing those councils.

When the king asked them to advise on how he should maintain his army and what answer he should give to the Scots' demands, they had responded with the practical guarantees needed to raise the loan from the City of London and the appointment of the lords commissioners to treat with the Scots. They had also taken the difficult decision to provide maintenance for the Scots occupying the northern shires. In all of this, according to Finch, the Great Council was 'all of [one] opinion, and his Majesty was pleased to be of the same opinion'. He finished by urging on

[5] Rushworth, iii.17. [6] Rushworth, iii.13.

his fellow peers the 'weight and importance' of the example set at York and the 'deep consideration it requires in our affection'.[7]

What the Lord Keeper had presented was a very partial view of proceedings that glossed over significant divisions. But his speech offers a valuable insight into the hopes and aspirations of those 'officers and ministers' by whom he said he had been advised. Finch was not renowned as a moderate, but in the proceedings at York, like most other councillors and peers, he had come to appreciate that there was no alternative to negotiating with the Scots. Now he was going further and advocating that in the current crisis it was incumbent on councillors and peers, through their involvement in the House of Lords, to take the initiative and provide a focus around which the king and the political nation could unite. This held out the prospect not only of healing the divisions opened up by the Scottish rebellion, but also enabling the king to regain some of the political initiative. Charles understood this, but at the same time he felt deeply frustrated and humiliated and was looking for an opportunity to reassert his authority and take revenge on his enemies.

This presented itself when Strafford reached London on 9 November. He had travelled south to bolster the king as he contemplated further dealings with the Scots. But, as John Adamson has shown, as soon as he arrived in London, Charles seized the moment to bring forward treason charges against the pro-Scots 'puritan party' that he had been contemplating since early in 1639. Strafford was to be their accuser and any opposition was to be overawed by the garrison at the Tower of London under the command of Lord Cottington.[8] However, rumours of what was intended leaked out and on 11 November the allies of the Scots launched a pre-emptive strike. The ground was carefully prepared in the House of Commons, with allegations of plots and threats to parliament's security that led to an order that Strafford himself be charged with treason and sequestered from appearing in the upper house. By the time John Pym appeared in the Lords to request their support, at around 5 pm, the peers were well aware of the gravity of the situation. They responded with considerable force and decisiveness. Strafford was prevented from taking his seat, while they entered into 'a serious debate' about how to deal with him. They then took the unprecedented step of ordering that he be sequestered and committed to the custody of the gentleman usher, even though no formal charge had yet been made against him. Finally they despatched a delegation to explain their actions to the king. Confronted by Arundel, Hamilton and Holland from among his own privy councillors, along with Bedford, Essex and Bristol, Charles meekly accepted

[7] *Ibid.*, 14–16. [8] Adamson, *The Noble Revolt*, pp. 99–101.

what they had done, and also agreed to dismiss Cottington as constable of the Tower and stand down the garrison.[9] The Lords' decisive action had narrowly averted a major political crisis and demonstrated to the king that they would not tolerate the use of force to deal with his political enemies. This was a position they were to stick to in the coming months; but it did not mean that they were aligning themselves with the crown's opponents.

Conrad Russell has described the House of Lords during the first session of the Long Parliament as the body that was best able to find 'the new political centre of gravity on which any new political consensus would have to rest'. It was generally able to maintain 'at least a working illusion of consensus' and it continued to place a heavy stress on achieving political compromise, maintaining unity and balancing the interests of king and people.[10] As we shall see, there is a good deal in this verdict. The Lords reflected a wide variety of opinion, with peers who were often intensely partisan and committed to pushing opposing interests. Issues such as the exclusion of bishops or the management of proceedings against Strafford regularly provoked fierce debate and bitter divisions. Yet, on a wide range of matters, the house was still able to reach workable compromises and move forward with at least a semblance of unity. It was also able to hold the balance between the king and the Commons, and sustain a working relationship with both parties. This placed them at the centre of the political stage and, arguably, gave them greater power and influence than at any other time since before James's accession.

The Lords' ability to work collectively – on which so much of their influence depended – was grounded in a strong sense of the need to uphold the order's privileges in a world in which they felt increasingly beleaguered and threatened. As Russell has demonstrated, this showed itself in the determination of the majority to protect the rights of even Catholic peers to sit in parliament, vote and avoid harassment.[11] More immediately it was a reflection of how seriously they took their status as *consiliarii nati* charged with continuing the role they had taken on at York. Moving towards the middle ground at Westminster, however, was a more complex process and required a significant shift of perspective. At York their discussions had mainly been directed towards meeting the needs of the king. They were asked to act as an expanded version of the Privy Council and provide him with the advice and support needed to negotiate a way out of the Scottish crisis. Once they were back sitting as the House of Lords, however, their remit broadened. They still felt

[9] *LJ*, iv.88–90; Adamson, *Noble Revolt*, pp. 109–11.

[10] Russell, *Fall of the British Monarchies*, pp. 210, 330–1. [11] *Ibid.*, 331.

a strong obligation to meet the king's needs and preserve his authority; but in the parliamentary setting they were conscious of an equally powerful obligation to serve the 'country' and devote themselves to the concerns and grievances of the people. This led to an important shift of perspective as they reverted to the terms of the Twelve Peers petition, which at least 23 of them had eventually signed. The petition offered a clearly defined agenda for reform. First, it recommended investigating the people's grievances, which were listed in detail as ranging from 'innovations in religion' and illegal levies, such as ship money, to the problems caused by 'the long intermission of parliaments' and the folly of the war against the Scots. Second, it advocated that the 'authors and counsellors' of these policies be subjected to trial and punishment. And third it urged 'that the present war may be composed . . . without bloodshed'.[12] This petition essentially provided the programme for proceedings in the House of Lords throughout the early months of the Long Parliament and its importance was formally recognised on 18 March 1641 when it was adopted as 'an act' of the house, and the text and list of original signatories was recorded in the *Lords' Journal*, 'for the honour of the Lords' petitioners'.[13]

At the same time as directing the Lords towards reform, the move to Westminster enormously enhanced the political influence and status of the pro-Scots 'puritan party' whom Charles had long identified as the leaders of the opposition within both the Lords and the Commons. By December 1640 they were sufficiently prominent in both houses for contemporary commentators to start referring to them as the 'ruling party' or the 'Junto'.[14] This pre-eminence was due to a variety of factors. The king was no longer breathing down their necks and stifling their manoeuvres as he had done at York; the crown was now negotiating with their Scots allies rather than treating them as rebels; and the adoption of the Twelve Peers Petition, in which they had been the prime movers, ensured that their views commanded respect and were listened to. Perhaps, their greatest advantage was that they were a bicameral grouping, able to operate across the two houses and coordinate the requests and initiatives that came up from the Commons. As John Adamson has demonstrated, their cohesiveness, debating skills and tactical sophistication were often enough to ensure that they could rally a majority of their 'independent-spirited and unmanaged colleagues'.[15] This gave them the ability to shape the agenda and make much of the running in the upper house; but it did not mean they were in control of it.

[12] *Constitutional Documents*, pp. 134–6. [13] *LJ*, iv.188–9.
[14] Adamson, *Noble Revolt*, p. 138. [15] *Ibid.*

In a house where the average attendance was around 80, the Junto was still a relatively small grouping, outnumbered by other contingents such as the privy councillors and the bishops. Their core membership, which endured throughout the first session of the Long Parliament (up to the recess of September–October 1641), consisted of just eight peers: Essex, Warwick, Saye, Mandeville, Wharton, Paget, Brooke and Howard of Escrick. In the early months they were joined by Bedford, who provided much of the leadership, and Hertford and Savile; but Bedford died suddenly in May 1641, and by this point Hertford and Savile were gravitating towards the royal court. Over the same period other senior peers such as Pembroke, Northumberland and Holland were gradually moving closer to them; and they also enjoyed the regular support of a group of less prominent members of the house which included Bolingbroke, Feilding, Roberts and Willoughby of Parham.[16] But, for the duration of this first session they remained a relatively small minority. To be effective they had to work with the grain of the house and form alliances within the 'independent-spirited' majority; however, this was by no means straightforward.

The obstacles and limitations that the Junto faced can, perhaps, best be illustrated by looking more closely at the concerns and attitudes of some of the other lords who had backed the Twelve Peers Petition. Most of these peers had aligned themselves with the 'puritan party' in the Short Parliament vote against pressing the Commons to resolve on supply. But this did not necessarily mean that they were with them on other issues. Lord North had signed the petition, but at York he had proposed that the needs of the royal army be met with a benevolence from the lords, which was certainly not an approach that the Junto wanted to encourage. Moreover, in a series of reflections on the early phases of the Long Parliament, (probably penned in March 1641), he made clear his concern that the balance was being tilted too far against the king and the existing status quo. After a spate of reforms in which 'the king may seem to have made himself a great loser by giving ground so much', he argued that what was needed, above all, was to repair the royal finances; and while he acknowledged the need for religious reform, he also urged that 'God forbid that we should yeeld to every fanatical opinion and to fal into a way of enthusiasts without any set forme of directory or liturgy.' North ended one of his letters by expressing the hope that he might 'keep myself an honest man, with an untainted conscience and reputation' which, as far as he was concerned, seems to have meant approaching each issue

[16] *Ibid.*, pp. 54, 100, 138–9, 150–2; *Oxf.DNB* articles on these peers.

with an open mind about where the balance was to be struck between the interests of king and people.[17]

This was also the approach of Lord Montagu, who had supported the Twelve Peers Petition, although he did not sign it. Montagu was renowned for his independent-mindedness and integrity. The diary he kept for the first three months of the parliament bears this out.[18] One of his chief preoccupations was to monitor and control the threat presented by Catholics, and this, together with his evident support for reform of grievances of the 1630s, such as ship money and the court of Star Chamber, made him a supporter of a number of Junto initiatives. But he was also a stickler for proper procedure and maintaining the privileges of the house, which led him to clash with Viscount Saye in January 1641 after the latter presented a motion against the Earl of Strafford on behalf of the Commons. Montagu was also impressed by Strafford's carriage and demeanour in response to the initial charges against him, and he appears to have been one of the peers who was reported to be turning in favour of the earl, or who were at least determined that he receive a fair trial.[19] The Junto peers had considerable advantages when it came to providing leadership in the upper house. But they had always to take account of the determination of individual peers to follow their consciences and balance their obligations to king and commonwealth.

They also had to operate within the conventions and traditions of a house that placed heavy stress on consensus and inclusiveness. The house's collective determination to bring together a broad range of interests and opinions is evident in the make-up of its committees. In the most thorough investigation that has been made of this topic, J.B. Crummett has shown that among the 12 peers most regularly appointed to serve on committee in the first session of the Long Parliament, eight were members or allies of the Junto. This is an impressive level of involvement made possible by the process of peers simply calling out the names of committee nominees, which gave the advantage to a well coordinated party grouping.[20] However, in spite of this bias, the overall composition of individual committees generally reflected a broad range of attitudes

17 North, *A Forest of Varieties*, pt. 3, 235–7.

18 HMC, *8th Report*, appx. 2, 57; Cope, *Life of a Public Man*, p. 180; HMC, *Buccleuch*, iii.386–413.

19 HMC, *Buccleuch*, iii.405, 407, 408, 412; HMC, *Cowper*, ii.273. See also the report of another 'petitioner peer', the Earl of Bath, quarrelling with Lord Brooke over the latter's apparent disrespect for monarchy: HMC, *Cowper*, ii.273–4.

20 Crummett, 'The Lay Peers in Parliament', pp. 261, 270–1; E.R. Foster, *The House of Lords 1603–1949* (Chapel Hill: University of North Carolina Press, 1983), pp. 87–92. The Junto members were Essex, Warwick, Saye, Brooke, Mandeville, Paget, Roberts and Wharton. The other four were Bath, Bristol, Manchester and Howard of Charlton.

and affiliations. For example, the large committee of 48 lords appointed on 6 November to receive petitions, while including ten of the Junto peers and a further eight of the signatories of the Twelve Peers Petition, also included eight privy councillors, eight bishops (five of whom were notable Laudians) and other peers who at York had kept their distance from the petitioners and followed the royal line, such as Maynard and Herbert of Cherbury. This was a particularly important committee because it had the power to investigate judicial decisions and effectively act as a court of appeal against the policies of the Personal Rule. But, although it was clearly sympathetic to the reformist approach, its membership was not dominated by 'radical critics of the crown' or 'the reformist Junto' as has been suggested.[21] Rather it was an expression of the concern to bring together a diversity of interests and rely on the peers' sense of responsibility to achieve a working consensus.

This inclusive approach was evident in the membership of other committees appointed in the early stages of the parliament.[22] It was a similar story with those whom the house chose to act on its behalf in conferences with the Commons and on delegations to the king. Junto lords were well represented, but the leading roles as spokesmen for the delegations were

21 J.S. Hart, *Justice Upon Petition* (London; Harper Collins Academic, 1991), ch. 2; Adamson, *Noble Revolt*, p. 124. Adamson remarks that 'the comprehensiveness with which the reformist peers came to dominate the new committee remains astonishing.' This conclusion appears to be based on inflating the category of 'reformist peers' in a way that can give a misleading impression of political loyalties. He includes in this category peers such as North, Montagu and Bath who, as we have seen, while supporting the Junto's reforming initiatives on some issues, distanced themselves and took a more independent line on others. He also includes Lord Herbert of Cherbury who, while he may have been swept up in the tide of support for reform, was not – to judge by his interventions at York – a natural bedfellow of the Junto peers: Adamson, *Noble Revolt*, p. 583n.

22 Another good example is the 28 man committee appointed on 14 November 1640 to 'examine the raising and ill managing of our armies in the northern parts', which again reflected a balance between signatories to the Twelve Peers Petition, bishops, councillors and allies of the court. As the Venetian ambassador observed, this had the potential to give a powerful lead in the inquest into those councillors responsible for the war, although in the event the committee's proceedings fizzled out in a series of cancelled meetings: *LJ*, iv.91,100; *CSP Ven. 1640–2*, 98.

For other important committees with a similarly broad based membership, see the committee to examine abuses in the courts of justice (*LJ*, iv.98), the committee to examine abuses in Star Chamber (*LJ*, iv.124), the committee to consider the Triennial Act (*LJ*, iv.147) and the committee to oversee the vacating of the ship money judgements (*LJ*, iv.156). The most obviously partisan of the committees during this period was the one appointed on 3 December to oversee the examination of witnesses against Strafford, which consisted of nine Junto allies and the Earl of Bath (*LJ*, iv.103) But this was very much the exception. The committee appointed five days later to supervise access to the earl in the Tower was much broader based and included the Earl of Southampton, who was identified as almost the only peer who at the time was sympathetic to Strafford: *LJ*, iv.106; HMC, *De L'Isle and Dudley*, vi.350.

generally taken by less obviously partisan peers. Bristol, who continued to perform a delicate balancing act between the interests of king and reformers and was managing to retain the confidence of both parties, was much in evidence, as were the ever-industrious Earl of Bath, the Privy Council workhorse, the Earl of Manchester and the Earls of Arundel and Pembroke, now regarded as the elder statesmen of the house.[23] These were lords with whom Charles felt he could do business and their prominence in the proceedings of the upper house indicated that the spirit of the Great Council was still very much alive.

In the aftermath of the failed coup of 11 November the Lords pressed ahead with reform and the king was forced to concede much of the political initiative to the Junto and its Scots allies. The committees of the upper house launched a series of inquests into the grievances of the 1630s, taking the Petition of Right as its benchmark for what could be considered legitimate. In tandem with the Commons, it also began to investigate those who had been responsible. Windebank and Finch were forced to flee into exile and Laud was imprisoned, again to face treason charges.[24] The Earl of Northumberland summed up the prevailing situation when he reported to his fellow peer, Leicester, that

> Both howses understand one an other so well and are so fully resolved upon a reformation of all things that I do verily beleeve we shall see many persons questioned that within these 6 months thought themselves in great securitie; and such are the king's necessities that he will not be any way able either to defend those men or to helpe himselfe.[25]

Charles did make a bid to exert some influence over the negotiations with the Scots commissioners by pressing to be allowed to attend their meetings that began in London on 16 November. But, although he secured a legal ruling that his attendance would not invalidate the negotiations, he was unable to persuade either the English or the Scots that his presence would be beneficial.[26] Otherwise, as Northumberland's letter indicates, his dependence on parliament for funds and the prevailing political mood left him little room for manoeuvre. He held meetings with his Privy Council throughout November and December, but – to judge by the council register – they transacted little business of significance and much of this had been referred to them by parliament; while in the Scottish negotiations a pattern emerged of the king at first stubbornly

23 Crummett, 'Lay peers in parliament', pp. 274–7; Foster, *House of Lords*, pp. 116–25; HMC, *Buccleuch*, iii.401, 405, 412.

24 Gardiner, *History*, ix.243, 247, 248–9.

25 HMC, *De L'Isle and Dudley*, vi.343.

26 BL, Harleian MS 457, fos. 4–8.

contesting proposals then having to give way.[27] There were indications that Charles himself was determined to cling on to some of the powers that would enable him to influence the developing political situation. He kept together his northern army, in spite of all the difficulties of paying for it, and refused to be rushed into making appointments to replace his disgraced ministers. But it was not until mid December 1640 that the first public signs emerged that he was once more able to exert some political leverage.

The event that made this possible was the start of negotiations for a marriage between his second daughter Mary and Prince William of Orange, heir to the *stadtholder* of the United Provinces. This opened up various options for Charles. It would deprive the Scots of the possibility of gaining Dutch support; it made it possible to consider another bid to regain the Palatinate by military means; and it might even allow the king to intimidate parliament. Commentators were agreed, however, that it gave the king fresh room for manoeuvre. He announced the impending treaty to the Privy Council on 10 December and when the Dutch envoys arrived on 1 January he handed over negotiations to those who had become his most trusted senior councillors: Arundel, Pembroke, Juxon, Northumberland, Hamilton, Dorset, Holland and Vane.[28] From this point onwards the king moved to regain some of the political initiative.[29]

Throughout January 1641 he held meetings with the Privy Council every few days and began to stake out the middle ground on which he would defend his kingship. The key to this strategy was once again to

27 TNA, PC 2/53, pp. 47–71; Russell, *Fall of the British Monarchies*, pp. 176–9; Donald, *An Uncounselled King*, pp. 275–9. Russell describes Charles's lack of grip during this period as a virtual abdication of power, leaving privy councillors and peers to fill the gap: *Fall of the British Monarchies*, pp. 207–8. This is an exaggeration, as John Adamson demonstrates: *Noble Revolt*, pp. 132–5. However, it was the case that during this period Charles's influence was probably at its lowest ebb.

28 Gardiner, *History*, ix.244–5; *CSP Ven. 1640–2*, pp. 107–8; *Ceremonies of Charles I*, pp. 295–9.

29 For a fascinating insight into the political strategy being canvassed at court, see the letter of advice from Sir John Suckling to the queen's principal counsellor Henry Jermyn (undated, but probably written late December 1640 – early January 1641): Sir John Suckling, *The Works of Sir John Suckling, vol. 1. The Non Dramatic Works*, ed. T. Clayton (Oxford: Clarendon Press, 1971), pp. 163–7. This argued that in the face of widespread condemnation of past policies the king must be seen to be proactive in cultivating 'the love of his subjects' and 'a union with his people'. It was also important for the queen to be seen to be thoroughly engaged in 'composing differences and . . . reconciling king and people', since she was perceived to exercise considerable influence on Charles and without her support it was thought that any reforms would be unlikely to stick. During the second half of January this advice was closely followed at court, with Charles embarking on what he clearly saw as a series of striking concessions and the queen, with Jermyn's advice, reportedly doing everything she could to encourage her husband in this direction.

work with the Lords. On 15 January, in response to the activities of a group of separatists in St Saviour's parish, Southwark, who refused to acknowledge the Royal Supremacy, the council discussed whether the king should 'provide a declaracon' that 'all matters eccl[esiastic]all and the eccl[esiastic]all government shalbe reduced to the former state as it was in the tyme of Q.Eliz which is and was esteemed the best of times.' It was decided to refer this to the upper house who obliged on the following day by issuing an order that henceforth divine service be performed according to the acts passed under Elizabeth.[30] This was a powerful statement of their joint determination to defend the ecclesiastical status quo.

Charles also began to engage with reforming agenda set out in the Twelve Peers Petition. Again on 15 January, Arundel and Pembroke announced in the Lords that henceforth his judges should be appointed '*quamdiu se bene gesserint*' (during good performance) rather than '*durante placito*' (during royal pleasure). This was designed to demonstrate that the king was siding with the Lords at a time when details were emerging of the complicity of Lord Keeper Finch and other judges in the excesses of the Personal Rule; and it was quickly followed by a series of reassuring appointments to senior legal positions.[31] Over the following days momentum appeared to be gathering for a more general settlement. There were reports that Charles was withdrawing his support for Strafford and that he was about to make a series of senior ministerial appointments, with Bedford as the new Lord Treasurer, Saye as Master of the Court of Wards, Pym as Chancellor of the Exchequer and Bristol as Lord Privy Seal. Sir John Temple, who kept his ear to the ground at court, reported his understanding that the king 'is brought into a dislike of those counsells that he hathe formerly followed and therefore resolves to steere another course'.[32]

Charles was under considerable pressure to move in this direction because it was being made clear to him that parliament would only fund the financial settlement that he so badly needed if he supported measures for reform. But he still had options when it came to determining the pace and direction of this reform, and how it was managed. His choices here were revealing. The 'projected settlement', with its 'bridging appointments' and royal concessions, has largely been presented by historians as a process in which Charles was forced to surrender to the Junto leadership, the aim being to 'Venetianise' the king by coercing him

[30] TNA, PC2/53, pp. 75–92; SP 16/476/19, fos. 45v–46r; *LJ*, iv.133–4.
[31] *LJ*, iv.132; Adamson, *Noble Revolt*, pp. 157–8.
[32] HMC, *De L'Isle and Dudley*, vi.367–8.

into accepting councillors approved by parliament.[33] There is a good deal in this. The Junto leadership was certainly pressing hard for the ministerial and conciliar positions that would enable them to influence future policy and afford a measure of security against themselves being tried for treason. The ability of Pym and Oliver St John to manage the financial proposals coming up from the Commons, and coordinate initiatives with their allies in the Lords, gave them the capacity to apply pressure on the king at his most vulnerable point.[34] However, these negotiations were not just about applying pressure. With a monarch who was as sensitive to slights and humiliations as Charles, too much pressure was liable to be counterproductive, particularly if it looked as if it involved stripping him of his prerogative powers. These reformist policies had also to be sold to Charles as a positive step towards enhancing the dignity and authority of his monarchy; and one obvious way of doing this was to present them as another means of binding the king to his peerage.

The three most influential figures in selling this to Charles appear to have been Hamilton, Arundel and Pembroke. Hamilton, a longstanding personal favourite of the king who was now also becoming closely associated with the Junto leadership, managed the court end of the negotiations over appointments and promotions.[35] Arundel and Pembroke acted as go-betweens with the House of Lords. These two men had emerged from the wreckage of ministerial imprisonments and removals to assume the leading roles on Charles's Privy Council. Arundel became the king's chief ministerial adviser on foreign policy and resumed the role of senior councillor that he had performed in early 1639. His willingness to advocate a summons of parliament in September 1640 also helped ensure that he was acceptable to the Junto; and steps were taken to shield him from recriminations over the high-handed policies of the Court of Chivalry by ensuring that these were blamed on the court's officers.[36] Pembroke had signed the Twelve Peers Petition and suffered a consequent loss of royal favour and influence. But since December 1640 he had been working to rehabilitate himself, combining with the king to ensure a safe exile for Lord Keeper Finch and promoting the royal line in defence of an Elizabethan-style church settlement.[37] With the guidance of the two senior members of the Lords, Charles could be talked into regarding

[33] Russell, *Fall of the British Monarchies*, pp. 207–8; Adamson, *Noble Revolt*, pp. 194, 213.
[34] Adamson, *Noble Revolt*, pp. 144–6; Russell, *Fall of the British Monarchies*, pp. 242–3.
[35] Cust, *Charles I. A Political Life*, pp. 273–7.
[36] *CSP Ven. 1640–2*, pp. 116, 124, 139, 146; Adamson, *Noble Revolt*, pp. 74, 80; *D'Ewes Journal*, pp. 375–8.
[37] Adamson, *Noble Revolt*, pp. 156, 169–71.

concessions less as a surrender to the Junto and more as part of a process for drawing closer to his peerage and re-establishing the pattern of cooperation achieved at York.

This approach bore fruit in two striking initiatives from this period. In the first Charles took the unprecedented step of referring final approval of the negotiations with the Dutch to the House of Lords. On 10 February he went in person to the upper house, explained the terms on offer, told them that he had come to seek their 'helps and counsels' out of 'that free trust and confidence which I expressed at the beginning of this parliament' and assured them that it was up to them to 'take or leave as you shall see cause'.[38] The Lords' ratification of the treaty was largely a formality, but this was still a significant concession on the king's part, given that the making of foreign policy and, in particular, the arranging of royal marriages had long been one of his most jealously guarded prerogative powers. It demonstrated his willingness to engage the Lords in decisions that lay at the heart of government and to continue treating them as an expanded version of the Privy Council. The other initiative was the Triennial Act.

This had been introduced in the Commons on 24 December 1640 as a bill 'for annual parliaments', based on statutes from Edward III's reign. It provided that if the king failed to summon a parliament by the due date local officials and, ultimately, freeholders were empowered to send out writs and organise elections. This caused some controversy in the Commons at the second reading on 30 December when Sir Simonds D'Ewes and others expressed concern at the 'popular' nature of this provision and the potential for 'disorder and confusion'.[39] However, the reaction of the Lords appears to have gone considerably further. The Venetian ambassador reported on 1 January that the

> upper chamber has not seemed entirely favourable, fearing lest such an alleviation of the royal authority and the frequency of parliaments might not augment licence among the people, with manifest danger that after shaking off the yoke of the monarchy they might afterwards apply themselves to abase the nobility also and reduce the government of this realm to a complete democracy.[40]

The ambassador was not reporting actual debate in the upper house because the bill was not presented there until 20 January 1641;[41] however, he does seem to have been picking up on views being voiced by the peers and councillors that he talked to, perhaps, particularly by Arundel

[38] *LJ*, iv.157.
[39] Russell, *Fall of the British Monarchies*, p. 225; *D'Ewes Journal*, pp. 196–7.
[40] *CSP Ven. 1640–2*, p. 111. [41] *LJ*, iv.136.

who was his one of his closest acquaintances. He also noted, significantly, that the king 'for his own interests encourages this idea'. Here he seems to have detected the early resonances of the crown's strategy to highlight and marginalise the more radical elements being encouraged by the Commons and claim the middle ground in partnership with the Lords.

This was spelt out in a major speech that the king made to the two houses on 23 January in which he demonstrated publicly, for the first time, that he was listening to his councillors and peers, and was determined to reach out to moderate opinion. His intention, he declared, echoing one of his most familiar refrains, was 'to reduce all things to the best and purest times as they were in the time of Queen Elizabeth'. He warned against those taking advantage of the parliament to push a radical agenda and who, 'more maliciously than ignorantly, will put no difference between Reformation and Alteration of Government'. But he then went on to make a series of commitments to the reformist agenda in the Lords. He declared that he would 'lay . . . down' any sources of revenue found to be 'illegal', remodel the courts of justice 'according to the law', punish those crown officers who had 'overstretched their power', appoint new ministers sympathetic to reform and, even, invite reform of the bishops.[42] Most strikingly of all, he also declared his readiness to give way on what had become the Triennial Bill.

This had received its first reading in the House of Lords on 22 January, still with its provision for local officers to issue election writs where necessary. The same day it was discussed in Privy Council and it was apparently out of this discussion that the king formulated his response on the 23rd.[43] 'The thing I like well', he declared; 'frequent parliaments are the best means to keep a right understanding between me and my people which I so much desire'. However, he could not accept the present bill that contained powers for 'sheriffs and constables and I know not whom to use my authority'. So, to protect 'my honour' and 'the ancient prerogative of the crown', he announced that he would ask his 'learned counsel' to prepare an alternative bill that would be placed before the Lords.[44] This was duly presented prior to the Lords' second reading debate on 28 January and it stipulated that the power to issue election writs should be placed in the hands of the Lord Keeper rather than local officers and freeholders. Once the Lords got their hands on the bill, however, it was further amended so that, in the event of the Lord Keeper failing to act, first of all the whole body of the peerage, and then 'any twelve or more', would be empowered to meet 'at the Old

[42] Rushworth, iii.154–5. [43] TNA, SP 16/476/19, fo. 51v. [44] Rushworth, iii.155.

Palace of Westminster' and 'issue out writs in the usual form'.[45] This formula – with its telling reference to the principle which underlay the Twelve Peers Petition – was eventually accepted by both the king and the Commons. It placed the Lords squarely at the centre of the emerging political settlement, as *de facto* custodians of the all important power to summon parliament.

There were indications that Charles was not entirely reconciled to the course he was now embarked on. When the carefully selected delegation of Arundel, Pembroke, Bedford, Hertford and Holland attended him to secure his consent to the Triennial Bill on 15 February, he reportedly became 'very angry' and insisted on more time to consider it. The problem appears to have been that he got cold feet as it was brought home to him what a massive and irreversible curtailment of the royal prerogative he was about to approve. But overnight he was persuaded that he had no alternative and eventually 'yielded to necessity'.[46] Over the next few days there followed a series of important initiatives which seemed to indicate that settlement was going ahead. On 17 February the Lords, in the face of strong Commons' pressure to commence the trial of Strafford, opted to give him more time to prepare. Significantly the motion was supported by several of the Junto peers (Bedford, Hertford, Saye and Savile), which indicated to one observer that they were now prepared to do a deal over his fate. The following day the upper house indicated the possible terms for such a deal when it suggested that the king be asked to sequester the earl from his offices.[47] Then on 19 February there was a bid by a group of privy councillors in the Lords to unblock the negotiations with the Scots, which had stalled over discussion of the eighth article proposing wide-ranging conditions for a settled peace. With the probable connivance of the king, the Earl of Berkshire proposed that the lords commissioners should bring their 'debates to an end, satisfy them with money and get them out of this land'; their continuing presence was 'like an open wound'. He was immediately supported by Dorset and Arundel, who 'wish't that all armies may disband together'. Nothing came of this immediately, but on 3 March the Lords sent a delegation to the Commons, headed by Arundel, which proposed that the commissioners urge the Scots to set down 'at once and together with convenient speed all their particular heads and demands'. This was resisted by the Commons on a division and when the issue returned to the upper house several of

45 PA, House of Lords Main papers, 28 Jan. 1640/1; BL, Harleian MS. 6424, fo. 12; *LJ*, iv.147, 150, 152; Rushworth, iii.189–90.

46 *CSP Ven. 1640–2*, p. 126.

47 SRO, D1778/1/i/14; HMC, *De L'Isle and Dudley*, vi.381.

the Junto peers objected to the haste that had been urged by Berkshire.[48] But it was now evident that a majority of the upper house supported the king's wish to be rid of the Scots as soon as possible. Charles responded to these moves by finally delivering on his promises to take the Junto peers into high office. On 19 February, Bedford, Essex, Hertford, Saye, Mandeville and Savile, along with Bristol, were summoned to attend the Privy Council.[49]

The initiatives and concessions of mid February could be interpreted in different ways. From the perspective of the Junto, and in particular Bedford and the other proponents of compromise, they could be regarded as the fruit of long and careful cultivation, with pressures being applied to the king by the Scots and the Commons and the king being led steadily down the road towards a 'Venetianised' commonwealth. In his darker moments, Charles himself no doubt read the situation in much the same way. But there were also enough positive developments to enable the likes of Arundel and Hamilton to persuade Charles that by aligning himself with the reformist agenda in the Lords he was developing an alliance that could give him back a measure of political control. The king's faith in his peers was demonstrated in an unexpected, personal bid to influence the outcome of the proceedings against Strafford.

Through the long drawn out preliminaries to Strafford's trial there were various indications that support for the earl was growing in the upper house. Respect for the earl's responses and the dignity of his carriage was combined with doubts about whether the treason charge against him would actually stand up in court.[50] This encouraged Charles to try to tilt the balance further in favour of the earl by appearing in person when he answered the charges in the upper house on 24 February. He took the Lords by surprise. None of them was wearing the formal parliament robes, which were their normal attire, when the king attended and they lapsed into silence as he took his place in the chair of state. He announced that his presence was not intended in any sense to 'alter or hinder the justice of the tryall', but, since the Edward III statute defined treason as an offence against his person and sovereign authority, it was appropriate that he should be there to assess the validity of the charge. He then proceeded, in spite of his disclaimer, to make it clear that he thought there was no charge to answer. When Strafford appeared he put off his hat to him 'graciously'; then, having listened to the answers given by the

[48] Russell, *Fall of the British Monarchies*, pp. 195–6; BL, Harleian MS. 6424, fo. 23; *LJ*, iv.175.
[49] Russell, *Fall of the British Monarchies*, p. 263; Adamson, *Noble Revolt*, p. 199.
[50] HMC, *Buccleuch*, iii.390, 394, 412; *Cowper*, ii.272.

defence counsel, he declared that the earl 'had done him no wronge for ought he knew and that he had spake all truth as far as concerned him, only conceived he was mistaken in that which he had spoken the 27th art'.[51] This was the article in which the earl was charged with levying a tax on Yorkshire on his own authority, to which his response had been that he was authorised by the Great Council of Peers. In exonerating the council from giving such authorisation Charles was able, once again, to emphasise his respect for their proceedings and also underline his impartiality. But this seems to have cut little ice with the peers and the king's rather ham-fisted attempts to cultivate their goodwill largely back fired. They moved immediately to make it clear that it was they who were in charge of proceedings. It was considered a breach of parliamentary privilege for the king to take notice of a debate or a bill that was under consideration, and on this occasion his intervention was taken to constitute a suspension of normal proceedings. As Viscount Saye later observed 'it was not a house whilst the king was there'.[52] So, having sat in complete silence, on his departure they ordered the Lord Keeper 'to resume the house' and then went through the whole process of having the charges read and hearing the earl's answers once again.[53]

This determination to assert themselves in control of proceedings against Strafford was emphasised in the arrangements for staging the trial. These were worked out in early March, mainly by Arundel, who was appointed Lord High Steward to preside over it, and Pembroke, who, as Lord Chamberlain, was responsible for courtly ceremonial. Impeachment involved the Commons acting as accusers while the Lords sat as judges, and previous proceedings had taken place in the upper house.[54] On this occasion, however, it was decided to construct a special court at the southern end of Westminster Hall that would allow room for the attendance of Lords and Commons, and up to 1000 spectators. The aim, as John Adamson has described it, was to create the impression that Strafford 'was on trial not only before his peers, but before the representatives of the entire political nation'.[55] This involved carefully sidelining the king. At the impeachments of the early 1620s James had left the Lords to supervise proceedings for themselves; but Charles had already announced his intention to be present. This put the managers in something of a quandary. They could hardly deny the monarch his wish; but at the same time they could not allow him to sit in the chair of state because

51 BL, Harleian MS 6424, fos. 26–39; *LJ*, iv.171.

52 Foster, *House of Lords*, p. 6; BL, Harleian MS 6424, fo. 52r.

53 *LJ*, iv.171.

54 C.G. Tite, *Impeachment and Parliamentary Judicature in early Stuart England* (London: Athlone Press, 1974).

55 Adamson, *Noble Revolt*, pp. 220–6.

this would invalidate their proceedings and also imply that he was acting as one of the judges. Their solution was to erect a small gallery behind the throne from which the king and queen could observe proceedings in a private capacity. The vacant throne and the relegation of the royal person to the back of the court created a powerful impression. As John Adamson has observed, it was virtually an 'allegory of England's post-Triennial Act constitution' in which the 'first person' of the 'traditional sovereign trinity of "king, lords and commons" had been marginalised from 'the real representatives and custodians of the "commonwealth", the Lords and Commons'.[56] Within this narrative, it was the Lords, sitting in two ranks of seats either side of the throne and, alone among those in the main court, with their heads covered, who were the main focus.

The Lords also remained at the centre of the king's political strategy. Charles was determined that the trial should go ahead and that Strafford should face his accusers and secure acquittal in order to vindicate his own style of government. He therefore refused to accede to suggestions, even from the earl himself, that he be allowed to resign and retire quietly from public view.[57] There was speculation as the trial approached that he would adopt the course he had taken at the time of Buckingham's impeachment in 1626 and create a number of new lords to make 'such a partie there as it will be carried by votes'. But Charles, invariably respectful of the integrity of the noble order, refused to go down this road and instead relied on intensive lobbying.[58] His aim was to exploit the obvious divisions over the issue. The Junto was still pressing hard for the earl's conviction, determined to ensure that the king renounced his policies so completely that they could never be repeated.[59] Aligned against them were a group of courtiers and friends of the earl who were resolved to defend him. But the majority of lords appear to have been relatively open-minded, willing to allow Strafford to make his defence and listen to it. The uncertainty over how they would decide on the case was underlined in a report picked up by Sir John Coke on 9 March that a Lords' committee voted by 26 to 14 against allowing Strafford counsel at his trial, only for the vote to be reversed by 20 votes when the decision was reported to the full house.[60] There was plenty for the earl's allies to work with as the trial opened on 22 March 1641.

Over the first two weeks the ponderous presentation of the Commons' case, the slow pace of proceedings and Strafford's robust defence left most

56 *Ibid.*, p. 225. 57 Russell, *Fall of the British Monarchies*, p. 285.
58 HMC, *De L'Isle and Dudley*, vi.384; *CSP Ven. 1640–2*, p. 128. Only one new peer was created at this time, Lord Seymour: *47th Report of the Deputy Keeper of the Public Records* (1886), p. 119.
59 Adamson, *Noble Revolt*, pp. 217–19. 60 HMC, *Cowper*, ii.273; *LJ*, iv.179.

observers with the impression that his acquittal was becoming more and more likely. In early April Sir John Temple reported that the majority of the upper house now believed that he 'cannot be found guilty of treason', but only of 'high and most transcendant misdemeanours'.[61] There was a telling incident on 10 April when a majority of the Lords determined that, if the Commons brought forward new material for the prosecution, Strafford 'should have the like liberties'. For the upper house this was a matter of the right of a fellow peer to equitable treatment before the law; but for the Commons, who had been pressing to speed up proceedings, it looked as if the Lords were simply conniving at further delays. The decision caused uproar, and the same day the lower house gave the first reading to a bill of attainder, which simply declared that Strafford was guilty as charged and therefore could be executed for treason. This was a manner of proceeding which had little support in the Lords. On 15 April, when the Commons requested them to postpone further hearing of counsel while they put the case for the bill, the peers expressed their determination to press on with the trial.[62] By this stage it was generally accepted that the majority of Lords would spare Strafford on the charge of treason.[63] But, in the event, they were denied the opportunity to pronounce on this. They continued to hear counsel's arguments on both sides; but the trial gradually petered out as it was superseded by the bill of attainder.

The bill was formally introduced to the Lords on 24 April by the Earl of Essex and immediately encountered resistance. The previous day the Venetian ambassador had picked up concern among his contacts in the upper house that it would take out of their hands 'the prerogative of judging the peers of the realm' and set a precedent for the Commons to condemn any peer who became unpopular with the lower orders, adding that the king was doing 'all in his power to encourage this idea'.[64] It was this argument that seems to have carried most weight in the initial debate. Savile, who was beginning to align himself much more closely with the royal court, insisted that 'the lower house did encroach upon the higher house's liberties and did not know their duties'. He was supported by Bristol, and, between them, they persuaded 'the major part' of the house to shelve the bill until there had been further conference with the Commons.[65] The issue also brought into the open divisions within

61 HMC, *De L'Isle and Dudley*, iv.398. See also Lord North's hopes that this would be the case: *Forest of Varieties*, ii.239.
62 BL, Harleian MS 6424, fo. 54r; Adamson, *Noble Revolt*, pp. 236, 242–4; *LJ*, iv.218.
63 HMC, *Cowper*, ii.278. 64 *CSP Ven. 1640–2*, p. 141.
65 Gardiner, *History*, ix. 339–40; Adamson, *Noble Revolt*, p. 258; P. Christianson, 'Obliterated portions of the House of Lords journals', *EHR*, 95 (1980), 344.

the Junto. The more conciliatory members (Bedford, Saye, Hertford and Pym) wanted to dilute the attainder to allow Strafford to escape with his life, so that they could persuade Charles to go on making concessions. But the hardliners (notably Essex, Warwick and Oliver St John) were determined to secure Strafford's execution, to remove, once and for all, the threat that he presented. The bill eventually received its first reading in the upper house on 26 April and it was agreed to hear the Commons' case for it at a joint conference on the 29th. At this point, the most likely outcome, according to most observers, was that the bill would be either rejected or watered down. Henry King, a London newsletter writer, estimated that 50 peers were 'against it' and 30 'for it'.[66] However, this appears to have been turned around by a remarkable speech from Oliver St John at the conference on the 29th in which he insisted that nothing less than Strafford's execution would ensure the safety of the realm. The Earl of Bath, who had probably been among those opposing the attainder, acknowledged that St John did 'excellently acquitte himselfe'; Maurice Wynn, from the vantage point of the Commons, observed that this 'did satisfie divers lords that before were verie scrupulous'; and King remarked that many of the 50 peers who had previously opposed it 'are come about'.[67] However, what finally tipped the balance in favour of attainder was the intervention of Charles.

The king had pursued his policy of working with the Lords and building support in the upper house through March and April. Towards the end of April, as discussion of the attainder reached a critical juncture, he offered a fresh round of concessions to the Junto. Hertford was made a marquis; Warwick, who had been omitted from the earlier appointments, was now promoted to the Privy Council; and Lord Cottington was finally persuaded to resign his offices, opening the way for Saye to become Master of the Wards and Pym Chancellor of the Exchequer. These moves, together with signals to the upper house about the need to maintain their privileges and strike the right balance over reform, had helped to create a scenario in which it seemed more than likely that Strafford would escape the death penalty.[68] But this was not enough for Charles. He understood the need to rely on tactical manoeuvre and party building when this was the only option open to him; but his preference was for acting more forcefully and, where possible, cutting through the fudge and compromise to achieve his ends by direct action. He still felt deeply

66 Adamson, *Noble Revolt*, p. 267; Bodl.L., Tanner MS 66, fo. 77.
67 Adamson, *Noble Revolt*, pp. 271–4; Kent History and Library Centre, U269, C267/12; National Library of Wales, Wynn of Gwydir MS, 1684; Bodl.L., Tanner MS 66, fo. 77.
68 Adamson, *Noble Revolt*, pp. 264–5.

wounded by the surrenders and concessions that had been forced on him in recent months and was looking for an opportunity to turn the tables and take revenge on his enemies with a decisive *coup de main*. This was what led him to lend his support to the First Army Plot.[69]

Conceived in late March, with the involvement of discontented army officers and leading members of the queen's court, this was originally a scheme for the northern army to march on London, release Strafford from the Tower and intimidate the parliament.[70] As news of the plot started to leak in early April, the two houses looked to the king for assurances that he would not countenance such action. They latched on to the disbandment of the new Irish Army, which it was alleged Strafford intended to bring over to subdue England, and gave Charles several opportunities to announce that he would stand it down. But this he pointedly refused to do, adding to suspicions that he and Strafford were planning a rerun of the attempted coup of the previous November. The most damaging refusal came in a speech to the two houses on 28 April when he agreed to disarm recusants and banish papists from his court, but indicated that he would only disband the Irish army when the Scots and English forces were stood down as well. This was the context in which, the following day, so many peers appear to have been swayed by St John's call for the ultimate sanction against Strafford.[71] What finally sank the resistance to attainder in the Lords, however, was the king's disastrous decision to go ahead with the Army Plot.

The revelations on 3 May, that there had been an attempt by Captain Billingsley and 100 men to seize the Tower of London and release Strafford, transformed the political situation. The Earl of Stamford speaking in the upper house described the 'plot' as 'greater than . . . the Gunpowder Treason. For by this time had not this been discovered . . . we had all been made slaves'.[72] The Lords were once again called on to avert a threat to the security of the commonwealth. They responded promptly and decisively. When the Londoners presented a petition on the morning of 3 May outlining the extent of the threat, they quickly ordered the Earl of Newport, as Master of the Ordnance, to secure the Tower. They then dispatched a delegation to the king to ascertain how much he knew about it. When it became apparent that he had given the order to Billingsley, without waiting for his permission, they ordered Essex and Brooke to join Newport in mustering 500 men from the City trained

69 Cust, *Charles I. A Political Life*, pp. 283–4; Adamson, *Noble Revolt*, p. 219.

70 'The First Army Plot of 1641', in Russell, *Unrevolutionary England, 1603–1642*, pp. 281–95.

71 *LJ*, iv.230–1; Adamson, *Noble Revolt*, p. 267.

72 BL, Harleian MS 6424, fo. 58v.

bands. After further revelations on 5–6 May, which included a scheme to seize Portsmouth and use it as a safe haven for the king and queen, and possibly as a bridgehead for a French invasion, they set up a committee to interrogate the ringleaders of the plot and ordered that a proclamation be issued to apprehend them before they could flee abroad. Mandeville was then sent down to secure Portsmouth and question the governor Sir George Goring; the trained bands of Hampshire and Wiltshire and the ships at Portsmouth were put in readiness to defend the port; and the house put pressure on Charles to appoint Lord Lieutenants that it could trust. He was told that they 'thought it fit' that Salisbury should serve alongside the unreliable Lord Cottington for Dorset and that Southampton be joined with Lennox and Portland in Hampshire. When Charles tried to appoint Savile for Yorkshire the house sent a delegation to 'move his majesty' that he be replaced by Essex.[73] The most far reaching measure of this period, however, was the bill against dissolving or adjourning the parliament, which stipulated that this now required the consent of the two houses. After being rushed through the Commons, it was given first and second readings in the Lords on 7 May and was immediately referred to a committee of the whole house, from which it emerged later in the day with the recommendation that its operation be limited to two years. This was rejected in conference with the Commons in favour of a perpetual provision; and the following day the bill passed the Lords on its third reading by the 'major part'. The readiness of a majority to give its backing to such a drastic curtailment of the royal prerogative was a measure of the extent to which, for the time being, the king had forfeited the trust of the political elite.[74]

These measures added up to a remarkable assertion of power and authority by the Lords, as both Conrad Russell and John Adamson have emphasised. Several of the initiatives it took were unprecedented: the proclamation to apprehend the plotters was the first and only one of Charles's proclamations to be issued 'by the advice of the Lords of Parliament'; the order to the attorney general to issue a commission under the Great Seal for Goring to be examined on oath was similarly novel; and the authorisation to Essex, Newport and Brooke to call out the London trained bands and to Mandeville to act for 'the securing and safeguarding' of Portsmouth was the first time the house had deployed military power on its own authority. Even more far reaching, was its insistence that the king bow to its wishes in the choice of Lord Lieutenants. This claim, essentially to determine who should fill senior offices, was without

[73] Adamson, *Noble Revolt*, pp. 285–7; Russell, *Fall of the British Monarchies*, pp. 298–9.
[74] Russell, *Fall of the British Monarchies*, pp. 295–6; *LJ*, iv.238, 241.

parallel in recent times and it prompted the Venetian ambassador to observe that 'parliament will not even let the king enjoy the use of appointments which is his sole prerogative'. To cap it all, the Lords had, in effect, completed the work begun with the Triennial Act and removed from the king's hands one of his most important and cherished prerogatives, the power to summon and dissolve parliaments. In Russell's words, this was 'the Lords . . . acting as the ultimate repository of supreme authority'.[75]

However, remarkable as the lords' claims were, they were not as unprecedented as might at first sight appear. Much of the motive force behind these measures came from the Junto peers, pushing, as Adamson has stressed, to ensure that the key military offices in England were concentrated in the hands of the Junto and those they could trust.[76] However, support for this came from the body of the peerage, taking on the role that was increasingly being assigned to it of acting as an expanded version of the Privy Council. Since the start of the Long Parliament the proceedings of the Privy Council and the upper house had been merging more closely together. In early 1641, when the council was relatively active, initiatives that were discussed there would quickly be referred for further debate and decision to the Lords. Towards the summer, as council meetings dwindled away, the Lords started to take on various conciliar functions, such as issuing instructions to local magistrates or ambassadors about to depart abroad.[77] Its actions in early May could be seen in some senses as a formalisation of this merging of roles. Drafting proclamations, issuing instructions to the Attorney General, putting trained bands into a state of preparedness, even recommending the choice of Lord Lieutenants, were all functions that had normally been performed by Privy Councillors sitting in council. In the power vacuum created by the king's breach of trust, councillors continued to act, but they now looked to the Lords to share the responsibility and provide the alternative source of authority that they needed. Hyde suggested that the new Junto-backed appointees of February had an important role to play in this role in persuading the Privy Council to align itself more closely to 'the sense of the two Houses, which . . . was his [the king's] Great Council by whose wisdom he was entirely to guide himself'.[78] This, then, was not some sudden, new departure. The attitudes and habits which made it feasible had been forming over the medium term, going back to the start of the parliament and the attempted coup in November 1640, and beyond this to the Great

[75] Russell, *Fall of the British Monarchies*, p. 299; Adamson, *Noble Revolt*, p. 295; *Proclamations*, ii.742–4; *CSP Ven. 1640–2*, p. 152.

[76] Adamson, *Noble Revolt*, p. 295.

[77] TNA, PC2/53, pp. 127–30; *LJ*, iv.236, 242.

[78] Clarendon, *History*, i.261–2.

Council at York when peers had taken responsibility for guiding king and nation out of the Scottish crisis.

In its handling of the measures taken to counter the Army plot the upper house was able to preserve the appearance of remarkable unanimity. The only evidence of a division was over the third reading of the bill against dissolving parliament, where some peers may have favoured the two-year time limit. But the response to the attainder bill, which was reintroduced into the upper house by Warwick on 4 May, was very different. Here the stresses and strains generated by the bill produced repeated divisions. The crowds thronging round Westminster considerably heightened the tension and gave those who had misgivings about the whole process further cause to delay it. Savile and Bristol, this time supported by Bath, responded to the reintroduction of the bill by arguing that proceedings should be postponed until the crowds had dispersed, 'or else they might be deemed to condemn him for feare of force, or else if they acquit him to be in danger of their own persons'.[79] This line – which was also being pressed on the house by the king – found favour with the majority and it was resolved to hold a conference with the Commons before any further action was taken. However, set against this was the continuing alarm at the threat posed by Strafford. This was brought home to the Lords on the afternoon of 4 May when they followed the lead of the Commons and solemnly subscribed, one after another, to the Protestation Oath. The Earl of Southampton objected to subscription, on the grounds that the preamble, with its recital of popish plots, evil counsels and acts of 'arbitrary and tyrannical government', was close enough to the charges against Strafford to prejudge the issue of attainder. His protest was brushed aside; but it clearly highlighted the way in which the continuing revelations kept bringing the peers back to the Junto's argument that nothing less than the earl's execution could secure the safety of the realm.[80]

Debate on the attainder continued on 5 May and immediately a number of peers indicated the pressures they were under by asking to be excused from voting. Some, such as the Earl of Cumberland, who were presumed to be supporters of Strafford, again complained of the risk of intimidation by the crowds; others simply offered excuses.[81] The attendance of lay peers in the house that had been over 80 at the taking of the protestation dwindled to between 45 and 60. On 6–7 May the Lords proceeded to vote on whether the allegations made in the Commons' articles against Strafford were true or not, in each case proceeding to a division

[79] BL, Harleian MS 6424, fo. 59. [80] *LJ*, iv.234; BL, Harleian MS 6424, fo. 61v.
[81] Russell, *Fall of the British Monarchies*, p. 297; BL, Harleian MS 6424, fo. 63r.

and resolving, 'by the major parte' that they were. The final articles – that Strafford had 'endeavoured to overthrow the fundamentall lawes of England and Ireland' and 'exercised a tyrannous and exorbitant power above and against the lawes of both kingdomes' – were accepted on the afternoon of the 7th. The house then consulted the judges to determine whether the earl deserved to 'undergoe the paines and forfeitures of high treason'. When the answer came back that he did, a final attempt was made by Southampton, Bath and Savile to delay proceedings by querying whether the judges had made their decision on the basis of statute or common law. This was headed off by Paget, Brooke and others arguing that it would take up too much time.[82] Finally late on the afternoon of the 7th the bill was given its third reading and voted through by a majority. The size of this is impossible to estimate accurately. Sir Henry Vane writing to his friend Sir Thomas Roe that evening reported that the bill had passed by 51 votes to only nine; but the other contemporary reporter of this division, the anonymous author of *The Brief and Perfect Relation*, recorded the much narrower margin of 26 votes to 19 when the bill received its final approval on the morning of Saturday 8 May.[83] These figures give very different impressions of the extent of opposition. But what is clear, at least, is that the passage of the attainder bill caused deep and bitter divisions that left a lasting legacy and ushered in a markedly more partisan approach to House of Lords politics over the months that followed.

In the short term, however, having made its decision to support the attainder, the upper house gave every appearance of pulling together to persuade the king to accept the bill. Through the weekend of 8–9 May Charles agonised over whether to set aside the promises that he had made to protect Strafford and give his assent to the bill. He consulted the Privy Council who probably advised him to sign, although there is no record of what transpired. He also summoned four of his bishops and asked them how he could square this with his conscience. Eventually, at 9 pm on the Sunday, he set down his signature. However, this was not the end of the matter. He still had to determine a date for the execution and issue

82 Christianson, 'Lords journal', 350–2; J.H. Timmis, 'Evidence and I Eliz I. cap.6: the basis of the Lords' decision in the trial of Strafford', *HJ*, 21 (1978), 682–3; BL, Harleian MS 6424, fo. 64v.

83 TNA, SP 16/480/20; *The Brief and Perfect Relation* (London, 1647), p. 89; Christianson, 'Lords journal', 352. Recent historians have been divided on which is the correct figure: Russell (*Fall of the British Monarchies*, p. 297) and Adamson (*Noble Revolt*, p. 297) accept Vane's estimate, although Russell points out that it is not certain which division it refers to; J.H. Timmis (*Thine is the Kingdom* (Tuscaloosa: University of Alabama Press, 1974), pp. 169, 176–7) accepts the *Brief Relation* figure which Adamson argues probably relates to one of the earlier divisions.

the writ to deliver Strafford from the Tower. It was at this point that the Lords stepped in and acted decisively. They declared on their own authority that the date of execution should be 12 May, and the Earl of Newport undertook, as constable of the Tower, to deliver the prisoner.[84] Then on 11 May Charles made a last bid for clemency, sending his son to the upper house with a personal plea that, 'if it may be done without discontentment to my people', Strafford be allowed to live out the rest of his life in confinement. The Lords latched on to this last phrase and, with Essex, Bristol and Saye to the fore, determined that 'neither the people would be contented without Strafford's death, nor quiet or safety in delay thereof'. They then dispatched a delegation to inform the king of this, again consisting of the symbolic number of 12 peers. Charles accepted what they had to say with good grace, thanked them for their care for Strafford's 'innocent children', then affirmed that he was 'content' that his letter 'be registered by you in your house'. 'In it', he declared, 'you see my mind. I know you will use it to my honour'.[85] This was a very significant transaction because it showed Charles, once again turning to his peers in a moment of crisis, still prepared to trust that they would protect his honour and advise him with honesty and integrity. He hoped that they could be persuaded to grant Strafford clemency; but if this was not to be then at least he could feel that he had shared the responsibility for the earl's death, and, perhaps, even received a measure of absolution, from those whose opinions he respected above all others. The Lords, for their part, while remaining determinedly united behind the majority line, did their best to let the king down gently. The spirit of the Great Council was still discernible.

Through the summer months which followed, up to the adjournment of the parliament on 9 September 1641, this spirit became much harder to sustain. Politics in the upper house became more obviously partisan and bipolar. In part this was due to the legacy of the Army Plot and the bitter divisions engendered by the attainder of Strafford. But it was also the consequence of a change of direction by the Junto, following the death of the Earl of Bedford on 9 May. As John Adamson has demonstrated, this removed from the scene the opposition leader who was most committed to the policy of the 'projected settlement' and achieving reform by persuasion and accommodation. Bedford had recognised the importance of not pushing Charles too far, allowing him to retain his dignity and acknowledging his authority within very clear limits determined by parliament. After his death, leadership of the Junto passed into the hands of

84 Russell, *Fall of the British Monarchies*, pp. 299–300; Adamson, *Noble Revolt*, p. 301.
85 BL, Harleian MS 6424, fo. 66r; *LJ*, iv.245.

Warwick and Essex who believed that their future security depended on stripping the king of most of his power and authority. They were prepared to force Charles to accept a 'Venetianised' commonwealth, in which control over the appointment of councillors and officers was largely in the hands of parliament and freedom to exercise his prerogative was severely curtailed.[86] This made it much harder to maintain unity in the Lords. The majority of peers continued to believe in 'mixed monarchy', based on the traditional pre-1640 constitution in which the king continued to exercise his discretionary power. While Bedford's approach was in the ascendant, and it appeared that change was being managed through persuasion and accommodation, they felt relatively comfortable supporting the reformist agenda. But once the approach became more openly coercive, and appeared to threaten the political and religious middle ground, divisions became more overt, debates grew more fractious, and a 'king's party' began to emerge in the Lords.

The first clear indications of this were the debates over the bishops exclusion. These took place against a backdrop of growing disquiet in the Lords about challenges to the existing hierarchy and the popular threat presented in the May demonstrations by what Lord Savile called 'a rable of the base multitude'. When a libel against the bishops was pinned to the door of the upper house on 18 May the house was quick to pass an order that 'if the people come in a tumultuous manner at the hearing of the bishops or any other cause' the house would adjourn.[87] This sense of alarm at the challenges from below helps to explain why large numbers of lay peers rallied behind the bishops when the Commons called for their exclusion from the upper house in late May and early June. This produced some of the bitterest exchanges and deepest divisions of the period in the Lords. There was a 'long and serious' debate on 24–25 May which was eventually resolved in favour of the bishops, with between 30 and 40 lay peers supporting them, while 25 were opposed. Lord Pierrepont, one of those who participated, insisted that their place in the house was sanctioned by custom, antiquity and the house's responsibility to consider the needs of the church as well as the commonwealth. He also warned that if one section of the Lords could be removed in this way it would set a precedent for the expulsion of others.[88] The upper house then appointed one of its most anti-reformist committees of the period to confer with the Commons and urge them to amend their proposal on the grounds that

86 Adamson, *Noble Revolt*, pp. 309–12.

87 BRO, St John of Bletsoe MS, 1384; BL, Harleian MS 6424, fo. 70r.

88 *Two Speeches spoken in the House of the Lords by the Lord Viscount Newarke* (London, 1641), pp. 1–4.

'by common statute law and long practice it was an unquestionable right for [the bishops] to sit in parliament'.[89] The Commons pressed ahead, however, and on the third reading it was reported that, following further acrimonious exchanges, 32 lay peers voted for exclusion and 28 against which, with the bishops also voting against, served to bury the issue for the time being.[90] In retrospect Hyde saw these debates as a significant turning point in the attitude of the upper house. Opposition to reformist policies had never before been expressed 'with such warmth and vigour' and he detected in this the beginnings of a backlash against 'the empire' that 'the governing party in both houses . . . had exercised over them'.[91]

There were other issues too on which the Lords was starting to question the Commons' aggressively reformist line. They willingly followed the lower house in abolishing grievances such as ship money, forest laws and knighthood fines, but when it came to putting an end to the court of Star Chamber there was more hesitation. The main debate in the Lords on 21 June occasioned a remarkable attack by the Earl of Manchester who insisted that it should be preserved because of its crucial role as 'a court that regulated all other courts of judicature . . . curbed the nobility and awed the gentry'. He then delivered a trenchant defence of the king's prerogative: it was soe 'rivitted and inhaerent in him that it could not be limited by any lawe, that he might take any cause out of any court of justice and judge it himselfe'. Given the general tenor of proceedings in the Long Parliament, this was an extraordinary pronouncement, one reporter describing it as 'the highest prerogative language that was spoken since the parliament began'. It provoked a series of angry responses in the upper house, with Essex retorting that 'having labored all this parliament to make themselves freemen and not slaves' to allow such 'an arbitrary court to be a continewall scourge over them, suted not with theire liberties and freedome'. There was speculation that Manchester might be faced with impeachment were it not for the protection offered by his son Mandeville.[92] However, there were also indications that the earl's declaration struck a chord. He was an old Privy Council hand, highly respected in the Lords as a moderating influence. There was a strand of opinion that recognised that it was essential to preserve some aspects of the prerogative if effective royal government was to continue and was alarmed by the sort of emotive language used by Essex. In the end the upper house passed the Star Chamber bill on a majority vote. But before they did so they cut out a clause designed to give statutory

89 BL, Harleian MS 6424, fos. 70v–71r; *LJ*, iv.258.

90 BRO, St John MS 1383; TNA, SP 16/481/21.

91 Clarendon, *History*, i.312–13.

92 BRO, St John MS 1386; BL, Harleian MS 6424, fo. 73r.

effect to the clause in the Petition of Right that prohibited commitment by the lords of the council without showing cause.[93] Increasingly it was recognised that a balance had to be struck if the traditional status quo was to be maintained.

There was also a sense that the Commons' actions were serving to divide up the political nation in ways which were damaging to the prospects of unity and settlement. This became evident when the Commons tried to make the taking of the Protestation oath compulsory at the end of July. After delaying the bill in committee, the Lords eventually rejected it by majority vote, with, according to Hyde, three-quarters of the upper house voting against, apparently on the grounds that it would have excluded all those who refused to take the oath from holding office or taking their seat in the House of Lords.[94] The Commons retaliated by issuing a printed ordinance enjoining all Englishmen to take the Protestation and spelling out the penalties for failing to do so. This led to an indignant collective response from the Lords who, on 3 August, voted that the ordinance constituted a 'great breetch of priviledge' in that it was against the 'rights of the subject' and the peers 'to have any such imposition layd upon them otherwise than by the lawes of the land'.[95] The use of the emotive term 'imposition' to describe a measure by the Commons was a telling indication that the upper house felt that it was going too far. As in the debate over bishops exclusion, the notion was gaining ground that the lower house was prepared to override tradition, statute and common law in pursuit of reforms that could only divide the nation.

In spite of this evidence of growing differences, however, when the nation's security was threatened the upper house was still able to work with the Commons to push through some drastic curtailments of royal power. Further revelations about the First Army Plot, and then rumours of a second one, stoked up fear of conspiracies and cast further doubt on how far the king could be trusted. Furthermore, on 19 June 1641, news reached London of a conspiracy engineered by the Earl of Montrose and other former Covenanters to accuse the Junto's main Scots ally, the Earl of Argyll, of treason. This was the more frightening because the king had recently declared his intention to travel north in July to attend the Scottish parliament. There was now the alarming prospect of him passing through the as-yet undisbanded northern armies and seeking a rapprochement with some of the Scottish nobles who had formerly been united against him. The Junto leaders in Commons responded by

93 Russell, *Fall of the British Monarchies*, pp. 354–5; *LJ*, iv.296.
94 Clarendon, *History*, i.357.
95 Bodl.L., Clarendon SP, vol. 21, 1603; Clarendon, *History*, i.356.

drawing up the Ten Propositions that were presented to the Lords on 24 June.

These constituted the most far-reaching attempt yet to restrict the royal prerogative and entrust the oversight of appointments to parliament. The third proposition urged the king to remove 'evil counsellors' and appoint only 'such officers and counsellors as his people and parliament have just cause to confide in'; and proposition eight picked up where the upper house had left off in early May and stipulated that only 'good' Lord Lieutenants and Deputy Lieutenants be appointed, and that they be identified by taking a 'special oath . . . prepared by the consent of both houses'. These were measures that only just stopped short of demanding parliamentary oversight of the appointment of councillors and crown officers. This time, however, the upper house supported them to the full, along with other propositions requesting the king to delay his Scottish journey, disband his northern army, banish papists from court, send home the papal nuncio and put the upbringing of the prince in the hands of persons it could trust.[96] As Russell has observed, the overall response to the Ten Propositions was 'a remarkable example of how far [the Lords] were prepared to go in taking power out of the king's hands'.[97] Where they were fearful of a coup, and doubtful whether the king could be trusted to exercise military power, they were quite prepared to assert their collective authority in a way that severely curtailed the royal prerogative. However, they still remained open to assurances from the king and appeals to maintain the status quo.

Charles responded to the Ten Propositions by tackling them piecemeal. He agreed to delay the journey to Scotland until 10 August, disband his northern army and dismiss the papal nuncio, Rossetti. On the matter of appointments, however, he held firm. On 12 July the Lords sent a delegation on behalf of both houses to ask for his answer to the third proposition. Charles told them that he 'knew of no ill counsellors' still in his service and insisted that this assurance should 'both satisfy and be believed, he having granted all hitherto demanded by parliament'. He also protested that the continuing allegations that he harboured such counsellors threatened 'to deter any that he trusts in public affairs from giving him free counsel'. This was a well-judged appeal. By invoking the issues of trust and his special relationship with his councillors, Charles appears to have placated the Lords majority, at least for the time being. When the delegation reported back to the upper house no further action

[96] *Constitutional Documents*, pp. 163–7; *LJ*, iv.285–7, 290; Russell, *Fall of the British Monarchies*, pp. 350–4; Adamson, *Noble Revolt*, pp. 335–7.

[97] Russell, *Fall of the British Monarchies*, p. 353.

was taken and, in the less febrile atmosphere in July, the matter was allowed to fizzle out.[98]

The issue of parliament's power to control royal appointments resurfaced in the days leading up to Charles's departure for Scotland; however, this time the majority of the peers sided with him. The whole issue was brought into focus by a Commons proposal at the end of July to appoint a *Custos Regni* while the king was away. This had been promoted by the Junto leadership, apparently in the hope of securing the appointment of either Pembroke or Northumberland who could be relied on to do their bidding. The powers envisaged for the new appointee were spelt out in a speech by St John which declared that he should be able to do 'all things a king might do, as well in parliament as out of it'.[99] However, the prospect of placing such far-reaching, viceregal, powers in the hands of one individual, albeit one of their own number, appears to have alarmed the majority of the upper house. They debated the issue on 4 August, the day after expressing their indignation at the Commons' ordinance on the taking of the Protestation. With feelings still running high over the Junto's willingness to override the traditional *status quo*, they opted for a commission rather than a single individual, and defined its powers narrowly as applying only to the passage of certain bills, which it then proceeded to list. The Commons responded by adding a power 'for removing of officers and placing others in the king's absence'; then followed up with a request that the Lords 'move his Majesty' that Pembroke be appointed Lord High Steward in place of Arundel, who had recently been assigned to accompany the Queen Mother on her journey home through the Netherlands, and also that Salisbury be appointed Lord Treasurer. This was a decisive ratcheting-up of the claims for parliamentary oversight of royal appointments advanced in the Ten Propositions. Had it been accepted, it would, as Russell and Adamson have observed, have led to 'a fundamental shift . . . in the location of sovereign power' and taken the English state several stages further down the road towards a 'Venetianised' commonwealth.[100] When the Commons proposals were presented to the Lords on 9 August, however, they refused to countenance them. Mandeville, Saye and others pressed the case for Pembroke's appointment particularly hard; but it was not enough to shift the majority.[101]

At this point the king himself seized the initiative. The previous day he had shown his determination to keep control over royal appointments

[98] *LJ*, iv.310–11; Gardiner, *History*, ix.405. [99] Adamson, *Noble Revolt*, pp. 339–40.
[100] Russell, *Fall of the British Monarchies*, pp. 365–6; Adamson, *Noble Revolt*, p. 341.
[101] BL, Harleian MS 6424, fos. 89v–90r.

and free himself from the influence of the Junto by conferring the English dukedom of Richmond on Lennox who, according to Hyde, alone among 'men of great quality and consideration' in recent months had refused to 'stoop or make love' to the Junto leadership.[102] Richmond had long been a personal favourite of the king and by elevating him above every other member of the English nobility – including Arundel who around this time was thwarted in his hopes of succeeding to his ancestral title of Duke of Norfolk and began to distance himself from active involvement in high politics[103] – Charles was signalling his adoption of him as his new first minister. At Richmond's behest he then made the increasingly 'royalist' Bristol a gentleman of the bedchamber and his son Lord Digby ambassador for the key posting to Paris. Finally he further enlarged the Privy Council, reportedly on Bristol's advice, by bringing in three of the

[102] Clarendon, *History*, i.361.

[103] The political eclipse of Arundel at around this time has passed largely unnoticed, but it was a significant event. Having been one of the most prominent royal councillors, and a very important link between king and Lords in early 1641, Arundel faded into the background in the latter half of the year and withdrew from Westminster politics altogether early in 1642. He surrendered his office of Lord Steward of the household to Richmond, but retained his place as Earl Marshal. How far all this might have been the result of a falling out with the king is hard to ascertain. Arundel must have felt snubbed by the king's reluctance to grant him the long-coveted dukedom of Norfolk (*CSP Dom. 1641–3*, p. 38); but the king may have done this simply out a desire to ensure that his cousin and new favourite, Richmond, was clearly established as the senior peer. John Adamson has argued that Arundel had for some time been gravitating towards the Junto in the manner of his fellow senior peer, Pembroke (Adamson, *Noble Revolt*, pp. 63, 191, 618n); but it is hard to find positive evidence for this. The earl was certainly no friend to Strafford, but his management of his trial appears to have been as even-handed as was feasible (Adamson, *Noble Revolt*, pp. 235–6, 617–18n). His instinct was to do everything in his power to uphold hierarchy and authority, oppose anything that might be construed as popular, and remain, as far as possible, above the political fray. This made him an unlikely recruit to the reformers. It seems more probable that he took the opportunity afforded by his honorific role in escorting the queen mother back to France in August–October 1641 to withdraw from a political conflict that he found increasingly distasteful (*CSP Dom. 1641–3*, pp. 74, 148; BL, Add. MS 78, 628, *passim*). He returned to Westminster at the end of October, escorted the king on his entry to London on 25 November 1641, sat occasionally in the Lords during December and attended the Privy Council at the start of January 1642 (*CSP Dom. 1641–3*, p. 148; Adamson, *Noble Revolt*, p. 442, PA, HL/PO/JO/5/1/8; TNA, PC2/53, pp. 207–11); but from mid January 1642 there is little sign of him being active in politics. He was engaged in escorting the queen and princess Mary to the Netherlands in mid February, then took up residence in Antwerp in May and thereafter remained abroad (*CSP Dom, 1641–3*, p. 284; Howarth, *Lord Arundel*, ch. ix). Another element in his willingness to withdraw may have been the emergence of his eldest son, Lord Mowbray and Maltravers, now aged 33, as a political force in his own right. He was a significant figure in the Lords, a credible leader of the Howard family interest, and a committed royalist (*Oxf.DNB*, 'Howard, Henry Frederick, 15th Earl of Arundel, 5th Earl of Surrey, 2nd Earl of Norfolk (1608–1652)'; Appendix 2, 'English Peers and allegiance, 1640–2').

peers who had kept their distance from the Junto: Bath, Dunsmore and Seymour.[104] These appointments demonstrated that he was now resolved to start building a royalist party among those elements of the nobility on whom he felt he could rely.

He followed up on 9 August with a council-backed proposal to replace the *Custos Regni* project with a commission to act in his absence and secured agreement for this in the Lords after 'serious debate'. The next day, just before his departure for Scotland he appeared in the upper house in person, gave his assent to several of the bills that they had listed, then announced that he had passed the commission, consisting of 22 senior councillors, under the great seal.[105]

The king's decisive action wrong footed the Junto and the Commons. He had demonstrated that he still had the capacity to take the political initiative and could draw on the support of the majority of the Lords. For the Earl of Northumberland, caught in the middle of these events, it indicated a significant shift in the balance of power. Writing three days after the king's departure he observed

> a strange alteration and change in the present affaires, ellse the king would never have given such a farrmacy to the parliament. If they swa[llow] this pill quietly there is no question, but the king will easily overcome all difficulties that can arise in that place.[106]

With the support of a revived royalist party at court and a majority in the upper house, Charles appeared to be on the way to recovering much of his political authority.

In what remained of the first phase of the parliament, up to the adjournment on 9 September, the pace of proceedings slowed. This was partly due to the departure of the king, but also because of the effects of plague that took hold in London from mid August and reduced attendance in the upper house to around 20.[107] Even in such a sparsely attended Lords, however, party divisions were increasingly evident. In his parliamentary diary, Bishop Warner started to identify what he called 'good lords' and 'adverse lords'. The 'good lords' were those who supported the bishops in their struggle against a new Commons bill to impeach them for their part in the Canons of 1640. The 'adverse lords' (among whom he named Essex, Saye, Mandeville, Wharton and Paget) were 'vehemently opposed' to allowing the bishops adequate time to prepare their defence.

[104] Adamson, *Noble Revolt*, p. 344; TNA, SP 16/483/34.
[105] TNA, PC2/53, p. 177; *LJ*, iv.354–7. [106] BL, Add. MS 78,268, fo. 11.
[107] HMC, *4th Rept., De La Warr*, p. 295.

However, the 'good lords' carried the day – by just 23 votes to 22 according to Warner – and the bishops trial was postponed to 16 September 1641.[108]

Warner did not specify who the 'good lords' were on this occasion, but one can get a clearer idea of those who were now resisting the Junto from the proceedings in response to the Commons' ordinance of 8 September. This was an order for the removal of east end altars and communion rails and the destruction of images and crosses, which could be viewed by its opponents as a dangerous extension of radical religious reform. The Lords debated the order in committee on the 8th and suggested some relatively limited qualifications pending further discussion. Without waiting, however, the Commons decided to press ahead and publish their ordinance as originally framed. The upper house interpreted this as a blatant snub and on 9 September retaliated by ordering the publication of their own order of 16 January 1641 requiring adherence to the ecclesiastical arrangements in place under Elizabeth. The Earl of Dover, one of the peers who supported this resolution described their action as an attempt to ensure that religion was practised 'accordinge to the lawe and the quiet of the church'. However, the Junto peers and their allies, alarmed at the prospects of a rift with the Commons and apparent backtracking on religious reform, proposed delaying publication until there had been a further conference. Those in favour of publication carried the day by eleven votes to nine. The ten peers who – in addition to Bishop Williams – formed the majority were a cross section of less prominent lords who over recent months had distanced themselves from the Junto. The Earl of Dover's 'Observations in this parliament' reflected his disenchantment at the aggressive tone of some of the reforms being promoted by the Commons and their encouragement of 'tumultuous assemblies'; Lord Capel had recently been elevated to the peerage and Lord Dunsmore to the Privy Council as part of the king's party building effort; Lord Pierrepont had opposed the bishops exclusion; the Earl of Portland was distrusted by the Junto as Lord Lieutenant of Hampshire; Lord Mowbray, Arundel's son, was suspected of Catholicism; the Earl of Cleveland and his son, Lord Wentworth, were two of Strafford's more obvious friends in the upper house; the Earl of Carnarvon had been implicated in the Army Plot; and the Earl of Denbigh, and Lord Coventry had kept a low profile on issues of reform. This was a group

108 BL, Harleian MS 6424, fo. 92; *LJ*, iv.340–1, 363, 367, 368. Another sign of growing division and tension in the upper house was the eruption of personal quarrels – between Arundel's son Lord Mowbray and the Earl of Pembroke in July 1641, and Lord Paget and Lord Pierrepont in August; Harleian MS 6424, fos. 82v, 90r.

that reflected unease at the pace and direction of recent reform and the threat that it presented to the traditional status quo.[109]

Perhaps even more striking than the evidence of a conservative backlash was the indication of a collapse in the consensual approach of the early months of the parliament. The defeated minority of Junto peers and their allies took the highly unusual step of exercising their privilege to register a written 'protestation' against a measure that they could not agree with. This right had rarely been made use of; but on this occasion they went even further and in addition to having the protestation recorded in the *Lords Journal* they had it printed and published, with the names of those voting on either side attached.[110] This deliberate opening up of divisions in the house to public scrutiny was an unmistakeable sign that earlier efforts to present a united front were breaking down. In the face of growing partisanship, sides were beginning to form and differences were becoming clearly exposed. The collectivist spirit, which had been established at York the previous September, was draining away. The consequences of this for the peerage were to become apparent during the autumn recess.

The House of Lords' ability to act collectively and maintain the appearance of consensus up to the final weeks of the first phase of the parliament is one of the more remarkable features of the politics of the period. While the king had oscillated between compromise and attempted coup, and the Commons had become increasingly partisan, the Lords navigated their way though successive crises holding positions somewhere near the centre ground. This capacity to balance the interests of crown and subject was deeply ingrained in the peerage's view of itself and its role within the political system. One of the difficulties of reconstructing the politics of these months is the paucity of correspondence or working papers for individual peers; but what survives – notably Montagu's parliamentary dairy, Lord North's reflections and the Earl of Dover's 'observations' – does suggest that they took very seriously their obligation as *consiliarii nati*, to serve both crown and commonwealth. Most peers appear to have felt much more comfortable balancing these demands and steering a middle course than choosing sides.

This approach was based on long tradition and experience, as Conrad Russell has emphasised.[111] But it was also grounded in their recent participation in the Great Council at York, where, with the eyes of the

109 Adamson, *Noble Revolt*, pp. 356–9; Russell, *Fall of the British Monarchies*, pp. 368, 370; Bodl.L., Clarendon SP, vol. 21, 1603; *Oxf.DNB* articles on these peers.

110 Crummett, 'Lay peers', pp. 283–5; Foster, *House of Lords*, p. 55; Russell, *Fall of the British Monarchies*, p. 370.

111 Russell, *Fall of the British Monarchies*, p. 210.

nation upon them, they had set about charting a course to extricate the nation from the disaster of the Bishops Wars. After two decades during which the noble order was threatened with decline and in danger of being marginalised, the experience of holding centre stage, being listened to and being taken seriously had a revitalising effect. At the start of the Long Parliament the upper house picked up where it had left off in the Great Council, doing its best to act in accordance with the spirit summed up in the Lord Keeper's opening speech, but with an enhanced sense of responsibility to the public welfare, which meant shouldering the heavy workload of the programme of reform and facing up to the difficult decisions required in handling the king. The revival of conciliar power at York also helped and the habit of acting as an expanded version of the Privy Council carried over into the parliament. Privy Council and Lords increasingly merged together as the former looked to parliament for authority to act and the latter behaved more and more like an arm of the executive. The consequences of all this were particularly apparent in the peers' handling of the various plots and crises from November 1640 onwards, most notably the First Army Plot. The collective resolve that it displayed, in heading off the threat of a coup and putting in place safeguards to prevent this happening again, was a remarkable display of its willingness to take on the responsibility for guiding the nation out of crisis. One of the consequences was to enhance the status and authority of the Lords to a new level, perhaps, best summed in the provisions of the Triennial Act, which gave them the ultimate responsibility for calling a parliament should the king and Lord Keeper fail to do so.

The collectivist approach, which was a feature of the Lords proceedings during the early phase of the Long Parliament, came under increasing pressure, much of it exerted by the king. As we have seen, Charles's investment in the power and welfare of the nobility was not just a matter of fulfilling the expectations of a 'good king' and enhancing the dignity of his monarchy. He was also aiming to build a 'royalist party' that could be relied on to side with him in periods of crisis. Securing the support of the Lords remained at the heart of the king's political strategy and he was prepared to make significant concessions to achieve it. The 'projected settlement' of early 1641 was a crucial part of this policy, aimed, as far as Charles was concerned, at winning the battle for the loyalty of the body of the peerage. His approach to this was best summed up in his speech on 23 January 1641, which combined appeals to protect tradition and defend the centre ground, particularly in the matter of religion, with warnings of the dangers of radicalism and the menace of popularity, as much a threat to the nobles as to the crown. While he stuck to this programme, and gave an appearance of working to achieve consensus, Charles could anticipate retaining the goodwill and support of a majority of the peers. The benefits of this were evident in the way in which he was able to draw on noble support to retrieve some of the political initiative during the early months of 1641, and again in August, when his mistakes had left him in danger of being marginalised. They were also apparent in the whittling away of support for the conviction of Strafford on a charge of treason. As the events of late 1641 and 1642 were to demonstrate while the king stuck to a policy of patient party-building and appealing to majority opinion among the peers, he put himself in a strong political position. The problem was that at key moments, notably in early May 1641, he departed from the script and made ill-judged attempts at resolving his difficulties by force.

At the other end of the spectrum, the upper house was being pushed by the Junto in the direction of radical reform. The Junto peers had the considerable advantage that at the start of the parliament the Lords had adopted the Twelve Peers Petition as a basic agenda for reform. Through careful management, debating skills and coordinating initiatives with the Commons, they were able to achieve an influence over the direction of proceedings out of all proportion to their small numbers. But this did not amount to control of the upper house. While the Lords were engaging with issues of reform, or responding to real or imagined plots, they were generally willing to follow the Junto lead. But when they moved on to issues that appeared to threaten the existing status quo – such as the exclusion of bishops, usurping the king's prerogative in choosing ministers, or the destruction of Strafford by a bill of attainder – they became much less biddable. During the summer months of 1641 one can discern the outlines of a conservative backlash, culminating in the vote to publish the order of 16 January. The willingness of a number of less prominent peers to defy the Junto and Commons' line on this indicated a sense that the reformers were overreaching themselves and that the balance was being tilted too far against the crown. Both Edward Hyde and Giovanni Giustinian, the Venetian ambassador, were quick to point out that noblemen recognised that their power and position derived from the king and that what threatened his authority would ultimately damage their own.[112] Although the default position for most peers was to try to maintain balance and unity between crown and people, in the final analysis, if they were forced to take sides, the majority would gravitate towards their monarch.

[112] Clarendon, *History*, i.193; *CSP Ven. 1640–2*, pp. 111, 284.

The formation of the Royalist party

The Earl of Northumberland's observation on 13 August 1641 that there had been 'a strange alteration and change in the present affaires', which had done much to restore the political initiative to the king, was well founded.[113] On the face of it the king's departure for the north had weakened his cause, as he adopted a much lower profile in English affairs and directed most of his attention to Scotland. Some of the earlier tension subsided as the Junto leadership had less to be anxious about and less to respond to. But behind the scenes Charles had begun building a royalist party that could take on the Junto, both inside and outside parliament. As we have seen, the first indications of this were apparent in the days leading up to his departure when he had outmanoeuvred his opponents over the appointment of a *Custos Regni* and gone out of his way to strengthen the anti-Junto group at court by adopting Richmond and Bristol as his leading councillors and elevating dependable allies to the Privy Council. This was the first time since the opening of the Long Parliament that he had felt sufficiently confident of his position to promote loyalists and defenders of the royal prerogative rather than trying to appease the reformers. During the weeks spent in Scotland his determination hardened and he directed his efforts increasingly to assembling a party of what he called 'my servants' and the 'well affected'.

His chief adviser and agent in this process was another of the new appointees of early August, Edward Nicholas. Charles had entrusted him with custody of the privy seal, with the assurance that he would soon be made Secretary of State. From the moment of the king's departure to the eve of his return, on 25 November, Nicholas conducted a remarkably frank, and revealing, correspondence with his royal master, supplying a stream of perceptive advice on how to strengthen his position at Westminster.[114] He saw a considerable opportunity for the king in the growing backlash against the ambition and corruption of 'King Pym' and his cronies, and, in particular, the row between the Lords and Commons just before the recess, which he interpreted as a sign that 'the partie of the Protesters' had overreached itself. Charles was quick to respond. His comment on this last report – that 'I am not much sorie at it' – summed up his approach. He now recognised that there was an opportunity to exploit the various divisions and discontents that had opened up in the loose coalition ranged against him and to drive a wedge between Lords

[113] BL, Add. MS 78,268, fo. 11.

[114] J.S.A. Adamson, 'Parliamentary management, men-of business and the House of Lords 1640–1649', in *A Pillar of the Constitution: the House of Lords in British Politics 1640–1784*, ed. C. Jones, (London: Hambledon, 1989), p. 23; *Evelyn*, pp. 751–94.

and Commons.[115] For the time being he was prepared to commit himself to trying to achieve his ends by party building and political manoeuvring – what he called 'policy' – rather than a violent coup.[116]

At the heart of his strategy for regaining the political initiative was the House of Lords. The events of August and September, together with Nicholas's continuous reports of clandestine meetings by the 'faccous party' in the upper house, persuaded the king to abandon his earlier approach of appealing to the Lords as a whole. Instead he now aimed to assemble an organised party of his own among the peers who, with the support of the bishops, would be strong enough to stymie Junto proposals for further reform. This policy originated out of a three way communication between Charles, Nicholas and the queen, who was left in charge of managing the Crown's interests in London. Nicholas and Henrietta Maria were conferring about the possibility of assembling a caucus of royalist supporters while parliament was still in session in August. The queen was determined, according to the Venetian ambassador, who had privileged access to her court at Oatlands, to 'encourage those . . . who although at heart supporters of his Majesty's greatness have not had the courage to declare themselves hitherto'.[117] Charles gave his blessing to the project in his apostil to a letter from Nicholas on 27 September reporting that the Junto leaders had been holding recess meetings at Lord Mandeville's house in Chelsea. 'It were not amisse', the king commented, 'that some of my servaunts met lykewais to countermynd ther plots, to which end speake with my wife and receive her directions'.[118] This was easier said than done.

With the king absent from London and many of his most conspicuous allies dispersed to their country estates, there was little prospect of organising a loyalist lobby during the recess. The queen and Nicholas therefore settled on the next best thing, a display of strength at the reopening of the parliament on 20 October. In consultation with Lord Dunsmore, they put together a list of 11 peers who could be considered reliable royal supporters: the Earls of Bristol, Bath, Cumberland, Devonshire, Huntingdon, Newcastle and Northampton, and Lords Cottington, Coventry, Poulett and Seymour.[119] On 8 October Nicholas wrote to each of them in the king's name requesting their attendance at the reopening of parliament. He appealed to their 'good affeccon to the service of his Majestie & the publique', their sense of obligation now that they knew that the king

[115] *Evelyn*, pp. 761, 767. [116] Cust, *Charles 1. A Political Life*, pp. 17–18, 299–301.
[117] Adamson, 'Parliamentary management', p. 23; *CSP Ven. 1640–2*, p. 208.
[118] *Evelyn*, p. 765.
[119] *Ibid.*, pp. 769–70; Adamson, 'Parliamentary management', pp. 23–4.

was taking a personal interest in their attendance and the flattering notion that they had been singled out to perform this loyal service.[120] Bath wrote back immediately from Tawstock in Devon promising to make all haste back to London even though he was about to carry out the annual audit of his estate rentals. Devonshire and Newcastle explained that they were detained for personal and health reasons, but pledged their service to the king on future occasions.[121] At the same time, with Henrietta Maria's blessing, Nicholas contacted Juxon to organise a similar rally of the bishops 'which are well affected'.[122] Once the session had opened the queen and the secretary designate continued to keep up the pressure. On the Sunday 26 October, the day before the crucial Lords' debate on bishops exclusion, it was noted that she entertained an unusually large number of peers at Oatlands. The same day Nicholas was conferring with her about Newcastle's proxy vote and passing on the latest intelligence, that 'the Bps p[ar]tie is like to ballance the other side.'[123] In early November the queen was anxiously speculating that the absence of 'many of the Lords that ar gone of in the countree' would reduce support in 'the businesse of the Bishops. She therefore sent to Nicholas to chase up the Earls of Carnarvon and Southampton, and Lords Cottington and Dunsmore, to ensure that if they were not able to attend at least their proxies were in reliable hands.[124]

This concerted lobbying and whipping appears to have paid dividends. The attendance details contained in the House of Lords draft minute book from 29 November 1641 to the brief adjournment on 5 January 1642, combined with evidence from committee nominations and the call of the house on 17 November 1641, indicate that of the 12 peers written to or lobbied by Nicholas and the queen only Cottington, Newcastle and Poulett failed to appear regularly.[125] In addition there was regular attendance from a further 28 peers who, from the evidence of the 9 September 1641 vote and later divisions, could be regarded as 'well affected'. These were Berkshire, Bruce, Carnarvon, Capel, Craven, Cromwell, Denbigh, Digby, Dorset, Dover, Fauconberg, Goring, Grey of Ruthven, Herbert of Cherbury, Hertford, Berkshire's son, Howard of Charleton, Lindsey,

[120] SHC, Braye Letters, G85/5/2/11. [121] BL, Add. MS 78,268, fos. 3, 73–4, 79–80.
[122] *Evelyn*, p. 769; SHC, G85/5/2/11; Adamson, 'Parliamentary management', pp. 24–7.
[123] Gardiner, *History*, x.38; SHC, G85/5/2/21.
[124] *Evelyn*, pp. 785, 790. The Lords' proxy book covering this period shows a certain amount of activity among the 'royalist' peers to ensure that their proxies were in safe hands: for example, Southampton entrusting his proxy to Dunsmore and Newcastle his proxy to Hertford who was now a reliable ally of the king. More obvious was the response of the Junto who were busy nailing down proxy votes among allies who might be absentees: PA, HL/PO/JO/13/3.
[125] PA, HL/PO/JO/5/1/8; *LJ*, iv.396–504.

Monmouth, Mowbray, Pierrepont, Portland, Rich, Richmond, Rivers, Savile, Southampton, Wentworth and Lindsey's son, Willoughby of Eresby. The episcopal lobby, organised by Juxon, was even more dependable, with 11 of the 13 bishops whom the Commons were seeking to disfranchise for their role in the Canons of 1640 sitting on an almost daily basis, together with Bishop Williams to whom Charles looked to provide leadership.[126] This provided a solid phalanx of around 50 royal supporters among the house's regular attenders, compared with around 26 for the reformist Junto[127] and a further seven regular attenders who are difficult to categorise and probably represented a floating vote.[128] In a house in which the daily recorded attendance between 29 November and 5 January was generally between 45 and 60 this gave the loyalists sufficient support to block most Junto-backed reforms.

The opening weeks of the reconvened parliament were dominated by the campaign to exclude bishops from the upper house and force Charles to seek parliamentary approval for his appointment of councillors. Nicholas and the king had anticipated this, and their correspondence during September and October was full of suggestions for disrupting the plans of the reformist Junto. When Nicholas reported that the persistence of the plague in London meant that the session might have to be adjourned elsewhere, the king was quick to encourage such a development, suggesting Cambridge as an alternative venue where support for his opponents would be much weaker. And when the secretary designate informed him that Bristol feared that he would be impeached in the coming session, Charles harked back to the events in June and urged Nicholas to 'put Bristo[l] in mynde to renew that dispute betwixt the two houses concerning the Parlament protestation which Southampton was so fearse upon.'[129] They were particularly careful when it came to preparing the ground for the debate on bishops exclusion. News of the king's slate of new Calvinist appointees to the bishops bench, designed to offset any accusation that he favoured papists or Arminians, was released in London on the eve of the debate. At the same time, Nicholas was

126 For more detail on attendance, see below, Appendix 2, 'English Peers and Allegiance 1641–2'; Adamson, 'Parliamentary management', p. 26n.

127 The regular supporters of the Junto were Bedford, Bolingbroke, Brooke, Clare, Essex, Feilding, Grey of Warke, Holland, Howard of Escrick, Leicester, Mandeville, Newport, North, Northumberland, Paget, Pembroke, Roberts, St John, Salisbury, Saye and Sele, Spencer, Stamford, Suffolk, Warwick, Wharton, Willoughby of Parham.

128 These were the Marquis of Hamilton, Lord Keeper Littleton, Carlisle, Conway, Manchester, Nottingham and Peterborough. On the difficulties of categorising some of these individuals, see Russell, *Fall of the British Monarchies*, p. 468.

129 *Evelyn*, pp. 771–2, 775. For Southampton's refusal to take the Protestation Oath, see p. 236, this volume.

circulating to 'divers lords and others' a pledge that he had extracted from Charles that 'I am constant for the doctrine and discipline of the Church of England as it was established under Queene Elizabeth and my father, and resolve (by the grace of God) to live and die in the maintenance of it.'[130] The message that the church and the Protestant religion were safe in Charles's hands was being spelt out very clearly.

The proceedings against the 13 bishops accused of promoting the 1640 Canons began in the Lords on 23 October 1641, with Essex, Mandeville and Brooke trying to push through a resolution for their impeachment. This would have resulted in their immediate suspension and removal from the voting strength of the house. But the crown lobby stood firm. Bristol, Bath and the Catholic peer, Lord Brudenell, were able to trump the argument, put forward in the Commons – that since the Canons themselves had already been condemned the bishops were *ipso facto* guilty – by reminding the house that when the Lords previously agreed to outlaw the Canons it was 'profest & promised' that the vote should not prejudice the bishops.[131] The eventual decision was to give the 13 bishops until 10 November to answer the charges. Four days later the bill for bishops exclusion was reintroduced into the upper house. Its opponents first tried to block it using an objection already canvassed between Nicholas and the king, that it contravened parliamentary procedure to reintroduce a bill previously defeated in the same session. They then appear to have fallen back on the argument that removing the bishops from the upper house would inevitably pave the way to the rooting out of episcopacy altogether. Finally, after a long and bitter debate, in which Southampton was prominent in the bishops' defence, it was again agreed to defer further proceedings to 10 November.[132]

The willingness of a majority in the upper house to stand by the bishops had been consistent ever since the matter had first been debated in May 1641. But parliamentary direction over the king's choice of councillors was a different matter. Here the Lords' majority shifted its stance significantly. There was a sense of crisis in the opening weeks of the parliament, with reports coming in as it reconvened of 'the Incident' in Scotland (in which there had allegedly been an attempt to assassinate Argyll and Hamilton, two of the Junto's main Scottish allies) and then, at the start of November, news of the Catholic rebellion in Ireland. On previous such occasions the Lords had been very willing to

130 *CSP Ven. 1640–2*, p. 236; TNA, SP 16/485/2; *Evelyn*, p. 779.
131 BL, Harleian MS 6424, fo. 97; Russell, *Fall of the British Monarchies*, p. 411.
132 *LJ*, iv.407–8; BL. Harleian MS 6424, fo. 98; TNA, SP 16/485/76; *Evelyn*, p. 778; Gardiner, *History*, x.40–1.

support interventions over the king's choice of councillors. But not this time. When Pym proposed an 'Additional Instruction' for the English committee of MPs advising the king at Edinburgh, he encountered stern resistance. The instruction stipulated that, since the current 'troubles' were the result of 'ill counsels', Charles must remove 'such counsellors and . . . take to him the counsell of parliament', otherwise they would not hold themselves bound to assist him.[133] This was debated at length in the Lords on 9 November; but the upper house concluded that because it was a matter 'of great consequence' a final decision should be deferred to 'a further time'.[134] This was a significant turnaround. The last time the peers had discussed such a motion, at the time of the Second Army Plot in June, they had supported the clause in the Ten Propositions that Charles be asked to appoint only 'such officers and counsellors as his people and parliament had just cause to confide in'.[135] The new motion went rather further in insisting on the removal of 'evil counsellors' and their replacement by others approved by parliament. But Charles had already agreed to accept such constraints in Scotland and, in the midst of a crisis in England, this could be regarded as a legitimate safeguard. However, the majority of the Lords were evidently not prepared to countenance it.

The reasons for this were diverse. Nicholas's discreet lobbying probably had something to do with it. When he informed the king of the proposal, Charles's instruction was that 'You must see to cross this in the Lords House if it be possible.'[136] He no doubt passed this on to his contacts among the peers. But, perhaps, of more significance was the change of mood in the upper house, evident in the confrontation of 9 September. The combination of the conservative backlash against challenges to the constitutional and religious status quo and resentment at the dictatorial approach of the reformist Junto and the Commons' majority had undermined the tradition of consensus-seeking in the Lords. There was a new, hard-edged, sense of partisanship and a determination to defend the king's remaining prerogatives and stem the assault on the church. In these circumstances, an issue on which the Junto had previously been able to carry the house was now blocked by the majority. Northumberland, one of their principal spokesmen, acknowledged as much. In a letter to Sir Thomas Roe on 12 November, he explained how the proposal for parliamentary approval of councillors, along with bishops exclusion, 'stops . . . in our house'. 'If these matters should occasion any breach between the houses,' he anticipated

[133] *LJ*, iv.431–2; *Evelyn*, p. 785; Russell, *Fall of the British Monarchies*, pp. 423–4.
[134] *LJ*, iv.435. [135] See pp. 242–3, this volume. [136] *Evelyn*, p. 786.

ruefully, 'some unhappy effects are much to be suspected'.[137] The 'unhappy effects' that Northumberland was worried about were precisely what Charles and Nicholas were striving to achieve.

The effectiveness of the loyalist 'party' in the Lords produced a significant shift in political momentum. For the first time since the start of the parliament the king had recovered a measure of political control. He could look forward to a situation in which control of the upper house would enable him to negotiate with the Junto from a position of relative strength and pick and choose which items of legislation he allowed to go forward. And if another scheme proposed by Nicholas at the start of November came to fruition he could anticipate an even brighter political future. This was a plan to summon all absentee members of the two houses to attend in person which, the secretary designate anticipated, would tip the balance of votes in the king's favour.[138] The proclamation to implement this was delayed while the king remained in Scotland because the Lord Keeper required his personal warrant. But it was eventually published on 12 December 1641 and copies were sent to 210 absentees, with a request that they attend by 12 January 1642.[139] This meant that the king could look forward to a more sympathetic parliament in which majority support, perhaps in the Commons as well as the Lords, would lie with him.

Hyde later summed this up as a period in which the Junto 'did very visibly lose ground in the House of Commons as the king's friends grew daily stronger in the House of Peers'.[140] With the political situation turning against them, the king's opponents mobilised their base of popular support in London and 'the country' by reviving the Grand Remonstrance, which was finally voted through by the Commons in controversial circumstances on 22 November. This was yet another catalogue of the ills associated with Charles's government and the malign influence of Catholics, bishops and 'evil counsellors'. However, in contrast to previous such manifestos there was no attempt to involve the upper house or seek their approval. Instead, the Lords – or at least a large section of them – were now being presented as part of the problem.[141] In early December Pym proposed drawing up a list of bills that had been stopped in the upper house and presenting them to the king with the approval of the Commons and 'such of the Lords that are more sensible of the safety of the kingdom'. This division of the upper house he justified on the grounds that while the Commons were 'the representative body of

137 TNA, SP 16/485/76. 138 *Evelyn*, p. 782; Adamson, *Noble Revolt*, pp. 464–6.
139 *Proclamations*, ii.754–5; *CSP Ven. 1640–2*, p. 263.
140 Clarendon, *History*, i.447n. 141 Russell, *Fall of the British Monarchies*, p. 428.

the whole kingdom . . . their lordships [sat] but as particular persons'.[142] Such an attempt to circumvent the resistance of the king's allies in the Lords smacked of desperation. It could only further antagonise the loyalist majority among the peers who were intensely jealous of their status and privileges. To be told that they sat 'but as particular persons' and cared less about 'the safety of the kingdom' was bound to increase the sense of resentment at what they saw as the Junto's high-handed and dictatorial approach.[143] The rupture that Northumberland anticipated was increasingly becoming a reality.

As Charles made his way south in late November, he had a solid political platform on which to build. His procession into London on the 25th was the most spectacular royal entry of his reign and also the most effective in terms of mobilising loyal support. He was able to reassure the 'better sort' of Londoners that he had their best interests at heart, with fulsome undertakings that he would protect the Protestant religion, the existing laws and the interests of the City.[144] He also succeeded in getting over the message that he was committed to his role as a constitutional monarch. In response to the recent allegations that he was surrounded by 'evil counsellors' and papists, he went out of his way to demonstrate that he was ruling in partnership with his natural councillors, the leading peers of the realm. In the procession into the city from Hoxton his immediate entourage was made up largely of his principal ministers and household officers, several of them closely associated with the cause of reform. The Marquis of Hertford, who was given the honour of bearing the sword of state, processed immediately in front of the king, flanked by the Earl Marshal and the Lord Great Chamberlain, the Earl of Lindsey. Before them rode Lord Keeper Littleton, Lord Privy Seal Manchester and Lord Chamberlain Essex, together with a further ten peers led by the Duke of Richmond; and bringing up the rear were the Earls of Salisbury and Holland, respectively Captain of the Gentleman Pensioners, and Lord General in the North. But perhaps the most significant participant was the Marquis of Hamilton who a month earlier had been reported as turning against his royal master. Now he took his place just behind the king and queen, leading the horse of state in his role as Master of the Horse.[145] The whole occasion, as John Adamson has described it, was

142 Adamson, *Noble Revolt*, p. 459; Russell, *Fall of the British Monarchies*, p. 438.

143 See the comment on this in the Earl of Dover's 'Observations': Bodl.L., Clarendon State Papers, vol. 21, 1603, fo. 56.

144 Cust, *Charles I. A Political Life*, pp. 313–14.

145 *Ovatio Carolina. The Triumph of King Charles* (London, 1641), pp. 13–16. The other peers in the procession were the Earl Rivers, the Earls of Bath and Cumberland, Viscount Conway and lords Coventry, Digby, Feilding, Goring and Mowbray.

'a *tableau vivant* of "good counsel"', providing powerful evidence that the king was served by ancient nobles and councillors 'who would honour and preserve the post-Triennial act political order'.[146]

Over the next month Charles persisted with this calculated appeal to moderate opinion. His principal advisers, apart from Nicholas, were the Earl of Bristol and his son, Lord Digby. Bristol managed his following in the Lords and Digby was in close touch with Hyde and his other allies in the Commons. The basic strategy was to exploit the issue on which the king had the strongest case, the church, and neutralise two of the weaker ones, 'evil counsellors' and Ireland. He began with a concerted effort to show that he was now the best person to safeguard the Church of England, following up the appointment of Calvinist bishops with a proclamation on 10 December that firmly aligned him with majority opinion in the Lords in favour of defending a Jacobean-style church against radicals and sectaries.[147] He also strenuously countered the suggestion that he was dominated by 'evil counsellors'. On December 2, the day after he was presented with the Grand Remonstrance, he appeared in the Lords in person to offer fulsome assurances of his continuing support for moderate reform. Just as he had no regrets about any of the legislation already passed for 'the good of my people', he declared, so he would 'yet grant what else can be justly desired for satisfaction in point of liberties or in the maintenance of true religion that is here established'.[148] He followed up by reviving the activity of the Privy Council, chairing a number of well-attended meetings during December and early January.[149] In public, at least, Charles gave every impression of continuing with the constitutionalist line on display at his entry into London.

Ireland was, perhaps, his most difficult issue, because it involved a contest for control of the army intended to suppress the rebellion. But here the loyalist lobby in the upper house were able to mount a very effective defence of the royal prerogative. The impressment bill, which had passed though the Commons with relatively little resistance in November, challenged the king's traditional power to compel men to perform military service outside their shires by establishing a precedent for raising an army with the consent of parliament. At the bill's second reading in the Lords on 6 December there was a long and fierce debate. Littleton and Manchester complained that its effect would be to take away from the crown a prerogative that it had enjoyed ever since the time of Edward III. Lord Saye countered by declaring that the abolition of ship money would

146 Adamson, *Noble Revolt*, pp. 442–3.
147 *Proclamations*, ii.752–4; Cust, *Charles I. A Political Life*, p. 315.
148 *LJ*, iv.459–60.
149 TNA, PC 2/53, pp. 199–211.

have been 'to little purpose . . . if the power of pressinge should stand in force as it had done'.[150] The house appointed a committee more or less evenly divided between the two sides to draft amendments 'according to the sense of the house' and the outcome was that the bill was shelved.[151] Charles then attempted to exploit the Junto's discomfort by again putting in a personal appearance in the Lords and promising to pass any impressment bill that did not infringe his prerogative. This was not entirely successful because the upper house, ever jealous of their privileges, voted that the king was interfering in a debate which had not yet been resolved.[152] But for the time being, at least theoretically, Charles remained in control of military service and the Junto was blamed for failing to take effective action to suppress the rebellion.

While this was happening the king was strengthening his party at court and working to free himself from some of the shackles that the Junto had imposed on him in the past. One of his first actions on his return to London was to allow Essex's commission as Lord General of the Army south of the Trent to lapse and to take the command back into his own hands. There were also rumours that Holland, Newport and Hamilton were about to be removed from their offices. At the same time, he displayed a fresh determination to reward those who were serving him loyally. On the way south he had conferred the treasurership of the household on Lord Savile who replaced the out-of-favour Sir Henry Vane; Richmond was now promoted to the position of Lord Steward; Southampton was made a gentleman of the bedchamber and privy councillor; and Nicholas received his secretaryship and a knighthood. There were also reports that Bristol would fill the vacant lord treasurership or else displace Essex as Lord Chamberlain, that Bath would take over Manchester's position as Lord Privy Seal, that Southampton would assume Holland's place as Groom of the Stool, and that Lord Digby would replace Vane as the other Secretary of State. Newsletter writers dropped dark hints about 'factions at court' and 'malicious plots' against the 'good lords' of the Junto; but, from a loyalist perspective, such comments were evidence of Charles's effectiveness in building a party that could take on his political enemies.[153]

His determination to regain his freedom of manoeuvre was, perhaps, most apparent at a council meeting on 11 December when he set up a commission to retrench and rebalance his revenues, so that he could

150 Bodl.L., Clarendon MS, vol. 21, 1603, fo. 56v; Russell, *Fall of the British Monarchies*, pp. 434–5; Adamson, *Noble Revolt*, p. 462.

151 *LJ*, iv. 463. 152 *LJ*, iv.473–4; Gardiner, *History*, x.99.

153 HMC, *Buccleuch*, i.286–8; *CSP Dom. 1641–3*, pp. 178, 188–9, 192, 194.

subsist without having to rely on temporary grants of tonnage and poundage. This was born in part out of his frustrations at being repeatedly promised a lasting financial settlement, but never actually having it approved. As he explained, he felt that it was 'dishonourable for him to accept any more' in the form of temporary grants when his predecessors had received tonnage and poundage for the full duration of their lifetimes.[154] However, as John Adamson has stressed, it was also an attempt 'to break free of the financial constraints which for over a year had kept him so humiliatingly dependant on parliamentary largesse'. The central plank of the post-Triennial Act settlement, as devised by Bedford and Pym, had been to make the crown dependent on parliamentary supply and to use this to force the monarch into concessions that gradually stripped away the crown's prerogatives. By turning his back on further temporary grants, and trying to devise a way to 'live of his own', Charles was seeking to regain his capacity for independent action and put a stop to the seemingly inexorable weakening of royal power.[155] As he put it, he would not 'suffer himselfe to be starved or bought out of any more flowers of his crowne'.[156]

Up to 23 December the king was more than holding his own in the power struggle. He was outmanoeuvring the reformist Junto in the Lords and mounting an increasingly effective opposition in the Commons. He was also re-establishing a core of 'well-affected' support in key positions at court, preparing the ground for a reassertion of royal authority and managing to keep control of the streets of London. The support of the loyalist Lord Mayor, Richard Gurney, meant that the trained bands could still be relied upon to disperse popular demonstrations. For many in the political nation it had come to appear that, whatever his faults, at least he stood for the maintenance of the status quo. Moreover, with the anticipated influx of absentees in January he could look forward to considerably enhancing his strength in parliament. The party building approach that he had been pursuing since August seemed to be about to pay dividends. At this point, however, with success apparently within his grasp, he threw away his advantage with a series of grotesque misjudgements.

The first of these was the decision to replace Sir William Balfour, the lieutenant of the Tower who had held out against Billingsley during the First Army Plot, with a former army officer, Colonel Thomas Lunsford, who had an unsavoury reputation for violence and was said by the Commons to be 'not right in religion'. Charles was probably hoping to reinforce his control of the streets by appointing someone willing to

[154] TNA, PC 2/53, pp. 200–1. [155] Adamson, *Noble Revolt*, pp. 448–9.
[156] TNA, PC 2/53, p. 200.

clear away the 'tumultuous petitioners' who since the end of November had once more been congregating around Westminster. But this was taken in some quarters as signalling the start of another attempted coup. On 23 December the Commons requested the Lords to join with them in a petition to the king to remove Lunsford from his post. 'After a long debate' the upper house, somewhat surprisingly, refused.[157] The next day the Commons tried again, having ratcheted up the rhetoric with references to 'the great and imminent danger of the kingdom through the designs of the papists and other persons disaffected'. They also dropped dark hints about the 'malignant party', which was causing 'delays and interruptions' in the Lords. The peers debated the matter once more and 'it was resolved by the major part' that any decision should be put off until the following Monday, 27 December. Feelings were running sufficiently high, however, that 22 of the defeated minority decided to formally enter their 'Protestation' against the deferring of a proposal, which so much concerned the 'good and safety of the kingdom'.[158]

As with the 9 September protestation, this was an indication that the unity and collective spirit, which had largely prevailed in the peers' deliberations during late 1640 and early 1641, was now considerably diminished. Some peers had become more concerned to vindicate themselves in the eyes of the public than preserve the appearance of consensus. In contrast to the earlier episode, however, this was no isolated incident. Over the following weeks there was a series of such protests, entered by both Junto supporters and loyalists. They were a sign that party divisions were now firmly entrenched. When set alongside the details of attendance recorded in Lords' draft minute book for this period, these protestations also make it possible to gain a much clearer picture of how the peers were voting. On this occasion the 22 protesters were all drawn from the ranks of those who by this stage appear to have been confirmed supporters of the reformist Junto, with the one exception of the Earl of Carlisle who was something of a floating voter.[159] The attendance list for the day shows that there were a further 26 lay peers and 11 bishops present, most of whom must have voted against joining the Commons.[160] One has, of course, to be wary of assuming that all of them did so. As on other

157 Cust, *Charles I. A Political Life*, pp. 317–18; *LJ*, iv.487.

158 *LJ*, iv.489–90; Russell, *Fall of the British Monarchies*, pp. 440–1.

159 LJ, iv.490. The protesters were the earls of Bedford, Bolingbroke, Brooke, Carlisle, Clare, Essex, Grey of Warke, Holland, Howard of Escrick, Mandeville, Northumberland, Pembroke, Newport, North, Roberts, Saye and Sele, St John, Spencer, Stamford, Suffolk, Warwick and Wharton.

160 PA, HL/PO/JO/5/1/8, 24 December 1641.

occasions, there may have been peers who were reluctant to join in the formal protest, but who voted with the protesters or were absent when the vote was taken.[161] Nonetheless, the likelihood remains that most non-protesters in attendance voted against the Commons. Given the parallels with the situation at the time of the First and Second Army Plots, this was a remarkable display of dissent. Lunsford so obviously personified the most dangerous type of plotter and 'swordsman' that the Commons had every reason to expect peers to join with them. The reluctance of the majority was due in part to the effectiveness of loyalist party organisation in the upper house. The non-protesting lay peers constituted a roll call of many of the king's most reliable supporters.[162] But it was also a measure of the resentment many of the peers felt at the Commons' increasingly blatant attempts at coercion and at being labelled allies of the 'malignant party'. In these circumstances they were prepared to defend the king's

161 Russell, *Fall of the British Monarchies*, p. 440n. This was probably the case with the Earl of Salisbury who was listed as attending, but was not recorded as protesting, although he was normally an ally of the Junto.

One of the puzzles in analysing votes in the upper house is the extent to which proxies were being counted in divisions. Unfortunately this is not something recorded in the Lords' Journals or minute books and we are largely dependent on diaries and other extraneous sources for references to these. Elizabeth Foster, on the basis of her investigation of Lords' procedure, points out that proxies were called for 'if need be . . . probably when an important vote was close'. She also cites evidence from Hyde that suggests that proxies were being used in the latter stages of the first sitting. However, it seems questionable whether they were used during the more partisan proceedings of late 1641 and early 1642. Where one can compare attendance lists with the names of those recording protestations and occasional division figures this suggests that proxies were not being used; and it may be that in the highly charged debates of this period – when Protestations were regularly being entered by both sides – it was felt that it would be inappropriate to register the votes of those who were absent: Foster, *House of Lords*, pp. 19–22, 195; Clarendon, *History*, i.413.

A further problem is that the attendance lists themselves are not entirely reliable. The clerk and his assistants who recorded these in the Lords' minute book were working under considerable pressure, which meant that sometimes names were listed twice or omitted altogether (when we know from other sources that these peers were attending). Peers would come and go during the day – as the differences between the am and pm lists drawn up for some days demonstrates – and if they did not happen to be present when the names were being entered they could be left out. In spite of these shortcomings, however, it remains the case that these lists do provide valuable evidence on attendance, largely corroborated by other sources: PA, HL/PO/JO/5/1/8.

(I am much indebted to Andrew Thrush of the History of Parliament for advice on these matters).

162 PA, HL/PO/JO/5/1/8, 24 December 1641. The non-protesting peers were Berkshire, Bristol, Carnarvon, Coventry, Craven, Denbigh, Devonshire, Digby, Dover, Dunsmore, Fauconberg, Goring, Hertford, Howard of Charlton, Huntingdon, Lindsey, Monmouth, Northampton, Pierrepont, Portland, Rich, Richmond, Savile and Wentworth, together with Littleton who may have been a floating voter and Salisbury who may have voted with the Junto.

prerogative of choosing his own officers, even when the choice fell on someone as unsuitable as Lunsford.[163]

When the upper house reconvened after the Christmas break, on Monday 27 December, the most pressing issue was the tumultuous crowds. Lunsford had been persuaded to resign after representations from the Lord Mayor and was replaced by the largely unexceptionable Sir John Byron. But crowds of apprentices were congregating around the entrance to the Lords, shouting 'No bishops. No popish lords' and spoiling for a fight with the ex-army officers and 'swordsmen' whom the king had gathered at the palace of Whitehall.[164] After several unsuccessful attempts by the gentleman usher to disperse the crowds, the Lords agreed to request the Commons to join with them in publishing a declaration of their 'distaste of the assemblies of the people' and petitioning the king to provide them with a guard. The conference took place that evening, but the Lords' requests received short shrift. At their debate the following day, the lower house resolved not to join with the peers, but instead ask that a guard be provided by Essex. The Earl of Dover noted in his 'Observations' the significant, and disturbing, remark by Pym that 'God forbid that the House of Commons should proceed in any way to dishearten people to obteine their just desires in such a way.'[165] Meanwhile the crowd actions had become more alarming. Stone throwing apprentices confronted the 'swordsmen' in Westminster Hall, and Bishop Williams was threatened and jostled as he got out of his coach, and had to be 'rescued' by Dover and Lord Fauconberg when a mob broke into Westminster Abbey. That evening the Marquis of Hertford advised the 12 bishops who were present in the upper house to shelter in the palace precincts because of the danger of being lynched. The following day only two of them braved the crowds and attended the Lords.[166]

The absence of the majority of bishops on 28 December made a considerable difference to relative voting strengths in the Lords; but amongst the lay peers the loyalists were still in the majority, by around 28 to 21.[167]

163 The reported response of the majority was that 'it was in his Majesty's power to make choyce of his officers and they would not intrench so farre upon his prerogative as to make any opposition therein': *Diurnall Occurrences* (London, 20–27 Dec 1641).

164 Russell, *Fall of the British Monarchies*, pp. 441–2; *CSP Ven. 1640–2*, pp. 271–2.

165 *LJ*, iv.491–3; Russell, *Fall of the British Monarchies*, pp. 442–3; Bodl.L., Clarendon State Papers, vol. 21, 1603, fo. 56v.

166 HMC, *Hastings*, ii.83; Gardiner, *History*, x.117–18.

167 This calculation is based on the voting pattern suggested in the Lunsford division on 24 December, with a further four attending whose allegiance is uncertain, along with two bishops: PA, HL/PO/JO/5/1/8, 28 December 1641. John Adamson has argued that the absence of the bishops on the 28th produced a decisive shift in the balance of power away from the loyalists to the reformist Junto: *Noble Revolt*, pp. 477–8. But this is not

This helped to ensure that the issue of 'tumults' remained at the top of the house's agenda. The peers sent a message to the Commons asking for a response to their request at the previous day's conference, and when it became clear that the lower house was not going to support them some started a debate about whether, in these circumstances, parliament could still enjoy its privileges and freedom of discussion. The outrage felt by many was conveyed in an unfinished entry in the Lords' minute book: 'Uppon the rabbells cominge and pressinge about the Parliament there was much dispute whether this parlt . . . '.[168] Lord Digby, sensing the mood and anticipating majority support, pressed the issue particularly aggressively. He accused the Commons of having 'invaded the privileges of the Lords' house and the liberties of the subject', and moved that 'This was no free parliament.' Eventually the matter was put to the vote and it was resolved – reportedly by just four votes in a house where the recorded attendance was 55 – that 'this parliament is at this present a free parliament.'[169]

This was a momentous division. Had Digby's motion carried the day it would have led to the suspension of all parliamentary business for the foreseeable future and invalidated current and, possibly also, past proceedings.[170] The Commons would have been powerless to act and the break-up of the parliament, which was what Charles was angling for in the long term, would have been brought that much closer. Faced with this drastic scenario, several lords who might have been expected to support the motion pulled back from the brink. Their sense of responsibility – that as peers they were under an obligation to continue working with the Commons to resolve the current crisis – appears to have carried the day. However, the narrowness of the vote and its conditional nature ('at this present') indicated that such sentiments were finely balanced against the upper house's indignation at the Commons-sanctioned bullying by 'the rabble' and the growing sense of partisanship.

At this point Charles made his second major mistake. Seeking to take advantage of the Lords' continuing alarm over 'tumults' he sanctioned a petition drawn up by Williams in the name of 12 of the bishops requesting that, since they could find neither 'redress or protection' from parliament against the assaults of 'the multitude', all proceedings in their absence

borne by the attendance list for the day, or by voting patterns during January when, with the bishops almost entirely absent, the loyalists still won a series of significant divisions.

168 PA, HL/PO/JO/5/1/8, 28 December 1641; see also the draft journal entry confirming this: PA, BRY/22C, 28 December 1641.

169 *LJ*, iv. 494, 495; Gardiner, *History*, x.119–20.

170 Adamson, *Noble Revolt*, p. 482.

should be declared 'null and of none effect'. This reopened the possibility of an adjournment, but in a particularly risky way because it directly contradicted the lords vote of 28 December. In the stress of the moment neither the king nor Nicholas appear to have scrutinised the petition sufficiently closely or recognised its hazardous implications.[171] When the Lord Keeper presented it on the 30th his fellow peers showed considerable irritation. For once the Junto supporters were able to use concern for privileges to their advantage and push through a resolution that the petition was 'a deep intrenching upon the fundamental privileges and being of parliament'.[172] As soon as this was communicated to the Commons, Pym seized the initiative, ordered the doors of the lower house to be locked and, with great drama, explained that this was the precursor to a forcible dissolution. The Commons then resolved that the bishops involved should be charged with treason. Later in the day this was also accepted by the Lords and 10 of the 12 were immediately incarcerated in the Tower.[173] The whole episode was enormously damaging to the loyalist cause. The line, which a majority of the Lords had held in defence of the bishops, had at last been breached and the loyalist vote significantly reduced. Something that Pym and the Junto had been struggling to achieve for months was handed to them on a plate, as a result of Charles's own misjudgement.

The biggest folly, however, was the attempted coup against the Junto leadership at the start of January 1642. John Adamson has argued persuasively that in origin this was another attempt by Lord Digby to seize the initiative in the upper house, this time by charging Lord Mandeville and five of the Junto leaders in the Commons with high treason. This would lead to impeachment proceedings which, even if they were eventually unsuccessful, would cause such disruption to parliamentary business that the Junto would be unable to push through reforms before the absentee members arrived to give the king majority support. Digby seems to have persuaded the king that the rejection of the bishops' petition had been a temporary aberration and that, given a clear lead, the majority of the peers were still firmly behind him.[174] Charles, therefore, instructed the Attorney General, Sir Edward Herbert, to deliver articles of impeachment as the upper house reassembled on 3 January when it seemed likely that the large attendance (55 lay peers and four bishops)[175] would ensure majority support. Digby was primed to speak up and offer to prove that

171 Clarendon, *History*, i.472–3; Gardiner, *History*, x.122–3. 172 *LJ*, iv. 497.
173 Gardiner, *History*, x.122–5; Russell, *Fall of the British Monarchies*, pp. 443–4.
174 Adamson, *Noble Revolt*, pp. 489–91.
175 PA, HL/PO/JO/5/1/8, 3 January 1641/2.

Mandeville had encouraged 'the rabble' to march on Whitehall. Once again, however, the king badly miscalculated. It quickly became clear that the Lords were not prepared to countenance such naked political aggression. Digby lost his nerve – perhaps, as Gardiner suggests, when he saw the reaction on the peers' faces as the charges were read out – whispered to Mandeville that 'the king was very mischievously advised' and promptly left the house.[176] Instead of moving to examine witnesses, as had been anticipated, the Lords appointed a committee evenly balanced between Junto supporters and loyalists to consider whether the Attorney General's proceedings were 'regular', according to law and precedent, and whether an accusation of treason could be made in this way against a peer. Later that day, in conference with the Commons, they voted that the searching of the studies of the accused was a breach of privilege. They also abandoned their earlier resistance to dictating to the king the choice of who should take charge of an armed guard for the parliament and agreed to joining the Commons in petitioning that this be someone 'approved of' by the two houses.[177] The evidence that his scheme had backfired, and that the Lords were turning against him, prompted Charles's fateful decision to go in person to arrest the accused members on the following day.

The king's 'Attempt on the Five Members', and his subsequent flight from London on 10 January 1642, undid the gains that he had made in the autumn of 1641. The strategy of party-building and lobbying had been a considerable success. It was at odds with the consensus-seeking traditions of the Lords and the spirit of the Great Council, but it was very effective in handing the initiative back to the king. During October and November the loyalists had been able to block the trial and exclusion of bishops, stymie efforts to dictate the choice of councillors and provide a platform for Charles to relaunch himself as a constitutional monarch and defender of the status quo. But most of this progress was then undone by the mistakes of late December. Once again the king's resort to coercion proved almost entirely counter-productive. It pulled the rug from underneath the support that had been building for him, both inside and outside parliament, transformed the mood in the upper house and led a number of loyalists to refocus on their sense of responsibility to the people as well as the crown. In an attempt to steer the nation out of a fresh crisis, they sided with the Junto to keep the parliament going, condemned the bishops and blocked the impeachment. Charles was forced into a humiliating retreat and once more conceded the political

176 Gardiner, *History*, x.130–1; Clarendon, *History*, i.484.
177 *LJ*, iv.501–2; Gardiner, *History*, x.132–3.

advantage to his opponents. Nonetheless, his earlier successes had taught a valuable lesson: that, given the right approach, he could call on a significant majority of the politically active peers to support him against the Junto.

The Royalist party and the outbreak of civil war

When the two houses resumed business on 11 January 1642, the loyalists in the upper house faced a very different set of political circumstances. The king's withdrawal, first of all to Hampton Court and then, from 14 January, to Windsor, left them without any protection against the hostility of the London crowds and with no obvious focal point around which they could rally. Delegations of councillors and peers made regular trips out to Windsor to visit the king, and instructions were still being relayed by Nicholas, who was at the king's side, and by Richmond and Bristol, who were now reinstalled as his principal advisers.[178] But in comparison with the situation before Christmas their ability to organise and coordinate their actions was severely weakened. They also had to operate in a much more hostile political environment. There was a growing public perception, assisted by the numerous divisions and protests, that the House of Lords was divided into two sides. On the one hand there were those referred to as the 'good peers' or the 'virtuous lords', who were seen as standing for reform, the 'safety of the kingdom' and the interests of parliament. On the other were the loyalists who, following the lead given by the Commons in December, were increasingly described as the 'malignant party'.[179] This was a conveniently vague label that could be used to proscribe almost any activity that the parliamentarians disapproved of and, as we shall see, its application provided the means by which a significant contingent of loyalist peers was driven away from Westminster. But this did not happen until February 1642. During January the king's support largely held firm, bolstered by relatively high attendance in the upper house – normally between 60 and 70, compared with 50 to 60 during December (see Figure 5.1a–c) – which was probably due in considerable measure to the attractions of the London season.[180] Up to the start of February these peers were able to mount an effective rearguard action in the upper house.[181]

178 Cust, *Charles I. A Political Life*, pp. 330–1; Russell, *Fall of the British Monarchies*, pp. 467–8.

179 *LJ*, iv.539, 558; TNA, SP16/488/56; 489/12; HMC, *Cowper*, ii.304, 306.

180 Stone, *Crisis of the Aristocracy*, pp. 385–92.

181 Russell, *Fall of the British Monarchies*, p. 467 has argued that the attendance among the king's supporters was falling during January as a number of potential allies (like the

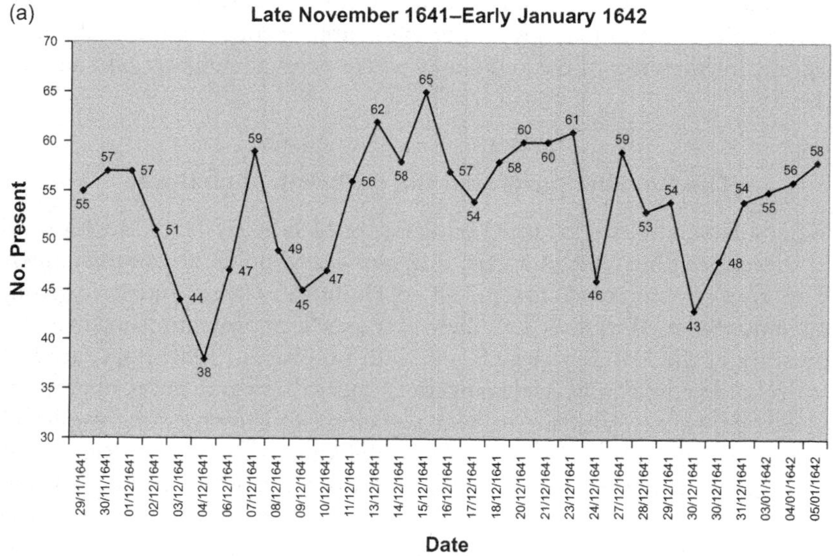

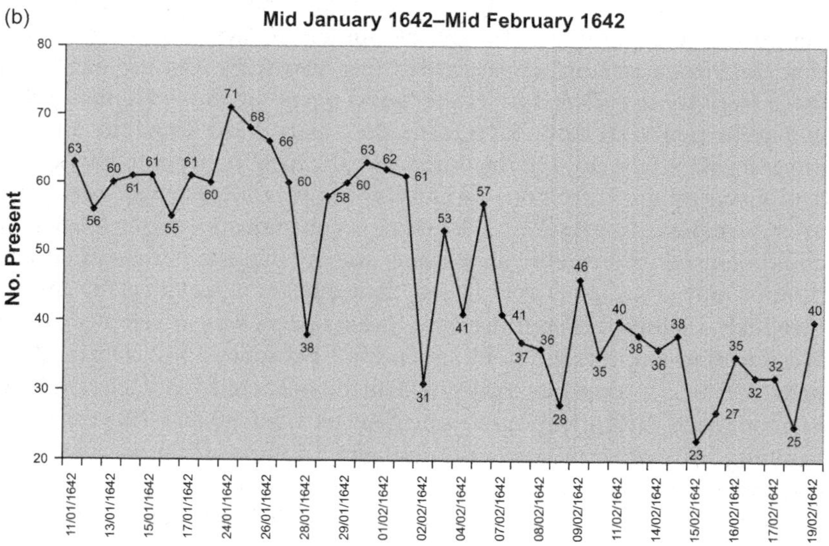

Figure 5.1 a–c Attendance in the Lords from late November 1641–late March 1642 (I am grateful to David Hughes for compiling these figures)
Source: Crummett, 'Lay Peers', Appendix X (based on PA, HL/PO/JO/5/1/8).

(c)

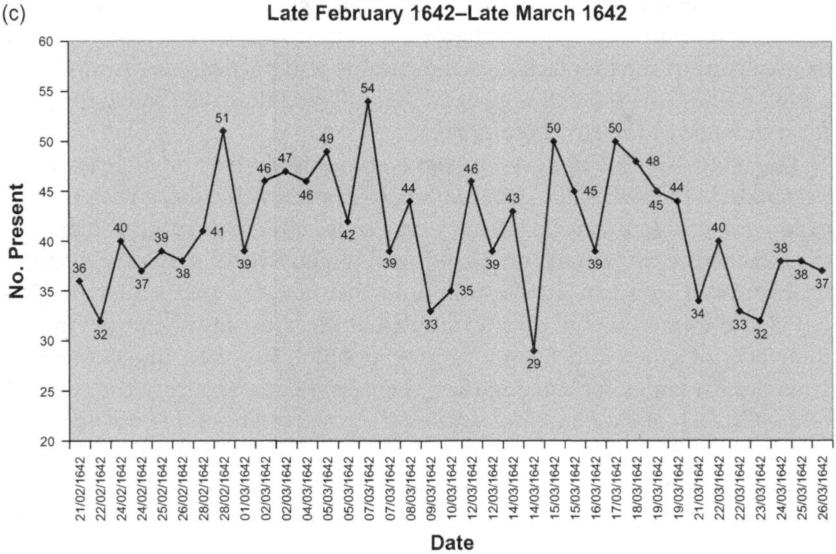

Figure 5.1 (*cont.*)

The loyalists attempted to negotiate the increasingly hostile atmosphere by falling back on a rhetoric of unity and moderation. The Earl of Monmouth, one of the most dependable of the king's allies, showed the way in a published speech delivered on 13 January. Reflecting on recent events, he appealed to his fellow peers to join with the Commons in a protestation to remove from Londoners their 'jealousies and apprehensions' and 'free his Majestie from his feares' that had driven him from Westminster. It was their responsibility to take the lead in such an enterprise because as noblemen 'God hath plac'd us (my Lords) in the medium betwixt the king and his people.' 'Let us play our parts', he urged,

> let us does our duties and discharge our consciences; let us really prove what wee are by name, Noblemen; let us endevour to work a perfect and a true understanding betweene the king and his people.[182]

This was an attempt to position the loyalists as the main proponents of unity and accommodation, those who were adhering most closely to the

Earl of Arundel and Lord Digby) absented themselves; but these losses were more than offset by the arrival of a number of loyalists who had not attended before Christmas, such as the earls of Westmoreland and Thanet, and lords Strange and Mohun.

182 *A Speech Made in the House of Peeres by the Right Honourable the Earle of Monmouth on Thursday the 13 of January 1641/2* (London, 1642).

aspirations of the noble order and seeking to revive the spirit of the Great Council of 1640. But it was a rhetorical stance born as much of necessity as idealism. In the increasingly inhospitable and partisan environment of early 1642, it was the one approach that allowed them the space to argue for a defence of the royal prerogative.

The king himself appears to have recognised this, or at least been persuaded of it by Bristol. After failing to make any headway with threats of force in mid January, he fell back on a more conciliatory approach. In a message to the two houses on 20 January, which Bristol may have drafted, he expressed concern at the 'manifold distractions' and undertook 'to equal and exceed the greatest examples of the most indulgent princes in their acts of grace and favour to their people'. He then urged them to consider measures for safeguarding their privileges, securing the religion of the Church of England and settling the royal finances. He was in effect falling back on Bristol's strategy for dealing with the Scots the previous March and, in Conrad Russell's words, calling 'on the Houses to state their uttermost demands'.[183] He was also offering an olive branch to offset some of the hostility aroused by his recent actions and make life a little easier for his supporters.

The loyalist peers were under no illusions as to the difficulty of their task or the magnitude of the stakes for which they were playing. The Venetian ambassador, Giovanni Guistinian, who had close contacts with the king's supporters in the upper house, provides some insight into their attitudes. He reported that in his conversations 'the majority of the upper house . . . sigh earnestly for a mutually satisfactory agreement.' The 'most prudent' among them, he reported, were being consistently intimidated with threats of being denounced to the people as 'enemies of the state'. However, they were determined to 'stand fast to their original opinion' and keep on arguing their case, because they recognised that 'if the lower house succeeds in beating down the royal authority it will afterwards proceed to reduce the prerogatives of the nobility as well' and 'establish a democratic state upon solid foundations'.[184] One has to make allowance for the ambassador's tendency to assume a natural alliance between monarchy and aristocracy against the forces of democracy. But nonetheless this offers a valuable perspective on what the king's supporters felt they were up against.

During January there were two crucial issues around which the divisions in the upper house revolved: first, the ongoing struggle to secure

183 *LJ*, iv.523–4; Russell, *Fall of the British Monarchies*, p. 465.

184 *CSP Ven. 1640–2*, pp. 284, 288–9. At this time he appears to have been particularly close to Berkshire's son, Lord Howard of Charlton who was the ambassador designate to Venice: *ibid.*, p. 269.

parliamentary control of the appointment of the king's officers and second the battle for command of the militia. The first issue hinged on whether the house would agree to support the Commons in a petition to the king that Sir John Byron be replaced as Lieutenant of the Tower. In spite of the fact that Byron was proving obstructive over an investigation into royal efforts to reinforce the Tower, the loyalists stood by him and when the matter was pushed to a vote on 17 January, they defeated the Commons' proposal, leaving 23 peers to sign a protestation.[185] Over the militia, the loyalists were more willing to present a united front with the parliamentarian peers. Measures to secure Hull and Portsmouth were approved without division, as was a general order from parliament to put the county militias into 'a position of defence'.[186] But when the parliamentarian leaders tried to extend this to a general request to the king that control of the militia be entrusted to 'such persons as shall be recommended unto your Majesty by both Houses of Parliament', they resisted. The proposal was voted down on 24 January in a particularly revealing division. As Conrad Russell has observed the 34 peers listed as protesting against this vote probably represented 'the high-water mark of the parliamentarian cause' in the Lords.[187] It included all the regular parliament supporters, but also a number of floating voters and erstwhile loyalists who had been sufficiently alarmed by the security threat to accept that control of armed force should be taken out of the king's hands, the likes of Clare, Peterborough, Nottingham, Viscount Conway and Lords Chandos and Hunsden. Significantly, however, the loyalists were still able to defeat them, by 40 votes to 32.[188] In spite of the loss of the bishops, the weakening of royal leadership and growing intimidation, then, the loyalists were still succeeding in holding back assaults on the royal prerogative.[189]

Their defences were finally broken at the start of February 1642 by a combination of increased intimidation and royal mismanagement. The opening of the breach was made on 26 January, when, after once more

185 *LJ*, iv.521. 186 *Ibid.*, iv.505, 509, 510.

187 Russell, *Fall of the British Monarchies*, p. 468

188 *LJ*, iv.533; *Private Journals*, p. 168n. The Lords Journal and parliamentary diary give different lists of protesters, 32 and 34 respectively, with Northumberland and Suffolk being added to the names in the Lords Journal. The division figures indicate that the lower number actually voted in favour of the militia proposal, with Northumberland and Suffolk presumably adding their names to the protest later: PA, HL/PO/JO/5/1/8, 24 January 1641/2; BRY/103, 24 January 1641/2.

189 The platform on which the loyalists were continuing to stand firm was summed up in the king's reply to the Commons' petition of 25 January, probably drafted by Bristol or Nicholas, in which he insisted that 'he was resolved only to deny those things the granting whereof would alter the fundamental laws and endanger the very foundation upon which the public happiness and welfare of the people is founded and constituted': *LJ*, iv.557–8.

rejecting the proposal to join the Commons' petition on the militia several peers suggested an adjournment of the house. They were probably mindful that on the previous day the first of several batches of county petitions, orchestrated by Pym and the parliamentarian peers, had been presented to the house, and there was every prospect of angry crowds growing in the days ahead.[190] The Marquis of Richmond, however, tried to take this further and proposed that it be put to 'the question whether we shall adjourn for six months'. After the experience of late December this remained a particularly sensitive issue and the house took immediate exception. The marquis was required to withdraw while they discussed whether to allow him to make an apology or impose more severe punishment. This led to one of the most heated debates of the entire period, lasting well into the night. Peers reportedly came close to drawing their swords on each other and Richmond's opponents threatened to go and sit with the Commons and publish the names of the other lords as 'enemies to the good and safety of the kingdom'.[191] Eventually the house voted (by 40 to 23) to allow Richmond to make his apology, but that was not the end of the matter. The next day the Commons launched their own investigation into Richmond's conduct, making it plain that they regarded him as an 'evil counsellor' and member of 'the malignant party' whose 'workes of darknes' were leading the king astray. The marquis tried to explain himself, pleading that he had always tried to live up to the ideals of a good nobleman, seeking 'the advancement of [the king's] honor, the maintenance of the public good of the kingdom, the union of the king and his people . . . and a right understanding and correspondence between him and his parliament'. But this cut little ice with some of his fellow peers and the next day they debated whether to support the Commons' petition that henceforth he be denied 'access to the persons or courts of the king or queen's majesty'. Again this was defeated (by 46 to 21); but the Richmond case had pushed the activities of 'evil counsellors' and 'the malignant party' to the top of the political agenda.[192]

Over the next few days the atmosphere of a witch hunt prevailed as members of both houses intensified efforts to identify anyone who could be regarded as 'an enemy to the publique peace and safety of the kingdom'.[193] The resultant pressures finally cracked the resolve of the loyalists. During the first week of February numerous of them

[190] *LJ*, iv.537–40.

[191] *Ibid.*, iv.543; HMC, *Beaulieu*, p. 145; Russell, *Fall of the British Monarchies*, p. 470; Bodl.L, Clarendon State Papers, vol. 21, 1603, fo. 57r.

[192] *LJ*, iv.550, 551; Crummett, 'Lay Peers', p. 290.

[193] *LJ*, iv.558; HMC, *Cowper*, ii.304, 306.

applied for leave of absence from the Lords, including the leaders of the loyalist lobby, Richmond, Bristol, Bath, Southampton and Dunsmore. Although not all availed themselves of this facility, attendance dropped off markedly, with nearly all the absences accounted for by regular supporters of the king.[194] Bath, who was plainly rattled, explained his reasons to Nicholas on 4 February. He felt he was now 'utterly unable to do [the king] service' in the upper house, 'by reason of the violation of the fundamentall privilidge of parliament which is the free debatinge and votinge, with safety and indemnity, without which no man is capable to sitte in any parliament'.[195]

The loss of morale among the king's supporters was not terminal. They were to rally during March to provide a vociferous and determined opposition to the parliamentarian majority. But from this point onwards they were almost always in the minority. The tipping point came late in the day on 1 February when the house reversed its earlier decision and resolved to join the Commons in petitioning the king to entrust command of the militia and royal forts to 'such hands as the parliament may confide in'. The loyalist Earl of Dover explained that this about turn was due to the vote taking place at night, 'many of' what he termed 'our lords being absent'.[196] The absence was because of a request from the king at Windsor. Earlier in the day he had panicked over reports that 1000 citizens were about to march out to present a petition to him and 'sent for some fourteen lords' to come to protect him.[197] The attendance list for 2 February showed a halving of the number of peers present (from 66 to 32), with most of the absentees loyalists who had apparently answered their monarch's call. By the next day of business, 4 February, attendance was back up to 53; but the damage had been done and the momentum was now with parliamentarian peers.[198]

Sensing their advantage, on 5 February, they reintroduced the bill for bishops exclusion, which had been shelved in late October 1641. Now, 'after a long and mature deliberation', the bill was passed, by 36 votes to 23. The parliamentarian majority was again boosted by some of those floating voters who had sided with them on 24 January; but the real story was the collapse of loyalist support. Conspicuously absent

194 *LJ*, iv.559–66, 571; Crummett, 'Lay peers', p. 291; Russell, *Fall of the British Monarchies*, pp. 470–1. The Lords attendance lists suggest that during early February those who absented themselves were the Duke of Richmond, the Earls of Bath, Bristol, Cambridge, Cumberland, Denbigh, Devonshire, Hertford, Southampton and Thanet and Lords Dunsmore, Goring, Mowbray and Willoughby of Eresby: PA, HL/PO/JO/5/1/8.

195 TNA, SP16/489/8.

196 *LJ*, iv.558; Bodl.L., Clarendon State Papers, vol. 21, 1603, fo. 57r.

197 TNA, SP 16/489/3; *LJ*, iv.558.

198 PA, HL/PO/JO/5/1/8, 1–2 February 1641/2.

from the ranks of those who stood by the bishops were the likes of Bath, Southampton and Bristol, who had been so effective in leading their defence in the past. The three bishops present in the house entered their protest; but, tellingly, none of the lay peers who voted alongside them was prepared to do so. This was not a time to be exposing themselves to public attention and rebuke.[199]

For the remainder of February the parliamentarians enjoyed an unchallenged supremacy in the Lords and were able to push through further bills that had previously been blocked. On the 8th the impressment bill, which had been held up before Christmas, was reintroduced and passed; and on the 9th they approved the Militia Ordinance giving powers to Lord Lieutenants nominated by parliament to appoint local officers and oversee the training of the militia.[200] The balance of power had tilted decisively against the loyalists; however, the conventions of cooperation and consensual action were still able to operate. Each time a delegation was sent to ask the king to give his assent to unwelcome requests it was loyalists who agreed to represent the views of the house. Monmouth and Craven presented the bill for bishops exclusion; Portland and Capel the impressment bill; and Lord Seymour and the Earl of Newport (who was gravitating towards the loyalists), a request at the end of the month that Charles return the Prince of Wales to Whitehall.[201]

Meanwhile, the king's strategy was to buy time until his wife and younger children were safely secured abroad, and he had his eldest son alongside him. On 7 February he despatched a soothing message to the Lords, offering to abandon the prosecution of the Five Members and appoint those whom parliament recommended to take control of the militia. He followed this up on 11 February by moving from Windsor to Greenwich – so as to be more accessible – and also finally agreeing to parliament's call for Sir John Conyers to replace Byron as Lieutenant of the Tower. Then, more surprisingly, on 14 February, he agreed to the bishops exclusion bill. This had originally been a measure on which the king was determined not to budge, as a point of principle. But he appears to have been persuaded that it was necessary to make a grand concession to dissuade parliament from preventing Henrietta Maria's passage abroad; and both he and the queen felt that it was preferable to concede on the bishops rather than the militia, which was essential for any future plans for military action against their enemies.[202]

199 *LJ*, iv.564; *Private Journals*, p. 284; Russell, *Fall of the British Monarchies*, p. 471; PA, HL/PO/JO/5/1/8, 5 Feb.1641/2.

200 *LJ*, iv.570, 572–3. 201 *Ibid.*, iv.565, 571, 614.

202 Gardiner, *History of England*, x.164–6; Russell, *Fall of the British Monarchies*, p. 475; Cust, *Charles I. A Political Life*, pp. 333–4.

Henrietta Maria boarded ship for the Netherlands on 23 February and, immediately, Charles reverted to a more aggressive political strategy. He sent personal letters to a contingent of loyalist lords, reversing his previous permission to absent themselves from parliament and requiring them to attend, because 'there is likely to be treated in parliament affairs much importing the public peace and good of our kingdom.' This was a rallying call to the 'well-affected', similar to the dispatches sent out by Nicholas the previous October and it had similarly positive results. A number of those who had been absenting themselves in early February returned to the fray. In a significant display of the partisanship that now dominated the proceedings of the upper house, the parliamentarian majority, which had previously done all it could to ensure attendance, interpreted the king's letter as a hostile move and launched an inquest into the 'evil counsels' that had prompted it.[203] Charles then set off towards York. According to the plan that he had devised with the queen, the aim was to establish a base there, in a part of the country that was presumed to be friendlier towards him than London, and then take control of Hull. He could then look to recruiting the military force he needed to intimidate parliament.[204]

The king's efforts to rally loyalist support in the upper house began to pay dividends in early March. The atmosphere was still extremely hostile, with continuing denunciations of the 'malignant party' and efforts to identify and punish 'evil counsellors'. But the loyalists succeeded in organising themselves and registering their opposition through a series of formal protestations against the majority decisions. The first issue on which they stood up to the parliamentarian majority was over the militia. Majority approval for the Militia Ordinance had been followed by an extended negotiation with the king to try to secure his assent. But it had become clear by early March that he was not prepared to yield on this issue, and this was accompanied by protests from the loyalists. On 2 March the upper house divided over whether to support a Commons' resolution that the kingdom be 'put into a posture of defence'. This was carried by 32 votes to 18, with 13 of the loyalists, led by Bath, Southampton and Dunsmore, entering their protest.[205] Three days later there was a loyalist attempt to block the engrossing of the Militia Ordinance by arguing that it contravened the Oath of Allegiance. This was defeated, but

203 *LJ*, iv.612–13. The peers who are known to have received Charles's letter were Bath, Berkshire, Dover, Howard of Charlton, Huntingdon, Lindsey, Mowbray, Northampton, Powis, Seymour and Southampton, although there were almost certainly others: *LJ*, iv.612, 618–19; HMC, *Hastings*, ii.83.

204 Cust, *Charles I. A Political Life*, pp. 332–3.

205 *LJ*, iv.622; PA, BRY/23B, Lords draft journal, 2 March 1641/2.

the final passage of the ordinance was approved by only 28 votes to 21, with 16 peers entering their protest against it. Further protests followed: on the 7th (over whether to support the Commons' 'declaration of fears and jealousies' – carried by 29 votes to 24), on the 15th March (against declaring that the Militia Ordinance was to be enforced by 'the fundamental laws of the kingdom'), on the 19th (against approving a message to the king about 'the safety of the kingdom') and on the 28th (in opposition to sending Bristol to the Tower for 'concealing' a loyalist petition to the Kent assizes).[206] In all some 20 loyalist peers were involved in these protests, including the Earl of Newport who had previously been one of the leading allies of the Junto. An additional six peers joined further protests during April.[207]

The achievements of this loyalist opposition were relatively limited. The only time they succeeded in defeating the parliamentarians was in preventing punishment of the Attorney General on 15 March after he had been impeached for his role in presenting the charges against Mandeville and the Five Members. The protests also attracted relatively little public attention. Newsletter writers and diurnall correspondents tended to report the final decisions in debates, leaving protests and even tight divisions largely unrecorded.[208] However, the fact that there were members of the upper house who were challenging the parliamentarian peers and continuing to make the case for the defence of the royal prerogative was important. It reinforced the arguments being made in the royal declarations published from mid March onwards that the maintenance of royal authority was essential to preservation of the constitutional status quo. It laid the groundwork for later royalist claims that the measures approved by the upper house lacked legitimacy because they had been pushed through in violation of proper procedures. And it provided a foundation for a royalist party when the king stepped up his efforts to rally political support in the spring and early summer.

By late March the political stakes for individual peers were being raised even higher as they started to face difficult public choices over allegiance. This first became apparent over the issue of whether to accept the new lieutenancy commissions conferred by the Militia Ordinance. In mid March the parliamentary leadership decided that it could wait no longer

206 *LJ*, iv.627, 631, 646, 656, 678; Crummett, 'Lay peers', pp. 292–5.

207 *LJ*, iv.697, 700; v.4. The 26 peers involved in protests were Bath, Berkshire, Capel, Cleveland, Coventry, Devonshire, Dover, Dunsmore, Grey of Ruthen, Howard of Charlton, Hertford, Lindsey, Lovelace, Monmouth, Mowbray, Newport, Northampton, Portland, Rich, Savile, Seymour, Southampton, Strange, Wentworth, Westmoreland and Willoughby of Eresby.

208 *LJ*, iv.645; HMC, *Buccleuch*, i.291–9; *Beaulieu*, pp. 148–51; *Perfect Diurnall* and *True Diurnall* for March and April 1642.

on this, and started to require the nominees to indicate acceptance of the commissions by appointing deputies. This was a process to which both the king and the news-hungry public paid a good deal of attention.[209] First to come into the firing line, on 22 March, was the Marquis of Hertford whose appointment as Lord Lieutenant of Somerset had been carried through the Commons by local MPs in the face of complaints that 'he had not gone right in the Lords House this parliament in his votes'. Hertford turned down the commission on the grounds that, although 'he should be very glad to obey this house and serve the commonwealth in what he may', he did not 'yet know that the king hath given his consent to it, without which he hopes your lordships will not impose it upon him'.[210] Within a few days the Earl of Cumberland and Lord Strange had followed suit, although their replies were rather more evasive.[211] The form of words chosen by Hertford was significant. He was still emphasising that, as a peer, he had an obligation to serve both king and commonwealth, and this remained the default position for most noblemen during the spring and early summer. Increasingly, however, the pressures exerted on them made this dual allegiance difficult to sustain.

These pressures increased once the king arrived at York on 18 March and started to look for peers to support him. He received a much more guarded welcome from the local inhabitants than he had anticipated and it soon became evident that if he was to establish a credible political presence in the north he urgently needed his peers to attend him, as they had done in April 1639. Yet, apart from Richmond, who accompanied him northwards, and Newcastle, who rode in on the day he arrived with an entourage of 'young gallants', there was no sign that anybody was prepared to turn out on his behalf.[212] The first device he used to try to boost attendance was to announce that the Garter Feast, prorogued from 1641, would be held at York on 18–20 April. Sir John Palmer, deputy chancellor of the order, sent out the individual summonses to the knights of the order while Charles was at Newmarket on 15 March; and on the 23rd the king followed these up by commanding Essex, Holland, Salisbury and Savile to attend, as his principal household officers. Meanwhile, in London rumours began to circulate that he was preparing to install a slate of new knights, including loyalists such as Hertford, Newcastle and Lord Strange.[213]

209 HMC, *Buccleuch*, i.293; *Cowper*, ii.309.

210 *Private Journals*, p. 346; *LJ*, iv.666.

211 *LJ*, iv.666, 672.

212 *The King's Entertainment at York* (London, 1642); *A letter written by Mr Simon Rhodes . . .* (London, 1642); *The Fairfax Correspondence*, 2 vols., ed. G.W. Johnson (London, 1848), ii.389–95.

213 Bodl.L., Ashmole MS 1108, fo. 135; *LJ*, iv.675; HMC, *Cowper*, ii.310.

These were shrewd moves on the king's part, drawing on the prestige and traditions of the order to mobilise support. But the parliamentarian leadership was alive to the dangers that they represented and a tussle ensued over the issue of attendance. On 22 March the Lords passed a resolution that the garter knights had a prior obligation 'to attend the weighty affairs of the kingdom discussed in parliament... by his Majestie's writ and the law of the land'. The next day these peers began to deliver their excuses to Palmer citing the house's order. Even the Earl of Berkshire, who was one of the loyalist protesters in April, felt sufficiently pressured to proffer his explanation for not travelling to York.[214] Charles retaliated by issuing a fresh instruction to the four household peers, this time warning that if Essex and Holland did not attend he would expect them to resign their offices. But it soon became clear that he had overreached himself. The upper house responded on 11 April with a series of resolutions declaring that this was a matter 'concerning the honour and privileges of parliament' and that the 'commands of the house' for Essex and Holland to attend took precedence over any royal summons or dispensation.[215] Significantly a number of loyalists supported these resolutions, an indication of the continuing power of matters of privilege to command a consensus. More surprisingly, the Lord Keeper refused to press the two peers for their resignation. He reportedly cited his obligation as a 'sworn councillor to his Majesty and the kingdom', and threatened to resign himself if the king persisted in an action 'so absolutely destructive to both'.[216] Littleton was one of the 'floating voters' in the Lords whose support Charles would need if his cause was to become politically viable. This robust refusal to cooperate was a measure not just of the extent of the king's miscalculation, but also of how far he still had to go in persuading his peers to provide the mandate needed to make his cause credible.

The Garter Feast, which eventually took place at York, was a much diminished affair, which underlined the weakness of the king's position. A special dispensation was required to hold the chapter because there were only four knights present: the Prince of Wales, the Elector Palatine, Richmond and the ever dependable Lord Great Chamberlain, the Earl of Lindsey. The attendance of other peers also fell far short of Charles's hopes. The Earl of Carnarvon and two of Richmond's younger brothers, Lord John and Lord Bernard Stuart, were knighted when James Duke of York was inducted into the order; Hertford and the Irish peer, Viscount Grandison, acted as supporters to the young prince; Lord Seymour bore

[214] Bodl.L., Ashmole MS 1111, fos. 54–7; 1132, fos. 27–41. [215] *LJ*, iv.712–13.
[216] HMC, *Buccleuch*, i.298–9; TNA, SP 16/490/8.

the sword of state; and Newport and Southampton were also present for part of the feast. But this was not the sort of attendance that the king had anticipated; and his hopes were further deflated when Seymour and Southampton quickly returned southwards, Seymour ostentatiously making his peace with the parliament.[217]

Chastened by his failure to attract support from his peers during his first month at York, Charles fell back on the advice that Sir Edward Hyde had given him on his journey northwards: 'to sit as quietly there as if you were at Whitehall' and avoid 'giving the least hint to your people that you rely upon any thing but the strength of your laws and their obedience'.[218] In a series of royal declarations, most of them probably drafted by Hyde, Charles set out to present himself as the constitutional monarch *par excellence*, champion of the legal and political status quo. This was probably the main aim behind his descent on Hull two days after the conclusion of the Garter Feast which, as Conrad Russell has pointed out, served to flush out his opponents and demonstrate to the world that they were in a state of rebellion against him. Hotham's defiance gave the king the upper hand in terms of the political debate and during May the declarations focussed principally on this and parliament's order of 5 May to execute the Militia Ordinance. Charles had a powerful case on both these issues. He could justifiably argue that Hotham's action amounted to 'no less than plain high treason' and that parliament's countenancing of it amounted to 'actual war levied against us'; while the Militia Ordinance could be seen as a challenge to the traditional view that the king was a part of parliament and that without his consent legislation was not binding.[219] This reinforced his basic claim that defiance of his authority was a rejection of the principles of property and the rule of law, and a direct encouragement to rebellion.

Armed with these arguments, and with the sense that parliament's support for Hotham had released him from any moral constraints against waging civil war, Charles began to adopt a more aggressive stance. When a parliamentary delegation arrived on 9 May to remonstrate with him over Hull, he made it plain that they were not welcome and threatened to 'clap' them up if they tried to 'make any party or hinder his service in the country'.[220] He held discussions with the Yorkshire gentry, which led to a pledge on the part of some of them to provide a guard for the defence

217 Bodl.L., Ashmole MS 1108, fos. 148–52; *LJ*, v.19; HMC, *Cowper*, ii.314.
218 *Clarendon SP*, ii.138–9.
219 *An Exact Collection of all Remonstrances, Votes, Declarations, Proclamations*... (London, 1643), pp. 163–7; Rushworth, iii.571–4, 588–99; Russell, *Fall of the British Monarchies*, pp. 510–11.
220 TNA, SP 16/490/34.

of the royal person. And, in an ambitious move to make his northern capital the new seat of government, he instructed the Lord Keeper to send out writs to hold the Trinity law term there, commencing in early June. The upper house took these various measures into consideration on 20 May and approved a resolution that 'the king, seduced by wicked counsel, intends to make war against the parliament.'[221] By this stage Charles did, indeed, appear to have made up his mind that the use of armed force against his enemies was both legitimate and necessary. But he still lacked the means to carry this through.

It remained imperative for the king, if he was to build a credible military challenge, that he secure a political mandate from at least a sizeable chunk of his peerage. Their endorsement was critical, both because of their capacity to command public attention and their role as Lord Lieutenants in controlling the local militia. However, during late April and early May Charles was still well short of securing it. The Earl of Stamford reported back to the House of Lords after a visit to York that the only peers he had seen there were Carlisle, Newport and Lord Rich; and Sir Hugh Cholmley, a member of the parliamentary delegation, noted that 'there was few about the king but souldiers of fortune'.[222] However, this situation did start to improve in late May, and what turned it around was another personal summons from the king.

From 20 May he started to send out batches of letters, addressed to individual peers, commanding them, on their 'allegiance', to come to York because 'we are desirous to speak with you concerning some affairs much importing the peace and good of this our kingdom'.[223] This combination of an appeal to 'allegiance' and a reminder of their obligations as noble counsellors was a powerful inducement. When the Earl of Salisbury, hitherto a staunch parliamentarian, explained to his fellow peers in late June why he had responded to the king's summons he emphasised that 'the king sent him an express command upon his allegiance to give his attendance which accordingly he did.'[224] Others took the same line, in some cases specifically citing the oath of allegiance, which each of the peers was obliged to take at the opening of parliament.[225] This was an

221 Rushworth, iii.614–19; *LJ*, v.67–8, 76.

222 *LJ*, v.19–20; *Memoirs and Memorials of Sir Hugh Cholmley of Whitby 1600–1657*, ed. J. Binns (Yorkshire Archaeological Society, 153, 2000), pp. 103–4.

223 *LJ*, v.83–4.

224 *Ibid.*, v.156. He took the same line in correspondence with his son-in-law, the Earl of Northumberland, citing his unwillingness to disobey 'a verbal command of the king's' or to 'displease the king': HMC, *Salisbury*, xxii.370–1.

225 *Remarkable Occurrences . . . 16–23 May 1642*, reported that when Savile, Seymour and Rich gave their reasons for refusing to attend the Lords they declared, explicitly, that

obligation that they clearly expected their fellow peers to recognise and understand.

The king's tactic worked. Salisbury and his son-in-law Devonshire slipped away unobtrusively from London and headed north on 24 May. Before long it was being reported that 'the lords fly away every day'. Dunsmore had set out on 21 May and Coventry, Capel, Dover, Mowbray, Northampton, Southampton and Westmoreland followed over the next week. The biggest coup for Charles was the defection of Lord Keeper Littleton. Charles had instructed him to send the great seal to York and despatched a royal page, Thomas Elliott, to receive it. But Littleton chose to deliver it in person, explaining to his friend the Earl of Essex, in what was becoming a common refrain, that he had again been swayed by the king's 'compelling commands upon him to bring him the seal, and upon no less injunction than his allegiance, which commands he could by no means disobey'.[226]

The flight to York among the peers in late May was widely covered in the news media and caused considerable consternation for those who remained in the House of Lords. It began to appear that not only was Charles winning the battle over attendance, but that there was also a significant danger that the credibility of their proceedings would be undermined. To start with, they adopted a somewhat heavy-handed approach, ordering the arrest of those who had departed without leave as 'delinquents'. But it soon became clear that such a policy was counterproductive. When they issued an order for Littleton's arrest on 23 May, eight of the loyalists who remained in the house registered their protest, pointing out the difficulty for those who received conflicting summons from both the king and parliament. More damagingly, several immediately headed off to York themselves.[227] This haemorrhaging of the membership of the upper house prompted a rethink. From the start of June, there was a concerted effort to shore up the parliamentarian support base among the peerage and win over those who were wavering. Lord Lieutenants, such as Rutland and Spencer who had not yet executed the Militia Ordinance were instructed to do so promptly, and on 10 June some 19 of the peers subscribed to a contribution of plate, money and horse for parliament's cause.[228] The parliamentarian leadership also embarked on a more measured policy to try to separate the irreconcilable loyalists from those who still appeared to be undecided. Those who clearly identified themselves

they were 'bound by the oath of allegiance to attend his Majesty'; Vallance, *Revolutionary England and the National Covenant*, p. 26.

226 HMC, *Buccleuch*, i.301–2; HMC, *Cowper*, ii.316–17.

227 *LJ*, v.80; HMC, *Buccleuch*, i.301–2.

228 *LJ*, v.96, 120.

as members of the 'malignant party' faced arrest and impeachment. A group of nine peers at York who, on 5 June, subscribed a defiant letter complaining that their summons to appear at the bar of the house was 'contrary to the dignity and privilege of peers' were condemned for 'seeking the destruction of parliament'; and Lindsey and Savile were voted to be enemies of the state and 'incendiaries between the king and his people' for preventing the king from receiving a petition for accommodation at the mass meeting of Yorkshire gentry and freeholders on Heworth Moor on the 3rd.[229] But for those reported to be willing to return to parliament the policy was very different.

An insight into the promptings and inducements that were deployed to coax them back into the fold is provided by the correspondence between Salisbury and his son-in-law Northumberland. Northumberland assured him that the upper house was resolved to 'make a great difference betwixt you and some others who, we hear, have expressed good affections to the parliament, and those nine lords whom we conceive fit to be made examples of'. If he returned promptly he promised that he would be 'well received' and would avoid any 'hard censure'. He would also go some way towards repairing his 'honour', which had suffered in 'the opinion [of] the world' because of his apparent betrayal of 'the Parliament'. For good measure, Northumberland then leaked a report that his father-in-law was about to return from the royal court because 'he values his conscience above his place'.[230] Such pressures achieved some success, with both Salisbury and the Earl of Clare returning to the Lords in late June. But the momentum remained with the king.

The procession of peers northwards was sustained well into June, assisted by further batches of royal letters.[231] By the 15th some 41 peers had joined the king, significantly outnumbering those who remained in parliament.[232] A visitor to York reported that the whole mood around the king had been transformed:

> the king, prince and duke of Yorke [are] well and cheerful, the court full of lords, many of the House of Commons and multitude of other brave gentlemen.[233]

This influx of supporters brought about a resumption of something like 'normal' politics around the king. Privy Council meetings were once again being held on a regular basis and the mechanisms for advising the king on policy, both formal and informal, were reactivated. Hyde, who

229 *Ibid.*, v.108–9, 126, 140–1.

230 HMC, *Salisbury*, xxii.370–1; HMC, *Buccleuch*, i.305.

231 *LJ*, v.100–1,169.

232 *His Majestie's Declaration made the 13th of June 1642 to the Lords attending his Majestie at York*... (London, 1642), p. 2; Clarendon, *History*, ii.186.

233 TNA, SP 16/491/21.

was in attendance from late May onwards, later recalled that most of the peers who had come up from London and were now attending regular council meetings were in favour of accommodation. His recollections are supported by contemporary reports, which referred to the likes of Bath, Dorset and Lord Chief Justice Sir John Bankes doing their best to talk the king out of any precipitate action that might lead to the onset of war.[234] However, as Bankes observed, 'all men give not the same advice' and there were those around the king prepared to advocate a more aggressive line.[235]

The identity of these individuals is something of a puzzle. The Lords and Commons remained convinced that the king was surrounded by 'pernicious counsellors and incendiaries' who were stoking his 'fears and jealousies' to the detriment of the public good. But they found it hard to pin down precisely who they were. The two most obvious candidates for this role, given their track record, were the queen and Lord Digby; but both were in exile abroad. Of those councillors attending at York, Richmond and Nicholas were probably closest to Charles on a day-to-day basis; but neither was regarded by contemporaries as a natural 'hard liner' – and publicly, at least, Nicholas was busy talking up the king's desire to 'tread the path of peace'.[236] In the absence of evidence to the contrary it would appear that it was Charles himself who was the main advocate of aggressive action – encouraged from afar by the queen who continued to ply him with a stream of advice about the dangers of accommodation and the gains to be made from taking a firm stand.[237] Certainly this was the assumption of two of the main proponents of accommodation, Bankes and Dorset. Both saw the most significant struggle as taking place in the king's own mind and Dorset placed his principal hopes of avoiding war in what he called 'the tractable and "counsellable" disposition of the king, who, though apt to take extempore resolutions upon the first impressions, yet upon pause and second thoughts changes to the better'.[238]

234 *Ibid.*, SP 16/491/17; Clarendon, *History*, ii.182–3; HMC, *Beaulieu*, p. 155; *Memorials of the Civil War*, ed. R. Bell, 2 vols. (London, 1849), i.13–14.

235 G. Bankes, *The Story of Corfe Castle* (London, 1853), p. 134.

236 Cust, *Charles I. A Political Life*, pp. 345–6; TNA, SP 16/491/17. The hapless Richmond, along with two grooms of the bedchamber Will Murray and Endymion Porter were formally accused by parliament of acting as 'evil counsellors'; but the evidence against Richmond was largely based on his ill-judged intervention on 26 January 1642, and neither Murray nor Porter was a major player, at any rate in English affairs: J. Greenrod, '"Conceived to Give Dangerous Counsel": William Murray, Endymion Porter, The Caroline Bedchamber and the Outbreak of Civil War' (University of Sheffield, M.Phil. thesis, 2003), ch. 7.

237 *Letters of Henrietta Maria*, pp. 70, 75, 79–80.

238 HMC, *Salisbury*, xxii.372.

The struggle over the direction of royal policy was played out during June in a series of exchanges between the king and the loyalist peers that took place around the council table and in more private meetings. Those who were trying to stave off civil war faced an uphill task. The king had a long list of grievances against parliament, which he insisted would have to be satisfied before any settlement could be reached. Bankes set these out in correspondence with friends and colleagues in London soon after his arrival at York in early May. First, there was the execution of the Militia Ordinance, which was no longer just a matter of parliament usurping the king's prerogative. Charles now felt positively threatened by it, and it was this, according to Bankes, that had prompted him to call up the guard of Yorkshire gentry. Second, there was Hotham's defiance at Hull, which had become a 'point of honour' for the king because it brought into question his capacity to command the loyalty and obedience of his subjects. Third, there was the failure of parliament to offer 'justice' against 'those who scandalise the king's person and government by speeches, sermons and pamphlets'. And beyond these there were the longstanding complaints about 'intrusions upon his prerogative', parliament's failure to settle the king's revenues and puritan assaults on the government and liturgy of the Church of England.[239] In the face of Charles's powerful sense of grievance, the most effective arguments that the proponents of accommodation could deploy, as Hyde later recalled, were first that it was crucial, from the point of view of gathering public support, that parliament be seen to strike the first blow, and second that the king lacked the money and arms to fight a war successfully.[240] These might hold Charles back for the time, but they did not offer a long-term solution. For this Bankes and his fellow councillors looked to their friends and colleagues still sitting in the House of Lords.

It is very likely, as Russell has surmised, that the surviving correspondence between Bankes, Dorset, Hamilton and Salisbury in York and Fielding, Northumberland, Saye and Wharton in London, was simply the tip of the iceberg.[241] During May and June there appears to have been extensive contact between peers and councillors on the two sides of the divide, much of it directed towards finding the basis for an accommodation. Two things in particular spurred the peers on in this task. One was a well-founded dread of the consequences of civil war. As Northumberland observed to Bankes, 'God forbid that either king or parliament should by power and force goe about to cure the present distempers: for that course can produce nothing but miserie, if not ruine, to both king and

[239] HMC, *8th Report, R. Bankes MSS*, p. 211; Bankes, *Corfe Castle*, pp. 134–5.
[240] Clarendon, *History*, ii.182–3. [241] Russell, *Fall of the British Monarchies*, p. 513.

people.'[242] The other was a continuing sense of the peerage's responsibility to bridge the gap between monarch and people and find a way out of the whole mess. Wharton posed the question to Bankes of whether 'all this kingdome [has] noe persons prudent enough . . . to prevent the ruine coming upon us'; then answered it by insisting that now was the time for those noblemen, including himself, who had 'the publique interests in the peace of this kingdom' at heart to stand up and be counted.[243] Such exchanges provided the context for the most concerted peace initiative of the summer, which resulted in the Nineteen Propositions.

The groundwork for this was laid in the House of Lords, by Bristol and Northumberland who launched what appears to have been a bipartisan initiative on 23 May. The preliminary was a lengthy speech from Bristol, which attempted to revive the proposals made in the king's address to the house on 20 January 1642.[244] Bristol started with the premise that what divided the two sides were 'fears and jealousies'. The king had given assurances for 'the settling all the liberties and immunities . . . for the propriety of our goods or liberty of our persons' and parliament had professed its willingness 'to make his Majesty a glorious king . . . support his dignity . . . and to maintain all his just regalities and prerogatives'. It should therefore be possible to find common ground and establish a basis for 'mutual satisfaction'. He then recalled how the commissioners at Ripon in 1640 had paved the way to a settlement with the Scots. And, finally, he urged the house to 'draw up Heads of Propositions' in which they could 'truly state and set down all things in difference betwixt the king and the subject, with the most probable ways of reconciling them'. This was a powerful and well-judged appeal, reminding the peers of the last time they had led the way out of an apparently insoluble conflict, a process in which, of course, Bristol himself had played a leading role. Northumberland promptly followed up with the proposal that 'a committee might be appointed to consider how there might be an accommodation between the king and his people.'[245]

242 Bankes, *Corfe Castle*, p. 123. 243 *Ibid.*, pp. 132–3.

244 Rushworth, iii.714–17. There is some question over the dating of this speech and whether Bristol delivered it. The printed version dates the speech to 20 May, but the 23rd is more likely, as Russell suggests, because the references to exculpating those peers who tried to obey summons from both the king and parliament was probably a response to the condemnation of Littleton earlier in the day, against which Bristol had protested. Bristol's disowning of the printed version of the speech stopped some way short, as Russell notes, of claiming that he had not delivered it. It is likely that he was protesting against the publication of a 'pirate' version: Russell, *Fall of the British Monarchies*, p. 514.

245 Clarendon, *History*, ii.119.

The 14 propositions that emerged from the committee's deliberations on 28 May were, however, considerably less bipartisan than the original intent behind the proposal.[246] There was no attempt to find a way of safeguarding the king's prerogatives or funding his financial needs, which Northumberland had acknowledged in his correspondence with Bankes were essential preconditions for any settlement.[247] Instead the committee of largely parliamentarian peers drew up a series of propositions that were likely to command support in the Commons. Their guiding principle, set out in the preface, was that 'the great distractions and distempers' of the current crisis had 'proceeded from . . . evil counsels'. It was proposed that parliament have the right to choose privy councillors and great officers of state, that safeguards be put in place to prevent the king's children being brought up as Catholics or marrying without the consent of parliament and that the king pass the militia bill. Before they were finally approved on 2 June, the Commons added a further five propositions, including a call for all forts and castles to be put in the hands of commanders chosen by parliament.[248] In spite of the uncompromising tone of the Nineteen Propositions, however, the peers involved in their drafting appear to have believed that they would, at least, provide the opportunity to open a dialogue with the king. Lord Feilding told his brother-in-law Hamilton, who had recently made the journey to York, that they 'have been brought downe to the lowest degree of moderation and respect'. He therefore urged him to do all he could to promote them as 'the only means' left to secure a settlement. And Northumberland, writing to Bankes in late June, after the king had rejected the propositions, argued that they had simply been intended as an opening bid to negotiate, couched in suitably deferential language, as a 'petition of grace, not right'.[249]

This was not how they were received at York. Bankes writing to Northumberland on 8 June indicated that they had met with a generally hostile response, prompting the earl to urge that 'harshe remonstrances and replyes might be forborne on all sides'.[250] There are hints that the advocates of accommodation were doing their best to persuade the king of the need to enter into a serious negotiation. A newsletter report that

[246] *LJ*, v.80, 89–90. It is notable that all eight of the loyalists who had protested over the treatment of Littleton earlier in the day, including Bristol were excluded from the committee.

[247] Bankes, *Corfe Castle*, p. 123.

[248] Gardiner, *Constitutional Documents*, pp. 249–54.

[249] National Records of Scotland, Hamilton Correspondence, GD 406/1/1655; Bankes, *Corfe Castle*, pp. 138–9. For other expressions of Feilding's desire for accommodation, see GD 406/1/1659, 1660; but for distinctly less conciliatory rhetoric from Saye, see GD 406/1/1658.

[250] Bankes, *Corfe Castle*, p. 130.

Bath and Dorset had given the king 'counsel very much against his expectation, though very good for the preservation of him and the state', may refer to efforts to put a positive gloss on the propositions; and there was an attempt by several peers in council on 11 June to reach out to parliament by accepting at least some of the ordinances.[251] But the king appears to have been unimpressed by these initiatives. Hyde suggests that, in the end, he simply bypassed the body of peers and entrusted the task of formulating a response to Sir John Culpepper and Lord Falkland.[252] Their *Answer to the XIX Propositions*, published on 18 June was a masterful statement of moderate royalism, defending the royal prerogative and the notion of a balanced polity in which the monarch must preserve his authority to enforce laws, defend the subject's liberties and curb the 'tumults, violence and licentiousness' of the people.[253] It was not, however, the opening to a meaningful dialogue that supporters of accommodation had been hoping for. It was at this point that Salisbury and Clare left York to return to London; and Northumberland was left to reflect that his hopes that 'we were growing into a very good temper and way of moderation' had effectively been dashed.[254]

The failure of the Nineteen Propositions to offer anything that resembled the basis for negotiation was a considerable blow to the advocates of settlement. Charles could point out, with some justice, that if this was the best that parliament could offer there was little point in trying to conduct further negotiations. As a consequence his hand was considerably strengthened when it came to binding the loyalist peers to his cause. During June, the royalist cause emerged for the first time in the public perception as a powerful and coherent entity. At last, it seemed that Charles had the political and, potentially, the military support to be able to challenge parliament. At the heart of this process was the king's success in extracting various commitments from the loyalist peers to stand and, if necessary, fight alongside him. The extent of his achievement in this regard has passed largely unremarked by historians. But given the weakness, and fragility of the royalist cause as recently as mid May, it was a considerable feat. And it owed much to Charles's ability to manoeuvre

251 HMC, *Buccleuch*, i.305; *Memorials of the Civil War*, i.13–14. It is worth noting that Bath wrote somewhat despondently to his wife from York on 3 June 1642 to say that he was about to 'acquaint the king with my intention of going home . . . for I am very weary of being here any longer where I can doe the king no service nor myselfe any good': Kent History and Library centre, U269, C267/13. In the event, Bath was persuaded to stay and does appear to have had some impact on the king's deliberations.

252 Clarendon, *Life*, pp. 154–6.

253 Cust, *Charles I. A Political Life*, pp. 349–50.

254 HMC, *Beaulieu*, p. 155; Bankes, *Corfe Castle*, p. 138.

and cajole a body of hesitant and largely reluctant peers into declaring their allegiance.

The first stage of this process was to amplify the differences between the peers at York and those who remained in London, and, at the same time, demonstrate that the House of Lords had become an unrepresentative and illegitimate rump. The defiant letter from the nine peers at York on 5 June was a starting point. It not only objected to the summons back to London as a breach of their privileges, but also complained that it was impossible to return to the upper house until they had been 'secured from all menaces, or demanding any account of our particular votes, and from tumultuous assemblies'.[255] The king followed this up by persuading

> the peers in council to set down in writing the affronts and violence which had been offered to them at London, by which their presence in the Great Council of the Kingdom was rendered both unsafe and dishonourable.[256]

It was in this context that Dover, one of the signatories to the nine peers' letter, drew up his 'Observations', outlining the pernicious effects of the various pressures exerted on the peers.[257] As Hyde described it, the text produced by the peers in council outlined the 'tumults . . . threats and menaces of the rabble at the doors of the house', 'the breach and violation of the old orders and rules of parliament . . . and reversing waiving or contradicting of motions made in a full house', and a specific incident of intimidation when Denzil Holles had demanded the names of 'those lords who refused to consent to the militia when the multitude without menaced and threatened all those dissenters'. This was a highly significant intervention because, if published, it would, once again, raise the whole question of whether this could be regarded as a 'free parliament'. A copy of the document was signed by various peers and presented to the king; but the following day, according to Hyde, 'many lords came to his majesty and besought him he would by no means publish that paper . . . saying that if it were published they would disavow it'. This forced Charles into agreeing 'never to make it public without their consent'.[258]

What appears to have happened is that those who originally subscribed to the document (presumably the nine peers and, possibly, others) were talked out of the original scheme by fellow nobles who recognised that publication on such a sensitive issue at this moment would undermine the delicate negotiations for accommodation. If this was, indeed, the case it indicates the divisions that were emerging within the ranks of the

255 Rushworth, iii.737. 256 Clarendon, *History*, ii.182–3.
257 Bodl.L, Clarendon State Papers, vol. 21, 1603, fos. 56–8. A similar, anonymous memorandum, dated 10 June, may also have been part of this process: TNA, SP 16/491/14.
258 Clarendon, *History*, ii.182–3.

royalist peers. None of the nine peers was referred to at the time as an advocate of accommodation; whereas Bath, who was mentioned, appears to have kept his distance from this initiative, in spite of making it clear on other occasions that he had been driven away from the parliament by 'scorns, menaces and affronts from the people'.[259] It would seem that the peers were beginning to split between those who continued to make accommodation their priority and those coming to insist that the pursuit of partisan political advantage should take precedence. In other words, there was growing evidence that Charles's efforts to take the battle to parliament were gaining support within the ranks of the peerage. From the king's perspective, however, it was not enough just to draw in a segment of the peerage. It was essential to engage all those who had journeyed to York in a binding commitment to the royalist cause. This he was able to achieve over a few days of intensive negotiation in the middle of June.

This stage of the process began on Saturday 11 June when Sir Thomas Fairfax, who was in York, reported that the king had made 'two propositions to the Lords: first if they would defend his person and raise him some horse; secondly whether they would obey an ordinance without his assent'. The first request was largely uncontroversial because no peer who was willing to respond to Charles's summons to York was likely to deny his obligation to defend his person. But the second prompted a group of lords – Hertford, Hamilton, Salisbury, Clare and Poulett were specifically named – 'to engage themselves further and [declare] that they would observe those ordinances of parliament which should be for his Majesty's honour and the safety of the kingdom'.[260] This would appear to have been a move on their part to try to rescue something from the breakdown of the Nineteen Propositions. By 11 June it had become apparent that the king was not going to agree to a meaningful negotiation over these, in which case this group of peers seems to have been hoping that they could move some of the way towards the position of the Lords in London by opening up a dialogue over parliament's ordinances. Equally, however, this was an opening that the king was determined to close down. His recent declarations had made it clear that those parliamentary ordinances which did not have the royal assent, in particular the Militia Ordinance, were illegal and unconstitutional; and he was resolved not to soften his line. Within two days Charles had got his way. Some 40 peers at York – including all those named as advocates of accommodation, except for

259 *LJ*, v.317. The nine signatories were Capel, Coventry, Devonshire, Dover, Howard of Charlton, Grey of Ruthven, Monmouth, Northampton and Rich: Rushworth, iii.737.
260 *Memorials of the Civil War*, i.13–14.

Clare – subscribed to an 'Engagement', which specifically renounced any compromise on the ordinances.[261]

The text of this was largely unexceptionable. The peers engaged themselves 'to defend . . . the true Protestant religion . . . the lawfull liberties of the subject . . . and just priviledges of your Majestie and both your Houses of Parliament'; 'not to obey any orders or commands whatsoever not warranted by the knowne lawes of the land'; and 'to defend your Majestie's person, crowne and dignitie, together with your Majestie's just and legall prerogative'. However, on the pivotal issue of parliament's ordinances they engaged themselves 'not to obey any rule, order or ordinance whatsoever concerning any militia that hath not the royall assent', to which the king added his own declaration 'that wee doe expect that you shall not yield to any commands not legally grounded, or imposed by any other'.[262]

This was the crux of the 'Engagement'. It cut off any possible avenue for opening up a dialogue with parliament over ordinances and constituted an unequivocal rejection of the Militia Ordinance. Moreover, it did so by means of what was variously described as a 'promise' or a 'profession' by the 40 peers who subscribed. This was different from a binding oath – and fell some way short of the controversial Military Oath proposed in 1639 – so that Salisbury, for one, appears to have felt few reservations about abandoning it later in the month when he returned to the Lords.[263] However, in political terms the distinction did not greatly matter. What was important was that the king had secured a signed undertaking to take sides with him against those challenging his power and authority. This was quickly published and in his regular dispatches to Sir Thomas Roe, presenting the 'official' royal line, Secretary Nicholas was able to gloss it as an unequivocal declaration of loyalty to the king's cause. The peers had shown

> that they were satisfied abundantly of his Majesty's goodness and promises and therefore resolved, with life and estate, to defend his royal person, prerogative and posterity, according to the laws and their allegiance to obey his commands; and to oppose to their utmost endeavour the new order for the militia and all other injunctions upon the subject which should not carry his royal assent.[264]

It is, however, something of a puzzle why those peers who had been holding out for accommodation were prepared to subscribe to such

[261] *His Majestie's Declaration made the 13th of June 1642*, p. 2.

[262] *Ibid.*, pp. 1–2; Clarendon, *History*, ii.184–5. The summary of the king's declaration in Hunt.L., Ellesmere MS, EL 7739, records the assent to the king's propositions as '*una voce*'.

[263] *LJ*, v.156.

[264] TNA, SP 16/491/17.

an emphatic declaration of allegiance. Considerable allowance must be made for the persuasive powers of the king, and pressure from fellow peers who began to gravitate towards the king's position as the uncompromising tone of the Nineteen Propositions became evident. But the explanation would also appear to lie in a clause in the 'Engagement' in which the king undertook not to 'engage you or any of you in any war against the parliament, except it be for our necessary defence and safety'. This was reinforced in a much fuller declaration of 15 June that he desired 'his nobility and council' to bear witness to the fact 'he always had and did abhor all such designs'. Thirty-seven of the peers signed this, with a supporting statement that 'we are fully persuaded that his Majesty hath no such intention.'[265] It would seem that the advocates of accommodation had been forced to recognise that for the time being the best they could hope for was to stave off the immediate outbreak of hostilities and keep open a space to continue working for peace. Part of the price of this was a willingness to subscribe to the Engagement.

In the meantime, however, on 11 June Charles had taken a step closer to open conflict by issuing the first commission of array. As the king saw it, this was an appropriate response to the execution of the Militia Ordinance, which had been proceeding apace, in spite of his proclamation of 27 May expressly prohibiting it.[266] The most provocative of the county musters – because of its relative proximity to York – had been held at Lincoln on 31 May by Lord Willoughby of Parham. Charles wrote to order him to desist and, when he refused to do so, contemplated going to Lincoln in person to enforce obedience to his own Lord Lieutenant, Lindsey. He was talked out of this by the Earl of Bath and, instead, began issuing his own Commissions of Array.[267]

This was a controversial expedient that was seen, with hindsight, as a serious mistake. Hyde later argued that it would have been better for the king to stick with the existing lieutenancy commissions rather than adopt this antique revival, which few had heard of and which, because it was issued in Latin, could be glossed by its opponents as making all sorts of demands for taxes and services 'not warranted by law'. But the king believed that this was not an option because the royal lieutenancy commissions had been condemned by parliament as illegal. The Commission of Array was the obvious alternative. Characteristically Charles sought legal and historical advice – probably from Lord Chief Justice Bankes who was well versed in the revival of medieval precedents from his days as Attorney General – and he discovered that the commission

[265] *His Majestie's Declaration made the 13th of June* 1642, p. 1; Clarendon, *History*, ii.185–6.
[266] *Proclamations*, ii.767–9. [267] *LJ*, v.102, 115–16; *Memorials of the Civil War*, i.13.

was sanctioned by medieval precedent, with the approval of parliament and the judges in Henry IV's reign.[268] This, the king firmly believed, gave him the legal and constitutional high ground in relation to the Militia Ordinance.[269] It also suited his immediate political ends because it enabled him to confer control of his military forces on nominees who were rather more obviously 'persons of honour, reputation and estate' than many of their parliamentarian counterparts. One of his objections to the Militia Ordinance was that it was a device 'to dispossess many of our ancient nobility of the command and trust reposed in them by us' and replace them with 'others who have no interest nor live near to some of the counties to which they are nominated for the lieutenancy'.[270] The Commission of Array entrusted command to a slate of senior commissioners for each shire, any one of whom had the power to call a muster. This enabled him to parade a considerably larger assemblage of noblemen in senior military positions than the Militia Ordinance – 55 members of the English peerage were nominated, compared to 28 on parliament's side. Moreover he was able to draw on peers who often had more experience and stronger local connections than their parliamentary counterparts, as was evident from the first batch of commissions which were issued 11–19 June.[271] The commissions of array, then, were a means not only of equipping the king with military force, but also enlisting large numbers of nobles to serve the royalist cause. The king consolidated this on 22 June by calling on his peers to fund a force of 2000 cavalry for three months, 'in defence of his royal person, the two Houses of Parliament, the laws of the land, the libertyes and property of the subject'. Thirty-seven peers responded with immediate offers of support, including the aged Lord Montagu who had not made it to York, but had sent the king another ringing affirmation of his loyalty.[272] The king also started to receive significant donations of money for the first time, particularly from the Earl of Worcester who was reputed to have paid £100 000 into the royal coffers in late June and early July.[273]

By late June, then, the king's political and military prospects had been transformed. For the first time he could look forward to fighting a civil

[268] Clarendon, *History*, ii.201–5; *Proclamations*, ii.777–81.

[269] See Hyde's account of the exchanges Charles initiated with John Selden on this issue: Clarendon, *History*, ii.205.

[270] Rushworth, iii.657–8.

[271] NRO, Finch Hatton MS 133; TNA, SP 16/491/21. For example, in the first batch of county commissions Northampton, Westmoreland, Newport and Lord Montagu considerably outweighed the young Lord Spencer in Northamptonshire: Finch Hatton MS 133, p. 46. See Appendix 2, 'English peers and Allegiance, 1640–42' for a full list of appointees.

[272] TNA, SP 16/491/29.

[273] Gardiner, *History*, x.207.

war on something like equal terms. Bankes, who was still angling for an accommodation, warned his friend Lord Saye that Charles was 'now in a condition not to have anything inforced from him' and this heralded a much more aggressive stance.[274] Soon after the first commissions of array had been issued royalist peers started to head off to their shires to execute them. The earliest attempt to do so was at Leicester on 16 June where Huntingdon's son, Henry Hastings, met resistance from the Earl of Stamford who had removed the county magazine to his house at Bradgate Park. As with Hotham's defiance at Hull, Charles took this as the cue for claiming that parliament 'hath actually levied war against us'; but this time he responded much more forcefully, ordering Hastings to arrest Stamford and 'his adherents' as rebels and traitors.[275] Dorset writing to Salisbury on 27 June attempted to put a positive gloss on this episode. He recounted that initially, on receiving news of Stamford's 'excessive zeal', the king had 'resolved *vim vi repellere* and concluded on a course that might have given beginning to a great deal of misery'; however, he was then 'altered by the more poised and wise advice of those that study how to preserve things from extremity'.[276] But whether Charles's action really constituted the climb down that Dorset perceived is questionable. By this stage the earl and his fellow advocates of accommodation were beginning to clutch at straws.

The final blow to their hopes was delivered in mid July, as Charles's confidence and readiness to fight continued to grow. On the 9th, after appointing Lindsey general of his army, he advanced out of York to Beverley with a force of 2500 men. His objective was Hull, but he held back initially in the hope that Hotham could be persuaded to surrender without a fight. On 13 July he made an excursion to Lincoln where he received a rapturous welcome from local inhabitants and 75 of the gentry undertook to support a further force of 400 horse for three months. He then returned to Beverley, to meet the Earl of Holland bearing a new petition for accommodation from the parliament.[277] Holland's account of the preparations in the king's camp was very revealing. Charles, he reported, was intent on building on his success at Lincoln by travelling to Nottingham and Leicester where he fully expected to command the same levels of support; and, although his forces were still small, it was being claimed by those about the king – and Holland believed them – that 'he may when he please call a very considerable number together that

[274] HMC, *8th Report Bankes*, p. 212. [275] HMC, *Hastings*, ii.84–5.
[276] HMC, *Salisbury*, xxii.372.
[277] Gardiner, *History*, x.211–12; C. Holmes, *Seventeenth Century Lincolnshire* (History of Lincolnshire, VII, 1980), pp. 147–50.

are ready on the least command to move towards him.'[278] This mood of aggressive optimism was to prove fatal for the chances of the earl's mission.

The Holland initiative was very much a last ditch attempt to avert the looming conflict. It was sponsored by a committee of the more moderate parliamentary peers, including Leicester and Spencer, who had entered their protests over votes to raise an army on 6 July. The conditions it proposed were a far more realistic basis for negotiation than the Nineteen Propositions. In return for the king agreeing to stand down his forces in the north, recall the commissions of array and 'come nearer to your parliament, and hearken to their humble advice and humble petitions', it offered to punish any 'tumults and seditious actions' that had caused him offence, restore Hull to the state it had been in before Hotham had become governor and 'settle the militia by a bill in such a way as shall be honourable and safe for your Majesty'.[279] This did not address the long-term divisions between the two sides, but it did offer a way to stop them fighting until calmer counsels could prevail. However, the king's response was to dismiss it out of hand. When Holland read the petition out, he immediately denounced 'the reproaches cast upon him by it' and retorted that 'he was sorry that they thought the exposing him and his honour to so much scandal was the way to procure or preserve the peace of the kingdome'. At a meeting, which took place soon after, 'peers and councillors' went further and insisted that, since he was 'ingaged for the vindication of his princely dignity and honour', the petition deserved an even sharper rejection than he had already given it.[280] This re-emergence of the language of honour, which had been relatively muted in recent royal statements, was very significant. It suggested that Charles was now thinking about the complex issues dividing the two sides primarily as a matter of personal honour; and past experience showed that once this happened it would be much harder to achieve compromise.[281]

In spite of the more aggressive outlook that now prevailed among the king's entourage, there were still some peers who were prepared to offer the 'more poised and wise advice' advocated by Dorset. Hyde, who was present throughout these negotiations recalled that, after discussion with Holland, several of them approached Charles and urged him to tone down his response because there was a good opportunity to gain concessions from parliament. His carefully scripted response provides one of the clearest statements we have of his attitude on the eve of civil war. He began by outlining the ways in which he had responded to the

[278] *LJ*, v.224. [279] *Ibid.*, 186, 207. [280] Clarendon, *History*, ii.230–1, 237–8.
[281] Cust, *Charles I. A Political Life*, pp. 230–1.

'great provocations' offered by parliament since the Grand Remonstrance with 'gentleness' and 'tender expressions', but had found that this had simply encouraged 'their insolence and irregularities'. The 'petitions and propositions' that they presented to him had been couched in 'so high a dialect, and with that sovereignty of language, as if he were subject to their jurisdiction'. This was not only profoundly humiliating, but, if allowed to pass unchallenged, it would 'lessen' his people's 'reverence to his Majesty'. To yield now would simply be to invite further affronts. It would also 'discourage those upon whose affections and loyalty he was principally to depend' as he prepared to take Hull by force. He was therefore 'resolved' to resist any further concessions and trust in God to uphold the righteousness of his cause.[282] This showed a much more confident and determined Charles. He now felt strong enough to set aside the fudges and hesitations of recent months, embark on a course of action that would redeem his slighted honour and follow the queen's advice to rally support by taking a firm stand.

For the time being, this was the end of the road for those advocating accommodation. Nicholas's regular dispatches to Sir Thomas Roe stopped mentioning the king's desire for peace and concentrated on the preparations for war. The day after rejecting Holland's overtures Charles advanced towards Hull and was repelled after a skirmish. On 22 July he visited Leicester where he again secured a commitment to fund a troop of cavalry. Then, after a brief return to York, he set out in early August on his recruiting drive across the midlands. The civil war was effectively under way.[283]

Those peers who were actively involved in politics faced a series of increasingly difficult decisions about allegiance in the spring and summer of 1642. In many cases they were being asked, as Michael Braddick has indicated, 'to choose between propositions which had not previously been understood as alternatives', backed by arguments which they had been brought up to believe were incontestable.[284] As a consequence of their high public visibility and the pressures being piled on to them by both sides, the nobility were often placed in a particularly uncomfortable position. Initially there were the decisions about how to vote in the Lords and how to respond to nominations for the lord lieutenancy under the Militia Ordinance. Then, as the king pushed harder for attendance at York and issued the Commissions of Array, and parliament responded with its own pressures to remain in London and execute the Militia

282 Clarendon, *History*, ii.238–40.
283 TNA, SP 16/491/84, 90; Gardiner, *History*, x.214–20.
284 M.J. Braddick, *Gods Fury, England's Fire* (Allen Lane: London, 2008), pp. 225–8.

Ordinance, the stakes became progressively higher and the choices more fraught.

Some sought to negotiate this by withdrawing from the political stage altogether. A good example was the Earl of Rutland who was alternately wooed and cajoled by both parties. He was a regular supporter of the parliamentarian peers in the Lords until he was nominated to the lord lieutenancy of Derbyshire in the Militia Ordinance in February 1642, at which point he sought to disengage himself by retreating to his country estates in Lincolnshire and Derbyshire. He ingratiated himself with the king in March by lending him his coach on his journey north; but then determinedly resisted the summons to York. After prodding by parliament, he did appoint Deputy Lieutenants, and held a meeting with them late in June. But he was not willing to go any further and by the late summer he was doing his best to distance himself from both parties.[285] There were opportunities, then, for peers to sit on the fence and opt out of taking hard decisions. In spite of this, however, the majority of the politically engaged peerage did effectively take sides in the summer and autumn of 1642, by attempting to execute the Commission of Array or the Militia Ordinance, taking up arms for king or parliament, or serving in a political capacity. There were 123 English peers in March 1642, of whom 27 largely excluded themselves from involvement in national politics. Of the remaining 96, 49 (51 per cent) were active supporters of the king and 22 (23 per cent) were active on behalf of parliament.[286]

In some cases the choice appears to have been relatively clear cut. Several of the parliamentary peers, such Brooke and Mandeville, followed a straightforward trajectory from the onset of the Scottish crisis to the outbreak of civil war, consistently aligning themselves with the opposition to the crown across a range of religious, political and constitutional issues and taking on leading roles in the summer of 1642.[287] Their counterpart on the royalist side was a peer like the Earl of Northampton, who after showing himself to be one of the most loyal and aggressive supporters

[285] *LJ*, v.96; HMC, *Buccleuch*, i.293, 303; *Cowper*, ii.309; A. Fletcher, 'Petitioning and the outbreak of the civil war in Derbyshire', *Derbyshire Archaeological Journal*, 93(1973), 36–9; L. Stone, *Family & Fortune* (Oxford: Oxford University Press, 1973), p. 200. He did eventually resume his place in the upper house in 1643: Clarendon, *History*, iii.287. Other peers who distanced themselves from the awkward choices involved in executing the Commission of Array or the Militia Ordinance in the summer of 1642, included the Earls of Leicester, Salisbury and Suffolk and Lord North, all of whom had hitherto been firm allies of the parliament: 'Robert Sidney, 2nd Earl of Leicester (1595–1677)', *Oxf.DNB*; C. Holmes, *The Eastern Association in the English Civil War* (Cambridge: Cambridge University Press, 1974), pp. 48, 52–3.

[286] See Appendix 2, 'English Peers and Allegiance 1641–2'.

[287] 'Edward Montagu, 2nd Earl of Manchester (1602–1671)', 'Robert Greville 2nd Lord Brooke (1607–1643)', *Oxf.DNB*.

of the king's desire to resume war with the Scots in the Great Council, then taking a leading role in the king's party at Westminster, responded to the summons to York and then rushed off to execute the Commission of Array in Coventry before he had even had time to get the commission copied.[288] For most peers, however, the choices were less clear and a variety of complex considerations often came into play before they made their decisions. We can trace some of the processes by looking again at one of the best documented among them, Edward Lord Montagu.

Now aged 80, Montagu had withdrawn from the Long Parliament at the end of January 1641 and retired to what he described as a life of 'privacy'. But he continued to take a keen interest in national politics, and his correspondence with his bother Manchester and his sons and nephews makes it possible to follow his reactions to the unfolding crisis. He felt very torn. The bedrock of his beliefs, as he told his nephew, George Montagu, was to stick to 'Solomon's rule': 'Fear God; honour the king.' 'That,' he declared, 'would bring all to perfection if it may be truly followed, which I pray heartily for'. At the same time he felt a profound loyalty and respect for parliament. 'My heart, hand and life shall stand for parliaments,' he told his son William; 'he is not of a true English spirit that would not shed life and all he hath for [its] maintenance and preservation'. Like so many of his fellow peers, he tried to reconcile this dual obligation by pinning his hopes on a settlement. 'My thought hath been but for an accommodation', he told his brother in June; and he urged that both the Militia Ordinance and the Commission of Array be 'quite vacated or at least laid aside for a time [which] would allay a great deal of heat and heartburning'.[289] However, even while he was expressing these hopes, he was taking steps which would land him firmly in the royalist camp.

Montagu's notes and meditations suggest that he experienced a period of anguished reflection, as he prayed and searched his conscience to find a way ahead. This reflection appears to have led him to lay much of the blame for the current crisis at the door of parliament. He was greatly exercised over its official sanctioning of the sin of 'usury' to raise money for the relief force for Ireland, which he believed would bring down God's judgements on their heads. More immediately, he was disturbed by parliament taking on itself to pass ordinances without the assent of the king, which he described as 'a violation of the privileges of parliament and common liberty of the subject'. In particular he was worried by the Militia Ordinance, which not only contravened legal and constitutional

288 *LJ*, v.163–7.
289 Cope, *The Life of a Public Man*, pp. 181–6; HMC, *Buccleuch*, i.295, 300; iii.414–15, 417.

precedent but also challenged the principles of order and hierarchy because it 'empowered one deputy, being never so mean a man, [to] command any of the peers of England'.[290] However, what finally prompted Montagu to come out of his retirement and openly support the king was not so much his reading of the political situation as Charles's personal summons to York. This forced him to come to a decision, and he reverted to his fundamental belief in the need for loyalty and obedience to his monarch. In a letter to Charles, he excused himself from attending personally on the grounds of age, but then, as in 1639, offered a trenchant declaration of his willingness to 'live and die for the maintenance of his Majesty's right'. He also pledged to fund 30 horse for three months. The letter was relayed to Charles by Montagu's son-in-law, Lord Willoughby of Eresby, who reported that when the king received it, he called some of the lords together and read it out loud, adding 'You may see how much I am beholding to this good man.' Montagu was overwhelmed, telling his brother that he was particularly gratified because 'I did think I had been as a dead man, quite forgotten and out of mind.'[291] When Charles followed up in early July with a personal letter telling him that he had been nominated for the Commission of Array in Northamptonshire – 'as a particular expression of our confidence in you and favour to you . . . taking notice that so constant and faithful have your services been ever to the crown' – the elderly peer decided he must act. At the meeting of the commissioners at Kettering on 15 August he joined the Earl of Westmoreland and Sir Christopher Hatton in ordering a royalist muster and requesting the Deputy Lieutenants to stand down the Militia Ordinance. In a county that had already shown itself to be staunchly parliamentarian this was a forlorn hope. A couple of weeks later, in spite of his age, he had been arrested and dispatched to confinement in London.[292]

We know much more about the considerations that shaped Montagu's decision on allegiance in the summer of 1642 than is generally the case. But it is likely that many of the peers faced up to the choices confronting them in a similar fashion. They would have sifted through a complex mix of ideological and personal concerns, and hoped that a belated accommodation would spare them the anguish of having to opt for one side or the other. Like Montagu, many of the royalist peers were profoundly uneasy about parliament usurping the king's prerogative and challenging legal and constitutional tradition through the passage of the ordinances,

[290] Cope, *The Life of a Public Man*, pp. 188–9; HMC, *Buccleuch*, i.292; iii.414–15.
[291] Cope, *The Life of a Public Man*, pp. 192–3; HMC, *Buccleuch*, iii.416–17.
[292] Cope, *The Life of a Public Man*, pp. 194–5; HMC, *Buccleuch*, i.307; *Beaulieu*, pp. 155–8; *Portland*, i.60–1.

in particular the Militia Ordinance. They said as much in the 'Engagement' of 15 June. Those who sat through the proceedings at Westminster were also alarmed by the threats and intimidation that they faced through late 1641 and early 1642. As the memorandum drawn up in conjunction with the nine peers' letter emphasised, this was the unacceptable face of parliament's efforts to mobilise popular support. And allied to these concerns – although less so in Montagu's case – there was often a deep-seated fear of radical Puritanism and the challenge it presented to the Church of England. A comparable mix of ideological considerations permeated the decisions made by those who supported parliament. Fear of popery, alarm about the influence of evil counsellors, and anxiety about plots and pre-emptive strikes to destroy the parliament and introduce tyranny, were woven together to provide a powerful rationale for the parliamentarian cause, for peers as for others. But these arguments were not necessarily enough in themselves to explain individual decisions on allegiance. The concerns they were picking up were shared across the political spectrum. The desire to maintain legal and constitutional traditions and keep in check the potentially destructive force of popularity was an abiding concern for many parliamentarians as well as royalists, and fear of popery and evil counsel caused alarm on both sides. In such circumstances, as Braddick has indicated, peers were being confronted with different types of choices at different moments. Their responses would often vary according to the questions they were being asked, who was doing the asking and the context in which this took place.[293]

Like Montagu many peers must have wrestled with their consciences, and sometimes they came up with surprising answers. Perhaps, no one behaved more unpredictably than Lord Paget. He had long been one of the most reliable allies of the Junto and the parliamentarian leadership, and was one of the first peers to execute the Militia Ordinance, in Buckinghamshire in late May 1642. But on 11 June he suddenly set off to join the king at York. In the published explanation that he issued, he readily admitted that his behaviour 'may seem strange' in one who had been so committed to seeking 'the reformation of all disorders in church and commonwealth'; however, he insisted that through all the struggles and divisions at Westminster he had never had the intention of actually fighting against the king. Now that it was evident that, 'under the shadow of loyaltie', there was 'a preparation of arms' against his monarch, he was convinced, by 'a good conscience' that he must declare his allegiance and 'throw myself down at his feet and die a loyall subject'. The cumulative pressure exerted by the king's summons, the direction of events and his

293 Braddick, *God's Fury*, pp. 225–8.

own sense of right and wrong appear to have finally triggered his decision to rally to the royal cause. After joining the king at York, in July he set off on a vigorous recruiting campaign in his home county of Staffordshire.[294]

Paget's inclination to throw himself on Charles's mercy and favour expressed the aristocracy's deep-rooted understanding that their very identity was tied up with the personal service and approval of their king. This was apparent on both sides of the divide. As we have seen, the Earl of Salisbury felt torn by his desire not to let down his king, and tried, unsuccessfully, to appease both sides. His friend and ally, the Earl of Pembroke, also wavered as a result of the royal summons. From late June he was conducting a lengthy negotiation via his son, Lord Herbert, and his friend Sir Edward Hyde over the possibility of being reconciled to Charles. He admitted to Hyde that he and the king had had their political differences, but assured him that his principal hope now was to 'be restored to his majesty's good opinion of me' and to 'ever live and die a faithful servant'. His son proposed various means by which such a reconciliation could be effected; but in the end Charles never quite managed to meet his requirements and Pembroke was held back by the 'scruple of honour' which, as in Salisbury's case, argued against his abandoning a cause with which he had aligned himself for so long.[295]

Many peers, then, faced complex choices in the summer of 1642 shaped by considerations that mixed ideology with the personal and the contingent. However, the end result was clear enough. It was to provide Charles with the platform for building a royalist party sufficiently powerful to take on parliament. From the beginnings of the formation of an identifiable loyalist lobby in October 1641 the king was able to rely on a cohort of around 40 'well-affected' peers who provided consistent support. During December 1641 and January 1642 they were strong enough in the upper house to hold at bay assaults on the royal prerogative and the king's authority. Even after their numbers had been reduced by the withdrawals of February 1642 they continued to vote *en bloc* and provide a focal point for defending the constitutional status quo. It was largely due to their efforts, and those of the royalist leadership in the Commons, that the king was able to keep fighting his corner and retain some degree of political agency during the spring of 1642 when to most observers he appeared bereft of support. Then, as he stepped up his efforts to recruit a royalist party in the early summer, it was the willingness of these peers to

[294] *The copy of a letter sent from the right honourable the Lord Paget unto the honourable House of Parliament*... (London, 1642); HMC, *5th Report Sutherland*, p. 141; R. Hutton, *The Royalist War Effort 1642–1646* (Harlow: Longman, 1982), pp. 22–3; 'William, 6th Baron Paget (1609–1678)', *Oxf.DNB*.

[295] *Clarendon SP*, ii.145–7.

respond to his summons that gave his cause political credibility. Finally, during late June and July, as he strove to draw together the critical mass of support needed to fight a war, it was their readiness to sign the Engagement, to subscribe to the regiments of royal horse and then go out into the shires to execute the Commission of Array that provided the basis for a royal army.

The contrast with the last occasion on which the peers had been summoned *en masse* to York, for the Great Council of September–October 1640, was a measure of the shift that had taken place in their circumstances and their relationship with the king. On the face of it there were marked parallels with the situation in September 1640. The king was summoning the Lords to York to give him the benefit of their advice; he was in desperate need of their support, which gave them considerable leverage; and there was much talk of the need for the peerage as a whole to stand up for 'the publique interests in the peace of the kingdome' and prevent 'the ruine coming upon us'. However, in other respects things were very different. The conflicts and grievances of late 1641 and early 1642 had produced a legacy of bitterness and distrust which made the prospects for settlement much more remote. The Nineteen Propositions, the only strategy for negotiation on the table, did not go nearly far enough in concessions to the king. Above all, the sense of unity and consensus, which had been so apparent at the Great Council and continued during the first phase of the Long Parliament, had been largely disrupted. This showed itself in the divisions among loyalist peers in the summer of 1642. Commentators continued to point to signs that the majority were pressing the king for accommodation, but their efforts were being undermined by those – like the nine signatories to the open letter to the Lords – who were prepared to put the pursuit of political advantage before the search for settlement. And Charles was able to exploit these divisions with considerable skill.

Conrad Russell has argued that Charles was much more successful as a party leader than as a king.[296] His effectiveness in building the royalist party in the summer of 1642 bears this out. He was now much more confident in his position and the direction of his political strategy than he had been in the autumn of 1640; and he displayed a sufficiently strong political conviction and determination to reassure the committed royalists that he would stand by what they believed in and do his best to protect them. The resilience of the loyalist party in the upper house, in the face of considerable intimidation, was testimony to the effect of this.

[296] C.S.R. Russell, *The Causes of the English Civil War* (Oxford: Oxford University Press, 1990), pp. 187, 209–10.

At the same time, with the help of Bristol, Hyde and others, he was able to reach out to the middle ground and rally moderate support in defence of constitutional monarchy and the Church of England. For much of the spring and summer of 1642 he accomplished the considerable tactical feat of steering a middle course between the line being advocated by Hyde and that of the queen. He also displayed a good understanding of how to manage his peers as individuals. After the abortive attempt to rally them to attend the Garter Feast in April, his approach of sending out personal summonses, appealing directly to their sense of allegiance, proved highly effective. And once peers were at York he was able to keep most of them there, partly by involving them in regular consultations and council meetings, but also through the coaxing and flattery that Montagu found so beguiling. But perhaps his greatest achievement was in manoeuvring a body of peers mainly bent on accommodation towards openly declaring their allegiance in the 'Engagement'. He exploited the divisions in their ranks very skilfully, sidestepping attempts to offer a compromise on parliament's ordinances, giving ground when it became clear that the memorandum in support of the nine peers' letter could not be published, and offering strong assurances that he had no intention of fighting a war except *in extremis*. Then when the moment came he was able to press home his advantage by clinching subscription to the 'Engagement'. Once this was published he appeared to have the mandate he needed for raising an army and preparing for war.

From the king's perspective, getting to this point was a significant achievement and it demonstrated the effectiveness of his policy towards his peerage. Amid complex ideological divisions, and in spite of repeated mistakes and misjudgements on his part, he was able to command the backing of around 60 per cent of the politically engaged English nobility and the active support of around half of them.[297] Given the 'get outs' and opportunities to sit on the sidelines and remain neutral that were available to peers, this was a considerable feat. It demonstrated that when they had to choose sides the majority of the noblemen would stand behind their monarch. This was, perhaps, less impressive testimony to the success of his long-term strategy of cultivating the nobility as natural supporters of the crown than the peers' response in 1639. A third of the politically

[297] See Appendix 2, 'English peers and Allegiance 1640–2', for these figures. The estimates of numbers backing the king are based on the signatories to royal declarations, pledges of support to raise cavalry and nominations to the Commission of Array (Arundel and Manchester have been omitted from the calculation of royalist numbers since, although both were named as commissioners, neither showed any open sign of backing the king at this time). Those who gave active support were those who tried to execute the Commission of Array, or served in arms or in some political capacity.

engaged peerage indicated their allegiance to parliament in the spring and summer of 1642.[298] But it demonstrated that the sense of obligation and allegiance that he had worked so hard to foster did have considerable resilience.

[298] See Appendix 2. This calculation is based on those who were nominated as Lord Lieutenants under the Militia Ordinance (and did not refuse to act, as in the cases of Hertford, Cumberland and Lord Strange) or who subscribed to fund cavalry for parliament. However, this figure does include the Lords Chandos, Paget and Spencer who ended up as active royalists.

Conclusion

Charles's understanding of his relationship with his aristocracy was in many ways summed up in the values and traditions of the Order of the Garter. He had grown up with the order; he had a strong emotional attachment to its rites and observances, and he saw it as epitomising everything that was most noble and most honourable about England's elite. It highlighted the chivalric values of courage, steadfastness and prowess in arms that were at the core of his own sense of honour and self-worth; and its traditions of loyalty and knightly companionship exemplified the ties and alliances he saw as sustaining his monarchy. The king was enough of a realist to acknowledge the conventional political wisdom that any monarch depended for support, above all, on his leading peers. Essex's description of the nobility as 'the very subalterne parts of the prince and the very shoulders whereon the head resteth', was echoed in his own remarks to the Short Parliament, that his peers having 'received honour from himself and his royal progenitors, he doubted not would . . . be moved in honour and dutiful affection' to serve his monarchy.[1] And his political experiences during the forced loan and the 1626 and 1628 parliaments brought home the need to cultivate the support of the Lords as a counterweight to the potentially obstructive Commons. But there was more to the relationship than simple political expediency. In his more idealistic moments Charles invested it with all the devotion and emotional attachment that attended his enthusiasm for the garter. He saw his nobles as a brotherhood in arms, bound to him by ties of fidelity and kinship, representing the old-fashioned martial ideals of valour and constancy and, through their 'good counsel' and political strength, partnering him in the government of the state. This was why he worked so hard to restore the order to its 'ancient luster', why he took such trouble over the upbringing and education of young nobles, why, after Buckingham's death, he resisted the temptation to dilute its prestige with new creations and why he strove so consistently to promote its welfare.

[1] Yale University, Beinecke Library, Yale MS 370; Rushworth, ii.1163.

But if Charles valued the aristocracy as his natural partners, and the mainstays of his monarchy, how did the peers view their relationship with the king? Here there was a powerful sense of a balance of obligations. They saw themselves as a nobility who were at the same time both 'dative' and 'native'. Their honours derived in part from royal grant and in part from ancient inheritance and birthright. Because the monarch had bestowed titles and recognition upon them and their families they owed him a duty of service; but equally because their birth, wealth and privilege had marked them out as leaders and spokesmen of the people they had a responsibility to serve the 'commonwealth' or 'country'. Dudley Lord North summed up this balance as the requirement on them to 'do good offices' between the king and his people and 'steare a course of justice indifferently betwixt both'.[2] The nobility's elevated position and consciousness of their birthright ensured that they did not lack self-confidence in their dealings with the crown. They expected to be treated as his 'natural counsellors' and to play a leading role in both advising the king and governing the realm. They also expected the king to show a proper regard for the rights and privileges of the 'honour community'. Hence Essex's implicit warning to Elizabeth that a good prince had a duty to maintain and honour the reputation of noble families; and the more explicit admonition of the English nobility to Charles, that to favour the Scottish and Irish peers would be to imperil the very 'foundacon of the grounds of honour layd in this kingdome'.[3] The assertiveness of the peers, however, was tempered by a strong sense that much of their personal honour and reputation was tied up with the validation of their service by the monarch. This was particularly evident in the confined arena of the royal court where a majority of noblemen competed for recognition. Here Charles's approval was everything and courtier peers, like Clifford and Newcastle, lived for the moment when they could tell their friends that the king 'seemed to be pleased with me very well'.[4] However, this was not restricted to the court. Service in office was generally seen as the *raison d'être* of the peerage and to be removed by the king was the ultimate humiliation. As the aristocratic loan refusers acknowledged, 'the displeasure of my prince' demonstrated by their recent suspensions was 'fully equal to close imprisonment' in the deep injury it inflicted on their sense of self-worth.[5] This rooted belief in the importance of personal service to their monarch helps to explain why the individualised messages that Charles sent to peers at the time of the forced loan and the Bishops Wars, and again in 1642, had such a powerful effect.

[2] North, *A Forest of Varieties*, pt. 1, pp. 85–7.
[3] Bodl.L., North MS b.1, fos. 55–6. [4] *Strafforde Letters*, i.101.
[5] *Proceedings in Parliament 1628*, v.466–8.

Charles has been seen by historians as a king with underdeveloped political antennae who was poor at reading how his actions would play with the various constituencies he was dealing with.[6] However, his relations with the peerage appear to have been an exception to this. Due to his own finely tuned sense of honour, and his instinctive understanding of its implications for those he had grown up with and in whose company he spent most of his adult life, Charles was notably sensitive to their views and concerns. This was evident not just in his care and understanding for their individual welfare, but also in the respect he showed to their claims as members of the 'honour community'. A good example is provided by the Holland/Weston duelling case in 1633 where he eventually acknowledged that for any nobleman the priority in such circumstances was to vindicate his honour. It was also evident in his readiness to retreat over the Military Oath in 1639 when he recognised that he was straining the loyalty of some of his most faithful supporters. But, perhaps, the most consistent demonstration of his respect for the concerns of the peerage was the way in which, after Buckingham's death, he went out of his way to ensure that senior members of the nobility were promoted to the offices in which they could fulfil their role as *consiliarii nati*. The elevation of the Earl of Northumberland to the Privy Council and Order of the Garter, and then to the lord admiralty, after succeeding to his title in 1632 was a case in point. While this depended in part on the queen's favour, it also reflected the king's recognition that a peer whom Wentworth and Laud identified as a particularly promising member of the 'ancient nobility' should be fast tracked into high office.[7] He demonstrated a similar approach in appointments to the Privy Council and lord lieutenancies during the 1630s, and he would have been mystified by the complaint made by opponents of the regime that his government was dominated by 'bedchamber men'.[8] This may have been a legitimate charge during the period of Buckingham's ascendancy, but it was one that Charles went out of his way to refute during the Personal Rule.

The king did not always get it right. In attempting to repair the damage done to the Earl of Worcester's local reputation after his demotion from the lord lieutenancy, he subjected the Earl of Bridgewater to the humiliation of appearing powerless in the execution of his office. And by

[6] Cust, *Charles I. A Political Life*, pp. 472–3; Russell, *Causes of the English Civil War*, p. 200.

[7] 'Algernon Percy, 10th Earl of Northumberland (1602–1668)', *Oxf.DNB*; *Strafforde Letters*, ii.42.

[8] Adamson, *Noble Revolt*, pp. 31–2.

no means all of his policies during the 1630s were noble-friendly. There were reports of widespread opposition among peers to the composition for knighthood fines when a number were summoned to answer before the Privy Council in February 1632. The Earl of Essex led the resistance, pointing out that like other peers he had waited on the king at his coronation and on numerous occasions since when 'he was ready to have received knighthood or any other honour his Majesty should have been pleased to vouchsafe on him'.[9] Fines for encroachments on royal forests were also a source of considerable grievance for several peers. Southampton faced a challenge to his title to lands in the New Forest in 1636, which would have reduced his rental income from £2500 to £500 pa; and when the justice seat moved to Rockingham Forest in 1637, Salisbury faced a fine of £20 000, Westmoreland £19 000 and Peterborough £5000. The peers were largely pardoned from these penalties after appeals to the king; but such behaviour toward them clearly rankled and must have caused considerable resentment among an order who were always extremely sensitive about their treatment at the hands of their monarch.[10] However, this sort of insensitivity to their concerns was not the norm. For the most part Charles went out of his way to defend their interests, even when – as in the case of the attempt to requisition Lord Brooke's house – this clashed with the claims of the royal prerogative. His systematic cultivation of the noble order was one of the features of his Personal Rule.

This raises the question of how successful the king and Earl Marshal were in their avowed policy of resurrecting the aristocracy. This was a policy that had two main elements, as Arundel's agenda of April 1625 indicated. The first of these – and the one to which Charles and Arundel devoted most of their immediate energies – was to restore the prestige and 'ancient luster' of the noble order. They began by putting a stop to the sale of honours, which was acknowledged as one of the principal reasons for the decline in respect. Grants of new titles were made so sparingly during the 1630s that there was an overall decline in the number of peers. This was followed by a policy of inflicting draconian punishments, first of all in Star Chamber and subsequently in the Court of Chivalry, on those guilty of defaming members of the aristocracy or challenging their authority. There was also a concerted effort to ensure that peers conducted themselves in a manner worthy of their order. The ceremonies and rites of the Order of the Garter were reformed to provide an exemplar

9 Sharpe, *Personal Rule*, pp. 114–16; *Court and Times*, ii.163, 171.

10 Gardiner, *History*, viii.86, 282; 'Thomas Wriothesley, 4th Earl of Southampton (1608–1667)', 'John Mordaunt, 1st Earl of Peterborough (1599–1643)', *Oxf.DNB*.

of the standards of decorum and behaviour expected of them; peers were given the opportunity to provide a virtuous education for their offspring at Sir Francis Kynaston's *Musaeum Minervae*; the Earl of Castlehaven was executed for behaviour that threatened to undermine the king's efforts to inculcate higher standards; and nobles were forcibly reminded of their duty to dispense hospitality. One of the most vigorous of these policies was the attempt to control the problem of duelling, which many regarded as not only displaying the unacceptable face of the honour code, but also threatening to set an example of defiance of royal authority. The Privy Council's declaration in the Holland/Weston case and the Star Chamber judgement against Apsley were followed by Arundel's efforts to resolve the problem once and for all by providing redress for 'scandalous words provocative of a duel' in the reformed Court of Chivalry.

The second element was a more general campaign to stabilise the honours system that was primarily the responsibility of the Earl Marshal and the heralds. It built on initiatives launched by Arundel's grandfather, the 4th Duke of Norfolk in the 1560s, which had extended the powers of heralds in conducting visitations, set up mechanisms for regulating the funerals of peers and gentry and attempted to establish the Court of Chivalry as a permanent entity. The implementation of these measures was patchy over the succeeding decades, but antiquarians and heraldic writers were successful in establishing a new 'genealogical science', which gave greater priority than hitherto to the claims of lineage and pedigree. During the first half of James's reign, the Earl of Northampton sought to revive and extend Norfolk's programme and made a concerted effort to establish the Court of Chivalry as a permanent arbiter of duels. But the earl received only intermittent support from the king and his efforts were largely undone by the outcry against sale of honours and the questioning of the crown's prerogative in such matters. After being appointed Earl Marshal in 1621, Arundel attempted, with some support from James, to reverse the damage done by sale of honours; but he was unable to overcome the opposition of Buckingham. It was not until the early 1630s that he got reform back on track, when a fresh round of visitations was launched and there were renewed efforts to ensure the registration of funerals. Moreover, in partnership with the civil lawyers, he was finally able to establish the Court of Chivalry on a permanent footing. The Earl Marshal and the heralds now had the powers they had long been pressing for and this, at last, appeared to offer the possibility of achieving the fixity and stability that so many contemporaries craved.

Gauging the success of these policies is, however, difficult. Much of the evidence is contradictory. Duelling continued largely unabated and social inferiors continued to insult and challenge the authority of peers.

The heralds' visitations of the 1630s appear to have been no more effective than those of previous decades and the Court of Chivalry – whose development was largely shaped by the civilians' quest for extra fees – directed most of its time and energy towards providing gentlemen with redress for defamation rather than supporting the heralds or cracking down on abuses against the peerage. However, there is some evidence that the Court of Chivalry's consolidation of its status as a regular forum for determining matters of honour did improve the position of the aristocracy. By the end of the 1630s there was much less talk of their declining status and more optimism that the crown and the heraldic establishment were getting to grips with the problem of stabilising the honours system. Alongside this the prestige and renown of the Order of the Garter appears to have been significantly enhanced and noblemen were becoming more aware of the standards of behaviour expected of them. However, in the final analysis, what did most to restore their prestige and authority was something that had little to do with deliberate royal policy: their response to the political crisis created by the Bishops Wars.

The Bishops Wars revived the traditional martial role of the 'ancient nobility' by encouraging them to take the field of battle alongside their monarch; but, more significantly, defeat had the effect of reducing the power of the king and, at times, forcing him to the margins of the political process. This put the body of the peerage centre stage in the search for political settlement and highlighted their capacity for arbitration and consensus building. Their finest hour was the meeting of the Great Council of Peers at York in September–October 1640. With the eyes of the nation upon them they provided the platform for a negotiated settlement with the Scots and were able to let the king down relatively gently, with much of his honour and his capacity for independent action still intact. The template established at York was carried into the early stages of the Long Parliament. There the peers were able to mediate between king and Commons in pushing reform of the abuses of the 1630s, and intervene to head off the attempted royal coups of November 1640 and the First Army Plot. Their enhanced prestige, and public respect for their efforts, was reflected in the central role they were given in the implementation of the Triennial Act and the trial of Strafford, and in the continuing readiness of those on all sides to look to them as the most effective mediators in the growing conflict. The status, authority and influence of the aristocracy, acting as a collective entity, was probably never higher during the early Stuart period than it was between 1640 and 1642.

In ways that he had not intended, then, Charles's actions had done a good deal to restore the status of the peerage. But what of his other objective, of fashioning them into a 'royalist party' that could stand alongside the Laudian bishops as one of the twin pillars on which he rested his monarchical authority? At the conclusion of the 1629 assembly he went out of his way to propose a compact in which he offered the Lords 'favour and protection' in return for loyal support. He was to prove as good as his word, making every effort, as we have seen, to promote their welfare and protect their interests. He also followed Newcastle's prescriptions for building a loyal and supportive nobility, by promoting a significant proportion to high office, taking care to respect their local interests and reviving 'Elizabethan' values. Above all Charles made considerable efforts to bring his peers to court and involve them in the round of 'ceremony' and attendance that Newcastle saw as such a powerful means of fostering a sense of obligation and allegiance. But there were limits to how far the king was able to go in cultivating loyalty among his peers. As we have seen, although his prerogative in matters of honour was theoretically absolute, in practice it was hedged about with qualifications and constraints. He was expected to do his utmost to protect the integrity of the honours system and at the same time respect the autonomous claims of the honour community. In the case of the Irish peers it prevented him from showing favour to a group that was conspicuously willing to pledge the loyalty, obedience and support for prerogative government that he craved. It may also have discouraged him from adopting the scheme for a new 'Order Military' in which noblemen would be granted privileges such as freedom from taxation and immunity from arrest in return for taking an 'oath of fidelitie' and pledging their military service. How seriously this was considered is unclear. Had it been adopted it could have opened the way to alliance of mutual self-interest between a highly privileged nobility and a more authoritarian crown of the sort that was to develop in countries like France and Brandenburg Prussia. But it would also have represented a considerable challenge to the rights of the existing aristocracy; and it seems likely that the senior councillors to whom it was referred for consideration talked him out of it because of this.

The question remains of how effective Charles was in cultivating the loyalty of his peers. Perhaps the most impressive testimony to his success was the commitment displayed at the start of the First Bishops War when peers were summoned to York. Of the peers 81 out of 93 either attended in person or pledged themselves to provide money or horse, including several who been expected to refuse. On this occasion Charles pitched his appeal in strongly personal terms, summoning his peers to fulfil their traditional obligation of taking their place alongside him on the field of battle. This was an appeal that, given their strong ethos of personal service to the monarch, they found very hard to resist. How far its effectiveness in 1639 was due to the king's earlier efforts to cultivate the loyalty of his peers is hard to assess. Some of the most fulsome expressions of support came from 'country peers', like Lord Montagu or Viscount Fauconberg, who had rarely ventured near the royal court where most of the king's efforts were concentrated. However, the involvement of relatively large numbers of peers in court ceremony and the sense of obligation and allegiance that this fostered did certainly have an impact when it came to getting some peers to set an example to others. The enthusiasm and leadership displayed by the likes of Newcastle and Clifford, for whom, as we have seen, the king's personal approval mattered a great deal, was crucial to the success of the service.

Personal service and the monarch's approval were certainly central elements in the peerage's understanding of their *raison d'être*. But, as we have seen, most peers felt an equally strong sense of loyalty to the 'commonwealth' or 'country'. Over the months following the Bishops Wars they were to demonstrate, again and again, their concern to balance these loyalties and fulfil the traditional role of arbiter between crown and people. Where the political agenda was focussed on the reform of the abuses of the 1630s, promoting the role of parliament and resolving the Scottish crisis, the bulk of the peerage would generally rally to the cause of the 'country'. But where Charles was able to shift the debate back to issues of personal loyalty, the defence of his honour, and the preservation of the royal prerogative and monarchical authority then he could generally rely on a sympathetic hearing and majority support. At the Council of Great Peers where the two sets of issues carried similar weight the nobles performed a masterful balancing act. Thereafter the effectiveness of the king's efforts to rally loyalist support depended on how far he could shift the political debate onto his own ground. In the early phases of the Long Parliament, with most attention focussed on reform this was difficult and the majority in the House of Lords were aligned behind the agenda of the Junto and the Commons, while still showing considerable sympathy for the king's concerns, particularly in the early proceedings against Strafford. By the autumn of 1641, however, the debate came to concentrate more on challenges to the royal prerogative and the constitutional status quo, and out of this Charles was able to fashion a very effective 'royalist party' among the peers. Finally, in the summer of 1642, the potency of his personal summons was once again demonstrated and he was able to draw a substantial body of peers to York where they provided him with the backing he needed to confront the parliament. Effective party building, then, was as much about the king being able to highlight the key issues that mobilised royal support as about building the sense of loyalty and obligation that had been the focus of his efforts during the 1630s. But both had important roles to play and both contributed to his success in securing the support of around 60 per cent of the politically active peerage in the summer of 1642.

Much of the recent historiography on the aristocracy and the causes of the English Civil War has concentrated on the role of opposition peers. Richard McCoy has traced the activities of those peers who from the 2nd Earl of Essex in the 1590s through to the 1620s rallied round appeals to 'aristocratic constitutionalism' and 'publick liberty'; Brian Manning has documented the discontents of the peerage against Charles and his policies; John Morrill has reflected on the efforts of the 'ancient peerage' to restore their dominant position around the crown; and John Adamson has traced the contribution to the outbreak of civil war made by 'The Noble Revolt'.[11] Adamson, in particular, has provided a powerful and compelling narrative to explain the ways in which a group of peers who had become alienated from Charles provided the political leadership for a struggle to 'Venetianise' the king, by stripping him of his military capacity and taking control of his prerogative powers to summon parliament and appoint councillors. Even Conrad Russell, who has given much fuller coverage than other recent historians on the House of Lords' efforts to hold the political middle ground, has still focussed primarily on the Junto peers and their Scots allies.[12]

The emphasis in this study has been rather different. By shifting attention to the king's efforts to cultivate a body of loyalist peers, and their responses to the political crises of 1640–2, I have tried to highlight aspects of the story that tend to get overlooked. This perspective, for example, has brought out the extent to which Charles shared the concern of many of his peers to rehabilitate the 'ancient nobility' and place them at the centre of his government. He was not always successful in the ways that his critics would have liked, but this was not for want of trying. My approach has also demonstrated that the influence of the loyalist peers on the developing political situation was rather greater than has often been allowed. Their contribution to the Great Council of Peers and their readiness to acknowledge and understand the king's position in the early stages of the Long Parliament enabled the king to retain a considerable degree of political agency at times when to many observers, and to later historians, he appeared to be almost entirely marginalised. Once Charles started to organise this support into a coherent 'royalist party' in the autumn of 1641, it proved to be a potent political force. It was strong

11 McCoy, 'Old English honour', pp. 133–55; B. Manning, 'The Aristocracy and the Downfall of Charles I', in *Politics, Religion and the English Civil War*, ed. B. Manning (London: Edward Arnold, 1973), pp. 37–80; Morrill, *Nature of the English Revolution*, pp. 10–14; Adamson, *Noble Revolt*.

12 Russell, *Fall of the British Monarchies*.

enough initially to hold back the assaults on his prerogative and authority in the House of Lords and, even after the withdrawal of many of his supporters in February 1642, it was still able to provide a rallying point for defenders of the constitutional status quo. In June 1642 it was these peers who gave him the political strength and credibility to assemble a royalist war effort a few weeks after he had appeared bereft of support.

This study tends to confirm the judgement made, from different standpoints, by Edward Hyde and Giovanni Giustinian, the Venetian ambassador, that there was a basic identity of interest between the crown and the body of the peerage.[13] This was about much more than the grants of title and obligations of service that Charles liked to dwell on; it rested on a recognition among many peers that the existing political and social order was under threat and that challenges to the hierarchy and the status quo would ultimately damage the aristocracy as much as the crown. When Charles was able to focus debate on these challenges he was able to draw on a readymade and relatively resilient body of political support. Arguably his biggest mistake of this period was to lose sight of this and attempt to resolve his problems though a series of political coups. Had he stuck consistently to a policy of party building and entrusted his political fortunes to the hands of the loyalist peers then the crisis of 1641–2 might have had a very different outcome.

[13] Clarendon, *History*, i.193; *CSP Ven. 1640–2*, pp. 111, 284.

Appendix 1
English peers and the royal court 1625–40

English Peers at the opening of the Short Parliament, April 1640	*Privy Councillor PC Minister M Court Officer CO*	*Knight of the Garter KG Named at Scrutiny N Appeared in Garter Ceremonial GC*	*Received Ambassador A Appeared in Masque M Other Court Ceremonial OC*	*Served in Court of Chivalry CC Castlehaven Case Juror J*	*Lord Lieutenant L Openly Catholic C*	*Service at York in 1639 Attended A Offered Excuse E Promised Attendance, Horse or Money P*	*Attended Council of Peers at York, 1640 CP*	*Category of Engagement with the Court Leading Courtier/Councillor LC Regular Courtier RC Occasional Courtier OC Country Peer C*
Marquis								
Winchester					C	A P	CP	C
Earls								
Manchester	PC M	GC	OC	J	L	P	CP	LC
Lindsey	PC CO	KG	A OC	CC	L	A		LC
Arundel	PC M	KG	A OC	CC J	L	A		LC
Northumberland	PC M	KG	A	J	L	P		LC
Pembroke	PC CO	KG	A OC	J	L	A P	CP	LC
Shrewsbury			A		C		CP	OC
Kent								C
Derby		KG			L			C
Worcester				J	L C	P		C
Rutland		N	A OC			A		OC
Cumberland		GC			L			OC
Sussex						E		C
Huntingdon		N	A OC	CC	L	P	CP	OC
Bath		N GC		CC		P		OC
Southampton			OC					OC

Bedford					N	GC	A		OC	CC	J	L					CP		RC		
Hertford					N	GC	A		OC			L					CP			OC	
Essex					N	GC	A				J	L		A			CP			OC	
Lincoln															E		CP				C
Nottingham					N		A					L			E					OC	
Suffolk	PC	M	CO	KG			A					L				P		LC			
Dorset	PC		CO	KG			A		OC	CC	J	L						LC			
Salisbury	PC		CO	KG			A				J	L		A		P	CP	LC			
Exeter	PC			KG			A		OC			L				P		LC			
Somerset																					C
Bridgewater	PC	M							OC			L				P	CP	LC			
Leicester	PC				N						J			A				LC			
Northampton					N	GC	A					L	A	A		P	CP		RC		
Warwick					N		A				J	L				P	CP			OC	
Devonshire					N	GC	A	M				L	A	A		P	CP		RC		
Cambridge	PC		CO	KG			A		OC				A	A			CP	LC			
March	PC	M	CO	KG			A	M	OC			L		A			CP	LC			
Carlisle						GC	A	M											RC		
Denbigh			CO		N	GC	A									P	CP		RC		
Bristol														A			CP				C
Middlesex																P					C
Holland	PC		CO	KG			A	M			J	L		A			CP	LC			
Clare						GC	A									P	CP			OC	
Bolingbroke												L				P	CP				C
Westmoreland							A						A	A			CP			OC	
Berkshire	PC			KG			A				J	L		A			CP	LC			
Cleveland					N		A					L				P	CP			OC	
Mulgrave				KG											E						C
Danby	PC			KG			A				J							LC			
Monmouth						GC	A										CP			OC	
Marlborough															E						C
Rivers							A													OC	

(cont.)

(*cont.*)

English Peers at the opening of the Short Parliament, April 1640	*Privy Councillor PC Minister M Court Officer CO*	*Knight of the Garter KG Named at Scrutiny N Appeared in Garter Ceremonial GC*	*Received Ambassador A Appeared in Masque M Other Court Ceremonial OC*	*Served in Court of Chivalry CC Castlehaven Case Juror J*	*Lord Lieutenant L Openly Catholic C*	*Service at York in 1639 Attended A Offered Excuse E Promised Attendance, Horse or Money P*	*Attended Council of Peers at York, 1640 CP*	*Category of Engagement with the Court Leading Courtier/Councillor LC Regular Courtier RC Occasional Courtier OC Country Peer C*
Newcastle	PC CO	N	A		L	A P		LC
Dover		N GC	A			P	CP	RC
Peterborough		N	A		L	P	CP	OC
Stamford		GC	A M				CP	RC
Kingston						P		C
Carnarvon			A M		L	A	CP	OC
Newport	PC M		A M			A	CP	LC
Chesterfield						P		C
Thanet						P		C
St Albans		GC			C	P	CP	RC
Portland			A		L		CP	RC
Strafford	PC M			J	L		CP	LC
Viscounts								
Montague					C	P	CP	C
Purbeck								C
Saye and Sele						A		C
Conway		N		J			CP	OC
Campden			A OC			P	CP	OC
Lords								
Mowbray				CC		A	CP	RC
Clifford		N	A	J	L	A	CP	RC

Abergavenny	N								C			P				C
Audley			A						C			P	CP		OC	
Strange	N		A	M				L		A			CP	RC		
Berkeley	N		A									P			OC	
Morley and Mounteagle									C			P				C
Dacres											E					C
Dudley												P				C
Stourton									C			P	CP			C
Vaux									C			P				C
Windsor									C			P	CP			C
Cromwell																C
Eure									C			P				C
Wharton		GC		M								P	CP	RC		
Willoughby of Parham			A		OC	CC						P	CP		OC	
Paget	N		A	M								P	CP	RC		
North	N		A		OC		J			A			CP		OC	
Chandos				M								P			OC	
Petre							J		C		E					C
Gerard																C
Stanhope											E					C
Arundel of Wardour									C			P	CP			C
Teynham									C		E					C
Kimbolton					OC							P	CP		OC	
Feilding	N		A	M	OC								CP	RC		
Brooke													CP			C
Montague										A		P				C
Grey of Warke													CP			C
Deincourt												P				C

(cont.)

(cont.)

English Peers at the opening of the Short Parliament, April 1640	Privy Councillor PC Minister M Court Officer CO	Knight of the Garter KG Named at Scrutiny N Appeared in Garter Ceremonial GC	Received Ambassador A Appeared in Masque M Other Court Ceremonial OC	Served in Court of Chivalry CC Castlehaven Case Juror J	Lord Lieutenant L Openly Catholic C	Service at York in 1639 Attended A Offered Excuse E Promised Attendance, Horse or Money P	Attended Council of Peers at York, 1640 CP	Category of Engagement with the Court Leading Courtier/Councillor LC Regular Courtier RC Occasional Courtier OC Country Peer C
Roberts						P		C
Craven			A OC					OC
Fauconberg						P	CP	C
Lovelace						P	CP	C
Poulett						A	CP	C
Harvey	CO		A	J		E		OC
Brudenell					C	P	CP	C
Maynard					L	P	CP	C
Coventry						P	CP	C
Howard of Escrick			A	J		P	CP	OC
Goring	PC CO	N GC	A	J		P	CP	LC
Mohun			OC			P		OC
Savile	CO		A			A	CP	OC
Dunsmore						A	CP	C
Powis	CO			J	C	P		OC

(cont.)

Herbert of Cherbury			N	A	M		P	CP		RC
Cottington	PC	M		A		OC	P		LC	
Finch	PC	M						CP	LC	

Sources:

List of English Peers April 1640: *LJ*, iv.45.

Privy Councillor, Minister, Crown Officer: TNA, PC2/48–52; *Oxf.DNB*: *G.E.C.*

Knight of the Garter, Named at Garter Scrutiny, Appeared in Garter Ceremonial: WCLA, MS X.7, Annals of the Order; Ashmole, *Order of the Garter*; Bodl.L., Ashmole MS 1110, fo.35, MS 1112, fos. 63–4.

Received Ambassador, Appeared in Masque, Appeared in other Court Ceremonial: Finet, *Finetti Philoxenis; Ceremonies of Charles I*; S. Orgel and R. Strong, *Inigo Jones. The Theatre of the Stuart Court*, 2 vols. (Berkeley: University of California Press, 1973); *Oxf.DNB*.

Served in the Court of Chivalry, Juror in the Castlehaven Case: *Cases in the Court of Chivalry*; Herrup, *A House in Gross Disorder*.

Lord Lieutenants, Openly Catholic Peers: Sainty, *Lieutenants of Counties, 1585–1642*; Questier (ed.), *Newsletters from the Caroline Court*.

Service at York in 1639: TNA, SP 16/413/117; 16/412 and 413 passim; E351/292; Warner, *Epistolary Curiosities*, p.199; HMC, *Rutland*, 504–7.

Attended Council of Peers in 1640: TNA, SP 16/466/42, pp. 37–8; DRO, Drake of Colyton MSS, 1700M/C/P/17; *Hardwicke SP*.

Appendix 2
English peers and allegiance, 1641–2

English peers in March 1642	*Short Parliament Vote on Supply 24 April 1640 Probably supported Council Motion [F] Against [A]*	*Supporter of the Twelve Peers Petition [TPP]*	*Voting on the Commons Ordinance 9 Sept 1641 Loyalist [L] Junto [J]*	*Summons to attend on the king's behalf 8 Oct 1641 [L]*	*Probable voting on Lunsford's dismissal 24 Dec 1641 Loyalist [L] Junto [J]*	*Attendance in the Lords 29 Nov–5 Jan*	*11 Jan–19 Feb*	*21 Feb–26 Mar 1641/2 Frequent [F] Regular [R] Occasional [O]*	*Signed Protestation in the Lords Jan 1642 Supporting the Parliamentarian line [P] Mar–Apr 1642 Supporting the Royalist line [R]*	*Signed Royalist Engagements or subscribed to fund cavalry at York [R] Parliament cavalry June 1642 [P]*	*Named to the Militia Commission March–July 1642 [M] Named to the Commission of Array June–July 1642 [A]*	*Active Royalist in 1642 [R] Active Parliamentarian in 1642 [P]*
Duke												
Richmond	F				L	F	R			R	A	R
Marquis												
Winchester	F										A	
Hertford	A	TPP			L	F	O		R	R	A	R
Earls												
Manchester			J			R	R	O			A	
Lindsey	F				L	F	F	F	R	R	A	R
Arundel	F					O					A	
Northumberland	F				J	R	F	F	P	P	M	P
Pembroke	F	TPP			J	F	F	F	P	P	M	P
Shrewsbury												
Kent	F											
Derby											A	
Worcester												R
Rutland						O	O				M A	

Cumberland	F					L			F	O				R			A	R	
Sussex																			
Huntingdon	F					L	L		F	O	F			R			A	R	
Bath		A	TPP			L			F	R	F		R	R			A	R	
Southampton		A							F	R	R		R	R			A	R	
Bedford					J			J	F	R	R	P			P	M			P
Essex		A	TPP					J	F	F	F	P			P	M			P
Lincoln		A	TPP							F	F	P			P	M			P
Nottingham		A							R	O		P				M			P
Suffolk								J	R	R	R	P				M			
Dorset	F								R	O	O			R			A	R	
Salisbury	F								F	R	R	P		R		M			
Exeter			TPP												P	M			P
Somerset																			
Bridgewater	F																A		
Leicester									F	F	F	P			P	M			
Northampton	F					L	L		F	F	F		R	R			A	R	
Warwick		A	TPP		J			J	F	F	F	P			P	M			P
Devonshire	F					L	L		F	R	F		R	R			A		
Cambridge	F								R	R	O			R				R	
Carlisle	F							J	R	O							A	R	
Denbigh	F			L			L		F	R								R	
Bristol	?		TPP			L	L		F	R	O			R			A	R	
Middlesex																			
Holland	F							J	F	F	F	P			P	M			P
Clare		A			J			J	R	F	F	P		R		M			
Bolingbroke		A						J	F	F	F	P			P	M			P
Westmoreland										O	R		R	R			A	R	
Berkshire	F						L		F	R	R		R	R			A	R	
Cleveland	F			L						F	R		R				A	R	
Mulgrave			TPP																
Danby																			
Monmouth	F						L		R	R	R		R	R			A		
Marlborough																			

(*cont.*)

(*cont.*)

English peers in March 1642	*Short Parliament Vote on Supply 24 April 1640 Probably supported Council Motion [F] Against [A]*	*Supporter of the Twelve Peers Petition [TPP]*	*Voting on the Commons Ordinance 9 Sept 1641 Loyalist [L] Junto [J]*	*Summons to attend on the king's behalf 8 Oct 1641 [L]*	*Probable voting on Lunsford's dismissal 24 Dec 1641 Loyalist [L] Junto [J]*	*Attendance in the Lords 1641/2 Frequent [F] Regular [R] Occasional [O]: 29 Nov–5 Jan*	*11 Jan–19 Feb*	*21 Feb–26 Mar*	*Signed Protestation in the Lords Jan 1642 Supporting the Parliamentarian line [P] Mar–Apr 1642 Supporting the Royalist line [R]*	*Signed Royalist Engagements or subscribed to fund cavalry at York [R] Parliament cavalry June 1642 [P]*	*Named to the Militia Commission March–July 1642 [M] Named to the Commission of Array June–July 1642 [A]*	*Active Royalist in 1642 [R] Active Parliamentarian in 1642 [P]*
Rivers						O	O			R	A	R
Newcastle	F			L			O			R	A	R
Dover			L		L	F	F	F	R	R	A	
Peterborough	F					F	F	R	P		M	P
Stamford					J	F	F	F	P		M	P
Kingston												
Carnarvon			L		L	F	R			R	A	R
Newport			J		J	R	R	R	R	R	A	R
Chesterfield											A	R
Thanet	F						R		P		A	
St Albans	F											
Portland	F		L		L	R	F	F	R		A	R
Viscounts												
Montague												
Purbeck												
Saye & Sele	A	TPP			J	F	F	F	P	P	M	P
Conway						R	R	O	P	P	M	
Campden	F										A	R
Stafford												

Lords																			
Mowbray	F			L					F	R	R		R	R			A	R	
Abergavenny																			
Audley	F																		
Strange	F								O	R	F		R				A	R	
Willoughby of Eresby									R	R	R		R	R			A	R	
Grey of Ruthven									F	F	F		R	R			A	R	
Berkeley																			
Morley and Mounteagle																			
Dacres										R	O	P				M			
Darcy										O									
Dudley																	A		
Hastings										O	F								
Stourton																			
Vaux																			
Wentworth				L		L			F	R	O		R				A	R	
Cromwell									R	F	R								
Eure																			
Wharton		A	TPP		J			J	F	F	O	P			P	M			P
Rich							L		F	R	F		R	R			A		
Willoughby of Parham		A	TPP						R	R	F	P			P	M			P
Paget		A	TPP						F	F	R	P		R	P	M	A	R	
North		A	TPP					J	F	F	R	P			P	M			
Chandos									O	F	R	P		R		M	A	R	
Hunsdon					J				O	R	F	P							
Spencer								J	F	F	F	P				M		R	
St John of Bletsoe							L		F	F	F	P			P				P
Stanhope	F								O	O	O								
Arundel of Wardour																			

(*cont.*)

(cont.)

English peers in March 1642	*Short Parliament Vote on Supply 24 April 1640 Probably supported Council Motion [F] Against [A]*		*Supporter of the Twelve Peers Petition [TPP]*	*Voting on the Commons Ordinance 9 Sept 1641 Loyalist [L] Junto [J]*		*Summons to attend on the king's behalf 8 Oct 1641 [L]*	*Probable voting on Lunsford's dismissal 24 Dec 1641 Loyalist [L] Junto [J]*		*Attendance in the Lords 29 Nov–5 Jan 11 Jan–19 Feb 21 Feb–26 Mar 1641/2 Frequent [F] Regular [R] Occasional [O]*			*Signed Protestation in the Lords Jan 1642 Supporting the Parliamentarian line [P] Mar–Apr 1642 Supporting the Royalist line [R]*		*Signed Royalist Engagement or subscribed to fund cavalry at York [R] Parliament cavalry June 1642 [P]*		*Named to the Militia Commission March–July 1642 [M] Named to the Commission of Array June–July 1642 [A]*		*Active Royalist in 1642 [R] Active Parliamentarian in 1642 [P]*	
Digby							L		R									R	
Mandeville		A	TPP		J			J	F	F	F	P			P	M			P
Feilding	F								F	F	F	P			P	M			P
Brooke		A	TPP					J	F	F	F	P			P	M			P
Montagu		A	TPP											R			A	R	
Howard of Charlton							L		F	F	F		R	R				R	
Grey of Warke	F							J	F	F	F	P			P	M			P
Deincourt		A															A		
Roberts		A						J	F	F	F	P			P	M			P
Craven							L		F	R							A		
Fauconberg							L		R	R	O			R			A	R	
Lovelace		A	TPP								O		R	R			A	R	
Poulett	F					L			O		O			R			A	R	
Harvey																			
Pierrepont				L			L		F	R	O			R			A	R	
Brudenell																			
Coventry	F			L		L	L		F	F	R		R	R			A	R	
Howard of Escrick		A						J	F	F	F	P			P	M			P
Goring	F						L		F	R								R	

Mohun									O				R	A	R
Savile		A	TPP				L	F	R	R		R	R	A	R
Boteler															
Dunsmore		A		L		L	L	F	R	R			R	A	R
Powis															R
Herbert of Cherbury	F							R	R	R				A	R
Cottington	F					L								A	
Seymour						L		F	F	R		R	R	A	R
Littleton					J			F	F	F			R		R
Bruce								F	R	F	P				
Capel								F	F	R		R	R	A	R

Sources:
List of English peers in March 1642: PA, HL/PO/JO/5/1/8.
Short Parliament Vote on Supply 24 April 1640: TNA, SP 16/451/39; *LJ*, iv.65–6.
Signatories to the Twelve Peers Petition: Adamson, *Noble Revolt*, 520–1.
Voting on the Commons Ordinance on 9 Sept 1641: *After debate about the printing and publishing of the Orders of 16 January last* (1641).
Summons to attend on the king's behalf 8 Oct 1641: SHC, Braye letters, G85/5/2/11.
Probable voting on Lunsford's dismissal 24 Dec 1641: *LJ*, iv.490; PA, HL/PO/JO/5/1/8, 24 Dec 1641.
Attendance in the Lords 29 Nov 1641 – 26 Mar 1642, Frequent – 70 per cent or more, Regular – 30–70 per cent, Occasional – 30 per cent or less: PA, HL/PO/JO/5/1/8.
Signed Protestations in the Lords Jan–Apr 1642: *LJ*, iv, v.
Signed Royalist Engagements and subscribed to cavalry for King or Parliament: *His Majestie's declaration*, 13 June 1642; Clarendon, *History*, ii.186; TNA, SP16/491/29; *LJ*, v.123, 163.
Named to Militia Commission and Commission of Array: *Acts and Ordinances of the Interregnum* 1642–1660, ed. C.H. Firth and R.S. Rait, 3 vols. (London: HMSO, 1911); *LJ*, v; NRO, Finch Hatton MS 133.
Active Royalist or Parliamentarian in 1642: *Oxf.DNB*; History of Parliament, draft biographies of peers; P. Young, *Edgehill* (Kineton, UK; Roundwood Press, 1967), pp. 62–70; Fletcher, *Outbreak of the English Civil War*, chs. 11–12; C. Holmes, *The Eastern Association in the English Civil War* (Cambridge: Cambridge University Press, 1974), ch. 3; P.R. Newman, *Royalist Officers in England and Wales* (London: Garland Publishing, 1981).

Bibliography

MANUSCRIPT SOURCES

ARUNDEL CASTLE, SUSSEX

Autograph letters	Correspondence of the Earl of Arundel
EM	Earl Marshal's Papers

BEDFORDSHIRE RECORD OFFICE

St John of Bletsoe MSS	Papers of Sir Rowland St John

BEINECKE LIBRARY, YALE UNIVERSITY

Osborn file 6115	Report of the Star Chamber case, Darcy v Markham 1616
Yale MS 370	Commonplace book belonging to William Camden

BODLEIAN LIBRARY, OXFORD

Ashmole MS 835, 836, 856, 857, 1108, 1110, 1111, 1112, 1113, 1132	Papers collected by Elias Ashmole
Bankes MSS	Papers of Attorney General Sir John Bankes
Clarendon State Papers, vols. 19, 21, 27	Papers of Sir Edward Hyde
North MS b.1	Papers of William Pope, Earl of Downe
Rawlinson MS B.210	Miscellaneous 17th century manuscripts including an anonymous account of the Scottish campaign of 1639
Rawlinson MS D.392	Historical Discourses by Sir Edward Walker including a diary of 1633–5
Tanner MSS vols. 66, 67, 142	Miscellaneous 17th century manuscripts and correspondence

BRITISH LIBRARY

Additional MS 6297	Miscellaneous documents relating to the Earl Marshal and Court of Chivalry

Additional MS 11,045	Papers of John Viscount Scudamore
Additional MS 12,514	Proposal for an 'Order Military' 1639
Additional MS 14,417	Heraldic papers of Nicholas Charles, Lancaster herald
Additional MS 34,727	Papers of the West family
Additional MS 35,331	Diary of Walter Yonge esq, 1627–1642
Additional MS 39,177	The 'Academ Roial' by Edmund Bolton
Additional MS 64,898, 64,918	Papers of Sir John Coke, secretary of state
Additional MS 70,499	Papers of the Earl of Newcastle
Additional MS 78,268	Papers of Edward Nicholas
Cotton MS Faustina C.VIII, Faustina E.1, Titus C.1	Papers of Sir Robert Cotton
Egerton MS 2816	New Years Gift Roll, 1627
Harleian MS 390	Newsletters of Joseph Mede
Harleian MS 456, 457	Sir John Borough's record of proceedings in the Great Council of Peers and the Scottish Negotiations of 1640–1
Harleian MS 1154	Miscellaneous heraldic documents, including an address by John Raven, Richmond herald
Harleian MS 1323	Miscellaneous documents relating to crown projects
Harleian MS 1368	Notebooks of Sir Henry St George, Norroy king of arms
Harleian MS 2240	Essex freeholders' book of 1634
Harleian MS 6103	Presentation copy of Edmund Bolton's 'Academ Royal'
Harleian MS 6424	Bishop Warner's diary of proceedings in the House of Lords, Jan. 1641–Jan. 1642
Harleian MS 7571	Miscellaneous documents relating to the 'Musaeum Minervae'
Harleian Roll T2	New Years Gift Roll 1638
Lansdowne MS 152	Council memoranda of James I's reign
Lansdowne MS 255	Memoranda by heralds
Royal MS 18A.LXXI	Presentation copy of Edmund Bolton's 'Cabanett Royal'
Sloane MS 1494	Duties of a gentleman of the royal household
Sloane MS 2904	Sir John Borough's review of the king's revenues

CAMBRIDGE UNIVERSITY LIBRARY

Dd.3.64	Papers relating to the Court of Chivalry and miscellaneous historical matters

COLLEGE OF ARMS

C.26	Office book of the Buckinghamshire Visitation, 1634
Chapter Bk 1	Chapter Book of the heralds 1623–1690

Curia Militaris	Papers and proceedings of the Court of Chivalry
Heralds MSS, vols. II, III, IV, V, VI, VII, VIII, IX	Miscellaneous papers belonging to the heralds
I.25	Earl Marshal's Book of Orders, 1601–1683
Partition Book 3	Book recording heralds' fees 1626–1640
Phillipps MS 13084, vols. 1, 3, 4, 5, 6, 7, 8, 10, 11, 12, 13, 14, 15	Miscellaneous papers belonging to heralds, including George Owen, York herald and Sir Henry St George, Norroy King of Arms
R.19	Miscellaneous documents of the Court of Chivalry
Sherard v. *Mynne*	Box of case papers for the Star Chamber and Court of Chivalry case, 1635–1639

DEVON RECORD OFFICE

Drake of Colyton MSS, 1700/M/C/P/17	Letter from the Great Council of Peers

FOLGER SHAKESPEARE LIBRARY, WASHINGTON, US

V.a.199	William Smith's memorandum on abuses by arms painters
V.b.7	Henry Howard's, 'Brief discourse on the right use of givinge arms'

HISTORY OF PARLIAMENT

Yale transcripts of Parliamentary Diaries 1624, Holland, Nicholas and Pym diaries

HUNTINGTON LIBRARY, CALIFORNIA, US

Ellesmere MSS	Papers of John Egerton, Earl of Bridgewater

KENT HISTORY AND LIBRARY CENTRE

U269/C267	Correspondence of the Henry Bourchier, Earl of Bath and the Countess of Bath

LEICESTERSHIRE AND RUTLAND RECORD OFFICE

DE1431	Papers of William Lord Sherard

NATIONAL LIBRARY OF WALES

Wynn of Gwydir MSS	Correspondence of the Wynn Family

NOTTINGHAM UNIVERSITY LIBRARY

Clifton MSS, Cl.C.	Correspondence of Sir Gervase Clifton
Ne.C. 15,406	Papers of John Holles, Earl of Clare

NORTHAMPTONSHIRE RECORD OFFICE

Finch Hatton MS 133	William Dugdale's Commissions of Array 1642

PARLIAMENTARY ARCHIVES, WESTMINSTER

BRY/22C	Draft journal of the House of Lords, Oct–Dec 1641
BRY/23B	Draft journal of the House of Lords, Feb–Mar 1642
BRY/103	'Scribble book' for the House of Lords, Jan–Mar 1642
HL/PO/JO/5/1/8	Minute book of the House of Lords, Nov 1641–Mar 1642
HL/PO/JO/13/3	Proxy book for the House of Lords 1640–2
Main Papers	House of Lords Main Papers

QUEEN'S COLLEGE, OXFORD

Oxford, MS 144	Papers of Sir Thomas Shirley
Sel.b.229, item 63	Proclamations and draft proclamations

STAFFORDSHIRE RECORD OFFICE

D661/11/1/5	Newsletters of Edward Dyott
D1778/1/i/14	Correspondence of William Legge

SURREY HISTORY CENTRE

Braye Letters, G85/5/2	Papers of Edward Nicholas
More of Loseley MS LM 1327/9	Letters and memoranda of George Viscount Chaworth

THE NATIONAL ARCHIVES

C115	Papers of John Viscount Scudamore
LC 5/180	Regulations of the Royal Household, *c.* 1629
PC2	Privy Council Registers
SO 1, 2, 3	Signet Office Letter Books
SP 14, 16	State Papers Domestic James I, Charles I
SP 63	State Papers Ireland
STAC 8	Star Chamber Cases, James I

WOBURN ABBEY, BEDFORD ESTATE OFFICE

Item 240	Star Chamber Reports, Jan–Feb 1633/4
Item 267	A letter about 'an Academie in London for the education of the young nobility'

WINDSOR CASTLE, ST GEORGE'S CHAPEL, LIBRARY AND ARCHIVES

MS X.7 Annals of the Order of the Garter

PRINTED PRIMARY SOURCES

A Calendar of the Docquets of Lord Keeper Coventry 1625–40, ed. J. Broadway, R.P. Cust and S.K. Roberts, 4 parts (List and Index Soc, special ser., 34, 2004).

A Collection of Miscellaneous Grants of Arms Part I, ed. W.A. Littledale (Harleian Society, 76, 1925).

A Collection of Rare and Valuable Tracts of the Most Interesting Subjects; but chiefly such as relate to the History and Constitution of these Kingdoms . . ., 13 vols. (London, 1809–15).

A letter written by Mr Simon Rhodes . . . (London, 1642).

Acts and Ordinances of the Interregnum 1642–1660, ed. C.H. Firth and R.S. Rait, 3 vols. (London: HMSO, 1911).

Acts of the Privy Council of England, ed. J.R. Dasent et al. (London: HMSO, new ser., 1890–1964).

After debate about the printing and publishing of the Orders of 16 January last . . . (1641).

An Exact Collection of all Remonstrances, Votes, Declarations, Proclamations . . . (London, 1643).

Ashmole, Elias, *The Institutions, Laws and Ceremonies of the Most Noble Order of the Garter* (London, 1672).

Bacon, Sir Francis, *The Charge of Sir Francis Bacon, knight, his Majestie's Attorney General touching duels upon information in the Star Chamber against Priest and Wright* (London, 1614).

Brathwait, R., *The English Gentleman, Containing Sundry Excellent Rules* (London, 1630).

Calendar of State Papers and Manuscripts Relating to English Affairs . . . in Venice, vols. 19–24, 1625–42 (London: HMSO, 1912–24).

Calendar of State Papers Domestic Series 1547–1625 (London: Longman, 1856–72).

Calendar of State Papers Domestic Series 1625–1649 (London: Longman, 1858–97).

Calendar of the Patent Rolls: Preserved in the Public Record Office: Elizabeth, vol. 2, 1560–3 (London: HMSO, 1948).

Cases in the High Court of Chivalry 1634–1640, ed. R.P. Cust and A.J. Hopper (Harleian Society, new ser., 18, 2006).

Cavendish, Margaret Duchess of Newcastle, *The Life of William Cavendish, Duke of Newcastle*, ed. C.H. Firth (London: Routledge & Sons, 1906).

Cavendish, William Earl of Newcastle, *The Country Captain and The Varietie. Two Comedies. . . .* (London, 1649).

Ceremonies of Charles I, The Note Books of John Finet 1628–1641, ed. A.J. Loomie (Bronx, NY: Fordham University Press).

Chamberlain, John, *The Letters of John Chamberlain*, ed. N.E. McLure, 2 vols. (American Philosophical Soc., 12, 1939).

Clarendon, Edward, Earl of, *State Papers Collected by Edward Earl of Clarendon* (Oxford, 1767).

Clarendon, Edward, Earl of, *The History of the Rebellion*, ed. W.D. MacRay, 6 vols. (Oxford: Clarendon Press, 1888).

Clarendon, Edward, Earl of, *The Life of Edward, Earl of Clarendon*, 3 vols. (Oxford, 1828).

Commons Debates in 1621, ed. W. Notestein, F.H. Relf and H. Simpson, 7 vols. (New Haven, CT: Yale University Press, 1635).

Constitutional Documents of the Puritan Revolution 1625–1660, ed. S.R. Gardiner (Oxford: Clarendon Press, 3rd edn, 1906).

Corona Minvervae or A Masque presented before Prince Charles . . . at the Colledge of the Musaeum Minervae (London, 1635).

Cotton, Sir Robert, *A Short View of the Long Life and Raigne of Henry the Third King of England* (London, 1627).

Court and Times of Charles I, ed. T. Birch, 2 vols. (London, 1848).

Diurnall Occurrences (London, 1641–2).

Edmondson, Joseph, *A Complete Body of Heraldry*, vol. 1 (London, 1780).

Ellis, H., *Original Letters Illustrative of English Histories*, 1st ser., 3 vols. (1824).

Evelyn, John, *The Diary and Correspondence of John Evelyn*, ed. W. Bray (London: George Routledge & Sons, 1890?).

Ferne, Sir John *The Blazon of Gentrie* (London, 1586).

Finet, John, *Finetti Philoxenis* (London, 1656).

G.F., *Duell Ease. A Worde with Valiant Spiritts . . .* (London, 1635).

Glover, Robert, 'Nobility, Politicke and Civill', in Thomas Milles, *The Catalogue of Honour* (London, 1610).

Greville, Fulke, *The Prose Works of Fulke Greville, Lord Brooke*, ed. J. Gouws (Oxford: Clarendon Press, 1986).

Guillim, J., *A Display of Heraldrie* (London, 1610).

Habington, Thomas, *A Survey of Worcestershire*, ed. J. Amphlett, 2 vols. (Worcestershire Historical Soc., 1895–99).

Hardwicke State Papers, 2 vols. (London, 1778).

Harrison, William, *Harrison's Description of England*, ed. F.J. Furnivall (London: New Shakespeare Society, 1877).

Harleian Miscellany, ed. T. Park, 10 vols. (London, 1808–13).

Hearne, Thomas, *A Collection of Curious Discourses*, 2 vols. (1775).

Hexham, Henry, *A True and Briefe Relation of the Famous Siege of Breda* (Delft, 1637).

Heylyn, P., *The History of that most famous saynt and souldier of Christ Jesus, St George of Cappadocia* (1631, 1st edn; 1633, 2nd edn).

His Majestie's Declaration made the 13th of June 1642 to the Lords attending his Majestie at York . . . (London, 1642).

Historical Manuscripts Commission: *Beaulieu* (1900).

Historical Manuscripts Commission: *Buccleuch and Queensberry*, vols. I & III (1899, 1926).

Historical Manuscripts Commission: *Cowper*, vols. I & II (1888).

Historical Manuscripts Commission: *De L'Isle and Dudley*, vol. VI (1966).

Historical Manuscripts Commission: *Hastings*, vol. II (1930).
Historical Manuscripts Commission: *Portland*, vol. II (1893).
Historical Manuscripts Commission: *4th Report, House of Lords MSS* (1874).
Historical Manuscripts Commission: *4th Report, De La Warr MSS* (1874).
Historical Manuscripts Commission: *5th Report, Sutherland MSS* (1876).
Historical Manuscripts Commission: *8th Report, R. Bankes MSS* (1881).
Historical Manuscripts Commission: *10th Report, Appx. 4, Earl of Westmoreland MSS* (1885).
Historical Manuscripts Commission: *Rutland*, vol. I (1888).
Historical Manuscripts Commission: *Salisbury*, vol. XXII (1971).
Historical Manuscripts Commission: *Various*, vol. VII, *MSS of Sir Hervey Bruce* (1914).
Ideology and Politics on the Eve of Restoration: Newcastle's Advice to Charles II, ed. T.P. Slaughter (Philadelphia, PA: American Philosophical Society Memoirs, 159, 1984).
James I, Edict and severe Censure against Private Combats (London, 1614).
James VI and I. Political Writings, ed. J.P. Sommerville (Cambridge: Cambridge University Press, 1994).
Journals of the House of Commons, vols. 1–2 (London, 1803).
Journals of the House of Lords, vols. 3–5 (London, 1802).
Legh, Gerard, *The Accedence of Armorie* (London, 1562).
Letters and Memorials of State, ed. A. Collins, 2 vols. (London, 1746).
Letters and Papers of the Verney Family, ed. J. Bruce (Camden Society, 56, 1853).
Letters of Queen Henrietta Maria, ed. M.A.E. Green (London, 1857).
'Letters on the claims of the College of Arms in Lancashire', ed. F.R. Raines, in *Chetham Miscellany* 5 (Chetham Soc., 96, 1875), pp. 1–38.
Life and Letters of Francis Bacon, ed. J.A. Spedding, 7 vols. (1861–74).
Lismore Papers, ed. A.B. Grosart, 10 vols. (London, 1886–8).
Markham, Francis, *The Book of Honour* (London, 1625).
Memoirs and Memorials of Sir Hugh Cholmley of Whitby 1600–1657, ed. J. Binns (Yorkshire Archaeological Society, 153, 2000).
Memorials of the Civil War, ed. R. Bell, 2 vols. (London, 1849).
Milles, Thomas, *The Catalogue of Honour* (London, 1610).
Munimenta Heraldica, ed. G.D. Squibb (Harleian Society, new ser., 4, 1985).
Naunton, Sir Robert, *Fragmenta Regalia*, ed. J.S. Cerovski (Washington DC: Folger Books, 1985).
Newsletters from the Caroline Court, 1631–1638: Catholicism and the Politics of the Personal Rule, ed. M. Questier (Camden Soc., 5th ser., 26, 2005).
Nicols, J., *The Progresses of King James I*, 4 vols. (London, 1828).
North, Dudley Lord, *A Forest of Varieties* (London, 1645).
Ovatio Carolina, *The Triumph of King Charles* (London, 1641).
Perfect Diurnall (London, 1642).
The Brief and Perfect Relation (London, 1647).
Proceedings in Parliament 1614, ed. M. Jansson (Urban, PA: Temple University, 1985).
Proceedings in Parliament 1625, ed. M. Jansson and W.B. Bidwell (New Haven, CT: Yale University Press, 1987).
Proceedings in Parliament 1626, ed. W.B. Bidwell and M. Jansson, 4 vols. (New Haven, CT: Yale University Press, 1991–6).

Proceedings in Parliament 1628, ed. R.C. Johnson, M.F. Keeler, M.J. Cole and W.B. Bidwell, 6 vols. (New Haven, CT: Yale University Press, 1977–83).
Proceedings in the Opening Session of the Long Parliament, ed. M. Jansson, 7 vols. (Rochester, NY: University of Rochester Press, 2000–2007).
Proceedings of the Short Parliament of 1640, ed. E.S. Cope and W.H. Coates (Camden Soc., 4th ser., 19, 1977).
Remarkable Occurrences... (London, 1642).
Reports of Cases in the Courts of Star Chamber and High Commission, ed. S.R. Gardiner (Camden Soc., new ser., 39, 1886).
Reports of Heraldic Cases in the Court of Chivalry 1623–1732, ed. G.D. Squibb (Harleian Society, 107, 1956).
47th Report of the Deputy Keeper of the Public Records (1886).
Rushworth, John, *Historical Collections*, 7 vols. (London, 1659–1701).
Rymer, Thomas, *Foedera* (1743 edn).
Scott, Thomas, 'A Discourse of Polletique and Civill Honour', in G.D. Scull, *Dorothea Scott, otherwise Gotherson and Hogben, of Egerton house, Kent, 1611–1680* (London, 1882).
Segar, William, *Honor, Military and Civill* (London, 1602).
Select Cases on Defamation to 1600, ed. R.H. Helmholz (London: Selden Society, 101, 1985).
Sir Kenelme Digby's Honour Maintained (London, 1641).
Six North Country Diaries, ed. J.C. Hodgson (Durham: Surtees Society, 118, 1910).
Smith, Sir Thomas, *De Republica Anglorum*, ed. M. Dewar (Cambridge: Cambridge University Press, 1982).
Spelman, Henry, *The History and Fate of Sacrilege* (London, 1698).
Stafford, A., *The Guide of Honour* (London, 1634).
State Trials, ed. W. Cobbett and T. Howell, 33 vols. (1809–26).
Stuart Royal Proclamations, ed. J.F. Larkin and P.L. Hughes, 2 vols. (Oxford: Clarendon Press, 1973–83).
Suckling, Sir John, *The Works of Sir John Suckling, vol. 1. The Non Dramatic Works*, ed. T. Clayton (Oxford: Clarendon Press, 1971).
The Acts of Parliament of Scotland, 12 vols. (1814–75).
The Complete Peerage of England, Ireland and Scotland, by G.E. Cokayne, 13 vols. (London: St Catherine Press, 1910–59).
The Constitutions of the Musaeum Minervae (London, 1636).
The copy of a letter sent from the right honourable the Lord Paget unto the honourable House of Parliament... (London, 1642).
The Diary of Sir Henry Slingsby, ed. D. Parsons (London, 1836).
The Diary of Thomas Crosfield, ed. F.S. Boas (London, 1935).
The Earl of Strafforde's Letters and Dispatches, 2 vols., ed. W. Knowler (London, 1729).
The Fairfax Correspondence, 2 vols., ed. G.W. Johnson (London, 1848).
The Jacobean Union. Six Tracts of 1604, eds. B.R. Galloway and B.P. Levack (Edinburgh: Scottish History Society, 4th ser., 21, 1985).
The Journal of Sir Simonds D'Ewes from the Beginning of the Long Parliament to the Opening of the Trial of Strafford, ed. W. Notestein (New Haven, CT: Yale University Press, 1923).
The King's Entertainment at York (London, 1642).

The Knyvett Letters, 1620–1644, ed. B Schofield (Norwich: Norfolk Records Society, 20, 1949).

The Letters of John Holles, ed. P.R. Seddon, 3 vols. (Transactions of the Thoroton Society, XXXI, XXXV, XXXVI, 1975–86).

The Private Journals of the Long Parliament 3 January to 5 March 1642, ed. W.H. Coates, A.S. Young and V.F. Snow (New Haven, CT: Yale University Press, 1982).

True Diurnall (London, 1642).

Two Speeches spoken in the House of the Lords by the Lord Viscount Newarke (London, 1641).

Visitations of the North, pt. 1 (Durham: Surtees Society, 122, 1912).

Walker, Sir Edward, *Historical Discourses on Several Occasions* (London, 1705).

Warner, R., *Epistolary Curiosities... Illustrative of the Herbert family* (London, 1818).

Warwick, Sir Philip, *Memoirs of the Reign of Charles I* (Edinburgh, 1813).

Wilson, A., *The History of Great Britain Being the Life and Reign of King James the First* (London, 1653).

Wyrley, W., *The True Use of Armories* (London, 1592).

SECONDARY WORKS

Adamson, J.S.A., 'Chivalry and Political Culture in Caroline England', in *Culture and Politics in Early Stuart England*, ed. K. Sharpe and P. Lake (Basingstoke: Macmillan, 1994).

Adamson, J.S.A., 'Parliamentary Management, Men-of business and the House of Lords 1640–1649', in *A Pillar of the Constitution: the House of Lords in British Politics 1640–1784*, ed. C. Jones (London: Hambledon, 1989).

Adamson, J.S.A, *The Noble Revolt. The Overthrow of Charles I* (London: Weidenfeld and Nicolson, 2007).

Adamson, J.S.A., (ed.), *The Princely Courts of Europe 1500–1750* (London: Weidenfeld and Nicolson, 1999).

Ailes, A., 'The Development of the Heralds' Visitations in England and Wales', *The Coat of Arms*, 3rd ser., 5 (2009).

Asch, R.G., *Nobilities in Transition 1550–1700* (London: Arnold, 2003).

Atherton, I., *Ambition and Failure in Stuart England* (Manchester: Manchester University Press, 1999).

Aylmer, G,E., *The King's Servants* (London: Routledge and Kegan Paul, 1974).

Baker, J.H., *An Introduction to English Legal History* (London: Butterworth, 2nd edn, 1979).

Bankes, G., *The Story of Corfe Castle* (London, 1853).

Barnes, S.J., De Poorter, N., Millar, O., Vey, H., (eds.), *Van Dyck. A Complete Catalogue of the Paintings* (London: Paul Mellon Centre for Studies in British Art, 2004).

Barnes, T.G., 'Star Chamber Litigants and their Counsel, 1596–1641', in *Legal Records and the Historian*, ed. J.H. Baker (London: Royal Historical Society, 1978).

Begent, P.J. and Chesshyre, H., *The Most Noble Order of the Garter 650 Years* (London: Spink, 1999).

Beltz, G.F., *Memorials of the Most Noble Order of the Garter* (London, 1841).

Billacois, F., *The Duel. Its Rise and Fall in Early Modern France* (New Haven, CT: Yale University Press, 1990).

Bindoff, S.T., 'The Statute of Artificers', in *Elizabethan Government and Society*, ed. C.H. Williams (London: Athlone Press, 1961).

Boynton, L., *The Elizabethan Militia 1558–1638* (London: Routledge and Kegan Paul, 1976).

Braddick, M.J., *Gods Fury, England's Fire* (Allen Lane: London, 2008).

Broadway, J., 'No Historie So Meete', *Gentry Culture and the Development of Local History in Elizabethan and Early Stuart England* (Manchester: Manchester University Press, 2006).

Brown, C.C., 'Courtesies of the Place and the Arts of Diplomacy in Ben Jonson's Last Two Entertainments for Royalty', *The Seventeenth Century*, 9 (1994), 129–48.

Brown, C.C., *Van Dyck* (Oxford: Phaidon, 1982).

Brown, K., *The Bloodfeud in Scotland 1573–1625* (Edinburgh: John Donald Publishers, 1986).

Butler, M., *Theatre and Crisis 1632–1642* (Cambridge: Cambridge University Press, 1984).

Christianson, P., 'Obliterated Portions of the House of Lords Journals', *English Historical Review*, 95 (1980), 339–53.

Clark, P., 'Thomas Scott and the Growth of Urban Opposition to the Early Stuart Regime', *Historical Journal*, 21 (1978), 1–26.

Cogswell, T.E., *Home Divisions. Aristocracy, the State and Provincial Conflict* (Manchester: Manchester University Press, 1998).

Cogswell, T.E., *The Blessed Revolution. English Politics and the Coming of War, 1621–1624* (Cambridge: Cambridge University Press, 1989).

Cooper, J.P., 'Ideas of Gentility', in *Land, Men and Beliefs in Early Modern History*, ed. J.P. Cooper, G.E. Aylmer and J.S. Morrill (London: The Hambledon Press, 1983).

Cope, E.S., *The Life of a Public Man* (Philadelphia: American Philosophical Society, 142, 1981).

Coss, P.R., *The Knight in Medieval England 1000–1400* (Stroud: Alan Sutton Publishing, 1993).

Coss, P.R., and Keen, M. (ed.), *Heraldry, Pageantry and Social Display in Medieval England* (Woodbridge, UK: The Boydell Press, 2002).

Cuddy, N., 'The Conflicting Loyalties of a "Vulgar Counsellor": The Third Earl of Southampton', in *Public Duty and Private Conscience in Seventeenth-Century England*, ed. J.S. Morrill, P. Slack and D. Woolf (Oxford: Oxford University Press, 1993).

Cust, R.P., 'A Rutland Quarrel, the Court of Chivalry and the Irish Peerage during Charles I's Personal Rule', *Midland History*, 35 (2010), 149–73.

Cust, R.P., 'Catholicism, Antiquarianism and Gentry Honour: The Writings of Sir Thomas Shirley', *Midland History*, 23 (1998), 40–70.

Cust, R.P., *Charles I. A Political Life* (Harlow: Longman, 2005).

Cust, R.P., 'Charles I and Popularity', in *Politics, Religion and Popularity. Early Stuart Essays in Honour of Conrad Russell*, ed., T.E. Cogswell, R.P. Cust and P.G. Lake (Cambridge: Cambridge University Press, 2002).

Cust, R.P., 'Charles I and the order of the Garter', *Journal of British Studies*, 52 (2013), 1–27.

Cust, R.P., 'Charles I, the Privy Council and the 1628 Parliament', *Transactions of the Royal Historical Society* (6th ser., 2, 1992), 25–50.

Cust, R.P., 'Patriots and Popular Spirits: Narratives of Conflict in Early Stuart Politics', in *The English Revolution c. 1590–1720*, ed. N.R.N. Tyacke (Manchester: Manchester University Press, 2007).

Cust, R.P., 'Sir Henry Spelman investigates', *The Coat of Arms*, 3rd ser., III (2007), 25–34.

Cust, R.P., *The Forced Loan and English Politics 1626–1628* (Oxford: Oxford University Press, 1987).

Cust, R.P., 'Was There an Alternative to the Personal Rule? Charles I, the Privy Council and the Parliament of 1629', *History*, 90 (2005), 330–52.

Cust, R.P. and Hopper, A.J., 'Duelling and the High Court of Chivalry in Early Stuart England', in *Cultures of Violence*, ed. S. Carroll (Basingstoke: Palgrave Macmillan, 2007).

Day, J.R.F., 'Primers of Honor: Heraldry, Heraldry Books and English Renaissance Literature', *Sixteenth Century Journal*, xxi (1990), 93–103.

Dewald, J., *The European Nobility 1400–1800* (Cambridge: Cambridge University Press, 1996).

Donagan, B., 'Halcyon Days and the Literature of War: England's Military Education before 1642', *Past and Present*, 147 (1995), 65–100.

Donagan, B., *War in England 1642–1649* (Oxford: Oxford University Press, 2008).

Donald, P., *An Uncounselled King. Charles I and the Scottish Troubles, 1637–1641* (Cambridge: Cambridge University Press, 1990).

Doran, S., and Freeman, T.S. (ed.), *The Myth of Elizabeth*, (Basingstoke: Palgrave Macmillan, 2003).

Doyle, W., *Aristocracy; A Very Short Introduction* (Oxford: Oxford University Press, 2010).

Elmhirst, E., 'The Fashion for Heraldry', *The Coat of Arms*, iv (1956), 47–118.

Elton, G.R., *The Parliament of England 1559–1581* (Cambridge: Cambridge University Press, 1981).

Elton, G.R., *The Tudor Constitution* (Cambridge; Cambridge University Press, 1960).

Elton, G.R., 'Tudor Government: The Points of Contact, III, The Court', *Transactions of the Royal Historical Society* (5th ser., 26, 1976), 211–38.

Englefield, W.D., *The History of the Painters and Stainers Company of London* (London: Painters and Stainers Company of London, 1923).

Ferguson, A.B., *The Chivalric Tradition in Renaissance England* (London: Folger Shakespeare Library, 1986).

Fissell, M.C., *The Bishops Wars* (Cambridge: Cambridge University Press, 1994).

Flemion, J.S., 'The Struggle for the Petition of Right in the House of Lords: The Study of an Opposition Party Victory', in *Peers, Politics and Power: The House of Lords, 1603–1911*, ed. Clyve Jones and David Lewis Jones (London: Hambledon Press).

Fletcher, A., 'Petitioning and the Outbreak of the Civil War in Derbyshire', *Derbyshire Archaeological Journal*, 93 (1973), 33–44.

Fletcher, A., *The Outbreak of the English Civil War* (London: Edward Arnold, 1981).
Fletcher, A., and MacCulloch, D., *Tudor Rebellions* (Harlow: Longman, 5th edn, 2004).
Foster, E.R., *The House of Lords 1603–1949* (Chapel Hill: University of North Carolina Press, 1983).
Gajda, A.M., *The Earl of Essex and Late Elizabethan Political Culture* (Oxford: Oxford University Press, 2012).
Gardiner, S.R. *The History of England 1603–1642*, 10 vols. (London: Longman, Green & Co, 1883–4).
Gelber, D., '"Hark what Discord": Precedency among the Early Stuart Gentry', *The Coat of Arms*, 3rd ser. III (2007), 117–44.
Gunn, S.J., Grummitt, D., and Cools, H., *War, State and Society in England and the Netherlands 1477–1559* (Oxford: Oxford University Press, 2007).
Hammer, P.E.J., 'How to Become an Elizabethan Statesman: Lord Henry Howard, the Earl of Essex and the Politics of Friendship', *English Manuscript Studies, 1100–1700*, 13 (2007), 1–34.
Hammer, P.E.J., 'The Smiling Crocodile: The Earl of Essex and Late Elizabethan "popularity"', in *The Politics of the Public Sphere in Early Modern England*, ed. P. Lake and S.G. Pincus (Manchester: Manchester University Press, 2007).
Hart, J.S., *Justice Upon Petition* (London: Harper Collins Academic, 1991).
Heal, F., *Hospitality in Early Modern England* (Oxford: Oxford University Press, 1990).
Heal, F., 'The Crown the Gentry and London: The Enforcement of Proclamation, 1596–1640', in *Law and Government Under the Tudors*, ed. C. Cross, D. Loades and J.J. Scarisbrick (Cambridge: Cambridge University Press, 1998).
Heal, F. and Holmes, C., *The Gentry in England and Wales 1500–1700* (Basingstoke: Macmillan, 1994).
Herrup, C.B., *A House in Gross Disorder* (Oxford: Oxford University Press, 1997).
Herrup, C.B., 'The Patriarch at Home; The Trial of the 2nd Earl of Castlehaven for Rape and Sodomy', *History Workshop Journal*, 41 (1996), 1–18.
Herrup, C.B., '"To Pluck Bright Honour from the Pale-Faced Moon"; gender and honour in the Castlehaven story', *Transactions of the Royal Historical Society*, (6th ser., VI, 1996), 137–59.
Hervey, M.F.S., *The Life, Correspondence and Collection of Thomas Howard, Earl of Arundel* (Cambridge: Cambridge University Press, 1921).
Hibbard, C., *Charles I and the Popish Plot* (Chapel Hill: University of North Carolina Press, 1983).
Hibbard, C., 'Theatre of Dynasty', in *The Stuart Court and Europe*, ed. R.M. Smuts (Cambridge: Cambridge University Press, 1996).
Hirst, D.M., *The Representative of the People* (Cambridge: Cambridge University Press, 1975).
Holmes, C., *Seventeenth Century Lincolnshire* (Lincoln: History of Lincolnshire Committee for the Society for Lincolnshire History and Archaeology, 1980, VII, 1980).

Holmes, C., *The Eastern Association in the English Civil War* (Cambridge: Cambridge University Press, 1974).
Holmes, C., 'The Strange Case of a Misplaced Tomb: Family Honour and Law in Late Seventeenth Century England', *Midland History*, 31 (2006), 18–36.
Holmes, P., 'The Great Council in the Reign of Henry VII', *English Historical Review*, 101 (1986), 840–62.
Holmes, P., 'The Last Tudor Great Councils', *Historical Journal*, 33 (1990), 1–22.
Howarth, D., *Lord Arundel and his Circle* (New Haven, CT: Yale University Press, 1985).
Hurstfield, J., *The Queens Wards* (London: Longman, Green & Co., 1958).
Hutton, R., *The Royalist War Effort 1642–1646* (Harlow: Longman, 1982).
Ingram, M., *Church Courts, Sex and Marriage in England, 1570–1640* (Cambridge: Cambridge University Press, 1987).
Jackson, W.A., 'Sir Robert Bruce Cotton's A Short View of the Long Life and Raigne of Henry the Third', *Harvard Library Bulletin*, 4 (1950), 33–4.
James, M.E., *English Politics and the Concept of Honour 1485–1642*, Past & Present Supplement 3 (Oxford: Past and Present Society 1978).
Jefferson, L., 'A Garter Installation Ceremony in 1606', *Court Historian*, 6 (2001).
Jessup, F.W., *Sir Roger Twysden 1597–1672* (London: Cresset Press, 1965).
Keen, M., *Chivalry* (New Haven, CT: Yale University Press, 1984).
Keen, M., *The Origins of the English Gentleman* (Stroud: Tempus, 2002).
Knowles, J., 'From Gentleman to Prince', in *Royalist Refugees. William and Margaret Cavendish in the Rubens House 1648–1660*, ed. B. Van Beneden and N. De Poorter (Antwerp: Rubenshuis and Rubenarium, 2006).
Levack, B.P., *The Civil Lawyers in England 1603–1641* (Oxford: Clarendon Press, 1973).
Levy, F.J., *Tudor Historical Thought* (San Marino, CA: Huntington Library, 1967).
MacCullough, P.E., *Sermons at Court. Politics and Religion in Elizabethan and Jacobean Preaching* (Cambridge: Cambridge University Press, 1998).
Manning, B., 'The Aristocracy and the Downfall of Charles I', in *Politics, Religion and the English Civil War*, ed. B. Manning (London: Edward Arnold, 1973).
Manning, R.B., *Swordsmen. The Martial Ethos in the Three Kingdoms* (Oxford: Oxford University Press, 2003).
Mayes, C.R., 'The Early Stuarts and the Irish peerage', *English Historical Review*, 58 (1958), 227–51.
Mayes, C.R. 'The Sale of Peerages in Early Stuart England', *Journal of Modern History*, 29 (1957), 12–37.
McCoy, R., 'Old English Honour in an Evil Time: Aristocratic Principle in the 1620s', in *The Stuart Court and Europe*, ed. R.M. Smuts, (Cambridge: Cambridge University Press, 1996).
Mettam, R., 'The French nobility, 1610–1715', in *The European Nobilities in the Seventeenth and Eighteenth Centuries*, ed. H.M. Scott, 2 vols. (Harlow: Longman, 1995).
Millar, O., *Van Dyck in England* (London: National Portrait Gallery, 1982).
Milton, A., *Laudian and Royalist Polemic in Stuart England: The Career and Writings of Peter Heylyn* (Manchester: Manchester University Press, 2007).

Milton, A., '"That Sacred Oratory"; Religion and the Chapel Royal during the Personal Rule of Charles I', in *William Lawes (1602–1645): Essays on His Life, Times and Work*, ed. A. Ashbee (Aldershot: Ashgate, 1998).

Morrill, J.S., *The Nature of the English Revolution* (Harlow: Longman, 1993).

Motley, M., *Becoming a French Aristocrat. The Education of the Court Nobility 1580–1715* (Princeton, NJ: Princeton University Press, 1990).

Munden, R.C., 'James I and "the Growth of Mutual Distrust": King, Commons and Reform 1603–4', in *Faction and Parliament*, ed. K Sharpe (Oxford: Oxford University Press, 1978).

'Museum Minervae', *Notes and Queries*, 3rd ser., vi (1964), 265.

Newman, P.R., *Royalist Officers in England and Wales* (London: Garland Publishing, 1981).

Orgel, S. and Strong, R., *Inigo Jones. The Theatre of the Stuart Court* (Berkeley: University of California Press, 1973).

Oxford Dictionary of National Biography; from the earliest times to the year 2000, ed. H.C.G. Mathew, 61 vols. (Oxford: Oxford University Press, 2004).

Palliser, D.M., *The Age of Elizabeth* (2nd edn, Harlow: Longman, 1992).

Peck, L.L., *Court Patronage and Corruption in Early Modern England* (London: Routledge, 1990).

Peck, L.L., *Northampton. Patronage and Politics at the Court of James I* (London: George Allen & Unwin, 1982).

Peck, L.L., 'Peers, Patronage and the Politics of History', in *The Reign of Elizabeth*, ed. J.A. Guy (Cambridge: Cambridge University Press, 1995).

Peltonen, M., *Classical Humanism and Republicanism in English Political Thought 1570–1640* (Cambridge: Cambridge University Press, 1995).

Peltonen, M., *The Duel in Early Modern England* (Cambridge: Cambridge University Press, 2003).

Portal, E.M., 'The Academy Royal of King James I', *Proceedings of the British Academy*, 7 (1915–16), 189–200.

Powell, W.S., *John Pory, 1572–1636: the Life and Letters of a Man of Many Parts* (Chapel Hill: University of North Carolina Press, 1977).

Powis, J., *Aristocracy* (Oxford: Blackwell, 1984).

Questier, M., *Catholicism and Community in Early Modern England* (Cambridge: Cambridge University Press, 2006).

Read, C., *Mr Secretary Cecil and Queen Elizabeth* (London: Jonathan Cape, 1955).

Roy, I., 'The profession of arms', in *The Professions in Early Modern England*, ed. W.R. Prest (Beckenham: Croom Helm, 1987).

Russell, C.S.R., *Parliaments and English Politics 1621–1629* (Oxford: Oxford University Press, 1979).

Russell, C.S.R., *The Causes of the English Civil War* (Oxford: Oxford University Press, 1990).

Russell, C.S.R., *The Fall of the British Monarchies 1637–1642* (Oxford: Oxford University Press, 1991).

Russell, C.S.R., *Unrevolutionary England* (London: Hambledon Press, 1990).

Sainty, J.C., *Lieutenants of the Counties 1585–1642* (London: University of London, Historical Society 1970).

Schwarz, M., 'Viscount Saye and Sele, Lord Brooke and Aristocratic Protest to the First Bishops' War', *Canadian Journal of History*, 7 (1972).

Sharpe, J.A., 'Social Strain and Social Dislocation, 1585–1603', in *The Reign of Elizabeth I*, ed. J.A. Guy (Cambridge: Cambridge University Press).

Sharpe, K., *Sir Robert Cotton 1586–1631* (Oxford: Oxford University Press, 1979).

Sharpe, K., *Politics and Ideas in Early Stuart England* (London: Pinter Publishers, 1989).

Sharpe, K., 'The Earl of Arundel, His Circle and the Opposition to the Duke of Buckingham, 1618–1628', in *Faction and Parliament: Essays on Early Stuart History*, ed. K. Sharpe (Oxford: Clarendon Press).

Sharpe, K., 'The Image of Virtue: The Court and Household of Charles I, 1625–1642', in *The English Court from the Wars of the Roses to the Civil War*, ed. D. Starkey (Harlow: Longman, 1987).

Sharpe, K., *The Personal Rule of Charles I* (New Haven, CT: Yale University Press, 1992).

Shepard, A., *Meanings of Manhood in Early Modern England* (Oxford: Oxford University Press, 2003).

Skinner, Q., *The Foundations of Modern Political Thought*, 2 vols. (Cambridge: Cambridge University Press, 1978).

Smuts, R.M., 'Art and the Material Culture of Majesty in Early Stuart England', in *The Stuart Court and Europe*, ed. R.M. Smuts (New York: Cambridge University Press, 1996).

Smuts, R.M., *Court Culture and the Origins of a Royalist Tradition in Early Stuart England* (Philadelphia: University of Pennsylvania Press, 1987).

Smuts, R.M., 'Public Ceremony and Royal Charisma: The English Royal Entry in London', in *The First Modern Society*, ed. A.L. Beier, D. Cannadine and J.m. Rosenheim (Cambridge: Cambridge University Press, 1989).

Snow, V.F., 'Essex and Aristocratic Opposition to the early Stuarts', *Journal of Modern History*, 32 (1960), 224–33.

Spence, R.T., 'Henry Lord Clifford and the First Bishops' War', *Northern History*, 31 (1995), 210–67.

Squibb, G.D., *Precedence in England and Wales* (Oxford: Oxford University Press, 1981).

Squibb, G.D., *The High Court of Chivalry* (Oxford: Oxford University Press, 1959).

Stater, V.L., *Noble Government. The Stuart Lord Lieutenancy and the Transformation of English Politics* (Athens: University of Georgia Press, 1994).

Stewart, A., 'Purging Troubled Humours: Bacon, Northampton and the Anti-duelling Campaign of 1613–1614', in *The Crisis of 1614 and the Addled Parliament*, ed. S. Clucas and R. Davies (Aldershot: Ashgate, 2003).

Stone, L., *Family and Fortune* (Oxford: Oxford University Press, 1973).

Stone, L., *The Crisis of the Aristocracy 1558–1641* (Oxford: Oxford University Press, 1965).

Stone, L., 'The Inflation of Honours 1558–1641', *Past & Present*, 14 (1958), 45–70.

Storrs, C., and Scott, H.M., 'The Military Revolution and the European Nobility, *c.* 1600–1800', *War in History*, 3 (1996), 1–41.

Stretton, T., *Waging Law in Elizabethan England* (Cambridge: Cambridge University Press, 1998).

Strong, R., *Henry Prince of Wales and England's Lost Renaissance* (London: Pimlico, 2000).

Strong, R., 'Queen Elizabeth I and the Order of the Garter', *Archaeological Journal*, 119 (1962), 245–69.

Strong, R., *Van Dyck: Charles I on Horseback* (London: Allen Lane, 1972).

Thomas, K., *The Ends of Life* (Oxford: Oxford University Press, 2009).

Thompson, I.A.A., 'Hidalgo and Pechero: The Language of "Estates" and "Castes" in Early-Modern Castile', in *Language, History and Class*, ed. P. Corfield (Oxford: Blackwell, 1991).

Thrush, A. 'The Personal Rule of James, 1611–1620', in *Politics, Religion and Popularity. Early Stuart Essays in Honour of Conrad Russell*, ed. T.E. Cogswell, R.P. Cust and P.G. Lake, (Cambridge: Cambridge University Press, 2002).

Timmis, J.H., 'Evidence and I Eliz I. cap.6: The Basis of the Lords' Decision in the Trial of Strafford', *Historical Journal*, 21 (1978), 677–83.

Timmis, J.H., *Thine is the Kingdom* (Tuscaloosa, AL.: University of Alabama Press, 1974).

Tite, C.G., *Impeachment and Parliamentary Judicature in Early Stuart England* (London: Athlone Press, 1974).

Treadwell, V., *Buckingham and Ireland 1616–1628* (Dublin: Four Courts Press, 1998).

Tuck, R., *Philosophy and Government 1571–1651* (Cambridge: Cambridge University Press, 1993).

Turnbull, G.H., 'Samuel Hartlib's connection with Sir Francis Kynaston's "Musaeum Minervae"', *Notes and Queries*, 97 (1952), 257–76.

Vallance, E., *Revolutionary England and the National Covenant* (Woodbridge, UK: Boydell Press, 2005).

Van Eerde, K.S., 'The Creation of the Baronetage in England', *Huntington Library Quarterly*, 22 (1959), 313–32.

Van Eerde, K.S., 'The Jacobean Baronets: An Issue between King and Parliament', *Journal of Modern History*, 33 (1961), 137–47.

Wagner, A.R., *Heralds and Heraldry in the Middle Ages* (Oxford: Oxford University Press, 2nd edn, 1956).

Wagner, A.R., *Heralds of England* (London: HMSO, 1967).

Wagner, A.R., *The Records and Collections of the College of Arms* (London: Burkes Peerage, 1952).

Wilcher, R., *The Writing of Royalism 1628–1660* (Cambridge: Cambridge University Press, 2001).

Worsley, L., Harting, V., and Keblusek, M., 'Horsemanship', in *Royalist Refugees*, ed. B. Van Benenden and N. De Poorter (Antwerp : Rubenshuis & Rubenianum, 2006).

Young, A., *Tudor and Jacobean Tournaments* (London: George Philip, 1987).

Young, P., *Edgehill 1642: The Campaign and the Battle* (Kineton, UK; Roundwood Press, 1967).

Zaller, R., *The Parliament of 1621* (Chapel Hill: University of California Press, 1971).

UNPUBLISHED DISSERTATIONS AND PAPERS

Ailes, A., 'Elias Ashmole's "Heraldical Visitacion" of Berkshire 1665–6' (Oxford University D.Phil thesis, 2008).
Crummett, J.B., 'The Lay Peers in Parliament 1640–1644' (University of Manchester PhD, 1970).
Cust, R.P., 'Charles I's Noble Academy' (forthcoming).
Cust, R.P., 'The failure of the Heralds' Visitations of 1634' (forthcoming)
Greenrod, J., '"Conceived to Give Dangerous Counsel": William Murray, Endymion Porter, The Caroline Bedchamber and the Outbreak of Civil War' (University of Sheffield, M.Phil. thesis, 2003).
Hammer, P.E.J., '"Base Rogues" and "Gentlemen of Quality": The Earl of Essex and his Irish Knights in 1599' (forthcoming).

Index

All members of the parliamentary peerage in April 1640 and March 1642 are listed, in order of precedence in Appendices 1 and 2.